# KEEP HOPE ALIVE

## Jesse Jackson's
## 1988 Presidential Campaign

A Collection of Major Speeches,
Issue Papers, Photographs, and
Campaign Analysis

Edited by

Frank Clemente

with

Frank Watkins

A Publication of the Keep Hope Alive PAC and
South End Press

Cover photo by Bob McNeely

Inside photos by Terry Gydesen (Nos. 2-8, 10-15, 17-21), Shepard Sherbell/Picture Group (Nos. 1, 23), Barry Thumma/AP Wide World Photos (No. 9), Kenneth Boone/Selma Times Journal (No. 16), Gregory J. Smith (No. 22), and Bob McNeely (No. 24). Copies of Terry Gydesen's photos are available from 420 N. Fifth Street, Studio 758, Minneapolis, MN 55401.

Text design and production by Richard Steele, Sheila Walsh and the South End Press collective.

Printed on acid-free paper by workers under union contract at Banta Book System, Menasha, WI.

PRODUCED BY WORKERS UNDER UNION CONTRACT

Printing and year correspond to last digits:
10 9 8 7 6 5 4 3 2 1
98 97 96 95 94 93 92 91 90 89

**Library of Congress Cataloging-in-Publication Data**

**Keep hope alive.**

1. Presidents--United States--Elections--1988.
2. United States--Politics and government--1981- .
3. Jackson, Jesse, 1941- . I. Jackson, Jesse, 1941- .
II. Clemente, Frank.
E880.K44 1988   324.973'0927   88-29527
ISBN 0-89608-358-6
ISBN 0-89608-357-8 (pbk.)

**South End Press, 116 Saint Botolph Street, Boston, MA 02115**

# ABOUT KEEP HOPE ALIVE PAC

The Keep Hope Alive PAC is a political action committee founded by Jesse Jackson as a direct outgrowth of his 1988 presidential campaign. The PAC's goal is to support progressive candidates for elective office throughout the nation by providing funding, resources and technical assistance.

The Keep Hope Alive PAC's president is Jesse Jackson, Jr. He replaced Ronald H. Brown, the PAC's first president, after Ron's gratifying achievement as the first African American ever to chair the Democratic National Committee. This victory was in large part made possible by the broad Rainbow Coalition built by Jesse Jackson in 1988.

We have travelled a long, long way from Fannie Lou Hamer being denied a seat at the 1964 Democratic National Convention to Ron Brown winning the Chair of the Democratic Party by acclamation! Times do change. We, the people, can win. We are, after all, still winning every day. And if progressives work together, we can "Keep Hope Alive!"

Steve Cobble
Executive Director
Keep Hope Alive PAC
733 15th Street NW, Suite 700,
Washington, D.C. 20005

# ABOUT SOUTH END PRESS

South End Press is a collectively run book publisher with over 150 titles in print. Since our founding in 1977, we have tried to meet the needs of readers who are exploring the politics of social and cultural change.

As a nonprofit educational foundation, South End Press is prohibited from endorsing candidates for electoral office. We consider *Keep Hope Alive* an essential contribution to the history of progressive movements in the United States, movements too often ignored or misrepresented by mainstream media.

The South End Press collective
116 Saint Botolph Street
Boston, MA 02115

# CONTENTS

# III. CREATING A HUMANE SOCIETY

# IV. RETHINKING NATIONAL SECURITY

# V. THE REVIVAL OF HOPE

# ADDENDUM

# FOREWORD

On the simplest level, this is "my" book, consisting as it does of my speeches and issue papers from last year's presidential campaign. At a deeper level, however, this book belongs to the seven million Americans who supported my bid for president. And at the deepest level, this book belongs to all of the martyrs for justice, to all those who struggled for progressive change — from Thomas Paine to Frederick Douglass to Harriet Tubman to Dr. Martin Luther King, Jr. Upon their courageous shoulders we now stand.

The Rainbow Coalition is a movement and a campaign of hope. Across America, hope has been reborn. A new broad-based coalition cutting across traditional dividing lines of race, religion, region, sex and sexual orientation has been built — and continues to grow daily.

As a result, America will never be the same again. We are building a progressive political constituency from the bottom up on the same people pillars upon which our country has been built. Many of us have not shared adequately in the promises of the American dream, and we are restless. And when the bottom shakes, everything resting on that foundation must move with it.

This new politically progressive coalition is demanding a new direction for the Democratic Party and the whole country — humane priorities and equal protection under the law for all at home, and peace through greater international justice, growth and cooperation abroad. A new *director* is not enough. We need a new *direction*.

Leaders must address the challenges of their day. It makes no sense to answer questions that no one is asking or answer questions that have already been addressed. In 1989, it is good, but not sufficient, to have been against southern American apartheid and the Vietnam War in the 1960s. It is now necessary to oppose economic violence and injustice, perpetuated by big corporations and government policies at all levels that institutionally favor the rich over the poor, the white and male over the black, brown, yellow, red and female in the 1980s and 1990s.

Our campaign had a winning message. It was imitated by other candidates because we discussed what was on the minds and in the hearts of the people. We had a clear message that came from listening to the grunts, the groans and the yearnings of average people. We did not hire consultants and pundits to tell us what to say. Leaders must know the people — their hopes, their dreams and their burdens. We knew the American people better than anyone running, and they heard our message and responded in record numbers.

Thus we set the agenda for the campaign and the nation with our message. Our message rallied the people, lifted their spirits, touched their hearts, revived their hopes and unleased their energy. This message brought new voters to the polls, inspired the young to care again and set in motion the demand for change and a new direction for our country. It has led to the recent victory of Ron Brown, the first African American chosen to head the Democratic Party. It is still leading us into the future.

The following speeches, issue briefs and position papers in *Keep Hope Alive* contain the content of our message as it was carried from South Carolina to Oregon, from Maine to Mississippi, and from Iowa to California. You may have gotten the general thrust and essence of our message from media reports on our campaign, but you certainly did not get the substance.

This book is designed to give you the *substance* of the 1988 Jesse Jackson for President Campaign. It will give the progressive political movement a concrete *agenda* around which to build and broaden its base for the 1990s and beyond. This is the agenda that nearly seven million Democrats voted for in primaries and caucuses in 1988. I offer you this book as my agenda for change. I believe it is our agenda for hope.

I must first give thanks to my family — for the support and guidance of my wife Jackie, the companionship and tireless campaigning of Jesse Jr. and Jonathan, and the comfort and encouragement of Santita, Jackie Jr. and Yusef. They are a constant source of joy and inspiration for me.

While many people contributed to the substance and issue development of my campaign, several people deserve special recognition. They are 1988 campaign staffmembers Frank Clemente, Issues Coordinator and editor and coordinator of the *Keep Hope Alive* book project; Robert Borosage, Senior Policy Advisor; Mark Steitz, Domestic and Economic Policy Advisor; Stephen Coates, Deputy Issues Coordinator; Dr. Jean Sindab, African Affairs Policy Advisor; Gerald Austin, Campaign Manager; Carolyn Kazdin, Deputy Campaign Manager for Farm and Labor; Ron Daniels, Deputy Campaign Manager for the South; Armando Guitierrez, Deputy Campaign Manager for Hispanic Affairs; Eddie Wong, Field Director; and Steve Cobble, Delegate Coordinator.

A very special thanks must be extended to Frank Watkins, my long-time aide and friend. Frank was the Political Director for the 1988 campaign. He helped start the Rainbow Coalition in the right direction, and America in a new direction, so many years ago. He has always been there when the people needed him.

Among the many non-staff advisors, there are several who significantly contributed to the materials included in this book. Carol O'Cleireacain was the campaign's chief economic advisor and greatly aided with overall issues development. Assemblywoman Maxine Waters, Roger Wilkins (who assisted with manuscript editing), and Ron Walters (the 1984 Jackson Campaign's Issues Director) as usual offered their astute political observations as events unfolded. Eleanor Holmes Norton and Ron Brown helped negotiate many of these proposals into the Democratic platform in Atlanta. David Gordon provided valuable economic analysis and contributed significantly to the "Paying for Our Dreams Budget." Ann Bastian and Teresa Amott made major contributions respectively to the campaign's education and family policies. Dr. Vicente Navarro, Dr. David Himmelstein and Dr. Steffie Woolhandler gave invaluable advice in the formulation of the Jackson National Health Care Program. Dan Lindheim gave sound advice on a wide range of policy issues. Iris Rothman provided expert editing at every turn in the campaign. And Terry Gydesen, the campaign's photographer, some of whose pictures are included in *Keep*

*Hope Alive*, deserves special recognition for her sensitive camera eye.

We regret that space does not allow us to mention the scores of others whose advice and counsel we depended on. We hope that the success of our campaign and its message is a sufficient testament to the value of your help.

Our hope is that you will read and seriously study the issues, policies and programs presented in *Keep Hope Alive*, debate them, argue about them, refine them and improve them. Share them with your friends. But above all, use them to build and broaden the Rainbow Coalition. For, in the final analysis, it will not be the progressive programs, but the *political power* to implement our agenda that is most important in keeping hope alive.

Jesse L. Jackson
Chicago, Illinois
August, 1989

# INTRODUCTION

Jesse Jackson's 1988 Democratic presidential campaign showed that the American people are open to a populist political message. Jesse Jackson's campaign for the presidency of the United States started out deep in the valley of doubt. The press, the pundits and the pollsters, cynical about the American people, discounted Jackson's prospects. The American people were said to be too close-minded, too divided and too self-absorbed to hear his message — much less support his candidacy. But Jesse Jackson had faith that if he could present his case — the case for economic justice at home and peace abroad — that Americans would respond. And they did, in large numbers.

Jesse Jackson entered the 1988 campaign viewed only as a great orator. He finished the campaign recognized by many as the great idea generator. More than any presidential campaigner in recent memory, and perhaps ever, Jackson laid out a substantive, coherent set of progressive proposals for wrestling with our economic troubles, rejuvenating our communities, strengthening our families and confronting the new, post-Cold War realities in the international arena. His ideas and policies captured the imagination of people within and outside his natural constituency, and propelled him forward to be a major political figure for the foreseeable future.

The 1988 election came at an important time in redefining what the Democratic Party stands for. Reagan's victory in 1980 seemed to have sent the message to Democrats that the New Deal and the Great Society were seriously wounded — if not dead. The party's ability to form a governing coalition — between business and labor, white southerners and minorities, the middle-class and the poor — had run out of steam in the late 1970s, a cumulative result of the backlash to the civil rights movement and other progressive movements of the 1960s and 1970s, and to the high inflation, ballooning interest rates and Iran hostage crisis of the Carter administration.

The 1984 election only added gasoline to the fire. Walter Mondale tried to pull together a winning coalition with the party's fractured interest groups and a tepid Democratic message. But he was trounced at the polls. He couldn't compete with Reagan's simplistic but pulsating and patriotic optimism, the more coherent and compelling ideology of the conservatives, and the superior fundraising and organizational ability of the Republican Party. As in 1980, the Democrats offered no strong alternative to the conservative ideology of getting the government off our backs; letting business and the market run free; extolling the virtues of patriotism, family and community (no matter how hypocritical the stance, or contradictory to civil liberties); and restoring American pride through an unprecedented military build-up and aggression around the globe.

In the early 1980s, there was no unifying personality or event to recast the Democratic Party's message to the American electorate. In the 1988 presidential campaign, Jesse Jackson stepped into, and in many ways filled, that void.

Jackson was the conscience of the Democratic Party in 1988. When the political winds of the Reagan era blew other Democratic politicians toward the center, Jackson stood his ground. He tried to pull the party back to its progressive populist roots — to the farm movement of the 1880s, the New Deal of the 1930s, and the civil rights and anti-Vietnam War struggles of the 1960s. While most candidates were interested in sound bites for the evening news, Jackson was interested in substance for the kitchen table. While the rest of the party couldn't decide where it should stand on foreign policy, Jackson articulated a bold new vision to take account of changes in the world economy since the 1940s, changes in the Soviet Union under Gorbachev, and changes in the Third World as it became clear that poverty, illiteracy and political oppression were the real enemies of democracy.

It was Jackson who attracted the huge crowds — of all races — who came to hear his message of inspiration and hope. He dominated the debates. His was a voice of reason, thoughtfulness and intellectual seriousness, whether or not one agreed with all his positions. He set the priorities and message of the Democratic campaign: stop drugs from flowing in and jobs from flowing out; invest in America; stop corporate greed and control corporate mergers; restore fairness to the tax system and reduce the deficit by making those who had "the party" — the rich and corporations — pay for the damages; provide debt relief and a Marshall Plan to the Third World; promote labor rights abroad and stop plant closings at home; expand the Democratic Party by passing a universal, on-site, same day voter registration bill; ensure pay equity for women; invest in Head Start, child care and prenatal care on the front side of life rather than jail care and welfare on the back side; declare South Africa a terrorist state.

In the United States, Jackson's program was called radical by many (in Europe, it's straightforward social democratic politics, and much of what he advocates is practiced by governments there). Why was Jackson's message so successful despite the American people's supposed fears about candidates who are "too ideological," "too radical" or "too controversial?"

Jackson's message reached people exactly because his message and vision transcend ideology and appeal to more fundamental values the American people hold dear. Jackson's message rested on three foundations: an economic populism which sought to democratize the economy to make it work better for everyone; upholding family and community values rather than purely individual values; and empowerment of the people.

## Economic Populism

Jackson's economic program might be called an updated version of American progressive populism — updated to take account of the internationalization of the world economy. Like the earlier populist movements, in 1988 his campaign attempted to build a coalition linking rural farmers suffering from shrinking markets and massive debt with urban workers faced with declining wages and increased competition from abroad. Despite the loss of U.S. jobs to overseas competition, Jackson didn't preach economic nationalism as some other candidates tried to do. Instead, he expressed solidarity with international workers and focused attention on the real problem: corporate policies which closed factories at home in search of cheap — and repressed — labor abroad.

While other candidates shied away from addressing growing class differences, Jackson eloquently defended workers and the poor who were being victimized by a wave of what he called "corporate and economic violence." Like earlier populists, Jackson called for greater control over corporate mergers, and he issued a Corporate Code of Conduct designed to bring greater justice — and improved productivity — to our economy. He did this despite the restored reverence for big business under Reagan. Jackson used class solidarity to find a common basis for workers — African American and white — to move forward. His eloquent refrain to workers — "When the plant lights go out, we all look the same in the dark" — met with knowing approval across the country.

Finally, he advocated a recently neglected staple of populist economics — a fairer tax system. He even prepared a comprehensive budget document to show how it could be achieved. None of the other candidates were courageous enough to make such a proposal — they were either too beholden to the interests of business and the wealthy, or they had too little faith in the electorate to trust that voters could understand that taxing the wealthy did not require increasing taxes on the poor and middle classes.

## Upholding Values

Like other successful populists, Jackson's message was a combination of economic radicalism with social conservatism. His "conservatism" is not the intrusive moralizing of the Moral Majority however, which advocates prayer in the schools, a ban on abortions, discrimination against homosexuals and infringements on civil or individual rights. Jackson's "conservatism" is his ability to feel for and deeply express how much he cares about and desires to build upon the core American values of family, community and patriotism. Our communities are being ripped to pieces by unemployment, drugs, crime and, in Jackson's words, "babies making babies." In ever-greater numbers, Americans are searching for comfort in the face of this destruction.

Jackson's campaign was a call to stand up and preserve the basic moral fabric of our country. Many times a week he would visit high schools, spend two hours with students and teachers and reach into their hearts, console them and bring them together to confront the scourge of drugs. He regularly stood shoulder-to-shoulder with white farmers — the backbone of the rural economy and of small town values — facing the loss of their land and their way of life. He stood with blue collar workers — often "Reagan Democrats" — who were struggling to keep their plants alive and their jobs in place.

The central role that morality — and religion — plays in Jackson's politics is what sets him apart as a visionary leader. The church is the main institution in working-class America to which people turn for hope and inspiration. Unlike the Moral Majority and the fundamentalist right, Jackson doesn't use biblical presuppositions to take public policy positions. Like the average person, in the best sense of religion, he simply views circumstances through a moral lens of what is right or wrong. And people understand that to enslave people in South Africa is morally wrong. That encouraging self-determination abroad is morally right. That "corporate barracudas" submerging our economy are morally wrong. That enhancing the economic security of working people is morally right. That refusing to stand up to drug dealers is morally wrong. That building stable families is morally right.

Jackson's morality placed him above politics as usual. He did not rely on focus groups, pollsters or pundits to tell him what position to take on an issue. He had the courage to articulate what is "morally right" and had faith that the American people would support him in that. As he said in his Democratic convention speech, "If an issue is morally right, it will eventually be political. If we're principled first, our politics will fall into place." Thus Jackson supported a two-state solution in the Middle East, not because it was politically expedient, but because it was morally right that the Israelis and the Palestinians should each be able to determine their own future free from outside interference.

Jackson's strength is that he transcends the debate over liberal versus conservative. The great liberal Democratic ideological failure of the 1960s was its isolation from the values of patriotism, loyalty to one's country, and love of family. But these are core values that drive middle- and working-class America. Jackson wrapped his vision of a new political direction in patriotic terms — "make America better and keep America strong" — because he believes in these values.

Jesse Jackson takes the values of American citizenship very seriously in large part because of where he has come from. His is the great American success story — born the son of an unmarried, poor, African American woman working as a maid in what was then racially-segregated South Carolina.

## Empowerment

Perhaps because of his past, Jackson's greatest gift — and the uniqueness he brings to politics — is his ability to help people move beyond despair to hope, to see beyond individualism to the potential power of collective action, empowerment, common ground, the rainbow quilt.

Jackson called on Americans to move beyond their divisions, to overcome their differences. His message was to cross racial, religious, rural and urban, even class divisions, and push people to move their private interests to a more collective, communal approach to solving their problems. His is the Rainbow Coalition. Rather than seeing groups — labor, women, environmentalists, minorities — as having competing interests which conflict with each other, he used their issues to cement them together. Jackson brought them together around the idea that they can't get what they want without each other.

Jackson made people understand their stake in the system. He called on them to be politically active; not to elect a candidate who would do things for them, but to act for themselves. He is not interested in government handouts. He is, however, interested in an activist government which promotes fairness, provides opportunity and protects those who are handicapped in the race for equality.

His appeal was not "Vote for me, I'll help you." Rather, it was a challenge to Americans — Get involved! He's not a politician in the traditional sense of someone who represents the public's interests. He relates to people as one of them. They call him "Jesse." They feel a stake in his campaign. They feel better about themselves. He, and they, have their dignity. This is a democracy. The message is united *together* — rather than behind a leader — we can run the country.

Jesse Jackson started this campaign against the odds, with low expectations from without, with little money or organization — only a message. *Keep Hope Alive* is that message. It contains the speeches, issue briefs and position papers that embodied Jackson's campaign.

## A Campaign of Challenge and Hope

Section I, "A Campaign of Challenge and Hope," provides an overview of the 1988 Jesse Jackson for President Campaign. "Building Progressive Political Power: 1983-1988," the first article in Section I, describes the political conditions which led up to the 1988 campaign and the major highlights of that effort — from the primaries and caucuses through the Democratic convention. This article concludes with an analysis of the general election and the future direction of the Democratic Party.

Jackson's two most important speeches of the campaign, his announcement speech in Raleigh and his convention speech in Atlanta, are included as bookends to this period in history. The announcement speech contained many references to the "New South," the core message Jackson carried throughout the region: the New South could heal old racial wounds and find common ground in economic and political empowerment.

Section I is completed by "The Revival of Hope: The Platform of the 1988 Jesse Jackson for President Campaign." Prepared in advance of the deliberations with the Dukakis campaign to facilitate negotiations over the content of the Democratic platform, this article underscores the coherence, comprehensiveness and boldness of Jackson's political program.

## Creating a Just Economy

Jackson's economic vision for America is outlined in Section II, "Creating a Just Economy." "The Message, the Mission and the Messenger," a speech to the Cleveland City Club, summarized the basic elements of Jackson's economic program: reordered budget priorities, including major new investments in people and productivity *along with* significant deficit reduction; expanded global growth through lowered interest rates, fair trade policies, debt relief and support for human rights in the Third World; responsible corporate citizenship to increase investments in products, not paper, and to improve the wages and working conditions of working Americans; and an "Invest America" plan using public pension funds, federally guaranteed, for rebuilding our communities.

In the position paper, "The Fundamentals of Economic Growth and Economic Justice," Jackson countered mainstream Democratic thinking that a strong dose of austerity (through consumer belt-tightening, reductions in federal spending and a possible across-the-board tax increase) for average Americans was needed to get the economy growing faster. Jackson took on the supply-siders and outlined how we can build a productive economy "up from the people," rather than by rewarding a wealthy few and waiting for some of their windfall to trickle down to the rest of us.

This section also includes Jackson's "Paying for Our Dreams" Budget. In all likelihood, this was the most comprehensive federal budget blueprint ever issued by a presidential campaign. Jackson put forth the budget plan not to prove that he could add or subtract, but to show that we could both reduce the budget deficit and afford social justice. It boiled down to a question of choices and political will.

Remaining speeches and issue briefs in this section fill in the details of Jackson's "Invest America" program, a unique contribution to the national political debate over how we can afford to rebuild our crumbling roads, bridges, water systems and rail lines. Also included are his trade policy, his plan for making corporations more accountable to the greater society — all of the stakeholders, not just the shareholders — and his "Worker's Bill of Rights." Jackson wrote this as a litany which workers recited at a Labor Day rally in Pittsburgh, and he used it as a touchstone with workers throughout the campaign.

### The Campaign In Pictures

From the cornfields of Iowa to the city of New York and from the coast of California to the convention floor in Atlanta, Jesse Jackson travelled hundreds of thousands of miles and touched millions of American hearts. Words alone cannot adequately describe the emotion — the joy, the hope, the affection — shared between Jackson and his supporters. The 24 photographs in *Keep Hope Alive* are not the usual campaign pictures of the candidate's appearance here and there. They are about the people that made this campaign — and make this country — great.

### Creating a Humane Society

In the papers and briefs collected in Section III, "Creating a Humane Society," Jackson reminded us that a just economy, indeed a just America, is not just about lowered deficits, lowered interest rates and increased productivity — it is about social justice for all of America's people. He reminded us that most people are dependent on welfare because they cannot find decent jobs, decent housing, decent health care or child care. Many of our youth are locked into lives of drugs and crime because they cannot find either the jobs or community support which might give their lives shape and meaning. Millions of our children's lives end up in the gutter because we do not care enough to put out a hand to pull them into the mainstream of the American community.

Jackson outlined a comprehensive approach to these problems through the issue briefs and position papers included here on the family, the elderly, drugs, housing, education, AIDS and health care.

"The Jackson National Health Care Program" is a sweeping proposal which would guarantee comprehensive coverage to all Americans while being fiscally responsible. Its soundness should provide a model for future debates on meeting our health-care crisis.

Perhaps one of the more remarkable events of the campaign period was Jackson's speech on Super Bowl Sunday at kick-off time to an overflow crowd of 900 in rural Greenfield, Iowa. In effect signaling the unofficial beginning of the campaign, the "Saving the Family Farm" speech included here outlined his call for a revival of earlier populist-era coalitions between farmers and urban workers. It was a rallying cry he came back to throughout the campaign.

Jackson sought to reclaim the dream for those Americans still suffering under the weight of discrimination. In other issue briefs in Section III, he called for an end to prejudice against the aged and outlined a plan to meet their needs. He called for deepening our commitment to affirmative action and effective government support for its objectives. He outlined an agenda for ensuring women's dignity and equality. He forcefully defended lesbian and gay rights and offered a plan for combatting the AIDS crisis. He provided renewed hope to immigrants, battered by an administration that has shown little commitment to cultural diversity or equal protection under the law. And he revived the spirits of the first Americans — the American Indians — with a plan for redressing past wrongs and confronting the challenges of the future.

Section III closes with an issue brief and speech on the environmental threats — and Jackson's far-reaching solutions — now facing this nation and the world, and an issue brief on "Exploring Space to Benefit All Humanity." Reporters and the public were often surprised to learn of Jackson's strong interest in space. His interest extends well beyond space exploration for technological purposes. It includes using space as a bridge to improved American and Soviet relations *and* to deepen our knowledge about the mysteries of the universe.

## Rethinking National Security

Clearly the most thoughtful yet provocative parts of the Jackson program are his views on defense and foreign policy. These issues have always been an Achilles heel of progressive politics — the American working-class may support economic populism, but it is still regarded as "jingoistic" when it comes to international relations. Conventional wisdom told Jackson to tone down this part of his message, but, as the materials in Section IV show, he constantly stressed a new direction in foreign policy as dramatic as his budget proposal.

In the speech "A New Realism in Foreign Policy," given to the American Society of Newspaper Publishers, and in the issue brief "Promoting Real Security," Jackson charted his course for moving beyond confrontation with and containment of the Soviet Union to fashioning "common security" arrangements. With the United States already capable of destroying major Soviet cities many times over, Jackson proposed that the United States initiate a moratorium on the testing of new nuclear weapons systems, and he challenged the Soviets to follow suit. With a bilateral and verifiable halt to new weapons development in place, he suggested that deep cuts in both superpowers' arsenals could be negotiated. Jackson further proposed significant and asymmetrical conventional force reductions between NATO and the Warsaw Pact. He also called for our European allies to pick up a greater share of the costs of their defense (should they deem it necessary) in place of our current massive expenditures.

In addition to improved U.S.-Soviet relations and a more stable nuclear and conventional force balance between the superpowers, Jackson's national security proposal called for a fundamental shift in how the United States deals with the Third World. Rather than viewing Third World changes in the context of superpower relations, Jackson defined a new doctrine to guide U.S. relations with Africa, Latin America, Asia and the Middle East. The Jackson Doctrine was based on four principles: support for international law, self-determination, human rights and the promotion of international economic justice and development. Section IV concludes with issue briefs which apply this "Jackson Doctrine" to Third World crisis points in southern Africa, Central America and the Middle East.

## The Revival of Hope

Section V, "The Revival of Hope," presents Jackson's strategy for building a new progressive majority in American politics. The key is voter enfranchisement, a "winning message" and organization building. In his speech, "The Promise and Politics of Empowerment," he called for passage of the Universal Voter Registration Act which would provide for same day, on-site registration.

This section concludes with "The Struggle Continues," a riveting speech Jackson made to his delegates (and to Michael Dukakis, Lloyd Bentsen and Paul Kirk, chair of the Democratic National Committee) on the morning after the Democratic Convention. In the speech Jackson reminded his supporters how close they were to where they were going, and how far they were from where they started. He outlined the many accomplishments of the campaign and the commitments made by the Dukakis-Bentsen ticket and the Democratic Party leadership to a progressive legislative agenda. Jackson also powerfully described what was at stake in this campaign and the need for activists to both gain influential positions within the Democratic Party structure and to remain active outside the Democratic Party (Jackson calls it "street heat") to bring about a truly progressive majority in America.

No book about the 1988 Jackson effort would be complete without presenting highlights of the campaign from each state. That was where much of the real story happened. Thus, an addendum to *Keep Hope Alive* contains state-by-state highlights as well as tables of election results.

## Now Is the Time

Now is the time when the themes, symbols and policies to which the national electorate responds are being redefined. There's an old axiom in politics that people alone can't change the course of history — conditions count, too. Now is the time for change.

The New Deal of the 1930s — a sweeping political realignment to the left — was a reaction to the tumultuous economic conditions of that time. The Socialist Party campaigns in the preceding two decades helped shape the course of that change in their advocacy for the 40-hour work week, collective bargaining across the land, Social Security and other "welfare state" legislation.

The "Reagan revolution" of the 1980s was also a reaction to the economic conditions of its time. For 40 years conservatives preached that the New Deal created inflation, big government and high taxes. In the failed policies of the 1970s this message finally played to sympathetic ears and succeeded in capturing the imagination of the electorate. But the Reagan era is ending.

Jesse Jackson views politics over the long term. In 1988 his campaign was a campaign of hope. It unleashed hope in the land, and it will keep hope alive. It has created a new permanent progressive force in American politics. It has only begun to forge a new progressive democratic majority. The outlines of such a majority are in this book.

# I

# A Campaign of Challenge and Hope

# BUILDING PROGRESSIVE POLITICAL POWER:

## 1983-1988

There is the status quo, and there are those who want to change the status quo — some by moving backward, others by moving forward. The Reagan-Bush administration set back our nation. The Rainbow Coalition of the 1988 Jesse Jackson for President Campaign is the best representative of those forces who want to move the country forward.

The Jackson forces call themselves progressive. "Conservative" means keeping things the way they are, or even retreating; "liberal" means moving things forward incrementally, tinkering around the edges of change; but "progressives" want fundamental change, what Jesse Jackson calls "a new direction."

Progressives are "radical" in the sense that they want to go to the root of the problem. A conservative asks for a study on corporations that pollute the air; a liberal wants to fund a program to clean up the pollution, and even wants the corporation to pay for it; a progressive argues for a program to stop the pollution at its source, and insists industry develop a fundamentally different means of production that is non-polluting.

Perhaps the single greatest accomplishment of the Jackson campaign was to bring progressive politics back as a serious force in America, back from the depths of the King and Kennedy assassinations. Progressive politics is stronger today than it has been since 1968. For a few brief days, between the Michigan caucuses and the Wisconsin primary, it even appeared as if Martin Luther King's dream of jobs, peace and justice for all Americans might come to life. This progressive coalition, which Jackson leads — united across race, ideology, region and religion — will surely be a growing force in the politics of the next decade.

Jackson dared Americans to dream about what kind of a nation we want, what kind of policies are necessary to get us there, and what work still needs to be done to make that dream reality. He offered the antithesis of the individualism and personal greed of the Reagan era, by offering a vision of the common good and a sense of community and united struggle for change.

He proved that politics didn't have to be based on pollsters, pundits and posturing but rather could be based on moral and political struggle. That's why he regularly made his campaign stops at places he called "the point of challenge." Jackson left Iowa only a few days before its critical caucuses to join in solidarity with autoworkers in Kenosha, Wisconsin, who had just been notified by Chrysler that their plant would be shut down — despite earlier guarantees that this wouldn't happen. He returned to McFarland, California, where there were few votes but where an extremely high number of children were being born with disabilities, and others were dying young, poisoned by pesticides used on the farms and seeping into the well water.

Jackson began to revive and invigorate a Rainbow Coalition based on common economic interests of poor, low- and middle-income Americans by appealing directly to workers and farmers and articulating their fears and concerns. Because the economy of 1988 was still clinging precariously to the edges of the artificial credit-card prosperity of the Reagan era, it was difficult for Jackson to break through all the barriers of race and age. However, he came a long way toward overcoming white voters' fear of an African American as president of the United States. His success with them bodes well for the success of a long-term progressive strategy.

The potential for such a movement was evident at the Democratic convention. In the midst of a convention sanitized to remove any hint of an appeal to "special interests," an international union president, William Winpisinger of the Machinists Union, put Jesse Jackson's name into nomination for the presidency. Other than Jackson speakers during the platform debate, and despite the fact that labor represented 25 percent of the delegates in Atlanta, Winpisinger's was the only appearance by a union official on the podium out of dozens of speakers over the four days. In fact, it was the first time a national union official ever nominated a Democratic candidate for president.

There is a non-ideological but politically progressive majority in this country. It has been kept apart and powerless by those in government, politics, business, education, religion and the press whose (primarily economic and largely unconscious) self-interest it is to protect the status quo — or take the country backwards. Those groups have divided the progressive movement by exploiting differences of race, culture, class, sex and age.

It is no accident that most "political education" in this country is ideological or programmatic and avoids discussions of power. People feel free to argue, debate or write about ideology or program but are made to feel afraid or ashamed about consciously seeking power to change their circumstances. Yet the solution to their material problems is achieving power.

The Jackson campaign taught progressives the error of focusing too heavily on ideology and program at the expense of seeking power. The "right" program and the "right" ideology simply are not enough. They must be linked to and supported by a broad-based political constituency — a majority democratic movement. Otherwise, even the "right" program and ideology can eventually reap a political backlash. When that happens, both the progressive and the progressive programs go.

In the simplest terms, power equals numbers. Most politicians understand perfectly at least one of the three R's. However well or poorly they can read or write, they do know how to count. Few are as candid about this matter as Senator Ernest "Fritz" Hollings (D-SC) was when he endorsed Jesse Jackson. The press asked, "Senator Hollings, you've said some very critical things about Jesse Jackson in the past. And you disagree with him on a wide range of issues. So why are you endorsing him?"

Senator Hollings went straight to the heart of the matter: "Jesse Jackson is from South Carolina. Jesse Jackson won South Carolina. I am running again for the Senate from South Carolina. Next question."

But the press, and those who deal with politics, too often count selectively: they skip over the figures that might add up to empowerment of the disenfranchised. For example, when Jesse Jackson was exploring a run for the Democratic presidential nomination, they counted him out. They said, "He can't win. He's not running to win. He's got another agenda."

Did they come to that conclusion based on the numbers, that no matter how large a percentage of the African American vote Jackson got, he couldn't get a winning majority? No.

Either they did not look at the numbers, or they looked and weren't telling.

Count it up yourself. There are about 175 million American citizens eligible to vote. Twenty million of them are African Americans. Thirteen million African Americans are registered — and seven million are not. In 1984, Walter Mondale won the Democratic nomination with a total of 6.8 million primary votes — a number not even equal to the number of unregistered African Americans and only half the number of those registered. Of the 37 million total votes Mondale-Ferraro got in November of 1984, about 10.5 million were African Americans — one-half of potential African American voters.

Perhaps to have told African Americans of their potential political power would have totally changed the 1988 election results — inspiring African Americans with the realization that their vote could make a difference, and thereby vastly increasing their turnout. But then, keeping people ignorant of their own power is one way of preserving the status quo.

## In the Beginning

Jesse Jackson started adding up the figures for himself before 1984. The African American community's liberation from the oldest and most powerful political machine — Chicago's Democratic Party — in America provided his initial motivation. In Chicago in 1983, Congressmember Harold Washington was bidding to become the first African American mayor of the third largest city in the United States — a campaign with tremendous symbolic, as well as material, importance.

Chicago had the largest concentration of African Americans of any city in America. The city was a majority "minority" city — 56 percent of African American and Hispanic descent. Chicago was the national center of African American business development and activity. A national civil rights organization — Operation PUSH — headed by a national leader — Jesse Jackson — was headquartered there. The strongest chapter of the National Urban League was based there, and the NAACP branch had a rich tradition and history. When Dr. Martin Luther King, Jr. chose to take his civil rights movement north, he went to Chicago to fight for open housing.

In 1979, Jane Byrne had been elected mayor with the vote of Chicago's African American community, but once elected she basically turned her back on it. The community had been given little political return on its investment and was insulted on countless occasions. The straw that broke the camel's back, however, was the appointment of an all-white board for the Chicago Housing Authority — which oversaw public housing more than 90 percent occupied by African Americans. When two African American women showed up at the CHA board meeting to protest, they were treated roughly, promptly arrested and thrown in jail. The community was outraged.

In the summer of 1982, to oppose Mayor Byrne's actions and to organize forces to oppose her 1983 re-election effort, a broad-based community coalition organized a boycott of ChicagoFest — a summer festival of food and entertainment which the entire city enjoyed.

The success of that boycott, the political education that took place and the enthusiasm it engendered, motivated the coalition to stay together around a massive voter registration drive. Harold Washington had said he would run for mayor if the community added 50,000 new voters and raised at least $100,000. In six months, the coalition registered 275,000 new voters and far exceeded its fundraising goal.

Despite the long history of struggle against the Cook County Democratic Party machine's oppression, and despite the importance attached to the mayoral race by the African and Latin American communities and progressive whites, Senator Ted Kennedy endorsed Jane Byrne in January of 1983, while Walter Mondale endorsed Richard Daley, Jr. Neither consulted the African American or Hispanic communities before they acted.

Their actions, more than any other single factor, signaled to Jesse Jackson and other African American leaders that if this was the way the "best" in the Democratic Party were going to treat them, then it was time for a new strategy — a new political equation. Their struggle for social, economic and political independence could no longer progress on the coattails of liberals. It must be led by themselves.

In March of 1983, due to a surge in African American voter turnout from 55 percent in 1982 to 80 percent a year later, Harold Washington was elected the first African American mayor of Chicago in what turned into a nationally publicized campaign. That same year, Wilson Goode became the first African American mayor of Philadelphia, the first African American astronaut went into space, and an African American woman was elected Miss America. The African American community started to feel, "We can do anything!"

After the Chicago race (and the Kennedy/Mondale endorsements), Jesse Jackson started talking with other African American leaders about an African American running for president in 1984. Jackson — always the tree shaker — preferred to advocate the idea and support someone else's candidacy. He even met with former Atlanta Mayor Maynard Jackson and current Mayor Andrew Young on several occasions to persuade them to run.

On May 13, 1983, Operation PUSH launched its "Southern Crusade," to focus on voter registration, voter education and voting rights enforcement — and to promote the idea that an African American could and should run for president in 1984.

Somewhere along the trail, at a voter registration rally, the crowd began to chant, "Run, Jesse, run." "Run, Jesse, run" became the rallying cry of the grassroots people's movement that literally propelled Jesse Jackson toward his candidacy.

Jackson's 1984 campaign early on was labelled a "for African Americans only" effort. True enough, in the beginning he spent a disproportionate amount of time campaigning to his potential strength — especially the African American church. There was a great deal of controversy, debate and tension inside the African American community over Jackson's run for the presidency. For Jackson to have a chance to win, or even to have a significant impact, he had to first solidify his grassroots base in the African American community. If he could not convince his base to support him, certainly few others would.

Besides Jackson's initial concentration on his African American support base, the press and pundits interpreted for the public that even the major themes of the campaign — the unfairness of party rules and the protection and expansion of voting rights — were primarily "African American issues." Nothing could have been further from the truth. With only half of all eligible voters participating in presidential elections, poor and working-class whites, progressives, African Americans and all minorities had a stake in opening up the process and expanding participation in the party and in the electorate at large.

There was little interest on the part of the press in understanding, analyzing or objectively reflecting on Jackson's point of view or interpretation of his own campaign. Framing Jackson's role in the 1984 campaign as "He's running against the party" made it easier to dismiss him as a serious contender for the presidency and to shape public opinion against him. Jesse Jackson was not running against the Democratic Party. He was running against the status quo of the Democratic Party.

The political professionals said Jackson was running not to win but to protest, to raise issues and to register voters. They also predicted that the maximum number of delegates Jackson could win in 1984 would be 175 to 200. After winning over 3.5 million primary and caucus votes, Jackson's delegate total reached 465.5. However, due to stacked party rules which did not distribute delegates strictly based on the proportion of the popular vote a candidate received, Jackson received 400 fewer delegates than he had earned in votes. Mondale got 400 more than he had earned.

In 1984, Jackson lost the Democratic nomination, but he won more than he lost. He made the centerpiece of his campaign the enforcement of the 1965 Voting Rights Act, the key to empowering the progressive movement. He inspired two million new voter registrations. In the teeth of Reagan's "landslide" victory for the presidency, the Rainbow constituency helped to elect Democratic candidates Paul Simon in Illinois, Albert Gore in Tennessee, Carl Levin in Michigan and Howell Heflin in Alabama — resulting in a net gain of two Democratic seats in the Senate.

In 1986, the impact of Jackson's 1984 campaign really made itself felt. The Democrats dramatically and solidly recaptured control of the Senate, 55 to 45. Democrats John Breaux of Louisiana, Wyche Fowler of Georgia, Terry Sanford of North Carolina, Richard Shelby of Alabama and Alan Cranston of California all won by margins in which the Rainbow Coalition, the people attracted to politics by the 1984 Jackson campaign, made the difference. In three other races, the Rainbow constituency played an important contributing role: Barbara Mikulski in Maryland, Bob Graham in Florida and Tim Wirth in Colorado. This expansion in the electorate, which resulted in Democratic control of the Senate, was largely responsible for the 1987 defeat of Reagan's ultra-conservative nominee to the Supreme Court — Judge Robert Bork.

### The 1988 Primary Campaign

Shortly after the Rainbow constituency helped return the Senate to the Democrats, Jackson had to confront the question of whether he would again become a presidential candidate in 1988. In political terms, 1988 presented a unique opportunity. For the first time in 20 years, there was no incumbent running for the presidency. One party would not be able to sit on the sidelines and watch the other party tear itself apart during the primary season. In 1988, both parties' candidates would have to compete for the nomination.

The Reagan-Bush administration's anti-people programs and policies had hurt so many at home (and alienated so many abroad) that there was great potential in 1988 for a populist campaign based on significant economic reform. In the past, hard times for those at the bottom had been used by national politicians to drive the races further apart and to drive a wedge between the poor and the middle-class. But now Jackson could use hard economic times for the poor and depressed regions of the country (such as the farm belt) and an uncertain future for everyone but the rich to pull people together across the dividing lines of race, class and sex.

None of the other potential Democratic candidates had a strong, built-in relationship with the national African American and Hispanic communities. There were no Humphreys, McGoverns, Kennedys or Mondales in the race in 1988. Even those African American leaders who might not have preferred Jackson had to acknowledge that there was no white candidate who had a civil rights record or history of involvement in the African American community who they could say more deserved the African American community's vote.

There would also be, for the first time, Super Tuesday — the 20 races focused in the South on March 8, 1988. Fifty-three percent of all African American citizens live in just ten southern states. The southern conservative Democrats created Super Tuesday as a way to push the party to the right and away from "special interests" advocating such things as labor law reform, equality for women and a cut in the military budget. But this time they didn't count very well. A New South of newly registered and newly motivated African American and progresssive voters had been born in 1984 and 1986, suggesting that Super Tuesday might be won by a people's coalition. Unprecedented African American support combined with an expanded white base could turn that conservative intent around. Jackson could run strongly on Super Tuesday and shift the ideological debate in the party to the left.

Also new this election year was the "15 percent threshold" candidates had to reach in an electoral district before they could receive delegates to the convention. The threshold had been lowered (though only slightly, from 20 percent in 1984), as a result of Jackson's pressure during the San Francisco convention. But with one national presidential campaign under its belt, plus an expanding constituency, the rule change would allow for a much fairer allocation of delegates.

With Ronald Reagan's religious fundamentalists and political conservatives on one side and George Bush's "blue blooders" on the other in the Republican Party, and with the Democratic Leadership Council (DLC) on one side and the National Rainbow Coalition on the other in the Democratic Party, both parties lacked clear ideological direction. Control was up for grabs. Thus, even though Gary Hart and George Bush were the early front-runners, it was by no means clear that they would wind up as the eventual nominees.

Republicans were very upset at losing control of the Senate in 1986, at the height of Ronald Reagan's popularity. Conservatives and religious fundamentalists were especially angry and were threatening to make all future Republican candidates "toe the line" on the Reagan platform and social agenda in 1988.

Democrats too were divided. Only Gary Hart and Jesse Jackson had run national campaigns. Hart, Jackson and New York Governor Mario Cuomo were the Democratic front-runners, but they were all "liberal" and thought potentially unacceptable to traditional southern Democrats and to the more moderate-to-conservative northern and western Democrats of the DLC mold. Senator Sam Nunn of Georgia and former Virginia Governor Charles Robb were being encouraged to run in order to give this constituency a voice and a candidate.

At this time, there was considerable concern in some Democratic Party circles that Jackson was not a loyal Democrat. Some Democrats feared that he would bolt the party and try to lead a third-party candidacy if he did not win the nomination or felt that he had not been treated fairly by the party. They forgot or chose to overlook the fact that while for two decades he had to fight to get into and participate in the Democratic Party, he had always been loyal to it and worked hard for its national ticket ever since 1964. In every election in which he was eligible to vote, Jackson had worked for the Democratic ticket.

In 1980, for example, he did not join the Kennedy rebellion against the incumbent President Jimmy Carter precisely because he thought it would weaken the Democratic Party against the Republicans in the general election. Kennedy sat on the sidelines during the fall campaign that year. Jackson did not. Thus, Jackson was being measured by a double standard when it came to party loyalty. Ultimately, the doubts voiced about his loyalty served to diminish his candidacy in the minds of average voters.

The uneasiness about Jackson triggered the "party loyalty" and "non-disruptive" pledge authored by Paul Kirk, Chairman of the Democratic National Committee (DNC), which all of the candidates were asked to sign. Jackson was the first to sign it. Unfortunately, the pledge was forgotten when another Democrat's fury was focused on Jackson. Not once during the attacks by Mayor Ed Koch during the New York campaign did Chairman Kirk try to restore civility by invoking the pledge.

Some others in the party seemed to wish that Jackson would just go away, or just deal with the so-called "fringe" or "locked-out" elements in the Democratic Party. Instead, in 1988, Jackson kept his base of African Americans and progressive whites and moved in on the American mainstream — farmers, workers, women, students and others traditionally part of the Democrats' constituency.

Those party professionals failed to understand how different the Jackson campaign's fundamental political strategy was from current Democratic Party thinking, and how close it really was to the party's roots. Jackson's formula for winning the presidency in 1988, and for the Democrats at the national, state and local levels in the long-term, was to *expand the party* — to bring back into it many of the 75 million voters who had failed to exercise their right to vote in 1984.

He understood that people of lower- and middle-class incomes who traditionally had voted Democrat were heavily concentrated in this "party of nonvoters" — fully half of the eligible electorate. He concluded that this major army of prospective voters had surrendered to apathy when they concluded that they could not make a difference. The Democratic Party had increasingly left them behind as it pursued big business, which provided large PAC contributions to incumbents, and more affluent voters, who voted more often.

With the collapse of liberalism in the 1970s, the party had entered a new era where it was believed to be easier to persuade a likely voter to vote for a candidate than to motivate a probable non-voter. The Democrats suffered from having no program to sell. In the absence of a populist economic program to motivate most Americans, the ideological ground was captured by the Republicans. Without a program of substance, Democrats were left with vague themes and appeals to competence, patriotism and optimism.

Jackson tried to change the formula. He recognized that while Democratic Party professionals were trying to blur the differences between Democrats and Republicans, just the opposite was needed. Roosevelt in the 1930s and Kennedy in the 1960s increased both the participation and enthusiasm of voters (and non-voters) precisely because they spoke to people's economic needs. With the economic uncertainty of the 1990s, the same appeal was needed in 1988.

Thus, while many Democrats, including some of the potential Democratic presidential candidates, had been intimidated enough by Ronald Reagan's economic policies that they were trying to imitate him, Jesse Jackson resisted all the way. He continuously fought Reagan's economic policies that so dramatically favored the rich and big business over the poor, the middle class and small businesses.

Jackson repeatedly attacked the administration's "Robin Hood in reverse" tax policies. He pounded the Reagan-Bush administration for doubling the military budget in peacetime while simultaneously declaring a war on the poor by cutting back on their food, education, health care and housing.

Jackson stood with farmers about to lose their farms to foreclosure; he stood with workers at the plant gate about to slam shut without notice; he stood with small businesspeople at the bank where they couldn't get a loan; he stood with service workers at the hotel where they couldn't get a contract; and he stood with the poor at the hospital where they couldn't get care.

While others said Reagan was racially insensitive, Jackson relentlessly exposed the Reagan administration for its "race conscious" policies, actions and decisions which were consciously designed to hurt people of color, as well as poor people. Jackson often pointed out that throughout Reagan's two presidential terms, he (and this was true of his entire term of office) had never had a formal meeting with the Congressional Black Caucus or a coalition of national civil rights leadership.

The Jackson critique of Reagan's foreign policy was not diluted by the president's popularity. He fought him, on principle, every step of the way. He did not see the U.S. invasion of Grenada — a poor and developing nation of 110,000 people without a standing army — as a great American victory, but as an elephant arrogantly and foolishly stepping on a gnat. He chastised the administration for locking the press out from covering the Grenada invasion.

He charged the Reagan administration with using the Grenada invasion to divert public attention away from the 241 dead Marines being brought home from Lebanon in body bags because they had been placed in danger by an ill-considered policy and left unprotected by a bad security plan.

Jackson always stood by traditional Democratic Party principles. In 1988 the people responded.

### The Greenfield Kick-Off

In hindsight, the Jackson campaign may have symbolically begun on Super Bowl Sunday, January 25, 1987. Jackson had been invited to speak at a church in Greenfield, Iowa, by Jay Howe, a co-chair of the county Democratic Party and by Rev. Bill Olmstead, a local Methodist minister. At the time the invitation had been accepted, Jackson's schedulers had not known it was Super Bowl night. When that

was discovered, Jackson staff inquired about a change of date, but the Greenfield organizers wanted him to come anyway.

He came and so did they — in record numbers at kick-off time. Over 900 people showed up for a church social, supper and service in tiny, rural Greenfield, Iowa. Jackson preached his heart out, and the people responded. It was clear that Jackson could get a hearing and a positive response from white citizens in America's heartland.

He began to travel the country, meeting with African American elected officials. If he was going to run again in 1988, he needed and wanted the African American community unified around his campaign. If it could be unified early, that would free him to spend more time expanding his base beyond his natural constituency. That unification effort largely succeeded. Early in 1987 Jackson was feeling secure that the African American leadership was behind him.

Jackson went back to Greenfield on March 19, 1987 to form and announce his exploratory committee. Six months later in Pittsburgh, Pennsylvania, on Labor Day, September 7, before the parade celebrating the 100th anniversary of the labor movement, Jackson indicated that he would again be a candidate in 1988. The final official announcement came on October 10, before 5,000 supporters in Raleigh, North Carolina, in an appeal to the New South and the nation.

The campaign was on again for Jesse Jackson. He had explored earlier, raised more money and had a better organization in place than in 1984. Willie Brown, the powerful and respected Speaker of the House in California, was chairperson of his campaign, bringing credibility and fundraising potential. Jackson hired Gerald Austin, an experienced professional campaign manager from Columbus, Ohio, who had twice played a principal role in the successful campaigns for Ohio Governor Richard Celeste. He secured the services of other political operatives for key staff positions. He put together a solid and professional campaign team for 1988.

In the debates and on the campaign trail, Jackson shone. His prior experience, his oratorical skills, his media presence, his ability to speak a language that common people could understand, and his ability to engender enthusiasm and motivate supporters all worked well for him in 1988. The biggest challenge he faced was political: to broaden his base of support.

The first opportunity, of course, was the Iowa caucuses. In 1984, Jackson had spent one day campaigning in Iowa. The results spoke for themselves: he got less than three percent of the vote and finished last in a field of eight. In 1988 he intended to run an all-out campaign in Iowa.

By doing well in Iowa, a predominately rural state whose Democratic electorate is 97 percent white, he could accomplish three goals: (1) establish the fact that he was indeed running a national campaign; (2) make a big dent in the "electability" issue; and (3) inspire African American voters across the country to turn out in even greater numbers than in 1984. The public would see that Jackson was running a "real" campaign for the presidency in 1988, not just a "symbolic" or "protest" effort as the media had portrayed it in 1984.

Jackson finished fourth in the Iowa caucuses — behind Gephardt, Simon and Dukakis — with 11 percent of the popular vote (9,773), beating three white candidates. That double-digit finish was significant for Jackson and, in fact, he might have done much better but for the peculiarities of the Iowa caucus system in which only 70 percent of the precincts reported in, and some of his strongest areas did not get recorded. In Waterloo, less than 50 percent of the precincts were counted. Some of the college communities where he did well also went uncounted. Jackson's finish is even more significant compared to the amount of time, money and staff invested in the state by other candidates. He was outspent five to one, outstaffed at least four to one, and spent many fewer days there than the other candidates who seriously competed for the vote.

Iowa did, in fact, begin to make a dent in the assumption that Jackson was not electable. He was not just getting African American votes. He continued to make inroads and to gain support from a broader constituency when he finished fourth (9,615 votes or nine percent) in conservative New Hampshire, a

state with an unemployment rate of two percent and a population that was less than one-half of one percent African American. He even beat Al Gore, the most conservative Democrat in the campaign, who spent ten times as much money and campaigned more days in the state.

He finished second in Minnesota, a state that is 1.3 percent African American. He placed second in Maine with 27 percent of the vote in a state with an African American population of 0.3 percent, and second in the beauty contest in Vermont with 13,044 votes — 26 percent of the vote in the whitest state in America, where only 1,134 African Americans live. These early contests demonstrated Jackson was likely to be a major force to be reckoned with in 1988.

The Super Tuesday primaries and caucuses which followed, 20 races in all, held primarily in the South and border states, proved Jackson's power. Jackson was expected to do well on Super Tuesday — and he did. He won the most popular votes that day (2,547,302) — and he was the only candidate to win delegates in every state that day.

In the 20 races, Jesse Jackson won 16 first or second-place finishes, while Dukakis won 12 and Gore 11. In the Deep South, Jackson received almost 10 percent of the white vote — about two and a half times more than he got in 1984.

On Super Tuesday, according to the *New York Times*, Jackson:

- Won the African American vote (91 percent);
- Won the liberal vote (37 percent);
- Won the labor vote (35 percent);
- Won the women's vote (30 percent);
- Won the 18-29 year-old vote (33 percent);
- Won the 30-44 year-old vote (35 percent);
- Won the 45-59 year-old vote (28 percent);
- Won among those making less than $12,500 a year (44 percent);
- Tied for first among those making between $12,500 and $25,000 a year (28 percent);
- Won among those who voted Democrat in 1984 (39 percent);
- Won among first-time primary voters (31 percent);
- Finished second among conservatives (23 percent);

- Finished second among Hispanics (21 percent);
- Finished second among Catholics (18 percent);
- Finished second among those who grew up in the South.

Jackson was on a roll and was headed for his home state of Illinois. In 1984, Mondale had won the state with 640,000 votes, while Jackson had laid claim to over half that number. In 1983, Harold Washington had been elected mayor with 600,000 votes in Chicago alone. There were now 912,000 registered African American voters in Illinois. Jackson had the momentum coming out of Super Tuesday. With Gore and Dukakis having both done well on Super Tuesday, and with the state's other favorite son, Paul Simon, in the race, the white vote would be divided. Jackson did indeed have a chance to win Illinois.

It had not yet quite hit the African American community that Jackson could actually win the nomination. But it had hit the white political leaders in Illinois, especially those in Chicago with whom Jackson had fought so hard over the past 20 years just to get into the local Democratic Party. It had hit those who had opposed Harold Washington's election as mayor.

Politics in Chicago were racially polarized in part because Jackson, together with the African American community, had fought the political machine for 20 years in order to expand the Democratic Party and move it in a progressive direction. In 1966, Jackson had helped Dr. Martin Luther King, Jr. to organize the first Open Housing march in Gage Park to combat the city's reputation as the most racially segregated community in America. Jackson had led the fight against Mayor Daley's "shoot to kill" order during the 1968 race riots. Jackson had fought Daley tooth and nail over police brutality and school desegregation. He had fought the building trades to provide access to employment and training for African Americans. He had confronted private industry and waged national boycotts against Anheuser Busch and Coca Cola to promote African American economic development.

When the *Chicago Sun-Times* ran a headline on the morning of the election, "Jackson Surging, Simon Sinking," that was all the signal the anti-Jackson forces needed to react. It was clear that Simon, having dropped out of Super Tuesday competition the week before, would not be the nominee. Yet Illinois's anti-Jackson forces gave Simon his first and only victory, with Jackson a strong second.

The experts said that Super Tuesday and the Illinois primary would be Jackson's peak, and the rest would be all downhill. The problem was they had forgotten to tell Jackson's supporters. In Kansas, Jackson ran a strong second (37 percent), winning three of the five congressional districts in the state and turning out more caucus voters than anyone else. In Puerto Rico, he won first place with 29 percent and 103,000 votes. He even won a surprise victory in Alaska, getting 35 percent of the vote.

Then came Michigan. It was possibly Gephardt's last stand. He was putting everything into it that he had. Dukakis had lost badly in Illinois and had yet to win in a northern industrial state outside of Massachusetts. He seemed unable to attract "working people" to his cause. Simon was not competing, and Gore did not seem to be a factor. The experts predicted Jackson maybe had a chance for a close second. As a long shot, he might even inch out a close victory. But no one, literally no one, anticipated the outcome in Michigan.

That Saturday caucus evening, all of the remaining candidates were at a banquet in Wisconsin. CBS Evening News had Michael Dukakis on the early evening news to congratulate him on his Michigan victory. Dukakis responded with caution, acknowledging his victory "only if the lead holds up." Richard Gephardt, taking his cue from media reports, used the occasion to congratulate Dukakis on his victory. One of the Boston papers headlined the Duke's Michigan win.

But Jackson won in a landslide.

Jackson won Michigan, beating Dukakis, his closest competitor, two to one. Michigan had a sizeable African American population for Jackson to draw on — but, by some estimates, Jackson got as high as 40 percent of the white vote in the Michigan caucuses. Jackson made the covers of *Time* and *Newsweek*, and the press was forced to seriously consider the possibility of a Jackson nomination.

Panic began to grip the Democratic Party establishment. Discussion began to surface of superdelegates — those chosen by virtue of their party office rather than by popular vote — as the way to "stop Jackson." The superdelegates could bring some political "sense, judgment, wisdom and stability" to offset the "emotional" appeal of Jackson.

Jackson, sensing the panic setting in, asked former Secretary of Defense, Clark Clifford, and former budget director, Bert Lance, to set up a meeting in Washington with key Democratic insiders to calm the party's fears.

Now "definition" in the campaign was changing. Press expectations had been raised for Jackson. The issue was no longer how well Jackson was doing compared to 1984, or his growing inroads into the white community. The standard became "Could he win?" and the watchword for journalists was *scrutinize* Jackson. But Jackson had been scrutinized from the beginning — personally and politically — more than any other candidate. On the issues, he clearly had been more specific than any of the other candidates.

The Connecticut and Wisconsin primaries and the Delaware and Arizona caucuses preceded the New York primary, now billed as the show-down state. Connecticut, Wisconsin and Arizona did not have large African American populations, so Jackson's expectations for victory were not high.

Jackson tripled his 1984 vote in Connecticut and Wisconsin, and his percentage of the white vote continued to rise. Huge crowds — workers, women, students and families — greeted the campaign everywhere it went. Clearly, Jackson was reaching across and breaking down ancient barriers of race and culture. He was having a tremendous impact.

But something had shifted. The race had narrowed. Babbitt, Hart and Gephardt were now gone; Simon was making his last stand in Wisconsin; and Gore proved to have little appeal in the northern industrial states. The race was coming down to Jackson versus Dukakis in late March — interviews with voters around the Wisconsin primary showed it.

They also reinforced the "yes, but" phenomenon which Dukakis quickly capitalized on. For Dukakis the television ad became, "Do you want a nominee who can defeat the Republicans in November?" It was painful to watch Wisconsin voters being interviewed by the press, speaking from the heart about how Jesse Jackson was the only one speaking to issues of concern to them, yet not wanting to take a chance with four more years of Reaganism. Not wanting to take a chance, they followed the conventional wisdom and voted for Dukakis over Jackson by 48-28 percent.

Because Republicans and Independent voters participated in large numbers in Wisconsin's open Democratic primary, by some estimates, the race was considerably closer among Democrats. A *Washington Post* article noted that only four points would have separated the first and second-place finishers among Democratic voters. And even in second place, Jackson's vote total surpassed Gary Hart's 1984 victory total.

After Wisconsin came two weeks of almost uninterrupted campaigning in New York. Only the Arizona and Delaware caucuses were squeezed into Jackson's schedule. On the eve of the New York primary, Jackson finished a strong second in Arizona and first in Delaware.

Thus, the stage was set for the show-down in New York between Jackson, Dukakis and Gore. If Jackson won, it would be post-Michigan all over again, with panic setting in among the party establishment. If Gore made a good showing, he would probably continue; if not, he would probably have to drop out. If Dukakis won by more than five percentage points over Jackson, he would be hard to catch.

Mayor Koch went on the offensive against Jackson saying, among other things, "that Jews would have to be crazy to vote for Jackson." Gore, trying to make inroads into the Jewish community in New York, attacked Jackson for his positions on the Middle East. Dukakis refused to be drawn into the fray, and Jackson generally succeeded in maintaining a posture above it.

When the results were in, Dukakis won New York 51 to 37 percent, in part because of the divisiveness injected by Koch. Gore won only eight percent of the vote and was now out of the race. Jackson pulled in about 225,000 more votes than he had gotten in 1984, but that wasn't enough to win. Jackson's statesmanship in the face of continuous and withering attacks won applause from all quarters. Mayor Koch's actions left the city more racially and religiously divided than ever before.

Dukakis was now clearly the front-runner, but Jackson vowed to continue to the end — to pursue the nomination as well as to carry the torch for economic democracy, equal opportunity and a just foreign policy all the way to the Democratic convention in Atlanta. Dukakis had a very small popular vote lead over Jackson going into New York, and even after New York, his lead was just 34 percent to Jackson's 30 percent.

Dukakis's delegate vote lead was relatively bigger because Paul Simon had put his campaign on hold, rather than dropping out, after his poor showing in Wisconsin, and Al Gore had done the same after New York. In the history of American politics, when it became clear that a candidate could not win the nomination and had stopped campaigning, the candidate would officially drop out and release his or her delegates. Jackson had placed second to Gore and Simon in states they had won. Under the rules, if they had dropped out, all of Simon's and most of Gore's at-large delegates would have moved to Jackson. If both of them had dropped out, as Dick Gephardt had done after the Michigan caucuses, Jackson and Dukakis would still have been in a virtual tie in terms of delegates, even after New York. By denying Jackson access to their delegates at a critical time in the campaign, they both in effect engaged in a "stop Jackson" effort.

Even though the race was still close, Dukakis was labeled the winner; Jackson was deemed to have no chance. Whereas after Jackson's Michigan victory the press theme had been scrutinize, scrutinize, scrutinize, it now seemed to be coronate, coronate, coronate. No one put Dukakis under close scrutiny, despite the fact that it was generally acknowledged he had been vague and non-specific on issues.

The press and party establishment said the race was over, but again the Jackson support-

ers failed to get the message. The largest crowds that Jackson drew throughout the entire campaign came after New York, after the press and party regulars said the campaign was over. In Ohio, at Ohio State University, Jackson drew 12,000 people to a rally on the eve of the primary. In Oregon, Jackson drew crowds of over 13,000 and 15,000 at Oregon State and the University of Oregon, with thousands who could not get into the gymnasiums standing on the outside. Jackson carried the campaign right through to Montana, New Mexico and New Jersey, to the last primary in California on June 7 — getting over one million votes in California alone.

Why was it important for Jackson to carry the campaign all the way to the convention in Atlanta? Jackson had to continue to keep rolling up popular vote totals and delegates. If he could at least equal Mondale's popular vote numbers for 1984 and get at least one-fourth of the convention delegates, he would have the power to be a progressive voice at the convention. The Jackson forces could keep Dukakis from moving to the right and give him a progressive political base to move toward if he were elected. They had to continue to make it clear to Dukakis and the Democratic Party the kind of political platform and agenda the American people wanted implemented in a new Democratic administration. Only by continuing to accumulate votes and delegates could they show them that. Jackson had contended from the beginning that what America wanted was not just a new director, but a new direction. The more votes he got, the more proof he had.

The Jackson campaign also had to continue its all-out battle for the nomination, even if winning was now a long shot, in order to keep people inspired and involved. It's what Jackson called, "Keep hope alive!" After all, in politics many things can happen. In any case the Jessecrats' votes were still needed if the Democrats were going to win in November.

For these reasons Jackson continued to press even harder the issues of the day: for a "Workers Bill of Rights" and a "Corporate Code of Conduct"; for a National Health Care Program; for reordering budget priorities; for declaring South Africa a "terrorist state"; for proposing a two-state solution in the Middle East — with security guaranteed to both the Israelis and the Palestinians.

While Jackson continued to campaign hard and to sharpen the focus on issues, to clarify the distinctions between himself and Dukakis, nevertheless, he wanted to avoid divisions that would leave scars and bring about a Democratic defeat in November. Jackson did not in any way want to contribute to a loss for his party, but rather to strengthen the Democrats' case as they drove for victory in November. Thus, he neither defamed Dukakis nor quit in disgust and defeat. Rather, he continued to lay out the arguments that he thought would help the party in the fall and he went all out until the Democratic convention in Atlanta in July, raising money, drawing huge crowds and getting the support of millions of voters. When Jackson said he had unleashed hope in the land, he had some powerful evidence.

### Winning Every Day

Overall, what did Jackson accomplish in the primaries and caucuses in 1988? He accumulated approximately seven million primary and caucus votes — double his total in 1984 and more votes than Walter Mondale accumulated in winning the nomination that year.

In terms of total delegates, Jackson finished a strong second. In the primary and caucus season, Jackson earned about 1,075 delegates to Dukakis's 1,790, a ratio of two to three. At the Atlanta convention, Jackson finished with 1,218.5, Dukakis with 2,876.25, a ratio of three to seven. The dramatic difference between "earned" and the "final" number of delegates was due in large part to the unelected superdelegates. No one else was even in contention. Jackson won 92 congressional districts in 32 states. By comparison, Jackson went into the 1984 convention with 384.5 delegates (and finished with 465.5 delegates) having won 60 congressional districts.

Jackson won ten states during the primary season: Alabama, Alaska, Delaware, Georgia, Louisiana, Michigan, Mississippi, South Carolina, Vermont and Virginia; he also won in the District of Columbia, Puerto Rico and the Virgin Islands. However, when delegations cast their votes at the convention, Jackson was taken to the cleaners; he won only four: the District of Columbia, Mississippi, South Carolina and the Virgin Islands — due to the inequity caused by superdelegates and the party's convention rules.

Jackson had narrowly lost Texas, but at the convention the delegate vote was 135 to 71 in favor of Dukakis. Because of Simon's and Gore's refusal to terminate their campaigns, instead of a minimum of 84 delegates in Illinois, Jackson got 57; instead of a minimum of 39 delegates in Tennessee, he got 20. Short of tearing up the convention, there was little Jackson could do. Despite the superdelegate inequity, Jackson still received the *most votes ever* by a runner-up for the presidential nomination.

Of 56 races, Jackson won 46 first- or second-place finishes. Jackson ran a strong national campaign because he ran very well in every region of the country — northwest, northeast, southern, border, western and midwestern states. (See the tables in the Appendix for a complete breakdown of the results.)

Overall, Jackson won the 18 to 29 year-old vote and essentially broke even in the 30 to 44 year-old vote. Thus he won the 18 to 44 year-old vote — the voice of a new generation. Jackson stepped into the vacuum left by Gary Hart and became a powerful force for the future direction of the party. As a Jackson staffer noted to a CBS correspondent: "Jesse Jackson is the future of the Democratic Party; if you don't believe me, go ask your kids!"

The Jackson campaign provided the nation with some of the primary election's very finest moments: Jesse in the pulpit of Ebenezer Baptist Church; Jesse on the Edmund Pettus bridge in Selma; Jesse comforting an aged Hispanic woman in a housing project in San Antonio; Jesse becoming the first candidate since Robert F. Kennedy to visit America's poorest whites in Appalachia; Jesse in Kenosha, Wisconsin, in subzero weather before 5,000 autoworkers; Jesse surrounded by white Wisconsin farmers as far as the eye could see; Jesse refusing to wallow in the mud with Mayor Koch; Jesse comforting people with AIDS all over the country; Jesse winning the stunning victory in Michigan; Jesse with 12,000 people in Columbus, Ohio, with overflow crowds even as late as Oregon, with a huge crowd of Native

Americans and rural Montanans on reservation land, filling the plaza in Santa Fe, marching with Cesar Chavez in California, and demonstrating with paperworkers everywhere.

The finest, most profound and continuing contribution was Jesse proving that white Americans would vote for an African American presidential candidate in numbers no one had believed possible.

## On to Atlanta

After the last primary on June 7, the focus of the campaign shifted from the primaries and caucuses to the Platform, Rules and Credentials Committees of the convention. Dukakis had wrapped up enough delegates to win the nomination, but Jackson, with over 25 percent of the delegates, was still campaigning and had put a sophisticated computerized delegate tracking operation in place.

Former New Mexico Governor Toney Anaya headed Jackson's Credentials Committee operation. Through skillful negotiations, he resolved all of the potential credentials fights before Atlanta — the first time that had happened since the McGovern credentials rule changes in 1972.

Harold Ickes, a New York attorney — whom some had characterized as a "neutron bomb" when Jackson appointed him — headed Jackson's thrust for changes in the Rules Committee. With skillful bargaining and creative leadership, Ickes negotiated major changes in the way future delegates will be selected so that they will better reflect the popular vote.

Changes won in the party rules for 1992 were:

- The number of Democratic convention superdelegates was cut by 240, or one-third. In 1988, superdelegates made up over 15 percent of the convention. In 1992, superdelegates will comprise less than 10 percent. This is a clear move toward more popular control of the Democratic Party.

- The "winner-take-all" primaries in effect in Illinois, Pennsylvania, New Jersey, Maryland, West Virginia and Puerto Rico were eliminated. No longer will a candidate who wins an election district by only 1% of the popular vote be given 100% of these delegates. "Winner take more," or "bonus" primaries, were also eliminated. From now on, all primaries will be proportional, a rule change that again promotes greater democracy and fairness.

- An incentive system was developed whereby if a state party reforms its procedures so that Democratic National Committee (DNC) members are elected by convention delegates (instead of by the State Executive Committee, as is often the case), they will be rewarded with an additional DNC seat. Over time, this change should help democratize the hierarchy of state parties, furthering the Jackson campaign's institutional goal of expanding progressive leadership in party structures.

Had these and other new democratizing rules been in effect in 1988, the delegate gap between Jackson and Dukakis in Atlanta would have shrunk by about 400 votes.

While progressives did not achieve the goal of nominating and electing Jesse Jackson to the U.S. presidency in 1988, they did enable the movement for social and economic justice to take a major leap forward. That movement now has more power — both within the political structure and in the streets — than it has ever had before. It is no longer a "fringe" movement. It is in the mainstream of the Democratic Party. Progressives have considerably increased their leverage and are getting closer to having the power to make their peace and justice agenda the policy of the government.

In Atlanta, as in the primaries and caucuses, Jackson and the progressive movement contributed significantly to the direction and tone of the convention. Polls showed that most Democratic Party activists in Atlanta agreed with Jackson's positions on the issues; they were kept in line supporting the governor's positions only by the Dukakis campaign's whip system. Almost every speaker borrowed words and thoughts from Jesse Jackson. The progressive program of justice at home and peace abroad became the rhetoric of the Democratic Party. While rhetoric is not policy, the party's adoption of Jackson's rhetoric provides new opportunities to build the progressive movement and achieve specific policy changes in the future.

Jackson's campaign created a "new equation" within the structure of the national Democratic Party that was evident in a growing respect traditional Democrats displayed for the progressive forces in the party, and concretely evident in the 20 new seats, including a vice-chairmanship for voter registration (selected by Jackson), added to the DNC.

Although the platform adopted by the Democratic Party was not the one that would have been put in place if Jackson had been the nominee, nevertheless it was a platform profoundly influenced by Jackson forces. The very goals of the platform — toward the meeting of human needs at home and at least "restraint" of militarism — were Jackson's goals and direction. Of the 13 platform planks in dispute between the two campaigns, Jackson lost only two. He negotiated and won major portions of nine of the 13 minority planks that were submitted — news that the press largely ignored.

Despite the Dukakis campaign's unwillingness to face the need for new taxes and spending commitments, it joined Jackson in calling for new priorities and investing in America — by requiring that "the wealthy and corporations pay their fair share." The Dukakis forces joined Jackson in pledging a "significant" increase in education funding. They joined Jackson in pledging to provide the "funding necessary to reach those unserved children" who qualify for WIC, prenatal care and Head Start — an estimated $10 billion per year expenditure. They joined Jackson in adopting language which recognizes the need to move beyond the Cold War, in agreeing to "promptly initiate a mutual moratorium on missile flight testing," to "support the sovereignty, independence and territorial integrity of Lebanon," and to implement a wide-ranging peace plan in Central America.

Jackson did lose on his specific proposals to raise $40-50 billion per year in new revenues from the rich and corporations and on the United States adopting a nuclear weapons "no first use" pledge. On a third minority plank — self-determination and a homeland for the Palestinians — Jackson won a moral victory. Never before at a national convention had a major public debate taken place over this issue.

But even prior to arriving in Atlanta, Jackson was able to do what no other runner-up ever had done before — sit down with the prospective nominee and co-write the *majority report*, the party's platform. The Democratic Leadership Council was nowhere to be found. Thus, the platform incorporated the Jackson position on the war on drugs, on saving family farmers, on preserving the environment and on achieving energy security. Because of Jackson it called for "major increases" in child-care funding, endorsed his pension fund reinvestment plan and supported universal, same-day voter registration. It incorporated key themes from the "Jackson Doctrine," which outlined a more equitable and respectful relationship between the United States and the Third World. It outlined Jackson's five-point plan for bringing democracy to southern Africa, including a U.S. declaration of South Africa as a "terrorist state." Such a declaration by the next president would have given him the power to immediately implement comprehensive sanctions and order all U.S. corporations out by a date certain.

The Democratic platform became a document that evidenced the progressive movement's growing strength. In practical terms, it also provides a standard by which candidates can be held accountable and deemed worthy of support.

Because of the prominence of issues in the Jackson campaign and the debate with Dukakis over the platform, Jackson received commitments from the leadership of the Democratic Party to support the following legislative changes:

- The Dellums Bill, which imposes comprehensive sanctions against South Africa.

- The Conyers Bill, which establishes same-day, on-site registration of voters. This would vastly expand the enfranchisement and empowerment of the millions of people who today remain outside the political process.

- Legislation to make the District of Columbia a state. This would not only benefit the people who live in the District by making them full citizens for the first time, but it is likely to also affect the entire country by adding two new members of the U.S. Senate and another governor, all of whom are likely to support progressive goals.

■ Comprehensive child-care legislation.

■ Economic set-asides for minorities, thus activating present "paper" policies that have never been enforced. The set-asides mean a guarantee that 10 percent of the billions of dollars a year that the federal government spends on goods and services would be invested in minority communities.

Finally, and perhaps the greatest victory of the Jackson campaign, is that a revolution took place. Progressives changed their minds about themselves. They saw themselves as winners. Their expectations were expanded. They won respect and legitimacy for the progressive movement of jobs, peace and justice that they are building at both the national and local levels.

Progressives who supported the Dukakis-Bentsen ticket did so not because the candidates represented everything progressives wanted nor because they represented the lesser of two evils. It's because they represented a party within which progressives now have considerable power. Dukakis-Bentsen represented a party that made important public commitments to progressives in terms of policies, platforms and direction for the future. Many progressives supported them because, if they helped put them in office, they could rightfully hold them accountable to their public commitments.

Some say that the choice between Dukakis and Bush was not significant. Jackson and many in the progressive movement disagreed. There was a difference between Dukakis and Bush on housing for the homeless, health care for every American, and jobs for all. There was a difference between Dukakis and Bush on foreign policy because Dukakis had a clearer, more rational and more humane view of U.S. interests and purposes in the world.

It would make a profound difference to the people of South Africa if a party came to power in the United States, South Africa's most powerful ally, that had stated that the government there should be declared a "terrorist state." It would make a profound difference to the people of Nicaragua if a president were in the White House who had pledged not to support the contras — and the Democratic nominee pledged that. It would make a profound difference to the people of Angola if the United States had a president who had promised to withdraw support from the murderers of UNITA. The Democratic nominee promised that.

The key to a progressive agenda, however, was not Dukakis-Bentsen. Jackson's Rainbow Coalition formed an alliance with the liberal-center and conservative wings of the Democratic Party because at that moment there was a mutual interest in defeating the Bush-Quayle ticket. More important than Dukakis being in office was who put him in office — his support base. If people of color and progressive whites helped put him in office — and if he wanted to be re-elected — he would be responsive to the people who elected him. If progressives did not turn out for him and he won, he would respond to those others who did vote for him. If progressives did not turn out for him and he lost, they would be blamed and their cause set back.

This is the strategy Jackson articulated. While the Jackson campaign supported the Dukakis-Bentsen ticket, it also continued to build an independent political force that was free to challenge. It organized from the bottom up, ran candidates for office, created new equations between the Rainbow Coalition and state Democratic Parties, engaged in reciprocal voting, insisted on shared slate-making, and shared responsibility for the future of the Democratic Party and the country.

The Jackson forces built state-by-state, congressional district-by-congressional district. They combined influence in the "suites" with "street heat" — pressure from the bottom up. They sought to place themselves, in Jackson's words, "close enough to serve, but distant enough to challenge." As Jackson told his delegates on the Friday after the Democratic convention, "'street heat' will have to continue even when I am president." Who puts you in office and holds you accountable after you are in office is what's most important in politics.

Thus Jackson, and his Rainbow Coalition, will continue to build their movement as an "independent third force" within the Democratic Party. With this campaign, the "third force" has become a main stream in the Democratic Party because it is addressing the real needs of the people of this country and drawing increasingly broad support from them. It is the heart and soul of the Democratic Party, and there is every reason to believe it can soon be the prevailing power in the party.

Some argue that the progressive movement won little in the 1988 primary season. Saying that, Jackson told his delegates in Atlanta, is like a hungry person sending someone to the store to buy a steak, and when he cannot find any steak, he comes home empty-handed. There was hamburger, beans, mashed potatoes and corn in Atlanta. The Jackson campaign brought them home, knowing full well that on the next occasion it will go back again and get the steak.

Some tell progressives they should not be in the Democratic Party at all because its purpose, design, organization and funding are not meant to turn the country in a new direction. But if progressives had not been working within the Democratic Party, it is unlikely that the movement would have reached seven million voters with its program in 1988. It is also unlikely that Jackson would have had the chance to lay out a progressive program before tens of millions of television viewers as he did July 19, from the podium of the Democratic Convention, in one of the most moving speeches in convention history.

So progressives moved into the 1988 fall election season with confidence — confidence in themselves, their program and their leadership — confident that their movement was now providing moral leadership to the country. As progressives worked to expand the base of the party, they felt confident that they would soon have the organized strength to achieve the power necessary to make their program the policy of the nation.

## Against the Odds

Special attention must be given to the manner in which the press covered the Jackson campaign. Since it could not fully accept an African American presidential candidate, the press effectively limited the early growth of Jackson's efforts.

While press coverage of the Jackson campaign was generally better in 1988 than it had been in 1984, its quality still fell far short of what a major — or even minor — candidate should expect. No one can say that Jackson did not or does not get press coverage — often very good press coverage. He did and does. But no matter how visible he was in the press in 1986 and 1987, Jackson was largely rejected when and where it counts — as a serious Democratic presidential contender.

In the beginning, the press rejected Jackson's candidacy, saying he could not win. Instead of analyzing the racial hurdle that Jackson had to overcome if he was to become a serious contender, much of the press concluded early on that he could never leap over it. Even when the situation was changing right before their eyes, the press found it hard to believe what they were seeing.

Gary Hart, according to all the polls, initially was the Democratic front-runner. Jackson was almost always a strong but distant second. Then Hart dropped out of the race in the spring of 1987. Over the next seven months, all the polls showed Jackson in first place among Democrats.

Normally, the press reports stories on polls and then concludes the reporting with a note that goes something like, "At this point the poll may only mean that the leading candidate has high name recognition" (not an insignificant advantage for a politician to have).

But when Jackson became the front-runner according to the polls, the normal concluding remarks ended up in the front of the story. The meaning of being first in the polls was changed from "front-runner" to the Democrat with highest "name recognition." Most stories went on to say, "No one, of course, expects Jackson to remain number one in the polls or to actually win the nomination." He was sometimes called the "statistical front-runner."

No one, of course, expected all seven candidates running to actually win the nomination. But only Jackson's candidacy was rejected out-of-hand before he had even taken the first test of the Iowa caucuses.

Other times, Jackson seemed to be Ralph Ellison's "Invisible Man." In early 1987, the *New York Times* wrote an article naming and giving an overview of the prospective Democratic presidential candidates. Jackson, the third-place finisher in 1984, then number two in the polls, with the largest voting bloc in the Democratic Party, was not even mentioned.

In another story, Lawrence Barrett of *Time* magazine wrote that Gary Hart was leading in the polls because, among other reasons, "He was the only Democratic candidate who had run a national campaign before." Later, *Time* followed up with a graph and chart showing Hart, Cuomo and Jackson in a close race, but with a story putting Jackson in the same category as Pat Robertson — both of whom were dismissed as religious misfits, not potentially serious political leaders. *Time*'s story gave one or two paragraphs to all the other "serious" candidates.

On the Friday before Super Tuesday, NBC's Sunrise Show was building up the day in which 20 races would be run. The commentator said it was coming down to a two-person race. Listeners might have anticipated her including Jackson among the two, since at that point Jackson had placed second in Minnesota, Maine and Vermont, and was expected to do very well in the South. Instead, she chose Gore and Dukakis — but she added there was a "wildcard" in the race who might actually win the most votes and the most delegates — Jesse Jackson. The person who gets the most votes and the most delegates is usually referred to as the "winner" or the "front-runner," not a "wildcard."

Jackson was often referred to as an "extremist" or dismissed for having "extreme" ideas and programs. Yet it was his ideas and programs that were emulated and borrowed by candidates of both parties, and he largely set the tone and the agenda for the entire campaign with his emphasis on drugs, workers and youth. Toward the end of the campaign,

Jackson laid out to the press — which was constantly asking him what he wanted — a wide-ranging "extreme" agenda on jobs, health care, education and housing. They were later stunned to hear that he was quoting from a 1940s speech by Franklin Delano Roosevelt.

The press's pre-judgment that Jackson could not win continued into the convention. A confidential CBS briefing report for its journalists in Atlanta characterized Jackson's in-roads in the white community as follows: "For all the efforts of the Jackson campaign to identify some kind of victory for their candidate, it is hard to find any way of looking at his performance (aside from his 92 percent showing among African American voters) that merits more than a nice try." Here's another way to look at it — how about history in the making?

The way press and pollsters put their questions can determine the answers they get. Polls on Jesse Jackson's "electability" sometimes revealed more about the attitudes of the person posing the question than the person answering it.

For example, if the University of Iowa had a basketball coaching vacancy and you asked Iowans if they wanted a new coach who could attract the best basketball talent in the country, could fill up the gymnasium, could win conference championships and possibly win a national championship, all of Iowa would say "Yes!" If you then asked, "Do you mind if the new coach is African American?", the overwhelming majority of Iowans would say, "No!"

If, on the other hand, you had the same coaching vacancy and your first question was, "Do you think the new coach should be African American?", most people might say "No."

The pollsters did not say to the people they polled, "Do you want a president who will fight for full employment and the rights of workers? a president who will fight to see that everyone pays a fair share of taxes? a president who will fight for a national health care program, the right of all Americans to live in decent, safe, sanitary and affordable housing, for an educational system that allows students to go as far as their interest and intellect will take them? and a candidate who offers bold leadership and a new direction?" If they had, the answer quite likely would have been "Yes."

If they had next asked, "Do you mind if such a candidate is African American?", the answer quite likely would have been "No." But when they ask, "Do you want an African American for president?" or "Do you think an African American can be elected president?", the answer was predictably "No."

The reporters who wrote, "Jackson is doing all the right things, but he can't win" (sometimes stating, but more often implying, because he's African American) did their profession, the Jackson campaign and the American people a disservice. They were engaging in prejudice — race-conscious, if not racist per se, pre-judgment. They were loading the question and tilting the playing field against the Jackson campaign.

The press, the pollsters, the pundits and the professional politicians largely failed to understand how America has grown and how Americans were trying to grow during the Jackson campaign. In large measure, they also failed to understand how Jackson had grown. These were major political stories in 1988 and the great majority of America's political journalists flatly missed them.

America is not the same as it was twenty years ago — or even four years ago — and neither is Jackson. Twenty years after the assassination of Martin Luther King, Jr., an African American was at the front of the national polls for seven months in the largest political party of the most powerful nation on earth. Things have changed and are changing!

So Jackson's moral challenge to the American people throughout the campaign — from Iowa to California — was, "If I am your first choice, why not vote for me and actively choose the winner, rather than passively settle for your second choice because someone has told you that I cannot win."

With all the concern in this country, in the Soviet Union and around the globe about achieving peace in the world, someone once said that in the final analysis, "Peace begins with me."

That was the very personal challenge of the Jackson campaign. The decision of whom one was going to vote for was in the hands, the hearts, the minds and the consciences of the American people. If the people thought he was the best candidate — if he was their number one choice — then he deserved their vote.

Perhaps the finest but most overlooked contribution the campaign made was the way it improved race relations in this country.

When Jackson started the campaign, racial violence was a national issue. The Goetz subway case in New York was fresh in people's minds. So was the Howard Beach murder in Queens and racial segregation in Forsyth County, Georgia. Racial incidents on college campuses were on the rise.

Given the explosiveness of race, the abandonment of civil rights by the Reagan administration and the dismal economic conditions facing many poor and working-class African Americans and whites, the Jackson candidacy could have dramatically increased racial tensions in our society. Instead, Jackson's candidacy persuaded the American people to come to grips with how they felt about the man's race, and to grow.

This confronting of race and the resulting creative tension and growth expressed itself in many ways. The size of the crowds (especially in almost all-white states such as Oregon, Connecticut and Wisconsin), the feeling of celebration, the obvious expressions of joy, the enthusiasm engendered, the often-stated, "He makes me feel good about myself, others and my country," were all expressions of this growth.

There were ugly incidents — for example, the St. Louis couple who plotted Jackson's assassination. But, as Jackson often pointed out, the very day that they were arrested, he got nearly 40 percent of the vote in Oregon. The glass one-quarter full of poisoned fear was three-quarters full of hope.

Over the years, Jackson has argued that sometimes you can think yourself into a new way of acting, while at other times you can act yourself into a new way of thinking. Both happened with Jackson, his staff, his supporters and the American people, because of the Jackson campaign.

While both thinking and acting are important, shifts in who has power in this country are probably the greatest determinant of a shift in attitudes. The attitudes and actions of the majority society, and those institutions that tend to dominate our perceptions of society, will shift in proportion to the economic and political power gained by African Americans — so too by labor, women, the poor, gays and other groups facing discrimination of one sort or another.

The greatest growth resulting from the Jackson campaign came in those in whom it was least expected — white workers, farmers and southerners. Many of the people conventional wisdom would predict to be the least sympathetic to a Jackson candidacy proved to be the most open and the most supportive. The classic example may be the people and place Jackson chose to make his initial state headquarters, Greenfield, Iowa, where only a few years ago the Ku Klux Klan thrived.

Together with the American people, the Jackson campaign showed how much America has grown in the last 20 years. Jackson made race less of an issue in American politics this year (unfortunately it was not enough to dilute the Republicans' favorite strategy of subtly playing on racial hatreds in the fall to win the general election). He made citizens feel pride and joy in their country, as they responded to a positive campaign. He called on us to make America better. He aimed at the best in our people, and his aim was true.

This openness of the American people to an African American who did not fit the conventional mold and did not mouth the conventional wisdom bodes well for future populist campaigns for social and economic justice. It serves as a basis to keep hope alive.

### Epilogue — Lessons from the 1988 General Election

The 1988 elections have come and gone. For progressives the results are mixed. On the one hand, Democrats lost the White House and with it the potential to reverse the most harmful policies of the past eight years. (One hopes that the Democrat-controlled Congress will fashion a more humane and progressive legislative and political agenda under Bush than it did under Reagan, by whom it was often intimidated.)

Yet, despite Dukakis's defeat, progressives can feel hopeful, especially about the long-term prospects for our political agenda. We can take comfort in growing public support for a government with compassion, a government that curbs corporate greed, that stops the scourge of drugs, that protects our families, that cleans up the environment, that ensures a decent education for our children, that ends homelessness, that provides health care for all Americans, that rebuilds our industries so we can better compete in the world marketplace, and that promotes human rights and just economic development around the globe.

Clearly, at the national level, the Democratic Party is at a crossroads. Largely because of the backlash to the progress of the civil rights and anti-Vietnam War movements of the 1960s, its old coalition of voters has been fractured. Lyndon Johnson predicted as much two decades ago, when he noted that passage of historic civil rights legislation meant the Democrats would lose the South for a generation. Because the party has failed to come to grips with these challenges — to address them head-on in a clear and principled way — and to actively build a new coalition, we've lost our way. The result: Democrats have lost the last five out of six presidential elections, only squeaking into the White House in the aftermath of Watergate in 1976.

But the 1988 election also signals an end to the era of conservative reaction ushered in by Reagan. Bush won only a mandate for a kinder, gentler nation from the voters (plus a mandate to curtail prison furlough programs and to recite the Pledge of Allegiance at public gatherings). He had no coattails: Democrats gained three seats in the House (usually the defeated party has a net loss of 10-15 seats), gained one seat in the Senate, added one governorship and kept their commanding majority in state legislatures, almost guaranteeing that Republicans will not control redistricting in 1991.

Bush did not even win convincingly in a time of relative peace and prosperity. In fact, as Table 1 on the next page indicates, Dukakis lost by a relatively narrow margin.

Dukakis won a total of 112 electoral votes from ten states and the District of Columbia. He lost 12 other states by four percentage points or less. In raw numbers, this translates

**Table 1:**

**Swing States in the Dukakis Victory Scenario**

| State | Electoral Votes | Percentage of Votes Bush-Dukakis | Margin of Dukakis Loss | Votes Needed to Switch | Number of Precincts | Voters per Precinct |
|---|---|---|---|---|---|---|
| Illinois | 24 | 51-49 | 94,999 | 47,499 | 11,696 | 4 |
| Pennsylvania | 25 | 51-48 | 105,143 | 52,572 | 9,459 | 6 |
| Maryland | 10 | 51-48 | 49,863 | 24,931 | 1,570 | 16 |
| Vermont | 3 | 51-48 | 8,556 | 4,278 | 300 | 15 |
| California | 47 | 51-48 | 352,684 | 176,342 | 23,627 | 8 |
| Missouri | 11 | 52-48 | 83,534 | 41,767 | 4,695 | 9 |
| New Mexico | 5 | 52-47 | 25,844 | 12,922 | 1,175 | 11 |
| Connecticut | 8 | 52-47 | 73,657 | 36,829 | 743 | 50 |
| Montana | 4 | 52-46 | 21,456 | 10,728 | 965 | 12 |
| So. Dakota | 3 | 53-47 | 19,855 | 9,928 | 1,153 | 9 |
| Colorado | 8 | 53-45 | 106,724 | 53,362 | 2,752 | 20 |
| Michigan | 20 | 54-46 | 289,703 | 144,852 | 6,645 | 22 |
| **Subtotal** | **168** | | **1,232,018** | **616,010** | **64,780** | **10** |
| Dukakis | 112 | | | | | |
| **TOTAL** | **280** | | | | | |

Source: ABC News Election Systems.

into 1,232,018 additional Democratic voters (see "Margin of Dukakis Loss" column), or only 616,010 voters needed to be motivated to switch from the Bush to the Dukakis column for Dukakis to have won. Considering that there were a total of 64,780 precincts in these 12 states, the number of votes needed to switch was less than *ten* votes per precinct.

These 12 swing states comprise an additional 168 electoral votes, for a total of 280 electoral votes — eight more than are needed to win. The 1988 election was closer than it has been portrayed.

With such a close loss, one can reasonably argue that a preoccupation with attracting Reagan Democrats, together with some tactical errors, cost Dukakis the election.

The strategic mistake was a failure to clearly identify the Democratic constituency and to adopt a clear ideology and a compelling message those voters could identify with. To recapture the White House, and to be the party of the future, Democrats must target four groupings: they have to mobilize *traditional* Demo-

crats, reach out to *potential* Democrats (those who are probable Democrats but aren't voting), appeal to *new* Democrats (our youth) and recapture *strayed* Democrats — the so-called Reagan Democrats. (Democrats must also copy recent GOP strategy, by finding issue "wedges" to campaign on which split Republican constituency coalitions at the presidential-election level.)

The principal rule of politics is to secure your base of support first and then incrementally increase your support among more marginal voters. The Dukakis campaign did just the opposite. Worse yet, it assumed that the goals of securing the Democratic base and attracting new support were antithetical. By focusing singular attention on the Reagan Democrats early on in the campaign, it ignored the core Democratic base of support — organized labor, women, African Americans and Hispanics, the poor, environmentalists and others. The campaign also assumed that Reagan Democrats were monolithic and that they could only be appealed to on the basis of fiscal conservatism and by appearing to be "strong on defense." In reality, the eight to twelve million Reagan Democrats suffered disproportionately from Reaganomics. They could have been strongly appealed to on populist economic themes.

Dukakis failed to exploit the common fears and the collective hopes of this potential Democratic universe. At no time did he systematically critique how the economy had been undermined by Reagan-Bush, how the rich and corporations had been indulged, the middle-class squeezed and the poor pummeled, or identify what Dukakis would do to change this. Dukakis only seemed to support a little tinkering at the edges. For instance, according to the *Baltimore Sun*, Bush's domestic proposals added up to $10 billion in new spending; Dukakis's totalled only $2.2 billion. Only in the last two weeks of the campaign — when Dukakis finally took up this populist message — did he begin to get back into the ballgame. From that point on crowds swelled, he reversed his steady slide in the polls since the second debate, and undecided voters broke his way — by a margin of 55 percent to 43 percent.

The Dukakis campaign's decision to avoid a debate about ideology meant they were left with promoting the candidate as a "competent manager." That message may work for the governor's office, but America doesn't look to its presidents — especially Democratic ones — for personal competence as much as for hope, a vision for the future, charisma, a caring warmth, toughness and strength. By personalizing the campaign so much and by not offering a compelling program that would take America into the future, Dukakis effectively took himself out of the "futures debate" — the one issue that every poll said would work to his advantage.

Ironically, avoiding ideology meant a passive rejection of the best that liberalism has offered: support for the "little person," protection from the ravages of big business, Social Security, Medicare, a progressive tax system, college loans, the G.I. Bill of Rights, child welfare, civil rights for all Americans, fair labor relations, the Atlantic Alliance.

Without a message, a program, populist symbols and a common language, traditional Democrats didn't feel they had a stake in Dukakis's campaign. Alienated voters didn't feel hope. Our youth didn't feel the pull of idealism and a call to service. And Reagan Democrats weren't called home. As a result, Bush was able to dominate the entire campaign by appeals to mainstream "values" — he had them and Dukakis didn't. And the rest is history.

In addition to the strategic miscalculation, there were some tactical mistakes which, when added to the mistaken strategy, made it difficult for Dukakis to win. The campaign's complacency after the Democratic convention and its assumption that Bush would self-destruct were naive at best. Early August was an ideal time for launching attacks on Bush's failures of leadership, on the administration's arms-for-hostages-for-drugs foreign policy, on the administration's slashing of programs for children and working Americans, and on the Republicans' callous and harmful economic policies which favored the rich over the rest of us.

Dukakis's failure to immediately and forcefully answer Bush's attacks on his patriotism and liberalism — essentially allowing Bush to define him and drive his negatives sky-high in the process — was a grave error. So were his fuzzy and sometimes downright confusing TV ads which were divorced from his message on the stump. The Bush campaign benefitted from a senior staff experienced in managing presidential campaigns, which Democrats do not have. The Dukakis campaign was also hurt by an insularity which often excluded Democratic Party regulars at the local level and left supporters and surrogates — from Senator Sam Nunn to Jesse Jackson — hanging, their advice ignored.

It was an election which was winnable — and it was not won.

## Which Direction for the Democratic Party?

Democrats have three choices. As in 1988, we can muddle along in the middle without a clear vision or message. We can move further to the right, trying to beat Republicans by being "better" Republicans. (But as Harry Truman noted, "When voters have a choice between a Republican and a Republican, they'll pick the Republican every time.") Or we can build on the best in the tradition that made the Democratic Party great.

The key to Democratic victory at all levels of government is *expansion and inclusion and a compelling political message.* On November 8, 91 million Americans voted, only half of those who are eligible — the lowest number since the 1924 campaign. Only 26 percent of all Americans of voting age elected George Bush. Unprecedented campaign expenditures are chasing fewer and fewer votes. Americans are turned off and tuned out. All studies report that a vast majority of those who have quit voting are poorer and less educated than their fellow Americans; they fit the classic Democratic voter profile. Indeed, if people with household incomes of $25,000 or less voted at the same rate as wealthier people, Democrats again would overwhelmingly be the majority party.

Yet the party — from its presidential candidates on down — is ignoring these possible voters and pursuing a shrinking electorate that is, on average, wealthier, better educated *and* more conservative. In fact, affluent people currently cast about one and one-half ballots for each ballot poorer people cast.

Three things are needed to counter this inequity: universal same-day, on-site voter registration (states that have it show a 10 percent to 15 percent increase in voter participation); a revival of economic populism throughout the party to attract the attention of these voters; and a rebuilding of the *grassroots* party apparatus — including a serious nationwide voter registration drive — to make sure these voters turn out from year to year.

Table 2 below illustrates the potential voting power of these non-voters, a large percentage of whom are African American. There were at least 12 states in which the number of unregistered and non-voting African Americans alone exceeded the number of votes by which Dukakis lost. With nearly nine out of ten African American voters supporting Dukakis, if these states could have been added to the 112 electoral votes that Dukakis won, he would

| Table 2:  States Where African Americans Could Have Made a Difference in the 1988 Election | State | Electoral Votes | Number of African Americans in Voting Age Population | Number of African Americans Who Voted in 1988 | Bush's Margin of Victory in 1988 | Number of African Americans Who Didn't Vote in 1988 |
|---|---|---|---|---|---|---|
| | California | 47 | 1,576,000 | 736,391 | 347,373 | 839,609 |
| | Illinois | 24 | 1,213,000 | 671,896 | 94,657 | 541,104 |
| | Georgia | 12 | 1,138,000 | 343,838 | 366,539 | 794,162 |
| | North Carolina | 13 | 993,000 | 424,433 | 323,458 | 568,567 |
| | Michigan | 20 | 896,000 | 473,581 | 289,703 | 422,419 |
| | Louisiana | 10 | 873,000 | 341,922 | 166,242 | 531,078 |
| | Maryland | 10 | 833,000 | 244,221 | 40,263 | 588,779 |
| | Pennsylvania | 25 | 783,000 | 402,770 | 105,143 | 380,230 |
| | Alabama | 9 | 697,000 | 275,695 | 266,070 | 421,305 |
| | South Carolina | 8 | 693,000 | 197,201 | 235,889 | 495,799 |
| | Mississippi | 7 | 587,000 | 209,907 | 193,969 | 377,093 |
| | Missouri | 11 | 370,000 | 188,391 | 83,534 | 181,609 |
| | **TOTAL** | 196 | | | | |

Sources: ABC News Election Systems; Joint Center for Political Studies. Number of African Americans who voted in the 1988 elections is a rough estimate based on exit poll data.

have had 308 electoral votes — and victory!

Besides universal voter registration and a beefed-up Democratic Party apparatus to mobilize voters, a fundamental overhaul of the Democratic Party message (or current non-message) is needed to inspire voters. In these precarious economic times, when the people at the top 10 percent of the income ladder control 70 percent of the country's wealth, it's time to renew the call for a more activist federal government — a government that supports progressive taxation, challenges corporate abuse, defends workers and their families, and promotes international cooperation and development. An appeal for economic justice for all Americans and a compelling program to rebuild America and offer security to our families will bring Reagan Democrats, and many independent voters too, into the Democratic Party — without moving it to the right.

Populist economic issues not only help Democratic Party constituencies find common ground despite race issues, they also widen the "gender gap," a fundamental building block in the Democratic Party's effort to recapture the White House in 1992 and to build a more permanent progressive majority in the United States. A majority of women differed with the majority of men in their presidential choice: 52 percent of women chose Dukakis while 54 percent of men chose Bush, according to ABC exit polls. At one point in the campaign the gender gap was as much as 20 percent. With women constituting 52 percent of the 1988 presidential vote, one Bush pollster noted that they considered the closing of this gap to be their biggest success of the 1988 election. How was it done? Essentially Bush took Democratic issues such as support for child care and health care, used "kinder and gentler" language, and focused on family symbols — staples of a more progressive Democratic message.

Seniors, 60 and older, who constituted 22 percent of the 1988 electorate, returned in large numbers to the Democratic fold, but not by enough to give Dukakis a majority. In 1984, Reagan overwhelmed Mondale among older American voters, winning by 60 percent to 39 percent. In 1988, Bush garnered 50 percent to Dukakis's 49 percent. Earlier in the year seniors were leaning Democratic by 13 points.

And they should be. Democrats initiated Social Security, and they must defend it, instead of hinting that it might be used for deficit reduction. Democrats initiated Medicare and Medicaid; it's time they insist that America join the rest of the industrialized world by enacting a universal and comprehensive national health care program. Democrats initiated nutrition and housing programs for seniors and other low-income Americans, and it's time they offered budget priorities that meet these needs.

Our 18- to 24-year-old youth, potentially one out of five voters, is another voting bloc that should sustain a progressive Democratic government. Only half of them are registered to vote. That compares to 68 percent for eligible voters as a whole. Once registered, however, young people vote at the same rate as other people. Youth (18- to 24-years-old) voted Democrat in every presidential election between 1952 and 1980. This changed in 1984, and in 1988 they gave Bush a modest 52 percent to 47 percent margin over Dukakis. But in congressional elections in 1988, they gave Democrats a 54 percent to 45 percent edge over Republicans, a clear turn back to the Democratic column.

Before Reagan, Democrats used to take the youth vote for granted (and did little to nurture it). Since Reagan, Democrats have written off the youth vote, assuming youth has lost its idealism and turned to materialism and conservatism. In reality, young people have been motivated by fear, the same economic fear that haunts African Americans, Hispanics, women, Reagan Democrats and seniors — a fear that should make them natural Democratic voters.

Jesse Jackson offered a program to deal with this fear — a program of hope. He showed that Democrats can offer an economically sound way out of our deficit mess — without raising the taxes of average working Americans — and leave significant sums for new investments. His program offered national health care, a fully funded war on drugs, affordable child care, protection for the environment and vast improvements in our educational and manufacturing systems to restore America's greatness in the world economy. His was a "family values" program. And with Jackson's hard-hitting anti-drug message and his challenge to corporate America to "clean up the suites," no one could question his position on crime.

The Republicans have no monopoly on patriotism either. Standing up for a strong and economically vibrant America, challenging the economic sinkhole of the military machine, confronting our world environmental challenges, creating a just economic growth and relieving Third World debt, and meeting the new challenges posed by a reform-oriented Soviet leadership — these are the new national security battles. There's no rational reason why we should build up arms just to build down. America can either get with the times — by Democrats having the courage to redefine the meaning of national security — or collapse under an arsenal which we cannot use.

Finally, Democrats need to deal head-on with the politics of race if we ever hope to overcome our minority party status at the presidential level and usher in a new, progressive majority. Bush's demagoguery around the Willie Horton prison furlough case was a not-so-thinly-veiled appeal to racist fear. It's no secret why the South is solidly Republican in national elections. Many of the so-called Reagan Democrats are actually Wallace Democrats, and some analysts estimate that as many as 60 percent of them have fled to the GOP because of racial prejudice.

Lee Atwater, George Bush's campaign manager and current Republican Party chairperson, openly underscores this point. In a recent interview in the *Washington Post*, he noted that "reformed segregationist" Strom Thurmond's southern strategy during Richard Nixon's 1968 race was "a model campaign." Atwater went on to explain, "I've used that as a blueprint for everything I've done in the South since then." This is not a blueprint for majority party control, as Atwater has lately pointed out. (He is currently "reaching out" to minorities for support, after 20 years of exclusion.) But it has been a very successful method for electing Republican presidents, ever since 1968.

On the other hand, African Americans represent 20 to 25 percent of the Democratic vote. They cannot be taken for granted, nor can they be ignored. Both because it is morally correct and for pragmatic political reasons, the Democratic Party has to look this racial cynicism straight in the eye and stare it down. In the New South and in urban areas of the midwest and northeast, Democrats can find economic common ground and move to a political higher ground.

Many of the Wallace Democrats and African Americans can be united around progressive economic issues and a populist appeal — there is no other way. At the same time, those swing voters who are irretrievably lost due to racial prejudice — and there are some — must be replaced with newly included "expansion voters." That is the winning Democratic formula into the next century.

Despite the Democratic Party's continued success at all office levels below the presidency, we must recognize that the Democrats have become the "opposition party" in presidential races — and we need to start acting like one, with clear and principled stands on the issues, as Goldwater did in 1964 to signal the beginning of the conservative surge and as Reagan did in 1980.

A progressive surge is possible in the latter half of the 20th century — a surge that challenges the greed of Wall Street, business PACs, agribusiness and the military-industrial complex. Republican administrations have done an excellent job of protecting and serving the interests of the very wealthy, domestically and internationally. It's time to return to a government "by and for the people," a government that acts as a protector and servant of the people. The Democratic Party must claim that role. The lessons that Jesse Jackson taught us in 1988 still apply. And progressives — a true American Rainbow Coalition — must lead the nation in a new direction. Only then can we hope to recapture the imagination of the electorate — and the White House.

# A CHANCE TO SERVE

Raleigh, North Carolina, October 10, 1987

Let me express my thanks to each and every one of you today for your coming to this great occasion. Many of you have come great distances. Others are from nearby. All have come to Raleigh, North Carolina, to witness an historic occasion—a presidential announcement.

But more important, you are here to "give witness" to your desire for a new direction for America—an America of jobs, peace and justice. I shall never be able to convey in full measure the depth of my gratitude for your concern and your support.

This is the 200th year of the United States Constitution. We've had to change the formula, add amendments and give new legal interpretations. We've made great progress—still, equal protection, justice and mercy for all are not assured. Unfinished business remains to make this a more perfect union.

Every generation faces critical problems and choices which constitute the basic challenges of its day. When it meets those challenges head-on and wins it's called progress.

Twenty-five years ago, the critical issue threatening to tear our country apart was racial violence. The South was the battleground, but the war against racial violence was a national war—as we soon learned. Twenty-five years later, racial violence is illegal. When racial violence does occur—such as in Howard Beach, New York or Forsyth County, Georgia —it's illegal and the perpetrators are put in the judicial system, tried and given their just punishment. Just as we displaced racial violence, we must replace economic violence with economic justice.

Economic violence is the critical issue of our day! When plants close on workers without notice, and leave them without jobs or training for new jobs—that's economic violence. When three to five million Americans are on the streets and homeless—that's economic violence. When merger maniacs make windfall profits and top management is given excessive bonuses, golden parachutes to aid a soft landing, while workers are asked to take a wage cut, a benefit cut and a job loss, a crash landing—that's economic violence. When our children are victimized with poor health care, poor education, poor housing, poor diets and more—that's economic violence against our children.

In foreign policy we are being led astray because our leadership has little vision or the wrong vision, and because it is weak. It wears a military fig leaf to cover up its impotence. Our foreign policy appears strong, but its leadership, its goals and its values are weak. We have the strongest military in the world, but weak leadership. We have guided missiles and misguided leadership.

That's why President Reagan invaded Grenada—a nation with 110,000 people and no standing army—when he was really mad at Cuba. The CIA paid off some of the surrounding states' leadership, and they pretended to invite him in as a cover to save some American students. President Reagan locked the press out so the American people could not learn what was really going on—all in the name of national security. The reality was that they were diverting attention away from the over 250 American boys killed without a chance to defend themselves in Lebanon. A strong military but weak leadership has left us with less moral authority in the world.

A strong military and weak leadership led us to mine the harbors in Nicaragua and dismiss the finding of the World Court, then send vulnerable Americans into the Persian Gulf when the Ayatollah did the same thing. A strong military and weak leadership has left us with less moral authority in the world.

A Jackson presidency would be characterized by strong leadership, a strong military, coherent policies, a strong economy and strong values—values that serve as a beacon of light for the free world and western civilization, values that aid others to find their way.

## Economic Common Ground
## Is the Key to Progress

It is indeed prophetic that we announce our candidacy here in the South. Many remember the Old South, the South of too much division, too little progress—rich soil and poor people. A few still wish to preserve that tradition. But we, in coalition—African American and white, Jew and Gentile—fought to end the worst in the Old South, and we won. The New South has the challenge to lead the nation in ending economic violence, finding peace, achieving economic justice and reaching common ground.

That's our challenge in a diverse region of people, customs and traditions—to find common ground. That's the key to a New South. That's the key to a new America. And that's the key to a new Democratic Party.

Today, my friends, we search for common ground. And we find it.

We find it at the plant gate that closed on workers without notice.

We find it at the shipyard where goods made in foreign countries by repressed labor undercut organized labor.

We find it at the schoolyard where a good mind can't get a scholarship, can't take out a loan, and teachers can't get paid.

We find it at the hospital where someone died because she didn't have a green or a yellow card to go upstairs to a bed that was empty waiting for the rich or insured to get sick.

We find it at the farm foreclosure where a family tradition reaches an end. Farmers fighting for fair prices and a return of their land and urban workers fighting for fair wages and a return of their jobs find common ground. Across lines of region, race or sex, in our fears and pain, we must turn to each other for help and consultation.

We find it at the funeral parlor where a family grieves for its child who sought drugs as anesthesia for his pain—only to find that the painkiller was a killer. The tears and fears bind us into a unit seeking common ground, sur-vival and human dignity. When the gates close and the lights go out, and we can't use crutches of color, sex or previous employment, in the dark we appear amazingly similar.

The New South not only liberated itself but it will help to change the priorities of the nation. The New South defeated narrow-minded and insensitive Republicans in 1984 and 1986. The New South defeated Robert Bork last week. But there are still challenges.

We must defeat toxic waste dumps.

We must defeat anti-union laws.

We must defeat those who would deny women the Equal Rights Amendment.

We must defeat runaway shops.

We must defeat the merger maniacs who take our jobs, capital, tax base and hope to foreign soil.

We must defeat the drug smugglers.

## More Jobs, Less Drugs

Today perhaps we face the greatest challenge of our lives—to protect the American family. We must protect the American family from two basic threats that are shaking the very foundation of our society. We must stop the flow of jobs out of our country. We must stop the deadly flow of drugs into our country.

I want to serve the American family. My candidacy offers hope for the American family and for our youth. My candidacy is a direct challenge to the cynicism and despair that led 75 million Americans in 1984 to surrender their franchise and not vote for anyone.

In our 1983 southern crusade and our 1984 campaign—and with the help of countless organizations and thousands of individuals—we were able to register and revitalize two million new voters, who voted Democratic. We formed the Rainbow Coalition. The years before, in 1980 and 1982, the Republican party registered a net gain of 12 Senate seats. By 1986, with our Rainbow Coalition providing the margin of victory in no less than seven races, the Democratic Party had reversed Republican gains and once again was in control of the Senate 54 to 46. An expanded and renewed Democratic Party, that makes room for old wine and new wine, is the key to victory in 1988 and beyond.

At the height of President Reagan's personal popularity, many within our party sought to move in his direction. Some cowered from the role of leadership against such a popular incumbent. The truth can be postponed, but not denied. The Rainbow Coalition provided the bold leadership, the new direction and the umbrella under which we are weathering Mr. Reagan's storm.

In 1984, despite President Reagan's landslide victory, we cut Mr. Reagan's coattails in the Senate. We were the difference for Senators Levin of Michigan, Heflin of Alabama and current presidential candidates Gore of Tennessee and Simon of Illinois. The Rainbow Coalition stuck to the true principles of the Democratic Party and to the true principles of America. The pendulum has now begun to swing in our direction.

In 1986 we cut President Reagan's coattails even more. He is now wearing a waiter's jacket. The Rainbow contributed to Senate victories for Mikulski in Maryland, Sanford in North Carolina, Graham in Florida, Fowler in Georgia, Shelby in Alabama, Breaux in Louisiana and Cranston in California. The result was the return of the Senate to Democratic control.

Now is the time for bold leadership and a new direction. Just a week ago I was in Key West, Florida where well over 85 percent of all the drugs that come into our nation enter. I went on a Coast Guard drug patrol and was briefed on the flow of drugs across our borders. The figures for 1986 alone were staggering:

- 178 tons of cocaine.

- 20 tons of heroin.

- 60,000 tons of marijuana.

Sixty percent of our high school seniors admit to drug use. Thirty-four percent of our students do not feel that trying cocaine is dangerous.

The American people have a $150-billion-a-year drug habit. That must stop. This is a time of great social and material need—millions homeless, millions in poverty, millions without medical care, millions not being educated, millions of families broken and children in despair. We must declare a war on drugs. A nation's first duty is to defend its borders from threats—and there exists no greater threat to

the American people today than drugs. We protect and patrol the borders of our allies in Korea, Japan and Europe. We can do no less than protect our own.

We must meet with the leadership of the nations where drugs are grown and help them develop alternative crops.

We must strengthen our Coast Guard and all of our drug interdiction programs. President Reagan has cut our sea and air patrol in half as the drug flow has increased. We have mine sweepers in the Persian Gulf, but there is a greater need for drug sweepers off the Florida Keys.

We must educate the American people, but especially our youth, to the dangers of drug use.

We must rehabilitate those with drug dependency.

We must end the demand for drugs. Some people are using drugs for pleasure. But more are using them as anesthesia from pain or escape from reality. They have lost a sense of purpose. There is power in purpose, so when purpose goes, power goes too. When purpose and power are lost, the loss of principle is not far behind. You find yourself doing things that in your right mind you wouldn't do.

**Reinvest in America**

Some of the despair and sense of powerlessness that leads to drug and alcohol addiction is rooted in the usurpation of the democratic control of our economy by multinational corporations who have no loyalty to America. Since 1980, 650,000 family farmers have been driven from their land with no place to go. This day, 37 million Americans have no form of health insurance. By the year 2000, it is estimated that there will be as many as 20 million homeless Americans unless we go in a dramatically new direction.

The great challenge to our party—for our party at its best is the party of the people—is to put America back to work at liveable wages. Every one percent drop in unemployment represents a $30 billion drop in our budget deficit. How do we put America back to work? We must move from divesting "outside" of America to investing "in" America. We need the five R's:

- Reinvest in America;

- Reindustrialize our productive capacity;

- Retrain our workers;

- Research for commercial development; and

- Recover more of our plants from making unnecessary weapons systems to necessary mass transit systems, steel for the rails, civilian and commercial space exploration and more.

We have the resources to do it! Now we need the leadership, the political will and the direction.

We must cut the military budget without cutting our defense. We don't need Star Wars to stimulate an arms race, militarize the heavens, and make us and the rest of the world less secure. We can do without Star Wars, but not Social Security, housing, health care, shelter for the homeless and education for our youth.

We must make corporations and the wealthy pay their fair share of taxes.

We must utilize a portion of the $2 trillion in public and private pension funds—government secured with a fair rate of return guaranteed—to capitalize the redevelopment of America.

We must also reverse the incentives to corporations to merge with other corporations, purge their work force, and in the process submerge our economy. American corporations must be accountable to the American people. Today corporations get a tax deduction when they close plants on workers. They get another tax break when they take our jobs, capital and tax base to repressed labor markets abroad. Slave labor anywhere is a threat to organized labor everywhere.

## The Jackson Doctrine

And then we must have strong leadership and a new direction in our foreign policy. I call it the Jackson Doctrine. The Jackson Doctrine consists of four principles. First, strengthen and support the rule of international law, including the role of the United Nations and the World Court. The United States has the most to gain in a world that respects the rule of law in international relations. We also have the most to lose in a world of anarchy and lawlessness because our interests are so broad.

Second, the Jackson Doctrine respects the right of self-determination, and third, it promotes human rights. That's why we support indigenous leadership in Central America like the Contadora process and the Arias plan. That's why we support Kenneth Kaunda of Zambia and the Organization of African Unity and the Frontline states in southern Africa and their plan to end apartheid. And we must measure human rights by one yardstick everywhere in the world.

The fourth Jackson Doctrine principle is support for international economic justice. That's why we reject two more aircraft carrier task forces—at a cost of $36 billion—for intervention in and containment of the Third World. The issue is not containment of their desire to be free and develop, but to raise their standard of living rather than lower our own. If we raise the standard of living in the Third World, we reduce Third World debt, reduce our deficit, take away the incentive of multinational corporations to take our jobs to repressed labor markets abroad, and strengthen our own and the world's economy through economic growth. We will have created a vast new market because they will then have the ability to buy what we produce.

I am making plans now to return to the Middle East—this time to visit our troops, to meet with their families, to lift their spirits, and to assure them that they are not alone in the Persian Gulf. We want to make it clear that our prayers and concerns are with them. It is not their fault that they are made vulnerable because of a misguided policy in the region.

Our soldiers are not legislators nor judges. They are our youth, our sons and daughters. They are trapped in a war without clearly defined objectives. It is to their lasting credit that they serve against the odds, that they are willing to die that America might live. These American soldiers deserve our support. Their families deserve encouragement. America may be divided over the Gulf policy but let us be unmistakably clear—we cannot be divided about our support for our troops and their families. We cannot repeat the mistake of Vietnam, where the Vietnam vet felt unsupported. We were not wrong in supporting the Vietnam vet. The Vietnam policy was wrong. We must continually make that distinction. Our challenge is to right bad American policy and to support good American soldiers.

## A New South Is Arising

My friends, we are here today in Raleigh, North Carolina, in the heart of the South. I was born in Greenville, South Carolina, went to college at North Carolina A & T, in Greensboro, and got my first chance to serve politically in Raleigh, North Carolina, as head of the North Carolina Intercollegiate Council on Human Rights. We sought to end the laws of apartheid that wrecked this region culturally, economically, politically and spiritually.

Twenty-five years ago I was appointed to be a member of the delegation of Young Democrats to their Las Vegas convention. The late Al House was elected their national president because of our coalition. Governor Terry Sanford gave me the opportunity to serve. I shall forever respect him for it.

It was clear then in national politics that a New South could arise, but we would have to rise together. Sons and daughters, locked away from each other by ancient and archaic customs, would have to find common ground. Once we found common ground, we could become national political champions and elect presidents as well as national basketball, football and baseball champions. This region of rich soil and poor people can lead America to its loftiest and highest ideals.

We are here today at the dawn, early in the morning, of the New South, early in the morning of our possibilities, early in the morning of our challenge to reach common ground, to end economic violence, and to assure economic justice to all of our people. We are early in the morning of the New South that elected new senators, the New South that defeated Judge Bork, and early in the morning of a New South characterized by humane priorities at home and human rights abroad.

The New South—where farmers and truck drivers, African American and white, male and female, the very able and the disabled, the secure and the threatened—can come together and raise the standard of living for everybody.

I'm a son of the South. I've spent all of my adult life trying to build a New South. As the poor of the South are liberated, the New South will lead the nation—with a commitment to liberal arts and science, peace and prosperity.

As a son of the New South, one who was born and bred here, developed in Chicago—urban America, the Midwest, the heartland of our nation—and one who has had the privilege to travel around the world to retrieve Americans from dungeons and foreign jails, as one who has had the privilege to meet the great leaders of the world, I can do no less than serve my country, offer my services, my skills, my energy and my commitment to its ideals. My broad-based American experience—from the humblest of beginnings to the boardrooms of corporations, the picketline, negotiating sessions with workers, the Pope at the Vatican, heads of state—has made my appreciation and love for America a part of my blood, my bones and my soul.

There is something wrong with our government's priorities today, the direction of its leadership—a cake and a Bible to Iran; hostages for arms; and in Central America, drugs for arms. This administration's priorities and its values are wrong. But there is nothing wrong with America. America is our land. America is God's country. America has been blessed and God bless America.

They say I'm number one in the polls because I have name recognition. I'm number one in the polls because I have service recognition. People know me because of 25 years of public service, not because my name is Jackson. If my name were Jesse Louis Kennedy and I was from Massachusetts, then name recognition might mean something. If my name was Jesse Louis Rockefeller and I was from New York, then my name might mean something. But my name is Jesse Louis Jackson from Haney Street in Greenville, South Carolina, and when I was born nobody knew my name.

Maybe if some of the other candidates had marched for public accommodations in Montgomery in 1954 and Greensboro in 1960, somebody would know their names. Maybe if some of the other candidates had marched in Selma for voting rights—and they were old enough—somebody would know their names. Maybe if some of the other candidates had caught bricks marching for open housing in Gage Park, Chicago, in 1966, somebody would know their names. Of if they had walked with Dr. Martin Luther King, Jr. when he was alive, maybe somebody would know their names too. I have name recognition, but I got it the old-fashioned way—I earned it.

My candidacy is a call to service. I have spent the last 25 years, not as a perfect servant, but as a public servant. My name has become synonymous with service, rescue, negotiations, struggle and strong leadership. That's why I want to be president: to serve the American people; to help make their lives more purposeful and complete; to provide equal protection under the law for all; to improve the quality of life for all; and to show that jobs, peace and justice are mutually reinforcing goals.

I want to serve my country. If I can be elected president, never again will women have doubts. Never again will race, sex or class threaten the American dream. The risks are great. The challenges are many. The path is treacherous. The traps abound. The forces of resistance seed the clouds of acid rain. But earth, wind and fire will not deter us from our mission or stop us. The job is difficult. But we have an obligation to serve—and I want to serve America.

I want to educate the children, make secure its senior citizens, and enable its disabled. I want to serve America.

I want to stop drugs from flowing into America. I want to stop jobs from flowing out of America. I want to provide an affordable health-care system. I want to house the American people. I want to stabilize the American family. I want to safeguard its liberties, its rights of privacy and its public obligations. I want to serve America.

For its 650,000 farmers driven from their land, for its 37 million without health insurance, for its millions who lost their jobs to plant closings and leveraged buy-outs, for its millions who have lost their small business opportunities, for its millions who wake up America every morning and put America to bed each night, who grow its food and whose shoulders energize our industries, whose sweat and blood fertilize our soil—I want to serve America.

I want to offer the highest and best service in our highest and most sensitive job, the job that has the most capacity to bring justice in our land, mitigate misery in the world and bring peace on earth—the office of president. Only in America is such a dream possible.

Today I offer my service to our country. I seek God's guidance and your prayers as we embark on this mission. Therefore, on this day, October 10, 1987, in Raleigh, North Carolina, I officially announce my candidacy to seek the nomination of the Democratic Party for the office of President of the United States of America.

# KEEP HOPE ALIVE

Atlanta, Georgia, July 19, 1988

Tonight we pause and give praise and honor to God for being good enough to allow us to be at this place at this time. When I look out at this convention, I see the face of America, red, yellow, brown, black and white, we're all precious in God's sight—the real rainbow coalition. All of us, all of us who are here think that we are seated. But really we're standing on someone's shoulders. Ladies and gentlemen, Mrs. Rosa Parks.

The mother of the civil rights movement.

I want to express my deep love and appreciation for the support my family has given me over these past months. They have endured pain, anxiety, threat and fear. But they have been strengthened and made secure by a faith in God, in America and in you. Your love has protected us and made us strong.

To my wife Jackie, the foundation of our family; to our five children whom you met tonight; to my mother, Mrs. Helen Jackson, who is present tonight; and to my grandmother, Mrs. Matilda Burns; my brother Chuck and his family; my mother-in-law Mrs. Gertrude Brown, who just last month at age 61 graduated from Hampton Institute, a marvelous achievement; I offer my appreciation to Mayor Andrew Young who has provided such gracious hospitality to all of us this week.

And a special salute to President Jimmy Carter. President Carter restored honor to the White House after Watergate. He gave many of us a special opportunity to grow. For his kind words, for his unwavering commitment to peace in the world, and the voters that came from his family, every member of his family, led by Billy and Amy, I offer him my special thanks, special thanks to the Carter family.

My right and privilege to stand here before you has been won—in my lifetime—by the blood and sweat of the innocent.

Twenty-four years ago, the late Fanny Lou Hamer and Aaron Henry—who sits here tonight from Mississippi—were locked out on the streets of Atlantic City, the heads of the Mississippi Freedom Democratic Party. But tonight, an African American and a white delegation from Mississippi is headed by Ed Cole, an African American, from Mississippi, 24 years later.

Many were lost in the struggle for the right to vote. Jimmy Lee Jackson, a young student, gave his life. Viola Luizzo, a white mother from Detroit, called nigger lover, had her brains blown out at point-blank range.

Schwerner, Goodman and Chaney—two Jews and an African American—found in a common grave, bodies riddled with bullets in Mississippi. The four darling little girls in church in Birmingham, Alabama. They died that we may have a right to live.

Dr. Martin Luther King, Jr. lies only a few miles from us tonight. Tonight he must feel good as he looks down upon us. We sit here together, a rainbow, a coalition—the sons and daughters of slaves sitting together around a common table, to decide the direction of our party and our country. His heart must be full tonight.

As a testament to the struggles of those who have gone before; as a legacy for those who will come after; as a tribute to the endurance, the patience, the courage of our forefathers and mothers; as an assurance that their prayers are being answered, their work has not been in vain, and hope is eternal—tomorrow night my name will go into nomination for the Presidency of the United States of America.

We meet tonight at a crossroads, a point of decision. Shall we expand, be inclusive, or suffer division and impotence?

We come to Atlanta, the cradle of the Old South, the crucible of the New South. Tonight there is a sense of celebration because we are moved, fundamentally moved, from racial battlegrounds by law, to economic common ground. Tomorrow we will challenge to move to higher ground.

Common ground!

Think of Jerusalem—the intersection where many trails met. A small village that became the birthplace for three great religions—Judaism, Christianity and Islam. Why was this village so blessed? Because it provided a crossroads where different people met, different cultures and different civilizations could meet and find common ground.

When people come together, flowers always flourish and the air is rich with the aroma of a new spring. Take New York, the dynamic metropolis. What makes New York so special? It is the invitation of the Statue of Liberty—give me your tired, your poor, your huddled masses who yearn to breathe free.

Not restricted to English only.

Many people, many cultures, many languages—with one thing in common, the yearning to breathe free.

Common ground!

Tonight in Atlanta, for the first time in this century we convene in the South. A state where governors once stood in school-house doors. Where Julian Bond was denied his seat in the state legislature because of his conscientious objection to the Vietnam War. A city that, through its five African American universities, has graduated more African Americans than any other city in the world. Atlanta, now a modern intersection of the New South.

Common ground! That is the challenge to our party tonight.

Left wing. Right wing. Progress will not come through boundless liberalism nor static conservatism, but at the critical mass of mutual survival. It takes two wings to fly. Whether you're a hawk or a dove, you're just a bird living in the same environment, in the same world.

The Bible teaches that when lions and lambs lie down together, none will be afraid and there will be peace in the valley. It sounds impossible. Lions eat lambs. Lambs sensibly flee from lions. But even lions and lambs find common ground. Why?

Because neither lions nor lambs want the forest to catch on fire. Neither lions nor lambs want acid rain to fall. Neither lions nor lambs

can survive a nuclear war. If lions and lambs can find common ground, surely we can as well, as civilized people.

The only time that we win is when we come together. In 1960, John Kennedy, the late John Kennedy, beat Richard Nixon by only 112,000 votes—less than one vote per precinct. He won by the margin of our hope. He brought us together. He reached out. He had the courage to defy his advisors and inquire about Dr. King's jailing in Albany, Georgia. We won by the margin of our hope, inspired by courageous leadership.

In 1964, Lyndon Johnson brought both wings together—the thesis, the antithesis—to create a synthesis, and together we won.

In 1976, Jimmy Carter unified us again and we won. When we do not come together we never win.

In 1968, division and despair in August led to our defeat in November.

In 1980, rancor in the spring and the summer led to Reagan in the fall. When we divide, we cannot win. We must find common ground as a basis for survival and development and change and growth.

Today when we debated, differed, deliberated, agreed to agree, agreed to disagree, when we had the good judgment to argue our case and then not to self-destruct, George Bush was just a little further away from the White House and a little closer to private life.

Tonight, I salute Governor Michael Dukakis. He has run a well-managed and a dignified campaign. No matter how tired or how tried, he always resisted the temptation to stoop to demagoguery.

I've watched a good mind fast at work, with steel nerves, guiding his campaign out of the crowded field without appeal to the worst in us. I've watched his perspective grow as his environment expanded. I've seen his toughness and tenacity close-up. I know his commitment to public service.

Mike Dukakis's parents were a doctor and a teacher; my parents, a maid, a beautician and a janitor.

There is a great gap between Brookline, Massachusetts and Haney Street, the Fieldcrest Village housing project in Greenville, South Carolina. He studied law; I studied theology.

There are differences of religion, region and race, differences in experiences and perspectives. But the genius of America is that out of the many, we become one.

Providence has enabled our paths to intersect. His foreparents came to America on immigrant ships; my foreparents on slave ships; we're in the same boat tonight.

Our ships could pass in the night if we have a false sense of independence, or they could collide and crash. We would lose our passengers. But we cannot seek a higher reality and a greater good apart. We can drift on the broken pieces of Reaganomics, satisfy our baser instincts, and exploit the fears of our people. At our highest, we can call upon noble instincts to navigate this vessel to safety. The greater good is the common good.

As Jesus said, "Not my will, but thine be done." It was his way of saying there's a higher good beyond personal comfort or position.

The good of our nation is at stake—its commitment to working men and women, to the poor and the vulnerable, to the many in the world. With so many guided missiles, and so much misguided leadership, the stakes are exceedingly high. Our choice: full participation in a Democratic government or more abandonment and neglect. And so this night we choose not a false sense of independence, not our capacity to survive and endure.

Tonight we choose interdependency in our capacity to act and unite for the greater good. The common good is finding commitment to new priorities, to expansion and inclusion; a commitment to expanded participation in the Democratic Party at every level; a commitment to new priorities that ensure that hope will be kept alive; a common ground commitment to D.C. statehood and empowerment—D.C. deserves statehood; a commitment to economic set-asides; a commitment to the Dellums bill for comprehensive sanctions against South Africa; a shared commitment to a common direction.

Common ground. Easier said than done. Where do you find common ground—at the point of challenge. This campaign has shown that politics need not be marketed by politicians, packaged by pollsters and pundits. Poli-

tics can be a marvelous arena where people come together, define common ground.

We find common ground at the plant gate that closes on workers without notice. We find common ground at the farm auction where a good farmer loses his or her land to bad loans or diminishing markets. Common ground at the schoolyard where teachers cannot get adequate pay, and students cannot get a scholarship and can't make a loan. Common ground at the hospital admitting room where somebody tonight is dying because they cannot afford to go upstairs to a bed that's empty, waiting for someone with insurance to get sick. We are a better nation than that. We must do better.

Common ground. What is leadership if not present help in a time of crisis? And so I met you at a point of challenge in Jay, Maine, where paper workers were striking for fair wages; in Greenfield, Iowa, where family farmers struggle for a fair price; in Cleveland, Ohio, where working women seek comparable worth; in McFarland, California, where the children of Hispanic farm workers may be dying in clusters with cancer; in the AIDS hospice in Houston, Texas, where the sick support one another, 12 of whom are rejected by their own parents and friends. Common ground.

America's not a blanket woven from one thread, one color, one cloth. When I was a child growing up in Greenville, South Carolina, and grandmother could not afford a blanket, she didn't complain and we did not freeze. Instead, she took pieces of old cloth—patches, wool, silk, gabardine, crokersack, only patches—barely good enough to wipe your shoes with.

But they didn't stay that way very long. With sturdy hands and a strong cord, she sewed them together into a quilt, a thing of beauty and power and culture.

Now, Democrats, we must build such a quilt. Farmers, you seek fair prices and you are right, but you cannot stand alone. Your patch is not big enough. Workers, you fight for fair wages. You are right. But your patch, labor, is not big enough. Women, you seek comparable worth and pay equity. You are right. But your patch is not big enough. Women, mothers, who seek Head Start and day care and prenatal care on the front side of life, rather than welfare and jail care on the back side of life, you're right, but your patch is not big enough.

Students, you seek scholarships. You are right. But your patch is not big enough. African Americans and Hispanics, when we fight for civil rights, we are right, but our patch is not big enough. Gays and lesbians, when you fight against discrimination and for a cure for AIDS, you are right, but your patch is not big enough. Conservatives and progressives, when you fight for what you believe, right-wing, left-wing, hawk, dove—you are right from your point of view, but your point of view is not enough.

But don't despair. Be as wise as my grandmama. Pool the patches and the pieces together, bound by a common thread. When we form a great quilt of unity and common ground, we'll have the power to bring about health care and housing and jobs and education and hope to our nation.

We the people can win. We stand at the end of a long dark night of reaction. We stand tonight united in a commitment to a new direction. For almost eight years, we've been led by those who view social good coming from private interest, who viewed public life as a means to increase private wealth. They have been prepared to sacrifice the common good of the many to satisfy the private interest and the wealth of a few. We believe in a government that's a tool of our democracy in service to the public, not an instrument of the aristocracy in search of private wealth.

We believe in government with the consent of the governed—of, for and by the people. We must not emerge into a new day without a new direction.

Reaganomics is based on the belief that the rich had too little money, and the poor had too much. So they engaged in reverse Robin Hood—took from the poor, gave to the rich, paid for by the middle-class. We cannot stand four more years of Reaganomics in any version, in any disguise.

How do I document that case? Seven years later, the richest one percent of our society pays 20 percent less in taxes; the poorest ten percent pay 20 percent more. Reaganomics.

Reagan gave the rich and the powerful a multi-billion dollar party. Now the party is over. He expects the people to pay for the damage. I take this principled position: let us not raise taxes on the poor and the middle class, but those who had the party, the rich and the powerful, must pay for the party!

I just want to take common sense to high places. We're spending $150 billion a year defending Europe and Japan 43 years after the war is over. We have more troops in Europe tonight than we had seven years ago, yet the threat of war is ever more remote. Germany and Japan are now creditor nations—that means they've got a surplus. We are a debtor nation—that means we are in debt.

Let them share more of the burden of their own defense—use some of that money to build decent housing. Use some of that money to educate our children. Use some of that money for long-term health care. Use some of that money to wipe out these slums and put America back to work.

I just want to take common sense to higher places. If we can bail out Europe and Japan, if we can bail out Continental Bank and Chrysler—and Mr. Iacocca makes $8,000 an hour—we can bail out the family farmer.

I just want to make common sense. It does not make sense to close down 650,000 family farms in this country while importing food from abroad subsidized by the U.S. government.

Let's make sense. It does not make sense to be escorting oil tankers up and down the Persian Gulf, paying $2.50 for every $1.00 worth of oil we bring out, while oil wells are capped in Texas, Oklahoma and Louisiana. I just want to make sense.

Leadership must meet the moral challenge of its day. What's the moral challenge of our day? We have public accommodations. We have the right to vote. We have open housing.

What's the fundamental challenge of our day? It is to end economic violence. Plants closing without notice, economic violence. Most poor people are not lazy. They're not Black. They're not brown. They're mostly white, female and young.

But whether white, black, brown, the hungry baby's belly turned inside-out is the same color. Call it pain. Call it hurt. Call it agony.

Most poor people are not on welfare. Some of them are illiterate and can't read the want-ad sections. And when they can, they can't find a job that matches their address. They work hard every day. I know. I live among them. I'm one of them.

I know they work. I'm a witness. They catch the early bus. They work every day. They raise other people's children. They work every day. They clean the streets. They work every day. They drive vans and cabs. They work every day. They change the beds you slept in at these hotels last night and can't get a union contract. They work every day.

No more. They're not lazy. Someone must defend them because it's right, and they cannot speak for themselves. They work in hospitals. I know they do. They wipe the bodies of those who are sick with fever and pain. They empty their bedpans. They clean out their commodes. No job is beneath them, and yet when they get sick, they cannot lie in the bed they made up every day. America, that is not right. We are a better nation than that. We are a better nation than that.

We need a real war on drugs. You can't "just say no." It's deeper than that. You can't just get a palm reader or an astrologer; it's more profound than that. We're spending $150 billion on drugs a year. We've gone from ignoring it to focusing on the children. Children cannot buy $150 billion worth of drugs a year. A few high profile athletes—athletes are not laundering $150 billion a year—bankers are.

I met the children in Watts who are unfortunate in their despair. Their grapes of hope have become raisins of despair, and they're turning on each other and they're self-destructing—but I stayed with them all night long. I wanted to hear their case. They said, "Jesse Jackson, as you challenge us to say no to drugs, you're right. And not to sell them, you're right. And not to use these guns, you're right."

And, by the way, the promise of CETA—they displaced CETA. They did not replace CETA. We have neither jobs nor houses nor services nor training—no way out. Some of us take drugs as anesthesia for our pain. Some take drugs as a way of pleasure—both short-term pleasure and long-term pain. Some sell drugs to make money. It's wrong, we know.

But you need to know what we know. We can go and buy the drugs by the boxes at the port. If we can buy the drugs at the port, don't you believe the federal government can stop it if they want to?

They say, "We don't have Saturday night specials anymore." They say, "We buy AK-47s and Uzis, the latest lethal weapons. We buy them across the counter at Long Beach Boulevard." You cannot fight a war on drugs unless and until you are going to challenge the bankers and the gun sellers and those who grow the drugs. Don't just focus on the children, let's stop drugs at the level of supply and demand. We must end the scourge on the American culture.

Leadership. What difference will we make? Leadership cannot just go along to get along. We must do more than change presidents. We must change direction. Leadership must face the moral challenge of our day. The nuclear weapons build-up is irrational. Strong leadership cannot desire to look tough, and let that stand in the way of the pursuit of peace. Leadership must reverse the arms race.

At least we should pledge no first use. Why? Because first use begets first retaliation, and that's mutual annihilation. That's not the rational way out. No use at all—let's think this out, and not fight it out, because it's an unwinnable fight. Why hold a card that you can never drop? Let's give peace a chance.

Leadership. We now have this marvelous opportunity to have a breakthrough with the Soviets. Last year, 200,000 Americans visited the Soviet Union. There's a chance for joint ventures into space, not Star Wars and the arms race escalation, but a space development initiative. Let's build in space together and demilitarize the heavens. There's a way out.

America, let us expand. When Mr. Reagan and Mr. Gorbachev met, there was a big meeting. They represented together one-eighth of the human race. Seven-eighths of the human race were locked out of that room: most people in the world tonight—half are Asian, one half of them are Chinese. There are 22 nations in the Middle East. There's Europe, 400 million Latin Americans next door to us, the Caribbean, Africa—a half a billion people. Most people in the world today are yellow or brown or black, non-Christian, poor, female, young, and don't speak English—in the real world.

This generation must offer leadership to the real world. We're losing ground in Latin America, the Middle East, South Africa, because we are not focusing on the real world. We must use basic principles: support international law. We stand the most to gain from it. Support human rights; we believe in that. Support self-determination; we'll build on that. Support economic development; you know it's right. Be consistent, and gain our moral authority in the world.

I challenge you tonight, my friends, let's be bigger and better as a nation and a party. We have basic challenges. Freedom in South Africa—we've already agreed as Democrats to declare South Africa to be a terrorist state. But don't just stop there. Get South Africa out of Angola. Free Namibia. Support the Frontline states. We must have a new, humane human rights assistance policy in Africa.

I'm often asked, "Jesse, why do you take on these tough issues? They're not very political. We can't win that way."

If an issue is morally right, it will eventually be political. It may be political and never be right. Fannie Lou Hamer didn't have the most votes in Atlantic City, but her principles have outlasted every delegate who voted to lock her out. Rosa Parks did not have the most votes, but she was morally right. Dr. King did not have the most votes about the Vietnam War, but he was morally right. If we're principled first, our politics will fall into place.

Jesse, why did you take these big bold initiatives? A poem by an unknown author went something like this: We mastered the air, we've conquered the sea, and annihilated distance and prolonged life, we were not wise enough to live on this earth without war and without hate.

As for Jesse Jackson, I'm tired of sailing my little boat, far inside the harbor bar. I want to go out where the big boats float, out on the deep where the great ones are. And should my frail craft prove too slight, the waves that sweep those billows o'er, I'd rather go down in a stirring fight than drown to death on the sheltered shore.

We've got to go out, my friends, where the big boats are. And then, for our children, young America, hold your head high now. We can win. We must not lose you to drugs and violence, premature pregnancy, suicide, cynicism, pessimism and despair. We can win.

Wherever you are tonight, I challenge you to hope and to dream. Don't submerge your dreams. Exercise above all else the right to dream. Even on drugs, dream of the day that you are drug-free. Even in the gutter, dream of the day that you will be up on your feet again. You must never stop dreaming. Face reality, yes. But don't stop with the way things are; dream of things the way they ought to be. Dream. Face pain, but love, hope, faith and dreams will help you rise above the pain.

Use hope and imagination as weapons of survival and progress, but you keep on dreaming, young America. Dream of peace. Peace is rational and reasonable. War is irrational in this age and unwinnable.

Dream of teachers who teach for life and not merely for a living. Dream of doctors who are concerned more about public health than private wealth. Dream of lawyers more concerned about justice than a judgeship. Dream of preachers who are more concerned about prophecy than profiteering. Dream on the high road of sound values.

And in America, as we go forth to September, October and November and then beyond, America must never surrender its high moral challenge.

Do not surrender to drugs. The best drug policy is a no first use. Don't surrender with needles and cynicism. Let's have no first use on the one hand or clinics on the other. Never surrender, young America.

Go forward. America must never surrender to malnutrition. We can feed the hungry and clothe the naked. We must never surrender. We must go forward. We must never surrender to illiteracy. Invest in our children. Never surrender, and go forward.

We must never surrender to inequality. Women cannot compromise the ERA or comparable worth. Women are making 67 cents on the dollar to what a man makes. Women cannot buy meat cheaper. Women cannot buy bread cheaper. Women cannot buy milk cheaper. Women deserve to get paid for the work that they do. It's right and it's fair.

Don't surrender, my friends. Those who have AIDS tonight, you deserve our compassion. Even with AIDS you must not surrender. You in your wheelchairs. I see you sitting here tonight. I've stayed with you. I've reached out to you across our nation. Don't you give up. I know it's tough sometimes. People look down on you. It took a little more effort to get here tonight.

And no one should look down on you, but sometimes mean people do. The only justification we have for looking down on someone is that we're going to stop and pick them up. But even in your wheelchairs, don't give up. We cannot forget 50 years ago when our backs were against the wall, Roosevelt was in a wheelchair. I would rather have Roosevelt in a wheelchair than Reagan and Bush on a horse. Don't you surrender, and don't you give up.

Don't surrender and don't give up. Why can I challenge you this way? Jesse Jackson, you don't understand my situation. You be on television. You don't understand. I see you with the big people. You don't understand my situation. I understand. You're seeing me on TV but you don't know what makes me me. They wonder why does Jesse run, because they see me running for the White House. They don't see the house I'm running from.

I have a story. I wasn't always on television. Writers were not always outside my door. When I was born late one afternoon, October 8th, in Greenville, South Carolina, no writers asked my mother her name. Nobody chose to write down our address. My mama was not supposed to make it. You see, I was born to a teenage mother who was born to a teenage mother.

I know abandonment and people being mean to you, and saying you're nothing and nobody, and can never be anything. I understand. Jesse Jackson is my third name. I'm adopted. When I had no name, my grandmother gave me her name. My name was Jesse Burns until I was 12. So I wouldn't have a blank space, she gave me a name to hold me over. I understand when you have no name. I understand.

I wasn't born in the hospital. Mama didn't have insurance. I was born in the bed at home.

I really do understand. Born in a three-room house, bathroom in the backyard, slop jar by the bed, no hot and cold running water. I understand. Wallpaper used for decoration? No. For a windbreaker. I understand. I'm a working person's person, that's why I understand you whether you're African American or white.

I understand work. I was not born with a silver spoon in my mouth. I had a shovel programmed for my hand. My mother, a working woman. So many days she went to work early with runs in her stockings. She knew better, but she wore runs in her stockings so that my brother and I could have matching socks and not be laughed at at school.

I understand. At three o'clock on Thanksgiving Day we couldn't eat turkey because mama was preparing someone else's turkey at three o'clock. We had to play football to entertain ourselves and then around six o'clock she would get off the Alta Vista bus when we would bring up the leftovers and eat our turkey—leftovers, the carcass, the cranberries around eight o'clock at night. I really do understand.

Every one of these funny labels they put on you, those of you who are watching this broadcast tonight in the projects, on the corners, I understand. Call you outcast, lowdown, you can't make it, you're nothing, you're from nobody, subclass, underclass—when you see Jesse Jackson, when my name goes in nomination, your name goes in nomination.

I was born in the slum, but the slum was not born in me. And it wasn't born in you, and you can make it. Hold your head high, stick your chest out. You can make it. It gets dark sometimes, but the morning comes. Don't you surrender. Suffering breeds character. Character breeds faith. In the end faith will not disappoint.

You must not surrender. You may or may not get there, but just know that you're qualified and you hold on and hold out. We must never surrender. America will get better and better. Keep hope alive. Keep hope alive. Keep hope alive. On tomorrow night and beyond, keep hope alive.

I love you very much. I love you very much.

# THE REVIVAL OF HOPE:

## The Platform of the 1988 Jesse Jackson for President Campaign

We are fast approaching the end of a decade of political reaction which embraced the past and feared the future. Reagan's false "Morning in America" is over.

America cannot be a first-rate world power with a second-rate economy. Eight years of Reaganomics have left our economy with a dangerous debt that compromises the American future and has spread its damage throughout the world economy. The gap between have and have-not Americans and between have and have-not nations has widened.

The Reagan-Bush administration promised that Americans would benefit from trickle-down economics. Instead, workers' paychecks have shrunk, home ownership is out of reach for young families, and the specters of poverty and homelessness haunt the streets of America unchallenged.

The Reagan-Bush administration promised a balanced budget. Instead, that administration added as much to the national debt as all the other presidents combined—from George Washington through Jimmy Carter.

The Reagan-Bush administration promised that deregulation and tax breaks for the rich would spark unprecedented investment and savings; instead, farms have been foreclosed, factories have been shuttered, and corporate takeovers have created debt instead of prosperity.

What should the Democratic Party stand for at home?

A federal budget that will pay for our dreams while making progress in reducing our deficit. Investment in people, not financial paper, and in our communities, not corporate takeovers.

Investment in families who need and deserve a fair and indexed minimum wage, pay equity for women, affordable child care, national health care, decent education, affordable housing and a real war on drugs.

A commitment to growth and economic opportunity, not economic austerity. Fair trade and more trade, not protectionism; global economic cooperation, not economic warfare.

What should the Democratic Party stand for abroad?

A fundamental reassessment of our national security priorities is long overdue. It must be grounded in a new realism about the world in which we live, and a sober reassessment of our real security concerns in light of profound changes in relations between the superpowers. Our national security policy today is still too often grounded in assumptions and institutions developed immediately after World War II. But new global realities dramatically demonstrate the increasing futility of relying primarily on military force to cope with the problems of the modern world. President Reagan and General Secretary Gorbachev lead the most powerful militaries in the world. Yet the President went to Moscow frustrated from failures in Nicaragua; the General Secretary who received him was defeated in Afghanistan. The mismatch between military might and political objectives was plain.

Bloated nuclear arsenals contradict the declining utility of military force to meet new threats to our security. We are less secure today not because of the spread of communism, but because American jobs are dependent upon a global economy over which we have less and less control. We are less secure today because a global drug trade overruns our borders, and because the health of our people is increasingly dependent upon a global environment that is growing ever more fragile. Huge investments in weapons cannot defeat these new enemies or win the wars they are waging in the heart of our communities.

The Democrats need an agenda for winning.

How can the Democrats win in 1988? First, we must expand the party. The issue is not the left wing or the right wing of the party. We must choose between leaving millions outside the democratic process or expanding the party to include the 75 million eligible voters who failed to exercise their right to vote in 1984. Millions of Americans will vote for a party dedicated to jobs, peace and justice.

The second key to victory will be our skill at healing divisions and building a winning coalition within our party. For the last eight years, we have had an administration in Washington that has divided and confused our nation. Old allies that together forged great victories in the past were now told they had little in common. Our task is to heal our nation as we build and expand our party into a broad-based winning coalition. That is why we stand with farmers who are about to lose their farms; with workers whose plant gates are about to close without notice; with small businesspeople whose banks will not give them loans; with children whose schoolyards are marketplaces for drugs; and with the poor who are shut out of medical care.

The third key to victory is a new direction for our country. Welfare reform is overdue, but so is corporate reform. As long as our tax laws give incentives to multinational corporations to export capital and jobs abroad, our jobs will not be protected. As long as we invest 70 percent of federal research and development funds and waste one-third of our scientists on military products, our economy cannot compete. As long as we champion the contras and affront other Latin Americans, our role in the world will decline. When our economic priorities are merging corporations, purging workers, and submerging the economy under a mountain of debt, we lose the ability to house our people, meet their health-care needs, and fight a war on poverty.

The Democratic Party is the party of hope, the party of progress, the party of the people. We know that if we stand together, we will win. If we turn *to* each other and not *on* each other, we can keep America strong and make America better. Together we can weave a quilt made of all the diverse patches—from the middle-class to the working poor, from farmers to urban workers, from steelworkers to environmentalists, from poor women with children to the elderly. The Democratic quilt follows a pattern designed by the people of our party, a pattern whose realization offers the promise of security and opportunity for every American.

Forty-four years ago one Democrat said it clearly:

"...That true individual freedom cannot exist without economic security and independence...In our day these economic truths have become accepted as self-evident. We have accepted, so to speak, a second Bill of Rights under which a new basis of security and prosperity can be established for all regardless of station, race or creed. Among these are:

- The right to a useful and remunerative job;

- The right to earn enough to provide adequate food and clothing and recreation;

- The right of farmers to raise and sell their products at a return which will give them and their families a decent living;

- The right of every family to a decent home;

- The right to adequate medical care;

- The right to adequate protection from the economic fears of old age and sickness and accident and unemployment; and finally,

- The right to a good education.

All of these rights spell security. And...we must be prepared to move forward in the implementation of these rights, to new goals of human happiness and well-being."

Once again we must revive Franklin Delano Roosevelt's dream.

## I. Charting a New Direction: A National Budget for Growth, Opportunity and Fiscal Responsibility

The federal budget sets the moral, political and financial direction for the nation. It shows what is important to us. It charts a course for living up to our values. And it indicates how deeply we are committed to them.

The Reagan policies have dug the economy into a deep deficit hole. We now find ourselves victims of the soldiers of austerity who were—in the words of Reagan's first budget director—hidden in the Trojan Horse of supply-side economics. If Democrats want to retain our identity and the hope that Americans have in us, we cannot let the Reagan deficits close off economic progress.

The next national budget must begin mobilizing the resources to meet urgent, realistic national goals while making steady progress toward reducing the federal deficit. We doubled the military budget in peacetime—we must now exercise restraint. We cut taxes on the wealthy and on corporations in the false hope that these cuts would produce an investment boom—we must now create a system of fair taxes. We shifted priorities away from investments in our children, our schools, our health and our communities—we must now reinvest in America to meet our national needs for the 1990s and beyond.

### Enact Fair Taxes

Upper-income groups, and especially the very wealthy, disproportionately benefited from the tax cuts of the last seven years. Elementary fairness requires that they contribute their share to deficit reduction. The poorest 10 percent of Americans are paying nearly 20 percent more in taxes than they did ten years ago; the richest one percent are paying over 20 percent less. By restoring the top tax rate to 38.5 percent, and by imposing luxury taxes and closing egregious tax loopholes, at least $25 billion more in taxes per year can be raised from the highest income individuals who have the greatest ability to pay.

Corporate taxes were substantially reduced in the Reagan years. The deficit cannot be reduced if corporations continue to get a public subsidy. Corporate tax loopholes alone grew from $10 billion in 1970 to $120 billion in 1986 and still remain near $40 billion per year, even after recent tax reforms. We support raising an additional $20-25 billion annually in taxes by returning corporate taxes (as a percentage of

net corporate income) to their previous levels.

### Promote Real Security

America must have a military force and a defense budget adequate to deter war, defend the people against external threats, defeat the enemy if we must fight, and protect our vital interests in the world. The Reagan administration doubled military spending during peacetime. These billions, poured so disproportionately into weapons systems, have undermined our most basic security, leaving us with a debt-ridden economy, excessive dependence on foreign energy and foreign capital, a devastating increase in the drug flow into our country, and an increasingly fragile national and global environment.

The combination of the most encouraging political changes in the Soviet Union in memory and a nuclear arsenal sufficient to destroy the world demand a reconfigured arms policy. Deferral of unneeded modernization of our nuclear arsenals is the rational first step today.

There are other opportunities created by these and other changing geopolitical circumstances.

We spend $150 billion per year for the defense of Europe. The Soviets have called for asymmetrical conventional force reductions there. The Europeans—now creditor nations—are better able to bear more of the burden of their own conventional defense even as we negotiate overall force reductions.

A Democratic administration must redefine our relationship to the Third World and reorder our military commitments to match a world in which foreign policy challenges increasingly arise in the developing world. Political and economic instability and upheaval will continue in developing countries unless poverty, illiteracy and political oppression are addressed.

A more business-like approach to management of Pentagon procurement will eliminate the huge waste that has produced an unprecedented scandal.

During this administration, military policy has often replaced foreign policy. With the two in greater balance, and an awesome array of military equipment in stock and on line, the country can afford a five-year freeze in the military budget. Indeed, it cannot afford to do otherwise. Such a freeze would save $60 billion annually by 1993 and still leave military spending 25 percent higher after inflation than it was in 1980.

## Invest in People and Families

A great and wealthy nation must not accept the conventional wisdom that the national deficit is a near-permanent fact of life and that we must defer urgent requirements for investment in the American future. We reject the defeatism that we cannot afford to have decent schools in the inner-city, health care our people can afford, child care so parents can work, or job training for employment opportunities. We can afford economic justice. We cannot afford to continue on our present path. It is irrational to deny prenatal care, when a dollar spent early in life saves more than seven dollars later in life. It is irrational to short-change schools, when the cost of welfare and jail care on the back side of life is so much greater than the cost of Head Start and day care on the front side of life. The next Democratic administration should enact a budget which meets sensible deficit reduction targets while substantially increasing investments in critical human needs.

### Wage a War on Drugs

Today the drug crisis is a greater threat to our national security than traditional foreign enemies. Our cities are being invaded by drugs. Sovereign nations are held hostage by the drug trade. A comprehensive approach must replace the patchwork of impotent and haphazard Reagan administration policies.

Five steps are immediately needed. We support the appointment of a national drug czar to coordinate a strong national offensive on drugs. We support vigorous foreign policy initiatives, including convening a western hemispheric summit with drug-producing countries to offer them incentives for alternative crops. We support a true coordinated offensive against the drug trade, including a strengthened Coast Guard, Customs and border patrol interdiction efforts, enlistment of the military to provide back-up patrols, intelligence assistance in detecting major drug transportation

routes, and expansion of local law enforcement efforts. We support an increase in federal resources to make treatment available to all who request it and to teach our children about the dangers of drugs from an early age. We oppose the tragedy of surrender that legalization would represent.

### Educate the Next Generation

Now as never before, educated citizens are essential to a productive economy, a healthy society and a stable democracy. Every child has the right to learn in classes free from the taint of segregation or discrimination and aided by the funds that are needed to provide equal education.

Recent changes in American society have made education a top priority for all Americans. The decline in the birth rate points up the importance of realizing the potential of every child. Revelations about the educational deficiencies of American children and workers compared with the citizens of other industrialized countries have shocked the nation. Therefore, we support a *doubling* of federal education funding over the course of the next administration. We should invest in children from the start by providing WIC, Head Start and pre-school education to all who are eligible. We must open the doors to higher education by making college aid available to all who qualify. We should invest in teachers by increasing training funds, improving career development opportunities and teacher enrichment programs and by establishing a National Teacher Corps to recruit teachers for tomorrow, especially minorities, with scholarships today. We must ensure equal opportunity by: restoring cuts in federal equity programs; offering incentives to equalize school district funding; expanding bilingual education, supporting historically African American and Hispanic institutions, and the education of those with special needs; and initiating a national literacy campaign.

### Provide Child Care for Working Parents

Child care is a necessary investment to safeguard family life so parents will be free to contribute fully to their families and to the economy. When child care is affordable and safe, parents are able to work and raise their standard of living. When child care is of high quality, children get the head start that enhances their education, helps realize their potential, and saves costs later on in life.

The Democratic Party should support a significant increase in federal support for child care for working parents, with assistance given according to need to low- and middle-income families, and aid provided to states to assist in building a child-care infrastructure, with standards for health, safety and quality. We support policies that promote long-range planning, research and coordination of child-care delivery in cooperation with the states and the private sector.

### Train the Future Workforce

The American economy and its workers are experiencing profound economic and technical changes, while our country lags far behind other industrialized nations in developing a flexible job training and vocational education system. We need to overhaul our approach to job training so that workers' skills can continually be upgraded for an ever-changing economy.

The next Democratic administration should significantly increase spending in order to improve job training and remedial education. We should especially target assistance for the long-term and hard-core unemployed, youngsters who cannot find work, and workers dislocated because of plant closings and cutbacks. Families cannot be expected to move from welfare to work without job training, job placement assistance, academic assistance and aid in language proficiency.

### Establish a National Health Program

Thirty-seven million Americans—more than one-third of them children—have no form of health insurance. Millions more have inadequate insurance that is tied to their jobs. No other nation spends so much on health care yet gets so little coverage in return. Current efforts to expand coverage must continue, but more fundamental reform is needed in order to reduce per capita costs while increasing the number of people covered and the comprehensiveness of that coverage. We believe it is time for the United States to join the other industri-

alized nations of the world by enacting a National Health Program which provides universal and comprehensive coverage to all Americans, including preventive, curative, long-term, rehabilitative and occupational health services. In order to adequately contain costs and to significantly reduce administrative overhead, such a program should be federally funded and administered.

### Solve the AIDS Crisis

The illness of AIDS is a challenge to modern technology, and to our health system. The fact of AIDS is a challenge to our compassion. The Democratic Party supports an acceleration of efforts and an increase in funding sufficient to quickly find a vaccine and a cure for AIDS. Resources must immediately be provided to ensure prompt review of new drugs and treatments. The country needs a major public education and prevention campaign to address AIDS.

We oppose all efforts to impose mandatory testing and quarantines, and we oppose discrimination in employment, education, housing and health care. These measures unfairly stigmatize victims and discourage efforts to identify the disease and prevent its spread. Instead we support voluntary testing and counseling, compassionate patient care and full civil rights for individuals with AIDS, ARC or who test positive for the HIV antibody.

### Renew Our Commitment to Decent Housing

Budget authority for low- and moderate-income housing has plunged from $28 billion to $11 billion since 1980, forcing millions of Americans into the streets and making the provision of shelter a hardship for millions of others. High prices, large down payments and high real interest rates have made it nearly impossible for many first-time home buyers to realize the American dream of owning a home. The Democratic Party must recommit itself to Congress' 1949 pledge of ensuring a decent place to live for every American.

We support a significant increase in housing funds with a goal to return spending on housing to pre-Reagan levels. We should attract new sources of capital, such as pension funds, to help finance construction and mortgages. We should assist the homeless and prevent further homelessness. We should preserve the existing inventory of public and subsidized housing. We should expand the production of affordable housing, emphasizing construction by non-profit developers to keep housing costs down. We should restore foreclosed government property to productive use. We should provide low-interest loans for down payments to first-time home buyers.

## II. An Economy That Works

Economic violence haunts the lives of too many Americans. Good farmers lose their farms to bad loans. Our children are victimized by poor education, poor health care and poor diets. Plants close without notice, while corporate raiders make windfall profits and top management award themselves excessive bonuses.

The American economy, which created the great American middle-class and offered hope to the poor, has turned on millions of workers who now find themselves victims of a new economic violence. The Democrats can offer a plan that can bring Americans relief and opportunity.

### A Worker's Bill of Rights

American workers have a right to expect a job with decent pay. Yet today, our country has 40 percent more working poor people than seven years ago. Most of the poor work every day. They carry messages between our offices, run our elevators, serve our meals, clean our bathrooms and sweep our floors. Most are white. Most are young. Most are female. They need economic justice. They deserve full employment at decent wages—the cornerstone of healthy families and a healthy economy. They need a Workers Bill of Rights which includes:

### A Fair Minimum Wage

We must support an indexed minimum wage of $5 per hour so that working people can support themselves through their own labor.

### Pay Equity

Working in a "woman's job" should not deprive a woman of comparable pay for work requiring skill, effort and responsibility equal to a "man's job." The federal government should take the lead by establishing a method for uncovering and correcting such pay discrimination.

### Family Leave Policies

Workers should not have to choose between their jobs and their families. The Democratic Party should support a national standard of parental and medical leaves to protect the jobs and incomes of workers who temporarily leave the workforce to meet family responsibilities.

### Union Representation

We must give workers the voice they need and the respect they deserve on the job. The right of all workers, including public employees, to organize and bargain collectively through the union of their choice is a precious American right that has been damaged by the Reagan administration. Many steps are necessary to protect the effectiveness of the right to organize. Among them are revisions in labor laws to remove cumbersome barriers to, and effective penalties against, management abuse of labor rights and other anti-union tactics. We must also ensure that there is no substandard wage competition for public contracts.

### Health and Safety

The health of workers on the job has been put in serious jeopardy during the Reagan years. By studious non-enforcement, this administration has deregulated occupational and health protection for American workers and increased both the harm and the risk of harm to them. Workers must have the right to know about hazards on the job. Nothing short of the revitalization of OSHA, its standards and its remedies can assure the protection workers need and deserve.

### Pension Security

A pension belongs to the worker, not to the company or public agency. We support the portability of pensions so that workers who change jobs will not be penalized. We will eliminate legal means which allow corporations to shed their pension obligations via bankruptcy or to remove assets from "overfunded" pension plans. We oppose efforts to reduce Social Security benefits. Social Security is self-financing and did not cause the budget deficit; its funds should not be considered for deficit reduction.

## Invest in America: Pension Fund Capital Can Help Meet Our National Needs

The physical structure of America's communities is in serious disrepair. Across our country a bridge closes every other day. Affordable housing and public transportation are not available to many. Small businesses cannot afford to borrow. Yet the Reagan administration has cut federal aid to local governments by more than one-third. New tax laws have restricted the use of public financing for economic development. And financial speculation has replaced real investment in jobs and in our communities. The Democratic Party should seek to shift a portion of our public pension funds from paper investments to investments in housing, small business development, neighborhood revitalization and infrastructure construction. Properly secured with federal guarantees, these pension funds can meet much of our growing investment needs.

### A National Investment Program

Using the model of Ginnie Mae and Fannie Mae, a National Investment Program would pool small investment projects overseen at the local level by a board of government, business and labor leaders. Federally guaranteed bonds would be issued to back these projects, which would then be sold to public pension funds that chose to buy them. Federal guarantees would ensure a fair rate of return to workers' pensions and reduced costs to borrowers.

### An American Investment Bank

To finance large infrastructure projects, an American Investment Bank is needed. Modeled on the World Bank, this Bank would receive an initial contribution of capital from the states, although only a fraction of the funds would need to be subscribed initially. This capital would back the Bank's bonds, which would be marketed to pension funds. In this way, we would leverage pension fund capital at a low enough cost to allow the Bank to relend the funds at a low interest rate for development projects. Experienced decision-mak-

ers—top leaders from business, labor and the public sector—would set the investment priorities and a professional staff would develop and screen feasible projects.

## Stop the Flow of Jobs Out of the Country

The competition for jobs in the new international economy is not between cities, but across borders; it is not confined to manufacturing but encompasses service jobs as well. Many American corporations have been roaming the globe looking for cheap, even militarily repressed, labor. Our quarrel is not with foreign workers. Jobs are being taken to low-wage labor markets by companies flying American flags who are loyal only to the short-term bottom line. They show little concern for the workers or the communities they leave behind, or for those they find abroad.

America needs more trade, fair trade and an administration willing to use all the tools available to better manage our trade to export more American goods and fewer American jobs. Protectionism is self-defeating and divisive. It pits American workers against American consumers and our workers against workers throughout the world. We need a president who is willing to use all of the tools available to manage America's trade within existing international frameworks. And we need to recognize that our choice is to help raise the wages and standard of living of workers in the Third World or to endure a lower standard of living ourselves.

### Enact Plant Closing Legislation

Before a plant closes its doors, workers and communities need six months advance warning to allow time to make the necessary adjustments. Experience with plant closings shows that advance notice has no harmful effect on employers, but that it does enable workers to make necessary adjustments and find alternative employment. It is cruel to leave workers jobless simply because they did not know they needed to look elsewhere. In the event of plant closings, businesses that are in sound financial shape should be responsible for extended health benefits, retraining and job placement assistance, and to return tax dollars they accepted as incentives to open the plant.

### Make the Violation of Worker's Rights an Unfair Trade Practice

We cannot fully safeguard the rights of American workers unless we safeguard the rights of workers abroad. Congress has passed legislation which denies duty-free access to goods coming from countries which violate workers' rights. President Reagan has never accepted the spirit of the law; systematic violations of labor rights such as the right to form and join unions, restrictions on the use of child labor, and limitations on the hours of work continue. Not only must the law be enforced, but we must work to reform the General Agreement on Tariffs and Trade so that violations of the basic rights of workers can be considered unfair trade practices which risk retaliation.

### Reform the Tax Code

Taxpayers should not subsidize corporations which disinvest from their communities and relocate abroad. Congress should end tax incentives—such as the foreign tax credit and deferred tax payments on income from foreign subsidiaries—which encourage investment abroad at the expense of employment at home.

### Establish a Coherent Program to Curb Corporate Abuse

Under the Reagan administration, corporations have been encouraged to pursue a course of irresponsible conduct that includes unproductive takeovers, monopolistic mergers, insider trading and golden parachutes for executives. Workers, meanwhile, often are left without even severance pay. We must reinvigorate the anti-trust and securities laws to ensure that large mergers are reviewed. We should change tax laws to discourage short-term speculation.

### Rebuild the Civilian Economy

The American economy continually faces transition and adjustment. In agricultural, energy, steel, the automobile industry, defense and other sectors, economic transitions have brought severe dislocation to our cities, towns and families. They cannot manage the effects of such changes alone. A Democratic administration should develop coherent policies to assist workers, industries and communities in making economic transitions. Preference in government contracting and procurement should be given to firms achieving certain standards of modernization and reinvestment, research and development and worker retraining. Readjustment in the balance between civilian and military research is necessary to strengthen our economy and restore American competitiveness. Because credit is crucial to rebuilding our communities, we should involve financial institutions as part of the solution by reforming and expanding community reinvestment laws, reversing the trend of financial concentration and deregulation, and encouraging special commitments in exchange when the federal government bails out our failing financial institutions.

### Reduce High Real Interest Rates

We must end the Reagan-Bush era of high real interest rates. The combination of loose fiscal policy and tight monetary policy has contributed to serious economic imbalances. High real interest rates have also redistributed money from debtors to the wealthy, feeding a speculative binge.

Loosening monetary policy is a vital accompaniment of deficit reduction—otherwise the economy will be plunged into a recession. We must urge the Federal Reserve Board to lower our interest rates in conjunction with lower rates in other developed countries. A combination of lower federal deficits and lower interest rates will begin not only to redress serious macroeconomic imbalances but also to chart a long-term course of more vigorous and stable economic growth.

### Achieve Energy Security

The Democratic Party recognizes that no country can protect its national security without a coherent energy policy. We need to fashion a Pan-American Energy and Environmental Security Alliance to develop our energy resources in this hemisphere. U.S. technology can be traded for oil from Latin America, thereby increasing trade, creating jobs and giving us a more secure energy source than we have now.

We oppose new offshore oil drilling sites because of the environmental risks. We need a vigorous effort to promote clean coal technology that would enable us to use our abundant coal reserves while preventing acid rain. We should pursue the use of natural gas, methanol, ethanol and other alternative transportation fuels. To reduce dependence on limited fossil fuels, we should make a major federal investment in researching and promoting renewable energy—from solar, hydro, wind and agricultural sources—and a major federal commitment to energy conservation. To prevent nuclear accidents such as Three Mile Island and Chernobyl, and to reduce the hazards of radioactive waste, we should phase out nuclear power.

### Protect the Environment

If a foreign power poisoned our air with acid rain, dumped toxic wastes in our water supply, and then took away the living space from our wildlife, we would see the threat to our national security. We are doing this to ourselves.

We need a new environmental policy that focuses on existing environmental abuses and threats and emphasizes changes in the production system to prevent pollution. The Democratic Party should support a vigorous federal research effort to discover new, environmentally sound production and farming technologies. We need vigorous federal support for recycling as a substitute to the construction of new trash-burning incinerators. Urgently required is the prompt elimination of unsafe toxic waste sites and aggressive enforcement of the Toxic Waste Superfund program. Industry should be made responsible for future clean-up costs as an incentive to stop polluting.

We strongly oppose attempts in recent years that have weakened the protection of national parks, refuges and forests. Instead, our national parks and coastal zones need more support, improved protection and management efforts. We must redouble our efforts to provide clean waterways, sound water management and safe, drinkable groundwater.

Essential to environmental policy is the promotion of international cooperation to confront worldwide environmental problems and, where possible, restoration of those natural resources that have already been harmed. We must, in international forums, address the depletion of the ozone layer, the "greenhouse effect," the destruction of tropical rainforests and other threats to the global environment. Indeed, we need to convene regular World Environmental Summits to bring the best minds and resources together to save our planet.

### Save the Family Farm

Reagan administration policies have brought deep recession to rural America, laying waste to family farms and Main Street businesses. The nation can solve recurring farm crises only by putting the economic development of the family farm and the rural business enterprise at the center of agricultural and rural development policy. We should apply the supply management policies of the Family Farm Act to serve world market and hunger needs while providing farmers with fair prices and eliminating billions of dollars in federal subsidies.

Instead of foreclosing on family farms and then packaging the seized land for resale to corporations, we should impose a moratorium on foreclosure of federally supported farm loans and help beginning, restarting and minority farmers purchase farmland now held by the federal government. We must support comprehensive programs of rural water quality protection and soil conservation. We must provide financing mechanisms and guarantees to farmers to help them diversify to meet new market needs and to become processors of the food and fiber commodities they produce. Government should work with farmers and ranchers to provide direct access to regional and international markets, now the private domain of large conglomerates and international shippers. We should convene an international conference of major food-exporting countries to stabilize the international market.

## III. Equal Justice at Home

America is not a blanket, woven from one thread. It is a quilt composed of many patches.

Every patch in the quilt is important. Together they make up "we the people" and give us our identity as a great and varied people.

## Defend Human and Civil Rights

The Democratic Party is the party of cultural pluralism. While the Republicans have become racially and culturally monolithic, the Democratic Party has become the party of all cultures and peoples. Our diversity is our strength. We celebrate and honor America's cultural heritage by ensuring full equality across all artificial barriers. We are proud of our multicultural and multiracial heritage and will work to preserve the rights of all Americans—from the most recent immigrants to the Native Americans.

No legacy of the Reagan years is more bitter than its abandonment of equal rights under law and its disregard for the rights of those who continue to experience discrimination.

We strongly support the ratification of the Equal Rights Amendment to assure women the same constitutional rights as men. We must guarantee women the right to make their own reproductive choices, without discrimination based on ability to pay.

African Americans continue to meet color discrimination and to suffer disproportionate economic, social, physical and psychological harm in this society. We must reverse the dangerous erosion in progress for African Americans visible in areas ranging from a sharp decline in college attendance to intolerable burdens of permanent unemployment.

Hispanics still suffer discrimination based on language, color and cultural differences. We oppose efforts to impose "English only" requirements and similar policies that have a discriminatory effect. Removing the barriers to the advance of America's fastest growing minority group is as urgent for the country as for Hispanics.

In a country of immigrants, millions of Asian Americans, Arab Americans and other ethnic groups from around the world still endure discrimination because of their national origin. Our immigration policy must be reformed to promote fairness, non-discrimination and family reunification, and to reflect our constitutional freedoms of speech, association and travel. The foreign born must not be discriminated against in education, in receiving services or benefits, or in their ability to participate in politics.

We must honor our treaty obligations with American Indian nations and take affirmative steps to end the scandalous conditions that now exist on reservations. New resources must be provided for adequate education, housing and economic development.

We must guarantee full civil rights for lesbians and gay men, ensuring their rights to privacy, equal protection and freedom from violence.

The physically disabled and sense-impaired must have their full civil rights, including the right to full access.

We must rebuild the civil rights enforcement machinery, assure equal protection under the laws, full expression of civil rights and freedom from discrimination based upon race, sex, religion, sexual orientation or handicapping condition. Strong affirmative action using all the available approaches, including numerical remedies, such as goals, timetables and set-asides for minorities and women, must be vigorously enforced. In employment, voting, schools, housing and business set-asides, efforts to redress historical discrimination must be made equal to the task.

## Support Political Empowerment

The right to vote is a cornerstone of the democratic process. Yet in 1984, 75 million Americans had the right to vote but did not exercise it. The core values and historic traditions of the Democrats require our party to assume responsibility for revitalizing the democratic process. We dedicate ourselves to bringing millions more Americans into the political processes that can change their lives. We must secure universal and same-day voter registration and facilitate registration by mail-in and agency-based methods. We must remove impediments to the one-person, one-vote principle by ending run-off primaries, at-large requirements, improper purging of election rolls, and other schemes that dilute the effect of an individual's vote. There must be no undercounting in the upcoming census. We must end discrimination against federal employees who are denied the right to full participation in the democratic process.

We should support statehood for the District of Columbia. We should support the rights of Puerto Rico, the Virgin Islands and all offshore territories to decide their future free from outside interference. We must rescue the Voting Rights Act from its beleaguered position and make its vigorous enforcement answer for decades of denial of the vote to the nation's minorities. We should encourage the nomination and election of women and minority candidates within our party and then in the general election, and we must minimize the domination and distortion of our elections by moneyed interests.

## IV. A New Realism in American Military and Foreign Policy

Defending the national security of the United States is the central responsibility of government. The foundation of real security is a healthy economy and a strong military. But the strongest foundation can be eroded if our policy is misguided. Our foreign policy must reflect the changing nature of threats to our security and respond to them in a fashion that is not alien to our values.

Democrats have always been committed to a strong national defense. But after the largest peacetime military build-up in our history, we have no shortage of military force. The demands of the time demand a new realism in defense and foreign policy.

### Reverse the Arms Race

The Democratic Party has always assumed leadership in nuclear disarmament. This priority continues even though the INF treaty was signed by Ronald Reagan, who had to fight sections of his own party to obtain approval of the treaty. Democrats, because they understand the peace process, should not simply follow the lead of Mikhail Gorbachev, but must take the leadership in redefining the relationship between the two powers. Common efforts are now possible, including action to settle world tensions, campaigns to reduce malnutrition and hunger in the Third World, joint space ventures, and more expansive cultural exchanges.

It is time to stop and reverse the nuclear arms race. This will not only reduce the risk of war; it will relieve the fiscal burden that has weakened the national economies of both the United States and the Soviet Union. We support a U.S.-initiated nuclear test ban moratorium and a challenge to the Soviet Union to join us in a mutually verifiable comprehensive test ban treaty. We should initiate an independent moratorium on missile flight testing, challenging the Soviet Union to join us in a mutually verifiable end to all new missile flight testing. We should continue the START process to achieve deep cuts in strategic arsenals. We should reaffirm strict adherence to the ABM Treaty and call for a ban on anti-satellite and other weapons in space. We should initiate a Space Development Initiative, not a Strategic Defense Initiative, and limit the Star Wars program to the most basic research. We should prohibit the production of nerve gas and work for a verifiable treaty banning chemical weapons. Working with our allies, we should reconfigure our forces and strategy to adopt a "no first use" policy on nuclear weapons. We must elaborate a defensive strategy that does not depend upon an impossible option that we cannot and should not exercise. Our policy should state clearly that nuclear weapons have only one purpose—to deter a nuclear attack on the United States or our allies.

### Increase Burden-Sharing and Opportunities for Conventional Arms Reductions in Europe

Forty-three years after World War II we are spending over $150 billion a year defending Europe against an implausible threat. The Europeans are creditor nations; we are a debtor nation. They have one and one-half times the population and twice the GNP as the Soviet Union. Yet during the Reagan years the cost to us of defending Europe has increased 20 percent. We can no longer afford to bear a disproportionate burden of their defense. While consulting and aiding our allies, we should reduce U.S. forces in Europe over the next five years and the Europeans must become more responsible for their own conventional defense. At the same time our primary concern should be to reduce the overall NATO defense burden. A Democratic administration should meet with our allies and negotiate mutual conventional force reductions with the Soviet Union.

## Bring Peace to Troubled Regions

The Reagan administration has undermined international institutions and international law and retreated from commitments to human rights and economic development. The Reagan approach is ineffective against the poverty, repression and despair most of the world faces. Against such adversaries, military force is of limited value.

The United States needs a new doctrine to guide our relations with the Third World. As the world power with the broadest global interests and concerns, we have the greatest stake in building a world at peace, governed by law. A Democratic administration should adopt a policy designed to support and strengthen the rule of international law and institutions; respect the right to self-determination; promote human rights and measure them by one yardstick; and support economic growth and development.

We must pursue this doctrine around the globe. We must work to protect human rights everywhere, for an end to discrimination in Northern Ireland, an end to oppression in Eastern Europe, and a beginning for democracy in Chile.

### Freedom in Southern Africa

The apartheid regime in South Africa is a uniquely oppressive regime in which every aspect of public life and private rights is determined by skin color. Even as it terrorizes its people at home, its state-sponsored terrorism destabilizes countries and people throughout the region. Its illegal occupation of Namibia has been sustained by its aggressive war against Angola. Its campaign of terror against its neighbors has culminated in the killing fields of Mozambique where its mercenary force, RENAMO, is carrying out a modern holocaust.

A Democratic administration should end all vestiges of the policy of constructive engagement and act boldly against apartheid by declaring South Africa a terrorist state. Such a declaration will allow the president to quickly implement comprehensive sanctions and create a climate for our allies and international organizations to join us. We should give U.S. corporations a date certain by which to cease doing business in South Africa if black majority rule is not established. We should enforce full sanctions against any country that provides arms, military equipment or military advisors to terrorist South Africa. A Democratic president, together with our allies, should convene a summit of the Frontline states, offering the development aid and security assistance needed to make them economically independent of South Africa. We should sever all ties with UNITA and establish diplomatic relations in Angola. We should seek implementation of U.N. Resolution 435 calling for a cease-fire and elections in Namibia leading to independence.

### Peace in Central America

The Reagan-Bush administration has wasted over $10 billion on a policy in Central America that has produced more violence, more economic disruption, more displaced people and more refugees. It is time to take a different course. In the region, we must turn from intervention to consultation, from imposing ideology to addressing debt and poverty. A Democratic administration must fully support the regional peace plan by ending all efforts to maintain the contras as a military force and by helping to reintegrate them into the region. We should end the military maneuvers and trade boycott which have failed in Nicaragua, and we should seek negotiations and economic incentives to encourage democracy.

Ironically, the countries that have made the least progress in implementing the goals of the regional peace process are El Salvador, Guatemala and Honduras—the countries where our influence has been the greatest. In El Salvador a Democratic administration should cut military aid and support a national dialogue leading to open elections. In Honduras we should stop consorting with drug smugglers in exchange for their support for the contras, reduce military aid, and encourage a true national dialogue and free elections. In Guatemala, we should terminate military aid until human rights abuses stop.

To address the crisis in Panama, a Democratic administration should engage our neighbors and allies and mold a coherent regional policy, including one that will cut the flow of drugs. To ensure that we do not repeat the profound failures of the past, we must conduct a full investigation of the relationship between the CIA, the Reagan administration and General Noriega.

As one indication of a new relationship to the region, we should join with the other countries of the hemisphere in recognizing Cuba, inviting that country back into the Organization of American States to begin to work out our continuing disagreements. By recognizing and negotiating with China and the Soviet Union thousands of miles away, we have achieved working relationships and reduced tension. We can do the same with Cuba on our doorstep.

### Justice in the Middle East

Our current Middle East policy has failed. Seven years of the Reagan-Bush administration have left more Americans dead, more Israelis dead, and more Palestinians and Arabs dead. We must do more than choose sides—we must act for peace. We must vigorously pursue a diplomatic solution to the Arab-Israeli conflict, building on the success of Camp David and dealing with the concerns of all parties.

Israeli security and Palestinian self-determination are two sides of the same coin. As Israel's friend and ally, we must do what it cannot do for itself: engage Israel with its adversaries and seek a settlement that can move Israel and the region beyond war. No settlement is possible without recognizing Israel's right to exist with security within internationally recognized borders, and the right of the Palestinian people to safety, self-determination and statehood. Any settlement must offer mutual security and mutual recognition and must trade land for peace. To achieve a just resolution of the conflict, we support a comprehensive, negotiated settlement under the aegis of an international conference that includes the designated representatives of the Palestinian people and of the Israeli government.

We remain committed to the sovereignty, independence and territorial integrity of Lebanon. We are committed to Persian Gulf security, an end to the Iran-Iraq war, freedom of navigation in international waters, United Nations efforts to achieve a negotiated settlement and an arms embargo to the combatants.

### Promote Global Growth and Development

Beyond our borders there is a world of opportunity and challenge. But this administration has not grasped the opportunities. Four hundred million Latin American neighbors are our allies and potential customers. Five hundred fifty million Africans are impoverished and need not only aid but trade.

Burdened with billions in debt, the less developed countries of the world have been forced into austerity programs as a condition for further credit. These policies have not only failed; they have been counter-productive, resulting in a slow-down in growth which helps neither debtor nor creditor. Indeed, such austerity may have been responsible for as much as 30 percent of America's lost trade in recent years. It has cost America more than one million jobs.

We must take the lead in helping to relieve these countries of their crushing debt burdens. American banks have already begun to write off bad debts, but there must be an international plan for debt forgiveness, relief or rescheduling. The banks must recognize that our government will no longer place their short-term financial interests over the economic and trading needs of the national and global economy. The International Monetary Fund's austerity policies must end and a program put in place which can improve fiscal responsibility while promoting growth.

We understood our mutual interest in developing Europe economically after the war. This policy is just as wise for the developing world. A Democratic administration should work with our allies to channel aid to the world's impoverished countries through a Marshall Plan for the Third World. This should be financed primarily through the trade surpluses of creditor nations, particularly West Germany and Japan.

The United States can make a significant contribution to improving the health of Third World economies by shifting foreign aid spending from military to economic programs and by increasing development assistance through direct grants. In 1980 development assistance accounted for two-thirds of total foreign aid, security assistance for one-third. The proportions are the opposite today. We must return spending priorities to earlier levels to promote true peace and development abroad.

# II

# CREATING
# A JUST
# ECONOMY

# THE MESSAGE, THE MISSION AND THE MESSENGER:

## An Economic Program to Make America Better and to Keep America Strong

Cleveland, Ohio, May 2, 1988

Political campaigns often highlight differences, provoke debate and accentuate the negative. Our campaign is a campaign of hope. One of its features is its positive tone. We have affirmed ourselves and our message, rather than negating the other Democratic candidates. We are detailing our differences with the other candidates. But we have not been divisive.

What almost everyone agrees with—the press, the candidates and the American people—is that my message is winning. I didn't start with the money, the ads, the polling or the endorsements. Instead, I have the message, which has brought me this far and I hope will carry me to the White House. My message has been borrowed and leased by the other candidates. I take that as a compliment—and a confirmation of my leadership. My message has set the pace for the campaign this year.

What is my message? Stop drugs from flowing in. Stop jobs from flowing out. Secure our farms, invest in our children, in our people and in our infrastructure. That's a winning message. That is a message that will make America better and keep America strong.

Today I want to speak on the subject: "The Message, the Mission and the Messenger." Part of my message concerns drugs: Up with Hope and Down with Dope. Part of my foreign policy message is the Jackson Doctrine: respecting and expanding the rule of international law; standing for human rights and measuring it everywhere by one yardstick; standing for self-determination; and supporting international economic development. Today, however, I want to focus and share with you my economic message and then urge you—if you agree with me—to vote for the messenger.

### We Must Reduce Our Deficits

After seven years, Reaganomics has left us worse off. We have moved from the world's largest creditor nation to its biggest debtor. Reagan has added more to our national debt than every president before him combined— from George Washington to Jimmy Carter.

Deficit spending—borrowing—has its place, but we have not been borrowing to invest in our people, in retraining our workers, in rebuilding our industries and infrastructure. We have been borrowing to fund the largest military build-up in peacetime history.

And now we no longer borrow only from ourselves. We are dangerously dependent on foreign capital, borrowing from foreign central banks to the tune of $22 billion in the first three months of this year alone.

These deficits cost us every day. They mortgage the future of our children. They lead us to forego necessary investments in children, in health, in roads and bridges, in our future. They choke small businesses with the high real interest rates necessary to attract foreign capital. They cannot be sustained.

How do you get out of this hole? The same way you got in. Reagan doubled the military budget in peacetime and gave the rich and powerful a multi-billion dollar tax break. Bush called it "voodoo economics"—before Reagan hired him. Now Bush can't even quote himself.

I offer a deficit reduction program that reduces our deficit while enabling us to invest in our future. It is a coherent strategy that reflects my priorities. Neither of my opponents has done the same. Bush promises to cut taxes to continue the Reagan military build-up and waves the magic wand of a balanced budget amendment. But we cannot magically legislate the deficit away.

Dukakis says he will collect Reagan's taxes, keep military spending about where it is and invokes the "Massachusetts miracle." But we cannot wish the deficit away. We must make choices and commitments.

I say freeze military spending at current levels, saving $60 billion a year by 1993. Even with this freeze, total military spending will still be higher than it was in 1980. We will still have the world's most sophisticated nuclear arsenal, the most powerful navy and air force, and over two million men and women in uniform. But we will have saved the resources necessary to build a secure economy.

Restore fair taxes. The Congressional Budget Office has demonstrated that the poorest 10 percent of Americans will pay nearly 20 percent more in taxes this year than ten years ago; the richest one percent will pay over 20 percent less. Tax the top 600,000 taxpayers at the 38.5 percent rate; move corporate taxes back toward the 1970's level. Together these two steps alone will raise $40-$45 billion per year by 1993.

We must commit ourselves to reducing the deficit, while we embark on important investment programs. We must show how we can pay for our promises. We cannot sustain Reaganomics, as George Bush suggests. We cannot manage Reaganomics, as Michael Dukakis suggests. We must reverse Reaganomics. Change our direction, reduce our deficits—and invest in America.

## We Must Lead the World to Global Growth

Our domestic economic health depends increasingly upon global economic growth. Growth abroad increases demand for our products and reduces our trade deficits. Global expansion will help put our industries and our workers back to work.

Global expansion requires that our developed countries, particularly the surplus nations of Germany and Japan, expand their domestic demand and lower their interest rates. This is one reason a candid U.S. deficit reduction program is vital, for it is a precondition for international cooperation to stimulate growth.

Beyond our borders, in the Third World, is a world of opportunity and challenge. But this administration has not grasped the possibilities: four hundred million Latin American neighbors, allies, customers; five hundred fifty million Africans in dire need of aid and trade.

Saddled with billions in debt, these countries have been forced into economic austerity as a condition for further credit. The result is a drastic reduction in their imports, and a drastic reduction in our exports. The resulting slowdown helps neither the debtor nor creditor. We must take the lead in relieving these countries of their debt burdens. American banks have already begun to write off bad debts. But only an international plan for debt forgiveness, relief and re-scheduling, combined with a Marshall Plan for the Third World, financed primarily by the surplus nations, will supply the resources necessary to create renewed growth in the Third World. The banks must recognize that our government will no longer place their short-term financial interests over the economic and trading needs of the global economy. The debtor countries, in turn, must ensure that relief results in broad-based economic growth, not subsidized capital flight.

## We Must Promote More Responsible Corporate Leadership

Our ability to raise living standards throughout the world needs the active participation of our corporations. Our jobs are not being taken from us by foreigners. They are being taken to low-wage labor markets by companies flying the American flag but loyal only to the bottom line.

Protectionism is not the answer. In the long run, it is self-defeating and divisive. We need fair trade and more trade and a president who is willing to use all the tools available to manage our trade.

Violations of workers' rights are violations of fundamental human rights.

As president, I would use American law. We can deny duty-free access to goods coming from countries that violate workers' rights.

President Reagan has been reluctant. I would do it vigorously.

If President Reagan vetoes the present trade bill, I would re-introduce a bill requiring notification of plant closings and sign it into law.

As president, I would use international law. Workers' rights should be protected by international law. Systematic violations of these rights—such as the right to form and join unions, restrictions on the use of child labor and limitations on the hours of work—should be considered unfair trade practices under the General Agreement on Tariffs and Trade. As we help raise standards for workers around the world, their demand for our goods rises and we, too, are better off.

As president, I would promote a Corporate Code of Conduct. Moving American jobs abroad and abandoning American communities is not in the national interest. Merger mania, leveraged buy-outs and CEO-subsidizing golden parachutes are not in the national interest. Fighting worker democracy is not in the national interest.

Cooperation is in the national interest. Our corporations need expanding markets, a productive work force and technological innovation. Our workers need decent jobs with real security, better pay to buy the goods they produce and a growing economy, too.

We all live and work by rules set by the government. We need a government sensible enough to have rules which defend the national interest. A government which can help to forge a new partnership between our corporations and our workers. And a government strong enough to enforce it.

The centerpiece of this new government policy is a Corporate Code of Conduct, based on democratic values and a common definition of the national interest. It establishes a set of responsibilities to accompany the right to do business, the receipt of government contracts, grants and incentives. It encourages participation of workers in their companies and in greater productivity.

A code of conduct would make corporations accountable not only to shareholders but to all "stakeholders," including the community and workers. Corporate boards would not be able to rubber-stamp their own golden parachutes or use workers' pension funds to finance the export of jobs. They would be encouraged to make democracy real in the work place.

My policies for changing corporate behavior and recognizing the role that corporate citizens play in our home economy and around the world do not sustain Reaganomics. They do not manage the damage. They reverse Reaganomics. I seek a mandate for that change. Jackson action will make America better and keep America strong.

## We Must Invest in America

America's communities are in need. Across our land, a bridge closes every other day. Affordable housing and public transportation are unavailable to many. Homeless people sleep in streets, under viaducts, or huddled in doorways.

Study after study—by presidential commissions, congressional agencies, business and labor groups—has pointed to our huge investment needs. The Joint Economic Committee found a trillion dollars of infrastructure needs over the next decade. A recent M.I.T. study stressed our desperate housing needs. A U.S. Office of Technology Assessment report examined a comprehensive approach to worker dislocation which would require billions in new investments.

Separately, each study meets with approval—and then inaction. President Reagan has cut federal aid to local governments by more than one-third. Speculation has replaced real investment. President Reagan's new tax laws have restricted the use of public financing for economic development, including joint private-public projects. His budget deficits have soaked up capital which we needed to make America more productive.

I have proposed a way out of this bind: a national investment program which would use federal guarantees to shift a portion of our public pension funds from paper investments to secure investments in housing, small business development and infrastructure.

There may be a number of ways to do this. At the moment pension funds and unions in Connecticut, Michigan and New York are forging their own approaches.

I would pool small investment projects—from local housing in Detroit to a neighborhood revitalization project in Birmingham—and then issue bonds backed by the projects but guaranteed by the federal government. We would then sell these securities to pension funds, with a fair rate of return guaranteed. Let us begin by using ten percent of the nation's $600 billion of public pension funds over a ten-year period: $6 billion of initial investment each year, overseen by a board of government, business and labor.

Federal guarantees mean that no retiree's pension is at risk. The pension funds could buy and sell the bonds on the market. The bonds would be a prudent investment, similar to the Fannie Mae and Ginnie Mae securities these pension funds now hold.

The participation of business, labor and public sector leaders at the local level will help to leverage the pension fund capital to generate an even greater amount of investment. For example, a project to finance low- and moderate-income housing for working people can receive a subsidy from the private sector by including higher-income units which would contribute a greater share of the revenues than they cost. Local government can lower the cost by donating and clearing the land or by providing initial property tax relief. State government mortgage authorities can provide subsidized mortgages. Together these subsidies can mean that $60 billion of guarantees and bonds sold to pension funds could produce more than double that amount of productive investment.

We also need a new initiative to finance large infrastructure projects. Why can't all the energy and enthusiasm that our brightest minds channel into Wall Street's investment banks work for an American Investment Bank? Modeled on the World Bank, this American Investment Bank would receive an initial injection of capital from all the states, although only a fraction of the funds would have to be subscribed upfront. Backed by this capital, the bank would issue bonds at a low enough cost to allow the bank to re-lend the funds for development projects.

The American Investment Bank would attract the country's finest minds. Experienced decision makers—top leaders of business, labor and the public sector—would set the investment priorities. A first-rate professional staff would develop and screen feasible projects. Properly managed, the bank could get the states to work together in a new kind of federalism, rather than fuel the cutthroat competition they face today.

Combining pension fund capital and federal guarantees will shift our priorities toward real investment. It does not sustain Reaganomics. It does not manage the damage. It is a creative way to reverse Reaganomics. Jackson action will make America better and keep America strong.

## We Must Invest in People

America has 40 percent more people working but still poor than seven years ago. Most of the poor work every day. They make the beds in our hospitals; carry messages between our offices; run our elevators; serve our meals; change our beds; clean our bathrooms. Most of them are white, young or female. Two out of every three workers at the minimum wage are women. They raise our children. Half of America's poor children live in a household headed by a single woman.

They need economic justice. They need a Workers' Bill of Rights and policies that make those rights real. We must raise the minimum wage and index it to at least half of the average wage. We must institute comparable worth and pay equity for women crowded into traditional "women's work" and use vigorous affirmative action to open up other jobs. We must provide child-care and family-leave policies so that workers are not forced to choose between job and family.

Workers need a voice and respect on the job. Unions should be recognized when more than half of the workers petition for it, and a first contract should be negotiated within six months. The National Labor Relations Board must no longer be a strike-breaking board. Safety and health laws must be honored and not breached. Workers should be on pension boards, with a say over how their savings are invested. This approach is not only right. We have the evidence that it is also productive.

We are told we cannot afford economic justice. Time and again we hear that we cannot afford to have decent inner-city schools, or health care for all our citizens, or child care, or job training programs.

The truth is we can't afford not to make these investments. The truth is that a dollar spent on prenatal care saves seven dollars later on. The truth is that a lifetime of illiteracy, drug addiction, jail care or welfare is more costly in every way than Head Start, basic education and drug treatment. The economic sense of such investment is obvious. As a recent report by the Committee for Economic Development (a group of businesspeople and educators) noted, "This nation cannot continue to compete and prosper...when more than one-fifth of our children live in poverty and a third grow up in ignorance."

We must shift our priorities from spending on weapons to investing in people. President Reagan has cut real spending sharply for education and training. As president, I would double education spending by 1993. President Reagan thinks it is enough to just say "No" to drugs. I have laid out a comprehensive program and budget for fighting drugs, including treatment on demand for addicts as recommended by the President's AIDS Commission.

I have laid out a plan to move from military spending to investment in people. I have explained how we will pay the bill. I am the only candidate for president who has. Perhaps we should ask how the others will pay for *not* making these investments.

What have I proposed? A plan to reduce the budget deficit in an orderly way. What have I proposed? A plan to stimulate global economic growth—to everyone's benefit. What have I proposed? A plan to generate responsible corporate behavior. What have I proposed? A plan to reinvest in America and to invest in our people.

That is my economic message and my economic program. It is coherent, comprehensive, relevant and timely. And it is necessary if America is to remain a first-rate economic power. It does not sustain Reaganomics—as Mr. Bush wants to do. It is not a technical fix designed to manage the damage—as Mr. Dukakis appears to want to do. It is a reversal of the cause of our crisis—Reaganomics.

This is a presidential campaign. My mission is clear: to make America better and keep America strong; to change the direction of our party and to redirect the course of our nation.

Many of you agree with this message and this mission. If you agree with me, you ought to vote for me. You ought to vote for me for reasons of conscience, conviction, consistency. Vote with courage for bold leadership and a new direction.

# THE FUNDAMENTALS OF ECONOMIC GROWTH AND ECONOMIC JUSTICE

*E*conomic violence is the critical issue of our day. When plants close on workers without notice—that's economic violence. When merger maniacs make windfall profits and top management is given excessive bonuses—that's economic violence. When two to three million Americans are on the streets and homeless—that's economic violence. When children are victimized by poor health care, poor education, poor housing, poor diets and more—that's economic violence against our children and it must stop.

—*Jesse Jackson*

Jesse Jackson has a vision and a program for the U.S. economy. He believes that we can prosper by encouraging and rewarding people, not by redistributing more wealth to the wealthy or imposing austerity on the rest of us. He believes that we must directly promote productive investment in people, machines, and ideas, not just cross our fingers and hope that paper investments and merger mania will somehow eventually make our economy thrive.

The Jackson campaign has prepared a wide variety of materials on the economy. This position paper reviews some of the underlying issues of economic performance with which every campaign must deal.

The first section reviews the Reagan record. The second section critically reviews the conventional wisdom that we can correct the economic distortions resulting from eight years of Reaganomic recklessness by ushering in a new era of economic austerity. The third section presents the Jackson program for a growing and just economy.

## Economic Misery, Paper Profits

President Reagan insisted after the October 1987 stock market crash that "the fundamentals are sound." Many seem to take solace from the fact that we have not yet, as of spring 1988, entered a recession.

That's the meager good news. The bad news is that the economy is sluggish and shaky. It has *not* been good for children and most other living things.

The bottom line is that the vast majority of U.S. workers and households have been forced to struggle to make ends meet.

Figure 1 on the next page shows the stagnation of workers' hourly earnings and of median family income since the early 1970s. Workers' real (inflation-adjusted) hourly earnings peaked in 1978. They are now lower than they were ten years ago. Real median family income still remained in 1986 below its previous peaks in 1973 and 1978. By this standard, American families were *not* better off in 1986 than they had been almost 15 years earlier![1]

## Figure 1:

### Austerity Continues

**Real Hourly Wages ($1986)**

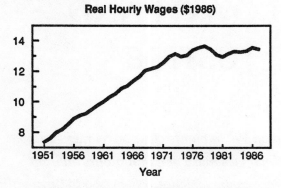

**Median Family Income (1986 $ in Thousands)**

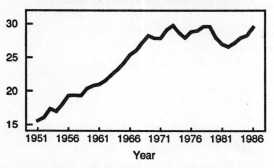

There are two main reasons for this stagnation in the living standards of most U.S. households.

- **The macro economy itself has stagnated:** Figure 2 presents trends for two main macroeconomic indices. The Republicans promised to revive the economy, but the rate of growth of real GNP itself fell even below its sluggish pace during the 1970s. They promised a supply-side revival by giving huge tax breaks to the wealthy and corporations, but the rate of net investment—net private productive investment as a share of net national product—has sunk even lower during the recent business cycle.[2]

- **There has been a major shift of income toward the very wealthiest:** Figure 3 shows that the top one percent of U.S. families dramatically increased their share of total before-tax personal income between 1977 and (projected) 1988. This gain came entirely at

the expense of the bottom 80 percent—the vast majority of American households.[3]

With stagnating opportunities and rising concentrations of wealth, distortions and instabilities in the economy have spread. Record-high real interest rates have squeezed private investment, undermined small businesses, pushed policymakers in other advanced countries to impose restrictive monetary policies on their own economies, and crippled Third World countries by increasing the burden of interest payments owed on their debt. U.S. corporate and personal debt are setting new postwar records with each passing year, while the personal savings rate has plunged.[4] Trade and budget deficits add to the vulnerability of our economy. Third World debt threatens to topple the world-wide house of cards.

Are these the "sound fundamentals"? Is this an economic record worthy of pride?

### Austerity to the Rescue?

Many among the wealthy, the pundits, and the politicians pontificate a stern solution to these problems. They tell us the party's over. They say that we have lived too long beyond our means. They warn that we must tighten our belts now or forever bear the consequences.[5]

As Peter G. Peterson, former Commerce Secretary under President Carter, notes, the Reagan administration "gave us ... a torrid consumption boom financed by foreign borrowing, an overvalued currency, and cuts in private investment, with debt-financed hikes in public spending and huge balance-of-payments deficits. It's the same script, proceeding toward the same woeful finale, that we have seen played out over the years by many a Latin American debtor."[6]

Part of this critique is correct, but the prescription will not cure the patient. There are two fundamental flaws in the logic of this austerity program:

- **The austerity program proposes to squeeze a stone which is already dry:** We have already seen [Fig. 1] that earnings have been stagnating for at least a decade for the vast majority of U.S. households. The federal government has already imposed an auster-

**Figure 2:**

**U.S. Macro Peformance**

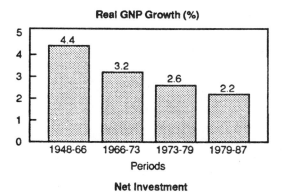

Real GNP Growth (%)

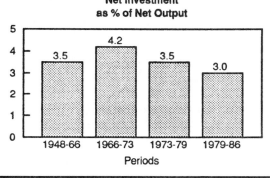

Net Investment
as % of Net Output

**Figure 3:**

**The Wealthy Grab a Bigger Slice**

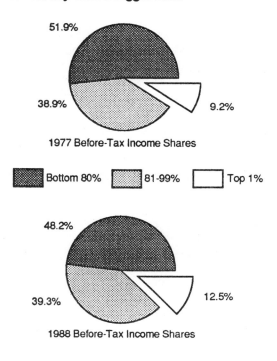

1977 Before-Tax Income Shares

Bottom 80%    81-99%    Top 1%

1988 Before-Tax Income Shares

ity regime for the past eight years on all but the very wealthy and large corporations. Figures 4 and 5 dramatize the tax and expenditure dimensions of these policies.

Figure 4 presents effective tax rates for each 10 percent and for the top one percent of the income distribution in 1977 and 1988. Even though the Tax Reform Act of 1986 undid some of the earlier damage from 1981 and 1982, it remains true that *every income class from the bottom 10 percent to the top 10 percent is paying a higher effective tax rate in 1988 than in 1977 while only the wealthiest one percent are enjoying a lower effective tax rate.*[7]

Figure 5, presenting the expenditure side of the story, traces changes in the composition of federal government expenditures between fiscal years 1979 and 1986. It shows that between 1979 and 1986 discretionary non-defense expenditures dropped dramatically as a share of federal expenditures while defense spending

and net interest payments rose significantly.[8]

■ **The most important tools of the austerity program have already been tried and have failed:** Despite huge redistributions of income from the vast majority of households toward those who can best afford to save, despite massively regressive changes in the distribution of government taxes and expenditures, savings and investment have plummeted, not soared. Personal savings rates have fallen dramatically: By 1987, personal savings as a percent of disposable personal income had fallen to 3.8 percent, by far its lowest level since the early 1950s. The total private savings rate—the ratio of gross private savings to gross national product—has also declined substantially, falling from 17.8 percent in 1979 to only 15 percent in 1987.[9]

Austerity proposals, in short, are part of the problem, not part of the solution.

## Toward a Growing and Just Economy

A growing number of Americans recognize that we must aggressively challenge the greed which has reigned in Washington for the past seven years.

The Jackson campaign believes that we can achieve both growth and justice, both a vibrant and a decent economy. We have made clear throughout our campaign the fundamental importance of achieving greater economic justice in the United States. We have also stressed the critical importance of revitalizing the economy in order to provide more opportunities for more people, to revive the hope of full employment and improving standards of living. We believe in promoting both growth and justice because all Americans have the right to work that is truly productive and to a decent and secure life and livelihood.

In order to pursue both of those critical economic objectives, we must overcome three principal imbalances which have plagued the U.S. economy for the past decade or more: the imbalance between the needs of the majority and the needs of the few; between fiscal policy and monetary policy; and between productive and unproductive economic activity. We cannot move ahead on economic policy until and unless we begin to correct all three.

### Peter and Paul

Some economists insist that we cannot address the needs of the many because we cannot afford to fulfill them. They argue that we must sacrifice wages and consumption to profits and savings.

But this argument represents a misguided approach to the revival of savings and investment.

Consider savings first. Reaganomics relied on savings by the wealthy. But depressed earnings for the many have forced them to *dis*-save in order to make ends meet. There is considerable evidence that U.S. households have been borrowing more over the past decade *not* because they have grown more greedy but because their incomes have grown much more slowly and sporadically than before.[10]

This suggests that we can begin to reduce

Figure 4:

**Robbing Many Peters to Pay a Few Pauls**

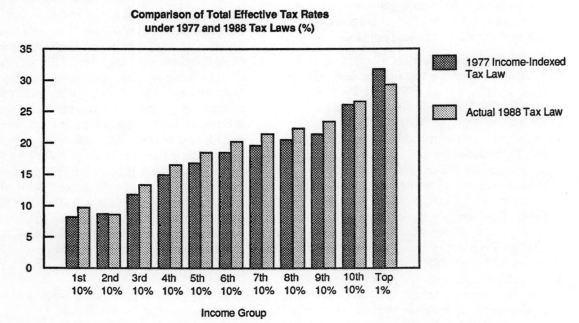

**Comparison of Total Effective Tax Rates under 1977 and 1988 Tax Laws (%)**

household borrowing by reviving a modest, steady, and predictable rate of growth in household disposable income. With higher earnings and resulting reductions in personal debt, households will be able to save much more of their wage-and-salary income.

Next consider investment. Economists recognize that businesses will not invest either if demand is stagnant or the real costs of borrowing are unusually high. Demand prospects will not be encouraging until and unless we commit the economy to a long-term growth path, at stable exchange rates, in which everyone can benefit through rising income. This requires a clear and firm commitment to a general growth in income. And we can hardly expect to encourage investment until and unless we bring real interest rates down further from their 1980s levels.

It does not follow, in short, that savings and investment can be boosted by penalizing the many and rewarding the wealthy. Savings and investment can be enhanced steadily and amply over the medium-term if we begin to reward and involve everyone in the growth process and begin to provide monetary stimulus and lower real interest rates.

**Fiscal Responsibility, Monetary Stimulus**

The Reagan administration has combined far too much fiscal stimulus with far too much monetary restriction. It is time to correct that imbalance as well.

The challenge is imposing. Staggering Reagan deficits have placed the American economy under severe strain. In order to raise the money to pay the government's bills, real interest rates have had to soar, and this in turn has caused an unparalleled overvaluation of the dollar. As a result, American industry was increasingly unable to contend in the highly competitive world marketplace for manufactured goods. The dollar has since come down in value, but the overhang of the trade deficit and a damaged industrial sector still remains.

Like us, the Japanese and West Germans have put off the day of reckoning. They have been able to sell their products here at good prices while also investing their money here at high interest rates. But their surpluses have been accomplished in an environment of slow growth and massive unemployment. They too know this situation cannot continue indefinitely. Sooner or later sustained U.S. borrowing from the rest of the world could result in a

Figure 5:

**More for Guns and Interest**

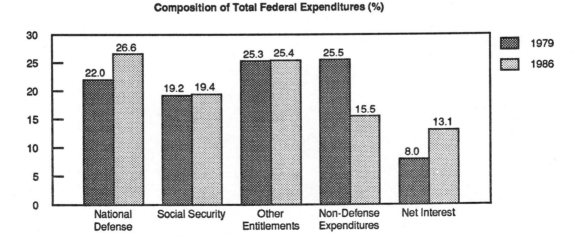

Composition of Total Federal Expenditures (%)

Figure 6:

**Record Real Interest Rates**

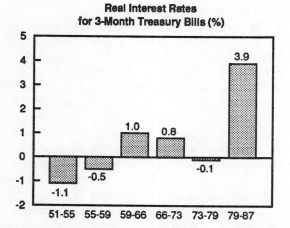

Real Interest Rates
for 3-Month Treasury Bills (%)

Figure 7:

**Businesses Bite the Dust**

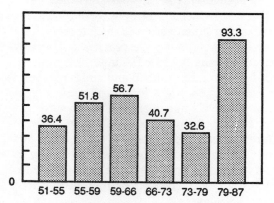

Business Failure Rate
per 10,000 Listed Enterprises (in Thousands)

sudden, panic-driven "run on the dollar" that would shake the financial system, drive up interest rates, and jeopardize growth everywhere. It was partly the concern that continued trade deterioration would force the U.S. to raise its interest rates in order to protect the dollar which precipitated the October 1987 stock market crash.

Meeting this challenge will require leadership on several fronts. Our nation needs lower interest rates and lower exchange rates, but we cannot simply decree them as long as we depend on foreign lenders for money. Nor are our interests served by economic brinksmanship that dares our allies to take their money and go elsewhere. With strong leadership, however, we can get our leading trading partners to cooperate.

The two critical steps are to present a credible plan for deficit reduction and a monetary policy designed to lower interest rates. Such a plan will meet the central demand of our main trading partners for deficit reduction. The dollar can then lower in value, without risking collapse, and our foreign trade deficit can be improved. Such a plan would force our allies to confront the need to "take up the slack" in the world economy, to lower interest rates and to raise demand worldwide.

The Reagan administration has not been

able to strike this deal because it has been unwilling to take the first step—to curb the appetites of its wealthy, corporate, and military friends in the name of deficit reduction. The Jackson economic program can provide an alternative, translating the moral imperative of fiscal responsibility into a credible plan for economic progress.

Fairer taxes and sensible military reductions will allow us to reduce the deficit and still substantially increase spending for education, housing, health care, environmental protection and rebuilding public infrastructure. Lowering the deficit will reduce our need to borrow, and allows us to promote lower real interest rates here and abroad through a less restrictive monetary policy.

In sharp contrast, the Reagan fiscal policies forced the Federal Reserve into perpetuating an era of high real interest rates. Figure 6 shows the trend in real interest rates since the early 1950s, underscoring the dramatically higher rates which have prevailed during the 1980s. Figure 7 dramatizes one of the most crippling effects of these lofty real interest rates, tracing the soaring business failure rates in the 1980s.[11]

With progress on the budgetary front, this era can end. Deficit reduction provides the preconditions for greater international coordination of interest rate policy, propelling the major economies forward in tandem.

We must also have an explicit exchange rate policy in order to stabilize currency markets. Export expansion and trade growth require an exchange rate that is more stable than the 100 percent swing the Reagan administration has given us. Never again can we have a hands-off attitude toward something so vital to our national interest and our prosperity as the value of the dollar.

Finally, we must redirect our trade policies. We need to reduce unfair trade barriers. At times we may even need to impose temporary limits to provide time for communities, businesses and workers to make needed adjustments to new economic circumstances. But more important, particularly over the longer term, we need to begin securing greater multinational corporate responsibility. We must work with the world community to establish laws requiring all corporations to abide by a code of conduct in their operations in other parts of the globe—adhering to environmental, safety, and labor standards comparable to those in the developed world. We should deny preferential trade treatment to offending countries that don't adhere to international labor standards and consider taxing imports and sales of all foreign corporations where these standards are not obeyed. And we should eliminate all tax subsidies that aid U.S. corporations to invest abroad.

Global coordination also requires, finally, that we work with our trade allies to restructure Third World debt. Austerity policies imposed on debtor nations not only have failed; they have been counter-productive, resulting in a slowdown in growth which helps neither debtor nor creditor. The lack of demand among debtors may account for as much as 30 percent of America's lost trade in the last several years. There are a number of policies we could vigorously pursue in order to restructure debt and offer debt relief. For example, if Latin American debtors were relieved of a little more than half of their current debt service, and if they were to use the freed-up foreign exchange earnings to buy U.S. goods in the same proportions as before their debt crises intensified, the result would be a surge of U.S. exports, adding roughly half a million new American jobs.[12]

## From an Unproductive to a Productive Economy

Our corporations are "hollowing" America, shortsightedly taking jobs and production abroad without consideration for the larger implications of their actions. We must make clear to U.S. corporations what we expect of them and what they can expect of the government.

Such a corporate policy will need to confront two critical sources of waste in our economy.

■ **There is the waste which results from our "casino economy."** In 1980-86 alone, investors spent $604.2 billion on paper investments—aimed at "increases in financial assets."[13] Since the years of the postwar boom, they have been spending a substantially higher proportion of funds on paper investments than they did during the long postwar boom. Such paper investments are costly to the economy. In addition to the productive investment which is lost, these numerous transactions take time, energy, and attention away from the real needs of our economy.

Some argue that the rising values of their shares is evidence that American corporations have never been better off. In fact, corporate raiders have driven up share prices, but no new real wealth is created in the process; rather, wealth is being transferred from workers to shareholders. Behind these rising share prices lies a major shift from equity to debt financing, without a proportionate increase in our productive base. This increased indebtedness has left American corporations, and thus our economy, more vulnerable and fragile.

Too much of corporate America has engaged in merger mania, purging workers, and submerging our economy beneath a mountain of debt. Figure 8 traces this mounting fragility, graphing the ratio of corporate debt to total corporate worth. As the graph shows, relative corporate indebtedness began to rise slowly during the late-1960s and the 1970s, compared to the period of the postwar boom, and has more recently soared during the speculative fevers of the 1980s.[14]

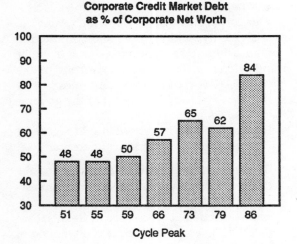

**Figure 8:**

**Rising Corporate Debt**

Corporate Credit Market Debt
as % of Corporate Net Worth

Cycle Peak

One cannot simply eliminate speculative investment with a wave of the hand. But systematic and sensible economic policies can begin to reduce its drain on the productive economy. Sustained growth and lower real interest rates would make productive investment look more attractive and place less of a premium on paper investment. Greater enforcement of anti-trust and securities laws would help limit harmful investment. A reinvest-in-America policy using federal guarantees will shift a portion of our public pension funds from paper investments to secure investments in housing, small business development and infrastructure, improving the ability of our capital markets to match the needs of small borrowers to the funds of huge institutional lenders. And a change in tax laws, with added taxes levied against securities transactions, debt financing and acquisitions, corporate dispositions, and tax loss mergers and transactions, could also begin to discourage this kind of casino behavior.

■ **Corporations presently engage in very wasteful practices in their treatment of workers and the environment.** Each year thousands of workers are killed on the job

and hundreds of thousands suffer injuries leading to workdays lost.[15] Corporations continue to dump toxic wastes and pollute the environment. Tens of thousands of workers lose their jobs as a result of plant closings.

We must increase support for occupational safety and health and environmental protection. We need a new excise tax on corporate emissions of chemical pollutants and increased funding for environmental protection.[16] Workers and communities need at least six months advance notification of a large plant closure to prepare for its effects. And corporations have a responsibility to provide job training and employment assistance as well as extended health benefits for those workers unable to find new employment at decent wages.

These specific measures should also be viewed within the more general context of a Corporate Code of Conduct. We need a new social contract that will level the playing field between workers, corporations, and the government. Corporations need a productive workforce, demand for their products, reasonable profits, and government policies that promote a stable and growing economy. Workers need good jobs with security, decent pay so they can afford to buy what they produce, and a stable and growing economy as well. Citizens need to feel secure about the health and future of their communities.

Government has a crucial role to play in ensuring that a new social contract is created. And this will require substantially greater standards of accountability for corporations in that relationship. Corporations must be operated in such a way that the interests of the broader community are upheld. They should begin to provide "maximum feasible consultation" with all parties affected prior to any decision which would significantly impact their workers or the broader community.[17] We can no longer afford to tolerate any less than this kind of understanding.

We can have economic growth and economic justice—not by balancing the budget on the backs of the poor and working Americans, not by lowering taxes on those floating by on golden parachutes, not by pursuing misguided foreign and military policies, not by squeezing dry the Third World. We can achieve these objectives by investing in the people, machines, and ideas that will make America, together with the rest of the world, grow and prosper.

1 The data for real hourly earnings are based on the series for real hourly compensation for all employees from the *Economic Report of The President, 1987*, Table B-43, and *Business Conditions Digest*. Data for real median family income are taken from Congressional Budget Office, *Trends in Family Income: 1970-1986* (Washington, D.C.: U.S. Government Printing Office, February 1988), Table B-1.

2 Trends in real GNP growth from data for real GNP in 1982 prices in *Economic Report of the President, 1987* and *Business Conditions Digest*. Trends for the rate of net investment based on data for real net private fixed non-residential investment and net national product in the National Income and Product Accounts, Table 5.3, line 6 and Table 1.10, line 3 respectively.

3 Graph is based on Congressional Budget Office, *The Changing Distribution of Federal Taxes: 1975-1990* (Washington, D.C.: U.S. Government Printing Office, October 1987), Table B-1.

4 These indices of debt and savings are defined as follows: (1) Corporate debt is commercial and industrial loans outstanding divided by total corporate profits; (2) personal debt is the ratio of consumer installment credit outstanding to total personal income; and (3) the savings rate is the ratio of total personal savings to total personal income. Based on *Business Conditions Digest*, (1) Series Nos. 101 and 35; (2) Series No. 95; and (3) Series No. 293.

5 Perhaps the most detailed presentation of this argument is provided by Peter G. Peterson, "The Morning After," *The Atlantic Monthly*, October 1987.

6 Peterson, "The Morning After," p. 49.

7 Figure 4 is based on data for effective tax rates in CBO, *The Changing Distribution of Federal Taxes*, Table 11. The numbers presented in the graph control for changes which have taken place between the two dates in the shares of income received by the respective groups in the income distribution, seeking to focus more directly on the effects of changes in the tax laws themselves.

8 Figure 5 is based on data for U.S. government outlays (net of offsetting revenues) in CBO, *The Economic and Budget Outlook: Fiscal Years 1989-93* (Washington, D.C.: U.S. Government Printing Office, February 1988), Tables G-5, G-7.

9 Data on personal savings rates from *Business Conditions Digest*, January 1988, Series No. 293. Data on total private savings rate based on *Business Conditions Digest*, January 1988, Series Nos. 290 and 298.

10 For one recent review of some of this evidence, with discussion of its implications, see Robert Pollin, "The Growth of U.S. Household Debt: Demand-Side Influences," *Journal of Macroeconomics*, Spring 1988.

11 The real interest rate in Figure 6 is defined as the interest rate on 3-month U.S. Treasury securities, adjusted for expected inflation (measured as a distributed lag on past values of inflation in the GNP price deflator). Interest rates from *Economic Report of the President, 1988*, Table B-71. Business failure rates in Figure 7 come from *ibid.*, Table B-95.

12 These estimates are based on Latin American debt service figures from International Monetary Fund, *World Economic Outlook, 1987* and trade figures from the Joint Economic Committee, U.S. Congress, "The Impact of the Latin American Debt on the U.S. Economy," May 1986.

13 See data on sources and uses of corporate funds, *Economic Report of the President, 1988*, Table B-92.

14 The variable in figure 8 is defined as the ratio of net non-financial corporate business (NFCB) credit market debt to total NFCB net worth and is taken from Board of Governors, U.S. Federal Reserve Board, *Balance Sheets for the U.S. Economy, 1947-86*, October 1987, pp. 21-25.

15 Data reported in *Employment and Earnings*, annual volumes.

16 See Jackson Budget Plan and Issue Brief on "Protecting Our Environment."

17 See Issue Brief, "A Corporate Code of Conduct," for more detail on steps toward creating such a new social contract.

# PAYING FOR OUR DREAMS:

## *A Budget Plan for Jobs, Peace and Justice*

*The federal budget sets the moral, political and financial direction for a nation. It shows how much we value human life. It charts a course for living up to those values. And it represents how deeply we are committed to them.*

—*Jesse Jackson*

Seven years of Reaganomics have left our country worse off than before. Real family incomes are no higher than they were in the early 1970s. We have moved from being the world's largest creditor to its largest debtor. We have lost economic leadership and power as our record trade deficits have mounted. At home, we have failed to invest in our children, our health, our roads or our future. We now find ourselves victims to the soldiers of austerity which were—in David Stockman's words—hidden in the Trojan Horse of supply-side economics.

We are told, time and time again, that we cannot afford to have decent schools in the inner city, health care all our citizens can afford, child care so people can afford to work, or job training that affords new employment opportunities. We are told we cannot afford economic justice. The truth is that we cannot afford to continue on our present path. It makes no sense to scrimp on prenatal care, when a dollar spent early in life saves more than seven dollars later in life. It makes no sense to have schools which can't afford to teach a poor child to read, when the cost of welfare and jailcare on the back side of life is so much greater than the costs of Head Start and day care on the front side of life.

We cannot let the Reagan deficits impede further progress. It is a fundamental duty of anyone who wishes to be the next president to set forth a plan to get out of the bind in which we now find ourselves.

The Jackson approach to the budget crisis is straightforward: We must get out of the deficit mess the same way we got in. We doubled the military budget in peacetime—we must now exercise restraint. We cut taxes on the wealthy and on corporations in the false hope that these cuts would usher in an investment boom—we must now create a system of fair taxes. We shifted priorities away from investments in our children, our schools, our health and our communities—we must now reinvest in America.

These changes can be made; making them requires no magic asterisks. It requires the courage to state a clear, bold new direction and then follow it.

Table 1 provides an overview of the Jackson approach to reducing the deficit. These estimates are based on the Congressional Budget Office (CBO) baseline estimates of deficits and, when available, CBO estimates of savings from proposed changes. Figure 1 indicates the substantially larger deficit reduction proposed by the Jackson budget approach as compared to current CBO baseline projections.

It should be noted that this is an outline and a guide to the Jackson approach, not a plan to which a Jackson Presidency would be bound in every detail. It is meant to set forth our priorities, as all candidates should, and to demonstrate that they can be met while being fiscally responsible. Changing circumstances —the state of the macroeconomy, for example— would of course lead to budget changes and adjustments.

But these changes cannot be used as an excuse to hide from critical questions of national priorities.

We face a 1993 deficit of well over $100 billion and urgent investment needs of at least $50-100 billion more. While the macroeconomy might cause this combined shortfall to vary, it will not make it disappear any more than cutting taxes did in 1981 and 1982.

A plan is needed. One option is government by commission, in which the bill for the Reagan-Bush economic extravaganza may well be divided equally—among those who attended the party and those who were excluded. Such a scenario is also likely to include an "agreement" that "the cupboard is bare" when it comes to making new investments.

Jesse Jackson offers a better plan. The Jackson years will reverse the distorted and harmful priorities of the Reagan years. They will restore the hope and power and potential of government to create opportunities so that all Americans may participate and prosper in our economy. Instead of bloating the military budget, we will rebuild the country's industrial base and revive America's cities. Instead of cutting taxes for the wealthy, we will have every group in society pay its fair share. In-

stead of excessive debt and fiscal austerity, we will create growth at home and abroad.

The Jackson budget plan reaches these ends by three main paths briefly summarized below: new investments, fair taxes, and cuts in military spending. Program-by-program descriptions can be found in subsequent pages.

The Jackson budget plan is not empty rhetoric, promising new programs without explaining who will pay the bills. It's a budget that accounts for how all of the elements can combine and how we can still achieve the goal of fiscal responsibility.

## New Investments

Federal expenditures are vital for growth in the economy and employment in the 1990s and beyond. The Reagan administration has cut real spending sharply for both education and training. The Jackson budget will double education expenditures by 1993. The Reagan administration says "no" to drugs. The Jackson budget says "yes" to action by increasing funding for law enforcement, drug treatment and education by 70 percent. The Reagan administration offers moral prescriptions for our families. The Jackson budget offers child care to three million more children, quality preschool education to every child in poverty, and

**Table 1:**

**A Budget Plan for Jobs, Peace and Justice— Summary Table**

| Fiscal Year | 1989 | 1990 | 1991 | 1992 | 1993 |
|---|---|---|---|---|---|
|  | | | ($ in Billions) | | |
| **Current Projected CBO Deficit**[*] | **$176** | **167** | **158** | **151** | **134** |
| **Revenue Plan** | | | | | |
| Tax Increases on the Wealthy | 19 | 46 | 55 | 59 | 65 |
| Corporate Tax Increases | 12 | 20 | 24 | 24 | 24 |
| Improved Income Tax Compliance | 1 | 3 | 5 | 7 | 9 |
| **Defense Spending Freeze** | 8 | 19 | 33 | 46 | 58 |
| **Non-Defense Spending Cuts & Federal Fees** | 4 | 15 | 21 | 23 | 24 |
| **New Investments** | (32) | (56) | (76) | (85) | (95) |
| **Modified Budget Deficit** | **$163** | **120** | **96** | **77** | **49** |

Totals may not sum exactly due to rounding to whole numbers.

*Projected federal budget deficit level assuming no changes in current spending commitments or tax rates and given CBO projections of economic conditions. From Congressional Budget Office, *The Economic and Budget Outlook: Fiscal Years 1989-1993, Part I*, February 1988, p. xxi.

Figure 1:

**Lifting the Burden— Comparing the CBO Baseline and the Proposed Jackson Budget Deficits ($ in Billions)**

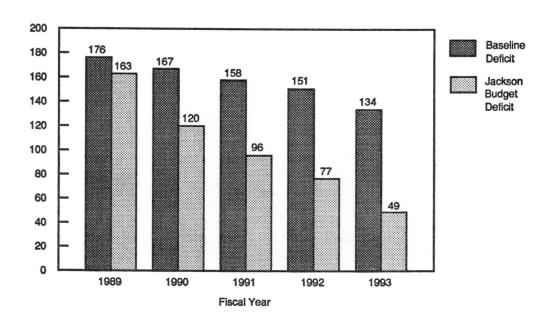

job training, health care and housing so that low-income families can afford to work and can live in dignity. The Reagan administration funds ever more exotic weapons of mass destruction. The Jackson budget redirects research talents and spends an additional $16 billion to find a cure for AIDS, to develop clean and secure sources of energy, and to make our industries more competitive in the world economy.

This budget offers hope. Its investments will total between $32 and $95 billion per year over the next five years. Figure 2 compares the growth in domestic spending under the proposed Jackson budget with CBO projections based on recent trends.

These increases must be kept in perspective. Compare them to the $150-billion-a-year Reagan defense build-up. Compare them to our trillion-dollar budget or to interest payments on the national debt, payments which will soon exceed $200 billion per year.

Most important, compare them to our needs. Study after study—by presidential commissions, congressional agencies, business and labor groups—has pointed to the funda-

mental investment needs in society. The Joint Economic Committee found a trillion dollars of needs over the next decade in infrastructure. A series of prominent education reports have pointed to the need for serious new investments in our schools and in support during the early years of life. A recent Massachusetts Institute of Technology study stressed our desperate needs in housing. The U.S. Office of Technology Assessment examined a comprehensive approach to worker dislocation which would require billions in new investments. The Children's Defense Fund annually presents a Children's Defense Budget outlining the most basic commitments we should make to our children and families.

Separately, each study meets with approval—and then inaction. We list responses proportionate to the problem—and then ignore them and offer instead a patchwork of minor proposals. We must break out of this pattern—fair taxes and a more sensible level of military spending offer the way.

**Fair Taxes**

Upper-income groups disproportionately

**Figure 2:**

**Domestic Spending— Actual/ Projected and Jackson Proposed Levels ($ in Billions)**

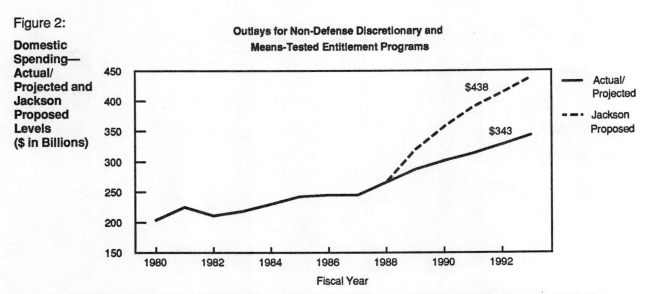

The actual/projected series in Figure 2 includes the sum of outlays for two spending categories in standard CBO allocations: "non-defense discretionary spending" and "means-tested entitlement and other mandatory spending," from Congressional Budget Office, *The Economic and Budget Outlook: Fiscal Years 1989-1993* (Washington, D.C.: U.S. Government Printing Office, February 1988), Tables G-5, G-7 for 1980-87 and II-7, II-8 for 1988-93. The figures for the Jackson budget for 1989-93 add all "New Investments" from the Jackson budget in Table 1 to the CBO projected levels. In order to maintain comparability between the projected and the Jackson budget figures, the CBO projections for "Social Services," at $5 billion per year, listed in non-means-tested entitlements, were added to the CBO projections for 1989-93.

benefited from the Reagan tax cuts. The Congressional Budget Office estimates that the poorest 10 percent of Americans will pay nearly 20 percent more in taxes in 1988 than they did ten years earlier; the richest one percent will pay over 20 percent less. Wealthy Americans can afford to pay more. Using CBO data, it is estimated that if the top 10 percent of taxpayers were taxed at the same rate in 1988 as they were in 1977, at least $55 billion per year *more* in revenues could be raised—nearly one-third of the federal deficit. The Jackson plan, by 1993, would raise at least this amount.

Figure 3 illustrates the distributional burden of these proposed tax increases on the wealthy. It shows the percentage of the increased taxes which would be borne by four different income groups, those with adjusted gross incomes above $50,000 annually. Nearly three quarters (71.5%) of the burden would fall on those earning $200,000 and over, while seven eighths (87.6%) would be borne by those

earning $100,000 and over. The burden of the proposed tax increases on those earning less than $50,000 is so small, at 0.08 percent, that it is lost in rounding and is too minuscule to show up on the graph. Since those earning $100,000 and over in 1988 comprised less than five percent of all households in the United States, these proposed tax increases would be targeted quite squarely on those who could best afford to pay them.

The corporate tax burden was also substantially reduced in the Reagan years. The Joint Committee on Taxation estimates that the cost of corporate tax loopholes grew from $10 billion in 1970 to $120 billion in 1986. Even after the 1986 Tax Reform Act, corporate tax breaks are expected to cost the Treasury $37 billion this year. The Jackson budget proposes returning corporate taxes as a percentage of corporate income roughly to their pre-Reagan levels. These levels will provide an insurance policy for business by stabilizing the economy while

**Figure 3:**

**Restoring Tax Justice**

**Distribution of the Impact by Income Size Group of Proposed Increased Taxes on the Wealthy**

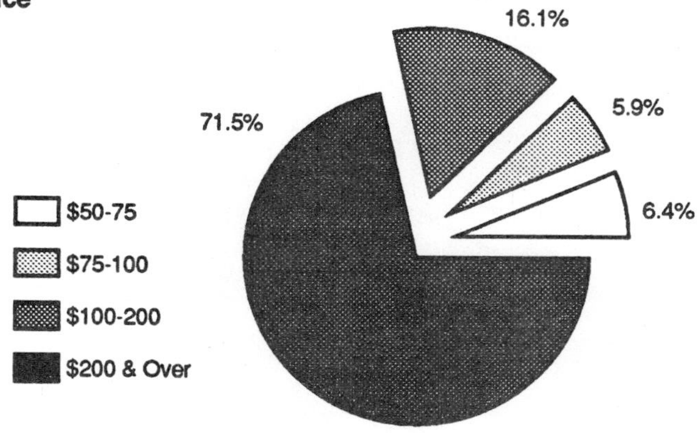

- □ $50-75
- ▤ $75-100
- ▦ $100-200
- ■ $200 & Over

16.1%

5.9%

71.5%

6.4%

Income Range (in $ Thousands)

The estimates are actually based on an allocation by income size group of four of the tax increase proposals: restoring the top income tax bracket to 38.5%, limiting mortgage interest deductions for the wealthy, raising the minimum tax on the top 2%, and the 5% surtax. These four items account for roughly two-thirds of the total revenues to be raised by the proposed tax increases on the wealthy. Based on discussions with staff of various tax committees and government agencies, it is reasonable to assume that the distributional effects of the additional revenues raised from the other proposed measures would be roughly the same as those shown in the graph. The estimates were prepared by the office of Rep. Charles Rangel (D-NY), member of the House Ways & Means Committee, based on the tax proposals summarized in the Jackson Budget Plan. In 1988, the estimated minimum income for those in the top five percent of the income distribution was $88,000: CBO, *The Changing Distribution of Federal Taxes: 1975-1990* (Washington, D.C.: U.S. Government Printing Office, October 1987), Table A-1.

still offering a tax rate below that of most other major industrialized countries.

Finally, improved tax compliance is an essential part of any deficit reduction program. Jacksons tax program would begin by ensuring that some uncollected taxes were paid; he would recognize, however, that the gains from improved enforcement are likely to come gradually and alone are not enough to compensate for the funds lost by our present system of tax breaks for corporations and wealthy Americans.

This tax plan—if implemented with due care—will provide serious deficit reduction at little overall economic cost. The justification for the tax cuts we propose to rescind was that they would stimulate investment and promote robust economic growth. Yet savings, investment and economic growth levels remain at historical lows. Cutting taxes did not increase investment; returning them to their previous

level will not decrease it. But, raising taxes on those who can most afford to pay will make much new direct public investment possible.

### Military Spending

The Reagan administration more than doubled the military budget in peacetime. Even after three years of no real growth, military spending remains at levels unprecedented in peacetime; measured in constant dollars, spending is now 48.5 percent above 1980 levels even after adjusting for inflation (Office of Management and Budget Historical Tables).

Yet increasingly our fundamental security concerns—a debt-ridden economy, excessive dependence on foreign energy and foreign capital, the devastating effect of drugs flowing into our country, the fragile global environment—cannot be addressed by military force. We can cut our military spending without cutting our defense.

**Figure 4:**

**Defense Spending—Actual/Projected and Jackson Proposed Levels**

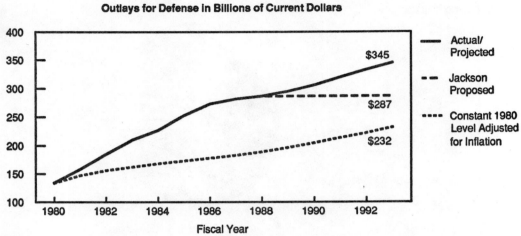

**Outlays for Defense in Billions of Current Dollars**

— Actual/Projected

– – Jackson Proposed

···· Constant 1980 Level Adjusted for Inflation

$345

$287

$232

Fiscal Year

The actual/projected figures are for total outlays, by fiscal year, for "National Defense," from *Economic and Budget Outlook*, Tables G-5 and II-7. The series for constant 1980 outlays adjusted for inflation is computed by adjusting the 1980 actual figure for increases in the GNP implicit price deflator, *Economic Report of the President, 1988*, Table B-3, and CBO projected increases in price deflator, *Economic and Budget Outlook*, Table I-7.

The size of our defense budget should not be determined in the abstract, or else "bigger" will always be defined as "better." Obviously, that is not the case. Under the Reagan administration, "bigger" has increased our insecurity. America must have a military force strong enough and a defense budget adequate enough to deter war, defend us against external threats, defeat the enemy if we must fight, and protect our vital interests in the world.

But cost overruns will not make us stronger; "sole source" contracts will not make us stronger; two additional aircraft carrier task forces (at a cost of $36 billion) will not make us stronger; $45 billion Midgetman missiles will not make us stronger; and Star Wars at $500 billion to $1 trillion will not make us stronger. They will, in fact, make us weaker; they will make the budget deficit bigger, make our economy sicker, and make us more vulnerable to forces beyond our control.

We cannot afford a foreign policy driven by guided missiles and misguided leadership. Thus, a Jackson administration would join with the Congress to undertake a thorough review of our global commitments and the military force structure necessary to meet them. Our commitments should not exceed our capacity to meet them.

The "new thinking" espoused by Soviet General Secretary Gorbachev and the sudden commitment to peace expressed by President Reagan open the possibility of significant reductions in the military burdens of both the Soviet Union and the United States. The recently concluded Intermediate-range Nuclear Force (INF) agreement is a good first step. Secretary Gorbachev has joined President Reagan in seeking to go beyond the INF to achieve deep cuts in our strategic nuclear arsenals.

A Jackson administration would build on the first steps already taken by President Reagan and test Secretary Gorbachev's sincerity. A nuclear weapons testing moratorium (which the Soviets unilaterally declared for 18 months in 1986-87) would provide the basis for a comprehensive test ban treaty. Agreements could be forged to end the testing of new missiles even as we reduce the arsenals at hand. With 26,000 nuclear warheads already in our arsenal (and nearly one-half of our strategic warheads in invulnerable submarines), the "modernization" that drives the arms race can be halted.

The Soviets have called for asymmetrical conventional force reductions in Europe, in which each side would reduce its forces to equal and lower levels. A Jackson administration would make a major effort to negotiate significant reductions in conventional forces. Our allies in Europe have twice the GNP and one and one-half times the population of the Soviet Union. They can afford to bear a greater share of the burden, even as we negotiate such reductions in troop levels.

A Jackson administration would also seek to redefine our relationship to the Third World. For the past seven years, the Reagan Doctrine has misguided relations with Third World countries. This Doctrine mistakenly assumes that most change and upheaval there comes from communist conspiracy rather than from poverty, illiteracy and lack of political freedom. Our relations with the Third World must move beyond superpower politics. It must be based on the four principles of the Jackson Doctrine:

- Support and strengthen the rule of international law.

- Respect the right of self-determination.

- Promote human rights.

- Support international economic justice and development.

A broad review of U.S. relations with the Soviet Union and with the Third World offers the potential for significant cuts in the defense budget. Yet, even prior to progress in these areas, the military budget can be cut without harm to our security—indeed, with scarcely noticeable change in our military forces.

Based on the new policy direction outlined above, defense spending can at a minimum be kept from rising above current levels. By keeping (nominal) defense outlays at roughly their 1988 level for the next five years the Jackson budget *saves* $164 billion through 1993. With these savings, total military spending after inflation will still be 27 percent *above* the 1980 level.

The graph in Figure 4 highlights this point. The solid line plots actual and projected out-

lays for national defense (in current dollars) from 1980. The line of dashes traces military spending proposed by the Jackson budget beginning in fiscal year 1989. The dotted line shows what military outlays would have been if they had been kept constant in real terms at 1980 levels and had increased since 1980 only to keep up with inflation. Even with the (nominal) freeze proposed in the Jackson budget, projected outlays in the early 1990s would still remain substantially above spending levels (adjusted for inflation) at the beginning of the 1980s—as shown by the distance between the line of dashes and the dotted line from 1989 through 1993. Outside of the second Reagan administration, military spending at this level would still be greater, in inflation-adjusted terms, than military spending in any year since World War II, with the sole war-time exceptions of the 1952-54 Korean War period and the 1967-70 portion of the Vietnam War.

The Jackson proposal is based on very conservative assumptions about the military budget. Indeed, with a more thorough review of our national security needs, larger reductions could likely be made without jeopardizing our security or that of our allies.

These savings may seem large to some observers, but a quick review of what will remain in the military budget testifies to their modesty. The U.S. would still have 12,680 strategic nuclear warheads to the Soviet Union's 10,340, giving us the ability to destroy all major Soviet cities 50 to 100 times over. The U.S. and its NATO allies would still outnumber the Warsaw Pact forces in Central Europe by 2.4 million to 2.3 million troops. The U.S. would still have 16 Army divisions (the same number as at the beginning of Reagan's term) and it would maintain the same number of air force wings (35), marine divisions (3), bomber squadrons (25), air lift squadrons and sea lift ships as the Reagan budget. The U.S. would still have 13 aircraft carrier battle groups, compared to one deployed by the Soviet Union. The U.S. would still have the same level of troops abroad outside of Europe (e.g., 44,000 in Korea, 16,000 in the Philippines, 47,000 in Japan). It would be a military force without compare in the world.

## Macroeconomic Effects of the Jackson Budget Plan

As we can see from the budget summary in Table 1, the Jackson policies make significant progress towards balancing the federal budget. In the absence of any counteracting proposals, however, reducing the budget deficit could increase the likelihood of recession—especially at this stage of the business cycle. The Jackson administration would pursue a number of different paths to avoid this outcome and to begin moving toward higher rates of economic growth.

First, we can negotiate with our trading partners a plan for expansion of the world economy. These negotiations are necessarily delicate but, under the Jackson budget, the United States would have met the major demand placed on us by other industrialized countries: reduce the deficit. In return, we can expect and demand fiscal and monetary expansion on their part.

The world economy has been in a state of stagnation during the 1980s, a problem that the U.S. cannot unilaterally solve. Two other leading industrial powers, West Germany and Japan, as well as the newly industrializing countries of the Pacific Rim, have had persistent trade surpluses, essentially placing the burden of demand on the remainder of the world economy. So far, American demand for foreign imports has helped stave off even greater world economic decline. The trade imbalance cannot continue indefinitely, however. Japan in particular must come to accept the fact that the U.S. no longer single-handedly manages world commerce as it did in the immediate postwar era, and that ultimately it is in Japan's interests to promote growth, not depression, in the world economy.

Second, it is no longer reasonable to imagine that the Third World will ever be able to pay off its massive debt. Even major banks have begun to adjust their books to reflect this reality. It is now time for the First World to help resolve the debt crisis through a flexible approach of bank write-downs and forgiveness, official lending, and innovative financing mechanisms. The banks must know that our government will not allow their financial interests to determine the fate of our country's economic and trade interests. And Third World countries receiving debt relief must ensure that our help is used to benefit broad-based economic growth, not to line the pockets of their elites.

Both of the above paths to global economic expansion should further reduce U.S. budget deficits. As the world economy expands, so will the U.S. economy and so too will the federal government's tax receipts.

The final part of the Jackson macroeconomic policy is to end at last the Reagan era's monetary tightness. Loosening monetary policy is a vital accompaniment of deficit reduction—otherwise the economy will be sent into recession. The next administration will face a difficult problem of macroeconomic management. Repairing the damage from Reagan's economic policies must not be allowed to cause the next Democratic administration to preside over recession. A Jackson administration will urge the Federal Reserve to lower nominal short-term interest rates in conjunction with a lowering of rates throughout the industrialized world. This should help to close the budget deficit even further. Expansion of the economy will raise tax revenues and the large interest payments that have plagued recent budgets will be lessened.

As with our budget plan, of course, interest rate reduction is a flexible goal and not a policy direction to which the Jackson administration would strictly adhere under all possible circumstances. There are a large number of ways in which the budget deficit, interest rates and the exchange rate can be combined. At the moment, interest rates are hostage to the exchange rate. But we expect that a combination of lower federal deficits and lower interest rates will begin not only to redress serious macroeconomic imbalances but also to begin charting a long-term course of more vigorous and stable economic growth.

A detailed analysis of the revenue and spending proposals in the Jackson budget are found on the next twelve pages.

**Table 2:**

**A Budget Plan for Jobs, Peace and Justice**

| | | | ($ In Billions) | | |
|---|---|---|---|---|---|
| **REVENUE PLAN** | **1989** | **1990** | **1991** | **1992** | **1993** |
| **Tax Increases on the Wealthy** | | | | | |
| Restore top rate on top 600,000 taxpayers to 38.5% | $6.3 | 14.5 | 19.6 | 21.2 | 23.3 |
| Reduce mortgage interest deductions for the wealthy | 0.8 | 2.3 | 2.7 | 3.1 | 3.7 |
| Luxury taxes | 0.7 | 0.9 | 0.9 | 0.9 | 0.9 |
| Close other loopholes | 2.1 | 9.5 | 10.5 | 11.8 | 13.2 |
| Securities transfer excise tax | 5.0 | 7.5 | 10.0 | 10.0 | 10.0 |
| Raise minimum tax on top 2% of taxpayers | 1.1 | 3.7 | 3.2 | 3.3 | 3.8 |
| 5% surtax on high incomes for deficit reduction— phases out when deficit hits $75 billion | 3.4 | 7.1 | 8.5 | 9.0 | 10.0 |
| **Subtotal** | **$19.4** | **45.5** | **55.4** | **59.3** | **64.9** |
| **Corporate Tax Increases** | | | | | |
| Raise minimum tax rate | 3.2 | 5.5 | 5.5 | 5.0 | 4.5 |
| Limit business meals deduction to 50% | 0.9 | 3.1 | 4.5 | 4.8 | 5.1 |
| Polluters tax | 5.7 | 7.4 | 7.9 | 7.9 | 7.9 |
| Close other loopholes | 2.3 | 4.3 | 5.9 | 6..4 | 7.0 |
| **Subtotal** | **$12.1** | **20.3** | **23.8** | **24.1** | **24.5** |
| **Improved Income Tax Compliance** | 0.8 | 2.8 | 4.8 | 6.8 | 8.7 |
| **Total** | **$32.3** | **68.6** | **84.0** | **90.2** | **98.1** |
| **DEFENSE SPENDING FREEZE** | **$8.0** | **19.0** | **33.0** | **46.0** | **58.0** |
| **NON-DEFENSE SPENDING CUTS & FEDERAL FEES** | | | | | |
| Supply management for farmers | 2.2 | 10.0 | 11.5 | 9.0 | 5.5 |
| Miscellaneous spending cuts & federal fees | 1.4 | 1.6 | 1.6 | 1.6 | 1.7 |
| Interest savings (after investment plan) | 0.6 | 3.3 | 7.6 | 12.1 | 16.9 |
| **Subtotal** | **$4.2** | **15.3** | **20.7** | **22.7** | **24.1** |

Table 2:
(cont'd.)

**A Budget
Plan for
Jobs, Peace
and Justice**

| INVESTMENT PLAN* | ($ in Billions) | | | | |
|---|---|---|---|---|---|
| | 1989 | 1990 | 1991 | 1992 | 1993 |
| Education & Job Training | $4.2 | 10.0 | 15.6 | 17.8 | 20.0 |
| Drug Enforcement, Education & Treatment | 2.8 | 2.9 | 3.0 | 3.1 | 3.2 |
| Housing & Community Development | 2.0 | 8.0 | 12.0 | 14.0 | 17.0 |
| Income Security & Social Services | 7.7 | 10.5 | 11.5 | 13.0 | 14.4 |
| Child Care | 3.5 | 4.9 | 5.5 | 6.0 | 6.5 |
| Health & Nutrition | 3.9 | 5.8 | 7.8 | 9.9 | 12.2 |
| AIDS | 1.5 | 2.0 | 2.2 | 2.5 | 3.0 |
| Energy | 0.4 | 0.7 | 1.9 | 2.3 | 1.7 |
| Environment | 1.3 | 1.4 | 1.5 | 1.6 | 1.7 |
| Transportation | 1.0 | 2.0 | 3.0 | 4.0 | 5.0 |
| Economic Adjustment & Diversification | 1.5 | 2.5 | 3.5 | 4.0 | 4.5 |
| Civilian Research, Development & Commercialization | 1.5 | 2.5 | 3.5 | 4.0 | 4.5 |
| International Economic Assistance (Debt relief, expanded development) | 0.2 | 2.5 | 5.0 | 3.0 | 1.0 |
| **Total** | **$31.5** | **55.7** | **76.0** | **85.2** | **94.7** |
| Pension Fund Reinvestment Plan (New guarantees, not expenditures) | $6.0 | 6.0 | 6.0 | 6.0 | 6.0 |

* Amounts represent increases above CBO Baseline Projections.

## I. Explanation of Revenue Plan

### Tax Increases on the Wealthy

#### Restore Top Rate to 38.5%

Tax law changes which took effect in 1988 lowered the rate paid by the top one percent of taxpayers (600,000 people earning more than $192,000 in net taxable income) from 38.5 percent to 28 percent. The result is that a secretary who is single with an annual income of $25,000 will be subject to the same 28 percent tax rate as the CEO whose annual income may be $300,000. The 38.5 percent bracket should be restored to recoup revenues from those who got the biggest tax reductions during the Reagan years. This new marginal rate is still considerably below the pre-Reagan level of 50 percent for earned income and 70 percent for unearned income.

*Source:* Calculation by Robert McIntyre, Citizens for Tax Justice, based on Joint Committee on Taxation, "Description of Possible Options to Increase Revenues," June 1987, p. 87.

#### Reduce Mortgage Interest Deductions for the Wealthy

The proposal limits deductions to $12,000 per return (single) or $20,000 (joint). Capping the deduction at this level would affect less than one-half of one percent of taxpayers and would retain the basic incentive for home ownership. There would be little disruption to home prices and home building because the caps are higher than the deductions taken by nearly all taxpayers. Roughly five-sixths of the revenue would result from limiting deductions. The proposal also phases out taxpayer subsidy of second homes.

*Source:* Congressional Budget Office, "Reducing the Deficit: Spending and Revenue Options—Part II," March 1988, pp. 319-321.

#### Luxury Taxes

To encourage savings and to increase progressivity of the tax structure, a 10 percent excise tax is imposed on aircraft and furs, on autos in excess of $20,000, and on boats and yachts in excess of $15,000.

*Source:* Joint Committee on Taxation, "Description of Possible Options to Increase Revenues," June 1987, pp. 45-47.

#### Close Other Loopholes

Various tax loopholes which largely benefit the very wealthy should be limited, including exclusions on estate and gift taxes, the avoidance of capital gains at death, pension breaks at very high income levels, like-kind real estate exchanges, and avoidance of taxes on interest earned by foreign investors.

*Source:* Omnibus Budget Reconciliation Act of 1987; Congressional Budget Office; Joint Committee on Taxation.

#### Securities Transfer Excise Tax

A 0.5 percent tax levied against certain kinds of securities transfers would reduce shorter-term speculative merger and acquisition activity and, instead, encourage longer-range investments. Japan, West Germany and the United Kingdom all have such a tax to discourage short-term trading.

*Source:* Joint Committee on Taxation, "Description of Possible Options to Increase Revenues," June 1987, pp. 82-83.

#### Raise the Minimum Tax on the Top 2% of Taxpayers

The minimum tax is designed to assure that no matter how many tax shelters are available to the wealthy (in this case the top 2 percent), they will still pay their fair share in taxes. The minimum tax should be raised from 21 percent to 25 percent.

*Source:* Congressional Budget Office, "Reducing the Deficit: Spending and Revenue Options—Part II," March 1988, p. 291.

#### 5% Surtax on High Incomes for Deficit Reduction

A special five percent surtax should be levied against the tax liability of those who most benefited from tax reductions since 1977. This surcharge would apply to people paying more than $10,000 in taxes (or earning about $75,000 or more). The surtax would raise their effective rate from 38.5 percent to about 40 percent. It would be lifted once the deficit is lowered to $75 billion for the previous year; thereafter it would be phased out over three years.

*Source:* Joint Committee on Taxation, "Description of Possible Options to Increase Revenues," June 1987, pp. 84-87.

*Note on Interactions:* Raising the top rate to

38.5 percent will increase the yield of several proposals, e.g., capital gains at death; conversely, however, the minimum tax revenues would be reduced by several other tax provisions. It is assumed that these effects will roughly cancel each other out.

### Corporate Tax Increases

#### Raise the Minimum Tax Rate

This proposal will insure that profitable corporations do not avoid paying the corporate tax. The rate should be raised from the current 21 percent to 25 percent. Our tax system will be more fair and the tax burden will be spread more evenly as a result of this plan.

*Source:* Congressional Budget Office, "Reducing the Deficit: Spending and Revenue Options—Part II," March 1988, p. 292.

#### Limit Business Meals Deduction to 50%

Business meal deductions are currently 80 percent of what is spent. Deductions for meal and entertainment expenses involve many abuses. There is no need for American taxpayers to subsidize the eating and entertaining habits of the well-off at that rate.

*Source:* Congressional Budget Office, "Reducing the Deficit: Spending and Revenue Options—Part II," March 1988, p. 308.

#### Polluters Tax

Chemical emissions and hazardous wastes which harm the environment are not presently taxed. An excise tax should be imposed on emissions and hazardous waste both to raise revenues and to reduce incentives to pollute. Sulfur dioxide and nitrogen oxide emissions which cause acid rain would be taxed at $250 and $200 per ton respectively. Hazardous waste would be taxed at $10 per ton. *Note:* The tax is low enough that energy costs would only be raised by a few percentage points (if at all) in a few regions of the country.

*Source:* Congressional Budget Office, "Reducing the Deficit: Spending and Revenue Options—Part II," March 1988, p. 308.

#### Close Other Loopholes

These include the completed contract cost accounting method used by defense contractors to defer tax payments; taxes passed by the House in 1987 (but not by the Senate) to discourage corporate mergers and acquisitions; and tax deferrals which benefit corporations that move overseas.

*Source:* Omnibus Budget and Reconciliation Act of 1987 (HR3545); Joint Committee on Taxation.

### Improve Income Tax Compliance

The Internal Revenue Service estimates that $85 billion in taxes was uncollected from individuals and corporations in 1987 due to their failure to file tax returns, understatement of income, overstatement of deductions, failure to pay taxes due on returns that are filed, among other reasons. The IRS believes that the maximum number of new staff for direct enforcement which the agency can assimilate in one year is 6,800. They further estimate that these 6,800 positions are capable of netting $800 million additional tax revenues in the first year and nearly $2 billion per year thereafter. The Jackson revenue estimates assume the addition of 6,800 new staff per year over the course of the next administration.

*Source:* Internal Revenue Service, "Income Tax Compliance Research: Gross Tax Gap Estimates and Projections for 1973-1992," March 1988; testimony by IRS Commissioner before numerous congressional committees.

## II. Explanation of Defense Spending Freeze: Real Security for the 1990s

The Jackson budget is based on five key principles which set the priorities for proposed levels of military spending:

- Reduce the risk of nuclear war by limiting nuclear weapons to their sole function of deterring nuclear war and by halting the development of the Strategic Defense Initiative.

- End the increase in aircraft carrier battle groups which have, at best, minimum utility against the Soviet Union and are not necessary to meet our security commitments to Third World countries.

- Increase burden-sharing and opportunities for conventional arms reductions in Europe.

- Bring the procurement process under control by eliminating overlapping and unnecessary weapons and limiting procurement inefficiencies and abuse.

- Fully fund military personnel and family benefits.

## Reduce the Risk of Nuclear War

The only value of nuclear weapons is to prevent their use. Existing inventories of nearly 13,000 strategic nuclear warheads (5,632 of them on invulnerable submarines) are more than sufficient for that purpose. Ongoing efforts to modernize the U.S. nuclear arsenal do not add to its deterrent capability. Instead, they are costly, unnecessary expenditures and, in some instances, highly destabilizing. With the Reagan modernization program, including the MX missile, the B-1 bomber and the Trident submarine, largely completed, further purchases have no justification. Absent arms control agreements with the Soviets, the Jackson budget leaves in place all weapons that have already been purchased.

Under the Trident II and the MX programs, missiles are designed to be able to destroy Soviet missiles in their silos. Their power, range and theoretical accuracy provide the image of a first-strike capability. This only increases instability, leading Soviet weapons to be placed on an even more hair-trigger status. Thus, ending any further purchases of Trident II or MX, while preserving C-4 missiles already placed on deployed Trident submarines, will add to rather than detract from our stable defense posture.

The Jackson military budget supports only the most basic research on ballistic missile defense, in the past scattered thoughout the Department of Defense. Most scientists concur that plans for an invulnerable missile defense shield are only wishful thinking—such a "defense" could easily be overwhelmed or underflown. The best defense is to eliminate as much of the nuclear threat as possible. Thus, the false promise of the Strategic Defense Initiative should no longer be used as an argument to forestall deep cuts in both superpowers' strategic nuclear arsenals. Its development should be halted.

## End the Increase in Aircraft Carrier Battle Groups

Much of the naval build-up is an increase from 13 to 15 aircraft carrier battle groups. The increase is designed to give the navy a capacity to corral the Soviet fleet in its ports in time of general war. This is a fool's game. There is no more tempting target for tactical nuclear weapons than a battle group that could be easily destroyed with little unintended damage.

In practice, the increased carriers will likely be used for showing the flag and for Third World intervention. Devoting such an extensive part of the naval budget to such forces is inappropriate. The number of battle groups should be reduced to 13, with a further reduction to ten to be considered for the long-term.

## Increase Burden-Sharing and Opportunities for Conventional Arms Reductions in Europe

According to Department of Defense reports, at least half of our military budget is devoted to preparation for fighting a World War II-style land war against the Soviet Union in Europe. The probability of such a war is close to zero. Moreover, should there be a war, the probability of it remaining conventional is even more remote. Most experts assume that such a war would turn nuclear within a matter of days.

Recent developments between the U.S. and Soviet Union (e.g., the INF Treaty, movement on a START Treaty, Gorbachev statements and actions, etc.) indicate that greatly improved relations are possible. This provides an opportunity for initiating significant reductions in this part of our military spending, as well as that of the Soviet Union. The next administration must seize this opportunity not only to reduce the threat of nuclear war, but to bring about substantial conventional reductions as well.

Many political commentators, both Democrat and Republican, from Henry Kissinger to Rep. Ronald Dellums (D-CA), suggest that the Europeans should become responsible for their own conventional defense. While increasing European defense burdens may be realistic in the short term, particularly given U.S. budget problems, the crucial concern is to reduce the defense burden of both NATO and the Warsaw Pact. Simply shifting the burden within NATO would still maintain needlessly high levels of military spending in Europe.

The U.S. has 325,000 troops in Europe. The Jackson budget calls for the U.S. to take the first step in reducing conventional troops by phasing out two divisions over four years (one would be decommissioned, one would return to the U.S.). These reductions can be made, even in the absence of negotiations, without affecting the security of our allies or the U.S.

With such an initiative the U.S. can challenge the Soviets to do the same. Considering previous Warsaw Pact proposals for significant reductions (in June 1986 they proposed cuts of 500,000 troops on each side) and recent statements made by General Secretary Gorbachev about the possibility of asymmetrical reductions (in April 1987 Gorbachev acknowledged the Soviet superiority in some areas and stated they are willing to remove the disparities), we can expect the Soviets to respond to our challenge. If they do not, our European allies would have the option of increasing their defense burden if they deemed such action necessary.

### Bring the Procurement Process Under Control

The massive increase in the defense budget during this decade has led to spending based on the availability of funds, rather than on necessity or mission. Inter-service rivalry has aggravated the process. The result has been the costly and inefficient purchase of both necessary and unnecessary systems.

The Reagan spending binge will not end when he leaves office. There is a backlog of over $270 billion in unspent appropriated funds facing the next president. This places enormous constraints on the next administration's ability to redirect military spending.

The next administration must take aggressive action to get weapon system procurement under control. Congress and the Pentagon must determine which systems are in fact of high priority. These should be efficiently purchased. Lesser priority systems must be cancelled. This is preferable to the current practice of maintaining a larger number of systems in production at inefficient, and costly, production levels.

The publicity surrounding Pentagon purchases of dime-store hardware items for thousands of dollars has forced Congress to insist on initial action in this area. This must go much further. In particular, sole-source contracts must be limited and competitive contracts increased. The "revolving door" between Pentagon officials and defense contractors must be severely constrained. Greater control over quality, efficiency and cost must be exercised by the Pentagon in all of its contract dealings. Whistle-blower protection must be assured.

Real reform, however, requires a change in the relationship between the Pentagon and the major U.S. military contractors who benefit from this relationship. Military contracts are a major source of profits for many of the largest U.S. industries; making the process more efficient, and presumably less profitable, will require substantial political commitment.

### Fully Fund Military Personnel and Family Benefits

Force level reductions are a necessary policy change. Nevertheless, once the appropriate force level is determined, all service personnel must be properly supported. This includes substantial improvements in living and other "quality-of-life" conditions for all members of the services and their families. In particular, military pay should be fully funded, and substantial increases provided for more and better family housing and dependent programs.

## III. Explanation of Non-Defense Spending Cuts & Federal Fees

### Implement Supply Management for Farmers

Our current farm policy provides massive subsidies to farmers in order to match their cost of production. Large corporate farms benefit most from this program. For example: in 1983 the largest 9.4 percent of wheat farmers received 42 percent of deficiency payments; the largest 12.8 percent of corn farmers received 40 percent of the payments; and the largest 7.6 percent of cotton farmers received 33 percent of the payments. A farm program based on supply management would set production targets to match demand, provide farmers with a fair price to match their production costs, and eliminate the huge and wasteful surpluses of the present system.

*Source:* Food and Agricultural Policy Research Institute, "Comparative Analysis of Selected Policy Options for U.S. Agriculture," February 1987.

### Miscellaneous Spending Cuts & Federal Fees

#### Improve Pricing for Commercial Uses of Public Land

The federal government leases out millions of acres of public lands for commercial uses such as grazing, mining and lumbering. Underpricing has led to lost revenues as well as overuse, endangering the environment. Better pricing could increase federal receipts while ensuring better environmental management.

*Source:* Congressional Budget Office, "Reducing the Deficit: Spending and Revenue Options—Part II," March 1988, pp. 196-201.

#### Include Foreign Deposits of U.S. Banks in the FDIC Insurance Base

Under federal law, the Federal Deposit Insurance Corporation (FDIC) insures domestic deposits against default. Deposits at foreign branches are neither covered by the insurance nor charged premiums. However, because the government has stated that it would not allow big banks to fail, it has implied coverage for foreign deposits. This policy gives big banks an unfair advantage over smaller banks which primarily have domestic deposits and should be changed.

*Source:* Congressional Budget Office, "Reducing the Deficit: Spending and Revenue Options—Part II," March 1988, pp. 209-210.

### Raise Charges to Cover Transportation Safety Programs

Federal safety programs provide a direct benefit to those who most benefit from them—vehicle manufacturers, transportation firms and users of transportation services. Raising the charges to cover the cost of federal safety services would eliminate the subsidy and treat users equally.

*Source:* Congressional Budget Office, "Reducing the Deficit: Spending and Revenue Options—Part II," March 1988, pp. 223-225.

### Reduce Federal Travel Expenses

Average annual travel costs per government employee have increased by 62 percent over the 1982 level, well above the rate of inflation. Better monitoring of costs, elimination of low-priority travel, and innovative savings methods can substantially reduce these costs.

*Source:* Congressional Budget Office, "Reducing the Deficit: Spending and Revenue Options—Part II," March 1988, pp. 279-281.

### Interest Savings

The combination of new investments, new revenues and spending cuts would result in substantial deficit reduction, thus significantly reducing interest outlays to finance the deficit. These savings are estimated based on CBO interest rate projections.

## IV. Explanation of Investment Plan

### Education & Job Training

Federal spending for education has dropped by more than 15 percent since 1980 (after accounting for inflation) and spending for employment and job training programs has dropped by more than 50 percent. The Jackson budget would double spending for education and job training by 1993. A top priority is to establish an Office of Pre-School Education (within the Education Department) which would oversee an enlarged Head Start program and develop parallel programs in child care centers and schools to ensure that every three- to five-year-old living in poverty receives a pre-school education. Other educational priorities include: restoring compensatory education to pre-Reagan levels; a doubling of college grants and loans; a new $1 billion Teacher Corps to provide college scholarships-for-service; quadrupling bilingual education spending; restoring all Reagan cuts made to Indian education; initiating a major adult literacy campaign; and providing federal incentives to help equalize spending between school districts.

The Jackson budget expands job training for families on public assistance to allow for longer-term training programs, higher reimbursement of child care costs, and reimbursement of transportation costs. Other job training priorities include expanded programs to help dislocated workers make the transition to new employment and for economically-disadvantaged youth.

*New Investments (1989-1993):* $67.6 billion

### Drug Enforcement, Education & Treatment

The Jackson budget proposes a 71 percent increase over current spending. Interdiction gets a substantial increase in funding, including for the State Department to cut drugs off at the source, as well as for beefed-up Coast Guard and Customs Service funding to secure our borders. Funding for local law enforcement would be more than doubled. The spending level suggested includes implementing the Presidential AIDS Commission recommendations on increased drug treatment programs so that addicts can get treatment on demand. Finally, the Jackson anti-drug program dramatically expands education and prevention efforts to cut demand.

*New Investments (1989-1993):* $15.0 billion

### Housing & Community Development

Appropriations for low- and moderate-income housing assistance have dropped from $32 billion to $8 billion from 1980 to 1988, forcing millions into the streets or into overcrowded living conditions, and impoverishing

millions of others. The Jackson budget funds a four-pronged approach to the housing crisis. It provides funds for the emergency needs of the homeless by providing housing allowances to pay for housing where they live. It meets the immediate needs of low-income people by modernizing public and other subsidized housing and by providing housing allowances to help families at the poverty level who are paying an excessively high percentage of their income for rent. It expands the supply of affordable housing by providing capital grants for new construction. The latter will emphasize construction by non-profit community-based institutions. Finally, the Jackson budget will aid first-time homebuyers by creating a low-cost revolving loan fund to help with down payments. (Note: federal funding for new construction will be significantly augmented by utilizing federally-guaranteed public pension funds in cooperation with state and local governments.)

*New Investments (1989-1993):* $53.0 billion

### Income Security & Social Services

For those parents who are unable to work and those who are working but are unable adequately to support their families because of low wages and the high costs of child care and health care, the Jackson budget provides a uniform national welfare benefit. Besides raising the AFDC cash benefit, the budget also liberalizes asset restrictions, increases the federal share of costs, and extends benefits to two-parent families, and increases work incentives. For the elderly, blind and disabled, the Jackson budget substantially increases spending for the Supplemental Security Income program. The increases will provide care to the one million people who are currently eligible but are not receiving benefits and will raise all beneficiaries up to the poverty level. The Jackson budget restores cuts made since 1981 to social services, community services, alcohol abuse and mental health programs, child abuse and family violence programs, child welfare services, juvenile justice and delinquency prevention, and programs for runaway and homeless youth.

*New Investments (1989-1993):* $57.1 billion

## Child Care

Currently, government spending for child care amounts to approximately $500 million through Title XX of the Social Services Block Grant Program and another $3.5 billion in tax credits which mostly benefit middle-income families. The Jackson budget takes the first steps toward creating a comprehensive national child care program which would make care available to every child in need at a price that everyone can afford.

To overcome the many problems created by our patchwork child care delivery system the Jackson budget creates a National Child Care Office to promote long-range planning, research, coordination and implementation of child care policy at all levels of government and in the private sector. Child care subsidies for low- and moderate-income Americans will be increased more than ten times to almost $7 billion more per year by 1993, enabling nearly three million more children to get care. As noted above in the Education & Job Training section, pre-school education (Head Start) would also be greatly expanded to serve every child who is eligible. About 1.8 to 2.0 million more children would be served by such an expansion. The Jackson budget would maintain the child care tax credit at current spending levels (adjusting for inflation) to assist the ten million families already taking advantage of this program.

*New Investments (1989-1993)*: $26.4 billion

## Health & Nutrition

The Jackson budget calls for the expansion of Medicaid to cover all pregnant women and children at or below 185 percent of poverty, and to ensure that families moving from welfare to jobs that do not offer health insurance benefits still have health care. Funding for the Women, Infants and Children (WIC) program is increased so that everyone who is eligible is served. WIC is one of the most effective federal programs, estimated to save $3 in long-term health costs for every $1 in prenatal spending. The Jackson budget also calls for increased funding for child nutrition programs, including increases in the school breakfast and restoration of the summer food program. Currently only 3.7 million children are reached by the school breakfast program, while 12 million benefit from school lunches. The Jackson budget will also raise the basic benefit level of the Food Stamp program to ensure that low-income families and elderly people no longer run out of food by the end of the month. It will do this by basing benefits on the Agriculture Department's Low Cost Food Plan rather than on the currently used and inadequate Thrifty Food Plan.

*New Investments (1989-1993)*: $39.6 billion

## AIDS

Current spending for AIDS research is $1.5 billion. The National Academy of Sciences has recommended that at least $2 billion in funding be made available for research by 1992. The Jackson budget funds above this level to accelerate research on a vaccine and a cure. Funding for public education programs is substantially increased to pay for advertising, community educational initiatives and special outreach to high-risk populations. The AIDS crisis points out the urgent need to establish a national health care program so that all who need care may get it no matter what their income (see discussion of National Health Care below). In the short term the Jackson budget expands eligibility and services for AIDS-related care through Medicaid and SSI. Funding is also increased to help meet the rising costs of charity care, as at least 20 percent of AIDS patients lack any kind of insurance, public or private. (Note: Increased funding for drug treatment is accounted for in the anti-drug portion of the budget.)

*New Investments (1989-1993)*: $11.2 billion

## Energy

The Jackson budget lays the groundwork for a transition from an energy economy based on nuclear power and an over-reliance on fossil fuels to one that relies more on renewable energy, co-generation and improved energy efficiency. The budget includes a substantial increase in energy conservation funding, both research and development and weatherization. Funding for renewable energy technologies would be returned to the levels of the late 1970s. The budget calls for increased funds to research clean coal technology so that our huge coal reserves can be used while minimizing acid rain and job loss to coal miners. The Jackson budget also calls for eliminating research for a second generation of nuclear power plants, which totals about $700 million per year. These savings should be used for nuclear waste disposal and nuclear plant decommissioning.

*New Investments (1989-1993): $7.0 billion*

## Environment

The budget of the Environmental Protection Agency and other programs charged with preserving the environment have been decimated under the Reagan administration. The Jackson budget would provide stable annual funding for land and water conservation, protecting national parks against environmental threats, and it would expand funding to ensure that existing environmental laws are fully enforced. More resources would be devoted to Superfund which is lagging in its mission to identify polluters and to clean up sites where no responsibility can be assigned. Extensive research into the numerous environmental threats we face (for instance, toxic waste clean-up, development of more environmentally-sound manufacturing processes, depletion of the ozone, the "greenhouse effect") are accounted for in the Research and Development portion of the Jackson budget proposal.

*New Investments (1989-1993): $7.5 billion*

## Transportation

Numerous studies have outlined the tremendous shortfall in funding for infrastructure by all levels of government. One report, by the National Council on Public Works Improvement, recommends that annual capital spending be doubled, a $45-billion increase, in order to sustain future economic growth. The Jackson budget proposes significant increases in federal spending for repair of urban arteries, repair and replacement of bridges on the national truck network, new road construction to alleviate congestion and improvements in water pollution systems.

The Jackson budget also raises spending for mass transit from the current $3.5 billion to $6 billion by 1993. Priorities include restoring operating subsidies to maintain existing urban mass transit systems; promoting regional mass transit systems linking city and suburbs so that inner city residents have greater access to suburban job opportunities; expanding van pooling and car pooling as a complement to existing rail systems; and providing expanded subsidies to the unemployed, the elderly, and low-wage workers who rely on public transportation as their major source of mobility. The Jackson budget would also change the current allocation formula enabling smaller cities to qualify more easily for federal matching funds ($1 billion is currently available but unspent). (Note: Additional monies for infrastructure development are assumed in the Pension Fund Reinvestment Plan described below.)

*New Investments (1989-1993): $15.0 billion*

## Economic Adjustment & Diversification

The American economy faces a continual problem of economic transition and adjustment, a process that can waste considerable productive resources in plant, equipment, and labor. Such transitions have torn the fabric out of communities and families whether they are involved or work in agriculture, steel, the automobile industry, or defense. Cities, towns, and families should not have to shoulder the effects of such changes alone, whether they occur because of a fall in farm prices, poor management decisions in the steel industry, foreign competition in the automotive industry, or because of a national political decision to eliminate a weapon system.

America needs a national policy that assists workers, industries, and communities in making these transitions in ways that maximize the productive use of our economic resources. New priorities in the Jackson budget, such as increasing spending for civilian research and development, will help create new employment opportunities for many workers who lose jobs in such transitions. However, some workers may be unemployed for an extended period of time and will need direct benefits, others will require extensive job retraining, businesses may require assistance in adjusting to new production requirements, and communities may require planning assistance in the process of economic adjustment and diversification. Thus, the Jackson budget includes funding for job training, income support and extended benefits to affected workers, and low-cost loans to business as initial steps in assisting in economic adjustment and diversification.

*New Investments (1989-1993)*: $16.0 billion

## Civilian Research, Development and Commercialization

Military research and development currently accounts for 70 percent of total federal outlays for research and development. In 1980, the military accounted for 50 percent of total federal R&D spending; at the height of the Vietnam War in 1970, the military accounted for only 53 percent of the federal total. This distortion has made industry less competitive and limited improvements in health care, the environment and other aspects of our standard of living.

The Jackson budget substantially increases non-military appropriations for R&D by lowering the military portion. The Jackson budget will significantly increase funding for health research; support the commercialization of technology to make our products more competitive in the international marketplace; work in partnership with industry to develop more efficient production techniques; support the development of renewable energy sources; and improve on our mass transportation technology, among other things.

*New Investments (1989-1993)*: $16.0 billion

## International Economic Assistance

The Jackson economic program recognizes the need for a strong U.S. commitment, in concert with our allies, to sustained world economic growth and expanded world trade. Meeting these goals requires a plan for debt relief, increased financial commitments from the developed world to international lending institutions (conditioned upon World Bank and International Monetary Fund participation in solving the debt crisis), and a restructuring of foreign aid. Priorities are development assistance to Africa and debt relief to Latin America.

The new investments in the Jackson budget include the following:

- An estimate of the federal revenue loss associated with substantial private bank absorption of Third World debt losses in 1989 and 1990.

- Increased financial commitments to international lending agencies. These would have comparatively small budgetary effects because the multi-lateral development banks are funded with small paid-in capital and receive most of their loans from the international financial markets at below-market rates.

- An increase in development assistance through direct grants and by shifting current foreign aid spending from military to economic programs. Foreign aid priorities have been completely reversed under the Reagan administration. In 1980 development assistance accounted for 67 percent of total spending and security assistance 33 percent. Today, the split is 36 percent to 64 percent (respectively). A major assistance effort would be targeted to the Frontline states in Southern Africa. This development aid would total at least $200 million per year in later years, four times the current spending level.

*New Investments (1989-1993)*: $11.7 billion

## Pension Fund Reinvestment Plan

A cornerstone of the Jackson program for reinvesting in America is the use of a small portion of public pension fund capital for small business development, neighborhood revitalization, and housing and infrastructure construction. Small, economically viable projects would be pooled to back bonds which, in carrying a federal guarantee, would be sold to the pension funds. In addition, an American Investment Bank would be established to create bonds, backed by government pledges, which would leverage pension funds for major development projects.

Six billion dollars per year in new loan guarantees would be provided under this investment plan. This capitalization would have no immediate effect on the deficit. The only impact would come in the event of defaults. Using very conservative assumptions, these would be unlikely to amount to more than a billion dollars in any given year, and even that amount would not show up until after the initial capitalization period of ten years.

## National Health Care

The Jackson budget includes relatively moderate spending increases for existing health programs, including Medicaid, and the Women, Infants, and Children nutritional program. These are necessary to assure immediate access to a full range of health care services for children and pregnant women. Funding is also provided for a significant increase in AIDS research. *Major health care increases are not accounted for in this budget plan* pending adoption of proposals to expand access and restructure how health care is financed.

Throughout the campaign Jesse Jackson has advocated making access to health care a right for all Americans. This right is guaranteed by all industrialized nations in the world, with the exception of the U.S. and South Africa. Jackson supports the creation of a national health program based on the principles of universality (i.e., all Americans have access) and comprehensiveness in coverage (i.e., providing a full range of preventive and curative services). To this end, one of the first acts of a Jackson administration would be to establish an expert commission to examine the range of options for achieving this goal.

One model that this commission will examine is the Canadian National Health Program (NHP). As discussed in the prestigious *New England Journal of Medicine* (February 13, 1986), the Canadian NHP offers a potentially interesting model for the U.S. Comparison with Canada is particularly germane, as the Canadian health care system was virtually identical to that of the U.S. prior to the introduction of the NHP in the mid-1960s. At that time, total health care spending as a percent of GNP was approximately six percent for both countries. As a result of savings from its NHP, Canada will spend about 8.6 percent of GNP on health care this year, providing full coverage for all Canadians. In contrast, the U.S. will spend about 11.2 percent of its GNP on health care, yet 37 million Americans will still be completely without insurance coverage and many

tens of millions more will have grossly inadequate coverage.

The Canadian NHP gives all citizens a free choice of physicians and hospitals (public or private) and has maintained very high levels of quality care. Infant mortality and life expectancy rates are common indicators of a nation's health level. Until it passed its NHP, Canada trailed the U.S. in both categories. It now leads in both. For example, the infant mortality rate in the U.S. is now 20 percent greater than that of Canada.

Much of the savings in Canada is due to major reductions in health administration costs. In the U.S. there is a huge administrative bureaucracy because of the patchwork system of health care coverage. There are special programs (with corresponding regulations and eligibility requirements) for the elderly, the poor, children, and others. Programs frequently vary by state, by insurer, by employment status, and the like. There is such a multiplicity of health insurance coverage that determining eligibility is a major part of the health system today. Under the Canadian NHP, providing universal coverage, none of this is necessary.

Other approaches may be more feasible in the short-term. To that end, if the best that can be attained in the short-term is a mandated-benefits proposal similar to that of Sen. Edward Kennedy (D-MA), then that should be considered. However, it will not adequately address the health care crisis. It would provide neither universality nor comprehensive coverage, and it would leave many of the uninsured still uncovered (e.g., the unemployed).

Similarly, the proposed catastrophic health care bills do not cover many of the most important catastrophic costs, particularly long-term care or catastrophic costs for the non-elderly. But in the short-term it may be necessary to seek passage of a comprehensive catastrophic bill (including long-term care) rather than focusing exclusively on a national health program. Most important, it is critical immediately to increase funding for maternal and child health programs so that we do not jeopardize future generations while sorting out present health care schemes.

# Investing in America

*When New York City teetered on the brink of bankruptcy, the federal government provided guarantees on the bonds sold to the city's pension funds. There is no reason why the federal government should not provide guarantees to pension funds and use American savings to reinvest in America. It won't cost anything to do it; it will be very costly if we do not.*

*—Jesse Jackson*

America's communities and the American people are in need. Over the last seven years, federal aid to local governments has dropped 38 percent. We have had tax cuts for the rich, spending cuts for the poor, military expansion and Medicare contraction. Workers, small businesses and many industries are staggering under the weight of corporate mergers. Thirty-three million Americans live in poverty, including one out of every five children under the age of six. Two to three million Americans are homeless. Affordable housing and public transportation are unavailable for too many in our nation.

It is time to turn back to the people: to reinvest in America. We can reinvest in America's infrastructure, retrain America's workers, and revitalize America's production even as we reduce the deficit. We can do this by using federal guarantees and a small amount of public pension assets. Using just ten cents of every public pension fund dollar would put to work more money than the Reagan administration has proposed using for economic development, mass transit and infrastructure over the next five years.

To create jobs and rebuild America, I propose a two-part Invest in America program:

## A National Investment Program

We need a National Investment Program which would use federal guarantees to back securities to finance small business loans, low-income housing, neighborhood revitalization and infrastructure investment. Currently, there are about $600 billion in assets in public pension funds. The funds are invested in both stocks and bonds. I propose to use a small portion—10 percent, or about $60 billion—to reinvest in America. This can be done prudently and securely. The federal government can provide a federally-guaranteed security—similar to Fannie Mae and Ginnie Mae bonds—to finance a pool of economically viable projects. Pension funds would be able to buy and sell these securities. The pension funds would get both market return and security on their investment. And at no risk to the pensioners, a small portion of their assets would be rebuilding America.

At the moment it is easier and more common for pension funds to purchase stocks and bonds of private corporations (often to fuel unproductive mergers and acquisitions) than to direct their assets into improvements in public and private infrastructure. Why? Because corporate stocks and bonds are what most investment managers know best. But it is not always in the best interests of the pensioner.

At the present time many housing or small business loans are too small or too new in concept to be easily marketable. A National Investment Program would bridge the gap between small projects and large pools of capital and offer as "low risk" a security as possible to pension funds.

## The American Investment Bank

Second, we need to establish an American Investment Bank to fund large projects. Modeled on the World Bank, the American Investment Bank would finance urban and rural development in America. All the states would contribute the initial capital, although only a fraction of the total funds would have to be subscribed up-front. This capital, backed by government pledges, would back the Bank's bonds. The bonds would be marketed to pension funds. This would leverage pension fund capital at a low enough cost to allow the Bank to re-lend the funds at a low interest rate for development projects.

Such a Bank would attract the country's finest minds and most experienced decision-makers. On its board would sit top leaders of business, labor and the public sector. They would set the investment priorities, aided by a professional staff to develop and screen feasible projects.

Properly managed, such a Bank can get the states to work together in a new kind of federalism, rather than compete against each other as they do today. A Bank-funded development project in one region could be required to use research and development, raw materials and technology from other regions of the country, thus promoting greater participation and cooperation among states.

This Invest America program would provide sorely needed employment for our people while filling our nation's need for more housing, improved roads and water systems, and better public transportation. America's people must go forward, acting in our own interests, using our own resources, living up to our own values, expecting and demanding leadership from our president and the backing of the full power of the federal government, as we build and rebuild our nation.

# INVEST IN AMERICA: REBUILD OUR CITIES

Nashville, Tennessee, June 15, 1987

To Mayor Riley, Mayor Washington, Mayor Barry and other mayors, I am delighted to have this opportunity to meet today with the people who have the most challenging day-to-day job in America. You are out there on the front lines of our society dealing directly with the challenges and opportunities of our cities. I want to congratulate you for the work you are doing to keep up in these difficult times of diminishing resources and increasing demands—and yet you persevere.

You are responsible for meeting the needs of your citizens, your business community, your educational system, your health care system and your infrastructure. Your responsibilities continue to grow—yet the revenue available to you is declining. I know, as you know, that your city's budget cannot be continued in isolation.

We live in an instantly changing world economy, where the competition for jobs is not between cities, but across borders; where even service jobs are being transported overseas; and local business are looking over their shoulders with fear at the merger maniacs—who pay themselves tremendous profits while they squeeze the productive capital and decent paying jobs out of our national economy. I know, as you know, that we must have a national economic policy that makes sense; a national urban policy that makes our cities a priority; and a national administration that once again understands that America's cities are critical to our national strength.

You are entitled to a president who stays awake and works as hard as you do; who takes his or her responsibilities to our nation's people as seriously as you do; and who will reach out to our nation's cities to forge a partnership of mutual respect and assistance; a president committed to a national agenda that includes housing, health care, transportation and education as part of our national security. You will have such a president if I can help it.

But let us be candid with one another.

As much as I would like to, I cannot promise that the next president of the United States will unlock the safe to find billions of dollars which should have been accumulating to the cities' accounts for the last seven years. The sad true facts of our national deficits are too well-known: a $2 trillion national debt; a trade deficit still near $160 billion; and little sign of improvement in America's competitive position in the world economy. We have a president who went into his hip pocket to pull out his tried-and-true "Soviet Scare and Scapegoat" tactic to divert attention away from an utterly failed economic summit in Venice. In addition to "Tear Down this Wall," where is the President's plan to "Rebuild our cities, rebuild our rural areas, and rebuild this economy"?

We cannot wait any longer for the White House plan to revitalize our cities. We must have our own action plan, use our own resources to trigger a new direction for our economy. We must have real ideas and real programs to address the real needs of our nation. This is why I want to talk about a policy of investment—a policy of investing in America.

Just as we have institutionalized the slogan—if not always the practice—of "Buy American," I believe we must raise the principle of "Invest in America." Investing in America means an economic policy that invests in people—as workers, as students, as homebuyers and as farmers.

Ranchers and farmers have fed America and the world. They deserve mercy, a moratorium, a restructuring of their debt, supply management, parity and markets. Farmers don't want a hand-out, they want a helping hand. If we can bail out Chrysler and Continental Bank; Europe and Japan; allow a $17 billion cost over-run on the B-1 bomber; propose to spend $36 billion on two carrier fleets for the navy; and construct 21 MX missiles they now say won't work; then we can bail out the family farmer and rancher. We intend to convene an international conference on food and agriculture in Chicago—an international conference at the site of the Trade Center—to give stability to world food prices and production, as we do oil, and correlate production with 500-to-700 million starving and undernourished people in the world.

Investing in America means spending more money on education—not less. Because only by improving the quality and access to education for all American young people will we ensure for this economy a chance to compete in the world markets of the future.

Education is not a dispensable social program. It is a defense act. When the Soviets launched Sputnik in 1957, we had to turn to education and science to catch up. It protects our national security. Four years at any state university costs less than $25,000, while four years in any state penitentiary costs more than $100,000. Schools are more efficient than jails. Schools at their worst are better than jails at their best.

Investing in America means investing in the community structures that keep this country at work—vital projects like roads, bridges, ports, harbors and water treatment.

That is why I bring before you today my suggestion for a new action plan that can begin to meet the needs of America's cities by making better use of some of the funds available to us right now. I urge you, the nation's mayors, to join me in supporting a national investment plan that can be the first step in rebuilding our economy.

This national investment plan will use a fraction of the nation's savings—pension funds that you have the ability to influence and control. This money would go to the five R's: reinvestment in America's infrastructure; retraining of America's workers; reindus-

trialization of America's productive capacity; research for commercial development; and recovery from a military to a peace-time economy. I propose a policy and incentive shift away from merging corporations, purging workers, and submerging our tax base and our capacity to be competitive.

Our challenge is to build an action plan which reflects a new vision of America's future; a vision of an America where Americans manage our own savings to provide for our own jobs, our own housing, our own transportation, and our own education to prepare our youth for the future; an America where American money rebuilds America's infrastructure, providing the most basic material need of Americans—socially useful jobs for all at livable wages. A job is as much a part of a people's infrastructure as the houses they live in, the streets they walk on, or the schools they go to. Jobs and education are the live alternatives to unemployment compensation, crippling welfare and despair.

I know the pain that destruction of personal infrastructure brings to the entire national family. When Len Bias died—without having fulfilled the promise of playing with the Celtics—something died in each one of us. As our children die daily from drugs, liquor, babies making unhealthy and unwanted babies, violence and suicide, we need to give our youth an alternative purpose and vision of their future in America.

You as mayors must be the leaders in a new "Forward Offensive" strategy for the economy. You can—and should—develop a national investment program. First, because you can identify the "Five R" needs. Who knows better than you, who have watched our most beautiful cities decay at the core, the major infrastructure needs? You, who see the unemployment lines swollen with a generation who has never known steady work and those who were once productive industrial workers, know the training needs! And you, who have watched the closed signs go up on plant gates and shop fronts as industry and the businesses that depend on it abandon your communities, know the importance of reindustrializing the economy.

This can be done because you have access to

the money. You are able to influence the assets to provide the infrastructure investments needed to revitalize your cities. You have influence with many of the people who manage your local pension funds. You can join together to find new ways to use these hard-earned dollars to fill your cities with humming workplaces again. We must protect the workers' pension funds by law in the name of "job security," just like, by law, we set aside F.I.C.A. funds for "Social Security."

Try to think of yourselves and, say, the country's top ten union leaders as an urban cartel—the OPEC of investment capital. That's what you are. The 25 largest pension funds in America have $500 billion in assets. This is a massive pool of capital which is being used ineffectively for the workers whose money it is. Fourteen of those funds are public, belonging to city, county and state workers. Together, public officials and public employees, taking just 10 percent of these assets, we can act to rebuild America.

I am not calling for pouring the hard-earned savings of America's public workers down the drain or into fly-by-night projects. Instead, I am calling for providing the trustees and investment managers of these pension funds with a wider range of opportunities to use the assets productively. There will be some projects you or the trustees or the investment managers will not invest in, just as now there are some private investments which are not considered good deals. But the choices will be larger, and the incentives for reinvestment in America will be expanded.

I want to talk at some length and detail about what you, as mayors, can do in a very practical sense to create a national investment program. But before I do, I want to put the program and the challenge I am posing to you in an international perspective.

What is the current economic context? The world has become much smaller. The American economy is more open to the rest of the world than ever before. Imports and exports are now more than 10 percent of the GNP—double what they were in the early 1970s. But those imports and exports are way out of balance. We have an economy which is much more open at the import end than at the export end.

More than goods are flowing across national borders. Savings are too. As long as we Americans spend more than we save, those countries which do the opposite send their savings to us. Right now a little over one out of every three dollars of the federal deficit is being financed by savings from some other country.

What do we have to show for it? This administration has turned America from the world's largest creditor to the world's largest debtor. There is nothing wrong with being in debt. As mayors, you have had to borrow. But you borrowed to build for the future. All this administration has left for the future is higher interest payments taking a larger and larger chunk of future tax revenues, leaving less and less for national priorities. This borrowed money has not been invested in America's future—American jobs, housing, transportation, infrastructure, health care or education. Because it hasn't, that reinvestment task now falls to us.

Meanwhile, business can roam to wherever the best deal is offered—where it can make the most profits. With new technology and methods of production changing daily, business has become footloose in its quest for profits and markets. In many ways we have created a system of incentives, directly or through the tax system, which has encouraged this footloose behavior.

As mayors, you know this only too well. Within America, you are each competing—and the governors of your states are competing too—in a mad, zero-sum game for business location. You know that something has to be worked out to reduce the senseless competition. That is another reason and role for the national investment program.

But our responses even in this area are fragmented and hit-and-miss. Further, there is no parallel program of capital and infrastructure investment. It won't do any good to have a highly-trained work force if business has taken all the jobs abroad.

For example, the media has put a lot of focus on the imbalance of trade with Asia, primarily with Japan, Taiwan, and Korea. But are they really the problem, or scapegoats who are victims themselves? Consider Taiwan. The U.S. trade deficit with Taiwan was $13 billion in 1985 and $16 billion in 1986. But who is the biggest exporter from Taiwan? None other than General Electric! Not far behind are Texas Instruments, Digital Equipment, General Instrument, Sears and dozens of other U.S. firms.

Bicycles illustrate just how self-inflicted some of America's Taiwan trade wounds are. Last year, Americans bought seven million imported bikes, 83 percent of them from Taiwan. Yet there isn't a Taiwanese bicycle company that competes in the U.S.—"No equivalent of a Honda or a Sony," says Jay Townley, the Vice President of Purchasing for the Schwinn Bicycle Company in Chicago. "It's only American brand names and American companies. The competition from Taiwan is us. You really can't consider Taiwan an exporting nation. Taiwan is simply a collection of international subcontractors serving the American market," he says.

Why do American and other multinationals go to Taiwan? In addition to a number of incentives from the Taiwanese government, worker rights are systematically violated. Assembly workers receive barely subsistence wages for eight-to-twelve hour days. They live in crowded company-owned dorms with no air conditioning, despite 100 degree heat. Health and safety regulations are lax or nonexistent. Strikes are all but illegal under martial law. The few unions that do exist are government-owned.

As multinational corporations grew, they arranged production in global assembly lines, with products such as cars made from parts from as many as 16 different countries. Plants are easily closed down in the U.S. communities and transferred elsewhere where workers are not organized. Through these global assembly lines, transnational corporations transformed world trade so that currently somewhere between 33 and 40 percent of world trade is simply transactions between different units of the same corporation. It is amazing that President Reagan can refer to this as "free trade."

It's good to focus on welfare reform, because we need welfare reform. But welfare reform without corporate reform represents little, if any, progress. As this example shows,

any attempt to deal effectively with transnational problems must deal squarely with transnational workers' rights.

Blaming or scapegoating others is no substitute for revitalizing our own economy. Blaming others will not put American workers back on the shop floor. Blaming others will not give back hope to America's youth. Led by you, we must forge a new equation. We have always forged it from the bottom up, not from the top down. Public accommodations laws did not come down from Washington, but up from a bus boycott in Montgomery. Open housing laws did not come down from Washington, but up from marches in Gage Park, Cicero and Chicago.

Revitalizing our economy offers America as deep a challenge as the civil rights movement faced. That is why I am challenging you, the nation's mayors, to serve as the front line in this "forward offense" of the American economy by breaking down the institutional opposition to using our pension funds for the "Five Rs" of reinvestment, retraining, reindustrialization, research and recovery from a military-dependent economy. I am throwing out to you today the challenge of joining me in the initial steps of a national investment program which will come from the grassroots in the best American tradition.

If you accept this challenge, begin now:

To evaluate your own city as to how it can exert greater control over its public pension and investment funds. What changes would you need to make in the governing bodies of those funds to exercise some control over their investment decisions? What are the local and state laws governing investment?

Convene the trustees, investment advisors and representatives of the workers whose pensions these funds represent to discuss targeting a small portion of the investments into the revitalization of the local economy.

You may wish to organize tripartite boards at the city level to consider how to focus funds on the housing, transportation, job and other infrastructure needs in your area.

Let us begin now to plan a national conference, which will take up the challenge of using pension funds to rebuild local infrastructures on a national basis. If you the mayors call such a conference, I can guarantee you that everyone will come—government officials, trade union leaders, corporate officials and financial experts. The very fact of this conference will be open communication among those who provide the capital: the pension funds themselves, the financial community which serves as the intermediaries for the investments, and the public officials who know so well where the needs of your communities are.

Finally, I suggest creation of a new entity—the American Investment Bank. This bank would act as a financial intermediary helping to fill America's infrastructure needs with America's largest pool of capital—pension fund assets.

A fraction of this capital—which has been increasing in size so rapidly recently, as the stock market has soared—can be put to use to revitalize America without any sacrifice of reasonable return to the workers whose pensions and savings these funds represents.

This is a domestic version of the World Bank to finance long-term investments in American housing, transportation, infrastructure and job creation.

Like the World Bank, this American Investment Bank would:

- Raise its capital by selling bonds;

- Pool the capital provided by public pension funds to lower the risk and the interest rate charged for development projects;

- Invest that capital according to priorities established by a tripartite board representing business, labor and government; and,

- Have a professional staff to help localities and states develop competitive investment opportunities.

The American Investment Bank is a unique version of federalism:

- It would not be government controlled; it would be tripartite.

- It would not cost any tax revenues; it would use American savings.

- It would not be a government agency; it would be privately administered.

The capital comes from state and local government workers; the investment opportunities and needs come from states and localities; the management represents a cooperation between public and private know-how.

Ultimately, it may well be that this will be so attractive that America's corporations and private pension funds will wish to change their rules to allow their participation.

You have every right to insist that the federal government provide support to your local efforts to reinvest. When New York City teetered on the brink of bankruptcy, the federal government provided guarantees on the bonds sold to the city's pension funds—similarly, with Chrysler. There is no reason why the federal government should not provide guarantees to pension funds providing American savings to reinvest in America. It won't cost anything to do it; it will be very costly to America if we do not.

I want to assure you that I will work hard to see to it that the federal government creates a guarantee for pension funds on securities which finance reinvestment in America. I have already spoken with a number of pension and investment experts along these lines. All assure me that, given a new federal mechanism to lower the risk of such investments, money could start flowing to meet American needs.

We must go forward, acting in our own interests, using our own resources, living up to our own values. In this way, we can address the plight of two-to-three million homeless; we can address the jobless who must construct the housing; we can rebuild transportation, bridges and railroads; our workers can make the steel, lay the rails, and assemble the trains. In this way—by rebuilding the infrastructures of our cities and our people—we turn tax consumers into revenue-generating taxpayers.

At the same time I promise you that I will continue to speak out on behalf of the nation's urban needs and of the responsibilities which others must help you meet. It is not right that the nation's cities should have to bear so much of the crushing burden of homelessness, of hunger, of overworked educational systems, overcrowded transportation systems and underfunded housing programs. It is not right that the problems of the cities should be ignored by the national media, as if cities were a relic of the sixties. It is not right that our national government should think nothing of spending billions on ill-thought-out and ultimately wasteful weapons systems while refusing to see the needs of our true national security—our people here at home.

Recently we have witnessed terrible scenes of spiritual despair: the racial violence at Howard Beach and Forsyth County, Georgia, on the campus of the University of Massachusetts and the Citadel in South Carolina; the suicides of farmers in the Midwest and young people in New Jersey and Illinois; the epidemic of drug-taking in our schools and of babies making babies in our neighborhoods.

Too many of our young people are losing hope. They do not see a future for themselves—no chance of getting a decent education or a good job. If we do not, as a people, take the lives of our children seriously, how can they? If we do not, as a nation, invest our resources in our children's future, what can

they look forward to? If we do not, as grown-ups, set them an example of working together and talking together among ourselves, what kind of example have we set for them?

It is time to fight—but not against each other. Fight for and with each other. Fight at a plant gate that's closing on workers without notice. Fight at a farm auction—for mercy and parity. Fight at a drilling site and increase our energy sufficiency and jobs. Fight at the site of a drug exchange that threatens to rot the welfare of our nation from within. Fight to be a strong nation. But that's not enough. Fight to be a good nation. Build the coalition that can turn this nation around.

I know there are storm clouds, and into each life some rain must fall. It's dark—but I know too that the morning will come. We have the will. We have the strength and we will find the way.

We will save the children, strengthen the cities, heal the land, invest in America, achieve peace in our time—now.

# SOLVING OUR TRADE CRISIS

*The solution to our trade crisis is economic cooperation, not economic warfare; world economic prosperity, not economic austerity; government investment in people, not government investment in bombs; and making multinational corporations answer to the American people, rather than making people subject to the whims of multinational corporations.*

—*Jesse Jackson*

Trade gives us all the opportunity to raise our standard of living, to build cooperation among nations, and to promote economic justice and world peace. However, in the last seven years, the policies of the Reagan administration have helped turn the world economy into a battleground—pitting American workers against workers from around the world.

The clearest result of this escalating global warfare is the U.S. trade deficit. In 1980, the U.S. was the world's largest creditor nation, running a small but manageable trade deficit. By 1987, our trade deficit had skyrocketed to $170 billion and lost us more than 1.3 million manufacturing jobs. To pay for this, we had to borrow more than $400 billion from the rest of the world, making us now the world's largest debtor. Ronald Reagan has made a hostage of the American economy, indebting us to foreign creditors and mortgaging future generations.

Reaganomics, which led to huge budget deficits, raised interest rates and the value of the dollar, making American agriculture and manufactured goods uncompetitive with those from the rest of the world. Some blame our trade deficit on American workers, claiming wages are too high and craftsmanship too poor. But workers' real wages have stagnated in the last 15 years. Some blame our trade deficit on unfair trade practices. But, "protection" abroad has not increased noticeably in the past seven years. Exploitation of workers, which should be an "unfair" trade practice, has.

We need to end unfair trade barriers. We can do this through the General Agreement on Tariffs and Trade (GATT). Unilateral protection is self-defeating and divisive in the long-run, setting the interests of American workers against American consumers and against workers and producers throughout the world. Solving our trade deficit requires getting the world economy growing strongly again. Without purchasing power there can be no trade.

To promote trade and growth I propose to:

## Promote Multinational Corporate Responsibility

Multinational corporations are pitting governments and workers in one country against those in other countries. They set up shop where they can get the cheapest labor, the best tax breaks, the weakest environmental and safety regulations, and the best deals. Footloose and without loyalties, except to the bottom line, if they don't get what they want they pick up and move.

The biggest exporter from Taiwan is not Taiwanese; it's General Electric. The American share of world exports has dropped from 15 percent in 1970, to 10 percent today, but U.S. multinational corporations' share has remained rock steady at 17 percent. The companies are American; the brand names are American; the workers, wages and conditions are not.

We must fight back against runaway corporations. Tax subsidies which aid U.S. corporations to invest abroad must be eliminated. Workers and communities need advance warning of plant closures to have time to consult and to act to avert job loss or arrange for a transfer of ownership. Businesses must pay their fair share of plant closure costs, including extending health benefits, retraining and job placement assistance, and the return of tax dollars used as incentives to aid the industry.

We must establish an international code of conduct for multinational corporations. Across the globe they must adhere to minimum accepted environmental, safety and labor standards. Violation of international labor standards should be an "unfair trade practice" allowing retaliation, including the denial of preferential treatment, and taxation and controls on imports. Corporations should be subject to penalties.

## Implement a Third World Marshall Plan

Nearly three-quarters of the world's population lives in the Third World. We need a comprehensive international approach to raise their living standards and restart the engine of economic growth. After World War II we had a mutual interest in aiding Europe's economic recovery. There is the same mutual interest today in expanding Third World economies and markets. We should ask Japan, West Germany, and other trade surplus countries to join with us to create a new capital fund for Third World development. We ourselves should redirect our $14 billion in aid to underdeveloped countries, prioritizing economic development over military assistance.

We must restructure Third World debt. Austerity policies have not only failed; they have been counter-productive, resulting in a slowdown in growth which helps neither debtor nor creditor. The lack of demand among debtors may account for as much as 30 percent of America's lost trade in the last several years. There are a number of proposals to restructure debt and to offer debt relief. They must be pursued vigorously. For example, if Latin

American debtors were relieved of a little more than half of their current debt service, and if they were to use as little as a third of the freed-up foreign exchange earning to buy U.S. goods, the result would be a surge of U.S. exports, adding more than half a million new American jobs.

## Stimulate World Economic Growth and Restore Financial Stability

Our tight money policies of the last decade have choked off credit and slowed economic growth throughout the world. We need instead to promote greater international coordination to lower *real* interest rates among the leading industrialized nations and propel the major world economies forward in tandem. A one percentage point drop in the interest rates of the United States, Japan, Great Britain, West Germany and Canada can, over the course of one administration, lead to a four percent growth in our economy: that's over $2,000 in increased income for every family; at least two million more jobs; and a $50 billion reduction in the federal deficit (due to lower interest costs and increased tax revenues).

Tight Federal Reserve monetary policies and foreign currency speculation by major corporations and banks has led to dramatic swings in exchange rates, contributing to the U.S. trade deficit and job loss. We must reduce these swings by confining exchange rate movements to a specified band. This could be done through a modest tax on large foreign exchange transactions made purely for financial speculation purposes. Never again can we take a hands-off attitude toward something so vital to our national interest and our prosperity as the value of the dollar.

## Reinvest in People

America must refuse to try to compete in the global marketplace as the newest entry in the low-wage labor sweepstakes. In the past, it was high wages and the expansion of public education which accelerated technical innovation and made the United States the economic wonder of the world. American workers' education, innovation, skill and commitment will be the currency of trade in the 1990s. We must double the federal education budget and make lifelong education and training programs available to all.

We must significantly reduce the share of federal research and development funds being devoted to military spending and redirect those funds to civilian industries—to make products we want to export, not those we hope will never be used.

These proposals for solving our trade crisis require a commitment to action coordinated between countries on a scale unknown before. But controlling multinational corporations whose only allegiance is to profit, joining in a true partnership with the Third World, and cooperating with our allies to reflate the world economy is the only course to follow to find peace and prosperity. Our present course leads only to a stagnant world economy and a declining standard living.

With Mrs. Rosa Parks
*Democratic National Convention*
*Atlanta, Georgia*

A Moment of Reflection
*On the Road*

Schoolchildren
*Chicago, Illinois*

Student Rally
*Canton, Ohio*

Community Rally
*Redmond, Oregon*

Delivering A Sermon
*Harlem, New York*

JESSE JACKSON'S WAR ON DRUGS BUDGET
Reagan Proposed
Jackson Proposed
Difference
(In Millions of Dollars)
· LAW ENFORCEMENT 2,878 4,101 +42%
· PREVENTION 611 917 +50%
· TREATMENT 425 1,685 +396%
· TOTAL $3,914 $6,703 +71%

Announcing His
"War On Drugs" Budget
*Los Angeles, California*

Jessie Jackson is the man
For President of this great land
Running for President
He's for everyone- big or small
If he's elected
He'll give his all
UNIVERSIT

Homeless Woman
*Jackson, Mississippi*

ST IN PEOP
ST IN AMER

r  Jesse Jackson

March to Save the Williamsburg Bridge
*Brooklyn, New York*

Housing Project Wall
*New York, New York*

One of Many Friends
*Chicago, Illinois*

Spontaneous Street Celebration
*Willingboro, New Jersey*

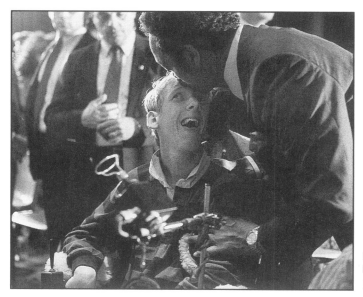

Rally for the
Physically Challenged
*Los Angeles, California*

March for
California
Farmworkers
*McFarland, California*

Drought Stricken
Farmers
*Egan, Minnesota*

At the
Edmund Pettus
Bridge
*Selma, Alabama*

Lesbian and
Gay Rights Rally
*Sacramento,
California*

Labor Rally
*Lancaster, Pennsylvania*

In Support of Striking Workers
*Philadelphia, Pennsylvania*

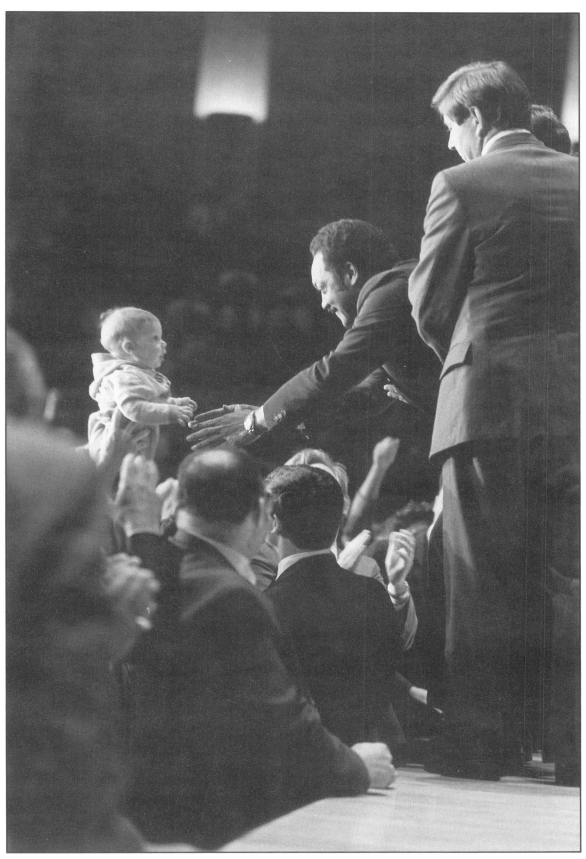

For the Next Generation
*Harrisburg, Pennsylvania*

Young Fans
*Albany, New York*

Rally for Peace and Freedom
*Washington, D.C.*

The Jackson Family
*Democratic National Convention*
*Atlanta, Georgia*

Keep Hope Alive!
*Democratic National Convention
Atlanta, Georgia*

*A beautiful color poster (36″ × 14″) of the photograph above is available for $6 from the Keep Hope Alive PAC, 733 15th Street, N.W., Room 700, Washington, D.C. 20005. Check or money order must accompany order.*

# A WORKERS' BILL OF RIGHTS

## 1. Workers Have a Right to a Job

People need jobs and there are jobs which need to be done. We can build the housing, roads and bridges that we need as well as provide care for this nation's people. We can end plant closings without notice and unemployment without hope.

## 2. Workers Have a Right to a Democratic Union

All workers, including public employees, should be able to organize themselves into democratic unions, have those unions recognized, and work under a collective bargaining agreement.

## 3. Workers Have a Right to a Living Wage

People who work full time should be able to rise out of poverty on their pay. American families need family wages. Young workers need opportunity.

## 4. Workers Have a Right to a Healthy Life and a Safe Workplace

Workers need affordable and accessible health care, a right to know the dangers at work, and good faith enforcement by skilled experts of the laws meant to protect their lives.

## 5. Workers Have a Right to Both Work and Family

No one should be forced to choose between a paycheck and a sick child, or between keeping their job and giving birth.

## 6. Workers Have a Right to Pension Security

A pension belongs to the worker, not to the company. Every worker is entitled to one as secure as Social Security. Workers should have a voice in ensuring that their pension funds be used in their own interest, not against them.

## 7. Workers Have a Right to Fair Competition

International trade needs a level playing field. Recognition of the basic democratic rights of workers at home and abroad to organize, bargain collectively, and to have enforced workplace standards is needed. Free labor cannot "compete" with slave labor.

## 8. Workers Have a Right to Freedom from Discrimination

There also needs to be a level playing field at home—affirmative action for those locked out of better paying jobs and pay equity for those locked into low-wage jobs.

## 9. Workers Have a Right to Education that Works

Workers need basic education for basic skills, vocational education for current jobs and life-long education for a changing economy.

## 10. Workers Have a Right to Respect

The contributions of workers, past and present, deserve a prominent place in the education of future workers. Those who give a life of labor deserve to have the companies for whom they work reinvest in their industry, in their community and in their country.

# A CORPORATE CODE OF CONDUCT

*There is nothing wrong with the American worker, the family farmer or the small businessperson. There is something wrong with the system. Economic violence is no accident. Deregulation, unchecked corporate greed, and incentives to merge companies, purge workers and submerge the economy are at the root of our economic problems. It is time to forge a new relationship between America's workers and its corporations.*

*—Jesse Jackson*

For generations, American workers and corporations have operated under an implicit unspoken agreement. In exchange for management having a free hand to run its own affairs, workers expected a secure job and decent pay. They also expected business would make America grow, that there would be continued reinvestment in the industries, communities and people of the United States.

But while American workers held up their end of the bargain, major corporations did not. Corporations closed down plants at home and moved abroad to exploit repressed low-wage labor. They've squandered their (and our) capital on mergers and acquisitions that produced only paper, instead of investing in factories and businesses. They invested in Wall Street instead of Main Street. Under Ronald Reagan's stewardship, corporations received huge tax breaks, polluted the environment, and endangered the health and safety of workers while the government turned a blind eye.

America needs a new partnership between its workers and its corporations. Our corporations need expanding markets, a productive workforce, technological innovation and government policies which promote a stable but growing economy. Our workers need decent jobs with real security, good pay so they can buy what they produce, and a stable and growing economy.

Workers forced to take pay cuts, threatened with job loss, and without a say in their workplace are, of course, less productive and their companies are less competitive. But when they are offered job security, a rising standard of living and a voice in managing the workplace, they actually will take the initiative in spurring productivity—and increasing profits.

Government must help forge a partnership between America's corporations and America's workers. Both must know their rights and recognize their responsibilities. Both must see that their cooperation is in the national interest. We must reissue the challenge of Franklin Roosevelt in his National Industrial Recovery Act—to bring labor and management together to provide "the assurance of a reasonable profit to industry and living wages for labor."[1]

The centerpiece of this new partnership must be a Corporate Code of Conduct.

## 1. Corporations Must Be Accountable to the Public

Corporations must be accountable, not just to their shareholders, but to all their "stakeholders"—their workers, their communities and their nation. Corporations cannot just pursue their own profits to the exclusion of the nation's needs. We must require our corporations to rise above "the bottom line."

We must:

- Require corporations to disclose information on their financial condition and their plans for future investment to appropriate government, community and labor representatives.

- Require corporations to extensively consult with all parties prior to any decision that would significantly affect workers or the larger community.

## 2. Corporations Must Make Productive Investments

From 1979 to 1986, corporate America squandered over $700 billion on 20,000 mergers and acquisitions.[2] Studies have shown that one-half to two-thirds of mergers don't work; that market share and profits fall.[3] Research, technology and productivity increases have suffered as corporate America's attention was dominated by searching for takeover targets or escaping hostile corporate raiders. We can change this desire to buy rather than build.

We must:

- Eliminate tax incentives which encourage mergers and acquisitions.

- Enact regulations that outlaw greenmail and extend the time period for reviewing takeovers.

- Vigorously enforce the anti-trust laws and guard against big mergers by dominant firms in major markets.

- Create a Merger Control Board which would grant merger approval conditioned on a firm's committing to new investment, modernizing facilities or providing assistance to adversely affected communities.

- Enact a Securities Transfer Excise Tax to limit short-term, speculative investments.

- Significantly increase funding for the Securities and Exchange Commission and appoint a chairperson who will enforce the laws at its disposal.

## 3. Corporations Must Reinvest in American Workers and the American Economy

Corporations must make a long-term commitment to economic growth by reinvesting in and modernizing their facilities, through ongoing programs of research and development, by introducing new technology (in consultation with workers affected), and by providing training and retraining for workers as the workplace and economy change.

We must:

- Engage government, business and labor around the country in developing long-range targets for employment, wages, prices and investment, thereby promoting economic stability. For example, tripartite groups would redirect public pension funds to invest in local housing, small business, neighborhood development and infrastructure needs.

- Offer "contingent protection" to industries challenged by foreign competition. For a fixed number of years, the government can provide threatened industries with interim protection, modernization and retraining assistance, in exchange for industry agreeing on a plan of action to make it competitive again. Once the plan is accomplished, protection would end.

- Give preference in government contracting and procurement to firms achieving certain standards of modernization and reinvestment, research and development, and worker retraining.

- Offer research grants to firms that undertake high-risk, long-term research into new production technologies and product designs.

- Establish jointly public-private funded industry research centers for corporations that adhere to the Corporate Code of Conduct.

## 4. Corporations Must Respect International Labor Standards

In the last two decades, the U.S. share of global exports has declined from 15 percent to 10 percent, while the U.S. multinational corporate share has remained constant at 17 percent.[4] This shift of production to other countries pits workers in the U.S. and abroad against each other and erodes worker rights and wages everywhere. American industry cannot compete unless we either lower our standard of living to match that of the Third World or raise their standard of living closer to ours.

Multinational corporations must respect the rights of workers in the Third World to organize free and democratic trade unions and to pursue decent wages and working conditions. Our long-range interest is to increase incomes in the Third World. Increased wages there, in combination with an international commitment to expand Third World economies, would provide the fuel for worldwide economic growth into the next century.

We must:

- Define the denial of workers' rights as an "unfair trade practice" (under the Generalized System of Preferences found in the General Agreement on Tariffs and Trade). Based on this we will be able to not only deny a country preferential trade treatment, but also retaliate against the unfair cost advantages these unfair labor practices produce.

- Make debt refinancing and development assistance contingent on these nations allowing free trade unions, rising wages and improved benefits and working conditions.

- Deny "Overseas Private Investment Corporation" insurance protection to investments of multinational corporations in countries which systematically deny workers' rights.

- Limit government contracting and procurement with companies that invest in "unfair labor practice" countries.

- Have a date certain by which all U.S. corporations must completely withdraw from South Africa.

- Enact into law the MacBride Principles which define corporate conduct in Northern Ireland.

### 5. Corporations Must Protect Workers and Communities From Plant Closings

Between 1979 and 1984, plant closings elim-

inated 11.4 million U.S. jobs.[5] Thousands of communities bore the cost of these closings, through increased unemployment, lost tax revenues and increased spending on social services. We propose a comprehensive federal plant closing policy to discourage corporations from divesting our workers and disinvesting from our communities.

We must:

- Require corporations to give at least two months notice for lay-offs and six months notice for moving or closing a plant of a set minimum size.

- Require corporations to work together with state and local officials to make a full accounting (during the six month notification period) of the estimated social costs involved in a plant shutdown.

- Ensure that corporate management negotiates with all the stakeholders—workers, community officials and local businesses that depend on the dominant firm—to seek alternatives to job loss. Employees must have the right of first refusal in any change of ownership and communities must have the right to convert the facility to an alternative use, if they so desire.

- Require that corporations pay their fair share of plant closure costs in consultation with state and local governments, including adequate severance pay, extended health benefits, retraining and job placement assistance, and the return of tax dollars used as incentives for the firm to locate there in the first place.

- Eliminate provisions of the tax code— such as the foreign tax credit and deferred tax payments on income from foreign subsidiaries—that encourage runaway plants.

### 6. Corporations Must Pay a Fair Wage for a Fair Day's Work

Women today earn only 67 cents for every dollar a man earns.[6] They are still largely segregated into low-paying "women's jobs" in the clerical, sales and service sectors. Minimum wage workers haven't received a wage increase since 1981, making their current $3.35 an hour equivalent to $2.45 in today's dollars. A minimum wage worker working a full 40 hours a week can't maintain a family of three above the poverty line. We need a wage policy that says that if you work for a living in America, you can make a living in America.

We must:

- Mandate that corporations provide pay equity: employees must receive equal wages for jobs requiring comparable skill, effort and responsibility.

- Increase the minimum wage to at least $5 an hour by 1992 and index it to 50 percent of average non-supervisory wages in the future.

- Require corporations to provide part-time employees with the same benefits (on a pro-rated basis) as full-time workers.

- Enact legislation mandating parental and medical leave.

- Require corporations above a minimum size to provide on-site child care or child care referrals so that parents (particularly single parents of pre-school children) can have the opportunity to go to work.

- Strengthen and enforce regulations to hire on a non-discriminatory basis, guaranteeing all workers, regardless of race, sex, ethnicity, religion or sexual orientation equal access to work and equal opportunity to participate in the economy.

## 7. Corporations Must Protect Employee Pension Plans

Over the past eight years, 1,400 corporations have siphoned off $17.5 billion in assets from employee pension plans, in large part to finance mergers and acquisitions that ended up costing workers their jobs.[7] Pension plans represent the savings of workers who passed up wage and benefit increases to provide for their retirement. Thus corporations have an obligation to use pension funds in ways that serve workers' interests. Corporations must adequately contribute to their employees' pension plans to provide security for their workers' retirement.

We must:

- Prohibit companies from tapping surpluses in pension funds to finance hostile takeovers or to make their balance sheets look better.

- Limit the ability of employers to terminate solvent employee pension plans.

- Reform pension, labor and tax laws so that every qualified pension plan has a committee composed of at least 50 percent employee representatives and that committee should have the ultimate fiduciary responsibility for the plan.

## 8. Corporations Must Safeguard Worker and Community Health and Safety

Each year approximately 6,000 workers are killed on the job and another 6,000 suffer serious injuries.[8] Exposure to harmful chemicals is rampant. According to the Labor Department damage done to workers health could range from $30 billion to $50 billion to treat.[9] We must have a safer workplace.

We must:

- Strengthen regulations and enforcement so that corporations provide safe working conditions, inform their workers and communities of possible hazardous conditions, and help preserve, not pollute, the environment.

- Require corporations to assume the full costs of and responsibility for environmental clean-up, such as required by Superfund.

## 9. Corporations Should Recognize and Respect Workers and Their Unions

Unions are workers' collective voice in running the economy. Corporations must bargain in good faith with existing unions and allow new unions to form when workers choose to be represented by them. Labor law reform is needed to ensure these goals and to provide workers with adequate job security.

The democratic rights that we take for granted in our society must be extended to the workplace and the shop floor, where hierarchical and authoritarian decision-making now threaten the productivity of U.S. businesses. Worker participation in businesses' day-to-day operations and in stock ownership has consistently been shown to result in increased worker satisfaction, a more productive workplace and more profitable companies. Removing the work rules, regulations and prejudices that restrict the full potential of working people will create a more productive America. We must strive for an America where we summon each worker to bring commitment and skill to the job, rather than resentment and hostility.

We must:

- Recognize unions when 55 percent of the workers sign up (the procedure now in place in Canada).

- Impose a time limit and arbitration on first contract negotiations when the employer is found not to be bargaining in good faith.

- Make it illegal for corporations to fire workers without just cause and due process, or to hire scab labor and lock out workers on strike so long as unions bargain in good faith.

- Provide tax incentives to firms that institute worker participation programs and workplace democracy.

- Limit government contracting and procurement with companies which lack workplace democracy programs and engage in anti-worker activities.

- Broaden representation on corporate boards to include all the stakeholders: owners, management, workers and the community at large.

Moving American jobs to low-wage countries and abandoning American communities is not in the national interest. Looking for short-run profits and putting them into mergers and paper acquisitions rather than into productive investments is not in the national interest. Endangering the health and safety of workers and polluting the environment is not in the national interest.

This Corporate Code of Conduct is based on our democratic values and our willingness to work together to keep America strong. It establishes a set of responsibilities to accompany the receipt of government incentives and grants. It encourages the participation of American workers in the health of their companies, increasing productivity and contributing to economic development.

Government must shape policies in the national interest. A president should implement policies such as these which build on our strengths and curb our weaknesses.

1   *The Public Papers and Addresses of Franklin D. Roosevelt*, 1938, Volume 2, p. 246.

2   *Merger and Acquisition*, May-June, 1987.

3   *New York Times*, June 21, 1987.

4   *Handbook of International Trade and Development Statistics*, U.N. Conference on Trade and Development, 1986.

5   U.S. Department of Labor Press Release, "Bureau of Labor Statistics Report on Displaced Workers, " November 30, 1984.

6   U.S. Bureau of Census, "1984 Census Bureau Report on Male/Female Differences in Work Experience, Occupation and Earnings," August 1987.

7   Figures from the Pension Benefit Guarantee Corporation (as of October 31, 1987) as quoted in the *Washington Post*, December 27, 1987.

8   Estimate by the National Institute for Occupational Safety and Health as quoted in *Corporate Crime Under Attack: The Ford Pinto Case and Beyond*, Franics T. Cullen, et al, 1987.

9   Estimate by the Department of Labor as quoted in *The Challenge of Hidden Profits*, Mark Green and John Barry, 1985, p. 706.

# III

# CREATING A HUMANE SOCIETY

# THE JACKSON FAMILY INVESTMENT INITIATIVE

*Protecting America's families is not simply a problem of the poor. It is a challenge to the entire society, a practical as well as a moral challenge. We will either raise the standard of living and quality of life for the poorest of us, or gradually lower the standard of living and quality of life for all of us.*

—*Jesse Jackson*

## Lost Years: A Decade of Neglect

A decade of neglect has taken its toll on our nation's families. Everyone agrees that repairs on our crumbling bridges and highways are overdue, but the situation is far more urgent for families. Put simply, Reaganomics has translated into a policy of disinvestment in families. The effects of this neglect have been devastating.

Today's families are caught between their dreams and the harsh economic realities that are the legacy of Reaganomics. After seven years of misguided policies—a doubling of military spending, cutting taxes on the rich and corporations, cutting social programs today without regard for the consequences of tomorrow—the gap between the rich and the poor is greater than it has been in the last 40 years. The share of income going to the middle class has fallen, as more and more families slide downward on the income distribution ladder. For nearly a decade now, more and more Americans have slipped below the poverty line. Children have replaced the elderly as the poorest of the poor, but many older Americans are still haunted by economic insecurity. Women must choose between their families and their jobs; men see their real earnings stagnate.

Why has this happened to our families? The causes are clear. Under Ronald Reagan, the federal government turned its back on young families, low-wage workers and single parents. Social spending cutbacks denied moderate-income families the support of government programs. Corporate pursuit of short-term profit left communities impoverished as jobs moved to the suburbs, to another state or to another country. A growing share of U.S. jobs pay low wages, offer few or no benefits and no opportunities for advancement, and are part-time or temporary.

Finally, social and economic policies in the United States today are based on the myth that the "average" family consists of a father receiving adequate wages and health benefits, a mother providing full-time child care, and children whose needs are met in the home. In a sense, we might say that the United States has an *implicit* family policy which flows from this myth. That implicit policy ignores the child-care crisis and condones below-subsistence welfare grants, jobs which provide no benefits, and budget cutbacks in vital social services.

The reality is that fewer than one in ten families today fits this outdated image. Even fewer minority families conform to the myth.

- In 1984, one in five white children and six in ten African American children lived with only one parent. Twenty percent of all births were to unmarried women.

- Over half of mothers of pre-school children and infants are in the workforce at least part-time. The vast majority of working women have husbands earning less than $20,000 a year.

- Over nine million people cannot earn enough to bring their families out of poverty. Over 37 million people have no health coverage.

- More than 13 million adults are unemployed or underemployed (working part-time because full-time work is not available). Unemployment rates for African Americans and Hispanics are twice as high as for whites.

- Young families are particularly at risk: nearly one-half of all children living in families headed by a person under 25 years of age are poor.

The effect of current policies has been most severe for American Indian, African American, and Hispanic families and for families of recent immigrants. By every indicator—poverty, unemployment, health status—minority communities are at grave risk.

Over the past seven years, we have heard too much empty talk about "family values." Protecting our nation's families requires a change in *social values*, as expressed in budget priorities and program initiatives. We must recover from the "lost years" of disinvestment by putting into place a set of policies which support and protect our families. The United States is the only industrialized country in the world which lacks a coherent set of proposals for family assistance. This must change.

Congress is attempting to take some steps towards solving the crisis, but these steps are too tentative—and some are in the wrong direction. Some bills cut needed programs in order to fund other initiatives, in the name of "pay as you go" budgeting. But the victims of economic violence—children and elders, dislocated workers, families in crisis—cannot pay as they go. They are in need of investment today for a more secure and productive future.

- Current welfare reform proposals do not make adequate provision for Medicaid and child care for families making the transition from welfare to paid employment.

- Current minimum wage legislation makes no provision for keeping up with inflation.

- Current family-leave bills make no provision for wage protection.

- Current child-care initiatives, while a step in the right direction, are underfunded relative to our crisis-proportion needs.

The Jackson "Family Investment Initiative" puts the federal government squarely on the side of families and proposes initiatives in three areas: "Work and Family," "Family Security," and "Looking to the Future." These programs are designed to help families close the gap between their dreams and their everyday reality of paying the bills, providing for their children, and caring for their parents. This family policy invests in the future of our nation—the next generation.

## I. The Family Investment Initiative: Work and Family

Combining work and family in the 1980s is a stressful endeavor. Like workers on an assembly line, families face a kind of "speed-up"—working harder than ever just to stay in the same place. For low-income families, the everyday effort of survival is exhausting. For middle-income families, every day is an effort to fend off downward mobility. Upward mobility seems a mirage.

In this environment, caring for children and disabled or older family members forces unconscionable choices on workers. Women must return to work sooner than they wish after childbirth, disabled family members must be hospitalized or family members must quit work to look after them. Persons who have earned the right to retire in dignity must continue paid work in order to cover expenses.

Leadership on work and family has to mean more than slogans. We must create economic expansion which makes possible good jobs at adequate wages and a national child-care policy, and makes practical a system of parental leaves.

### Good Jobs at Adequate Wages

Full employment at fair wages is the cornerstone of a family policy which meets human needs. When the economy stalls, workers cannot support their families nor can government meet their needs. The Jackson program begins by reorienting economic policy toward opportunity through economic expansion.

We need significant new federal investments in people and in our communities, paid for by increasing taxes on corporations and the wealthy and by cutting the military budget without cutting our defense. We propose an American Investment Bank which would use federally-guaranteed loans from public pension funds to rebuild America—financing small business development, low-income housing, neighborhood revitalization and infrastructure construction. We have outlined a Corporate Code of Conduct that would ensure long-term, job-creating investments in productivity rather than short-term job-destroying investments in paper. We have committed ourselves to upgrading the skills and productivity of U.S. workers by expanding the quality and quantity of education and job training programs. Finally, we offer a plan for global growth that combines a Marshall Plan and debt relief for the Third World with a coordinated lowering of interest rates among the industrial powers. Such a program will spur growth and create millions of new jobs in the United States.

## Ensure Pay Equity and Affirmative Action

The Family Investment Initiative guarantees an opportunity to earn a living wage to those families historically disadvantaged by racism and sexism—minority families and families headed by women. Full employment is necessary but cannot alone guarantee equal access for minority workers, particularly minority women. Therefore, we commit ourselves to affirmative action and comparable worth in order to ensure equal opportunity for all to hold good jobs at adequate wages.

A major cause of poverty for single-mother families is women's concentration in low-paying jobs in the service sector and in the lowest paid manufacturing jobs, such as apparel and textile work. Minority women are even more heavily concentrated in such female-dominated occupations and are much more likely to head their own families. As a result, they stand to gain a great deal from pay equity initiatives which would raise pay in women's jobs to the same level as that in men's jobs requiring comparable skills, effort and responsibility.

The Family Investment Initiative sets clear comparable worth goals. The Federal Employee Compensation Equity Act of 1987 funds a study to ascertain the extent of sex- and race-based pay discrimination among federal workers. We pledge to act to eliminate any pay discrimination found as a result of the study. The federal government should take the lead in promoting pay equity by starting with its own personnel. We will also work to pass legislation requiring a review of wage rates in the private sector and establish a timetable for equalizing the discrepancies.

In recent years, our government has turned its back on affirmative action. We pledge to increase enforcement by government agencies charged with ensuring equal access to employment regardless of age, race, color, creed, sex, sexual orientation or disabling condition.

## Raise the Minimum Wage

A key element of the Family Investment Initiative is an increase in the minimum wage. We support raising the minimum wage to $5 per hour and indexing it to half the average hourly manufacturing wage, to ensure its purchasing power in the future. Unlike the empty pro-family rhetoric of the past seven years, increasing the minimum wage is really pro-family.

Since 1981, when the minimum wage was frozen at $3.35, inflation has caused its purchasing power to fall by one-third, in turn causing substantial hardship for U.S. families. Adults account for 70 percent of the nearly seven million Americans earning the minimum wage or less. Nearly half of minimum wage jobs are held by heads of households and married women who work out of economic necessity. Taken together, women and minority workers are the vast majority of those minimum wage earners.

The costs of raising the minimum wage are insignificant in comparison to the benefits. Economic studies have shown that restoring the minimum wage to its historic level would have a minimal impact on teenage employment, on the unemployment rate and on inflation. In addition, raising the minimum wage would lighten the burden on U.S. taxpayers who must presently pay the cost of welfare for workers who cannot adequately support their families.

## Comprehensive Child and Dependent Care

Child care is a sound investment for our families and for our nation's economy. It is an essential aspect of creating economic opportunity and integral to the Family Investment Initiative. Affordable child care increases work force participation, particularly by single parents. Productivity rises when parents don't have to lose time on the job worrying about their children's safety. And children in high-quality child-care settings get a head start on their education.

By 1995, two-thirds of all pre-schoolers and four-fifths of all school-age children will have mothers in the workforce. But today there is already a child-care crisis. Accessible, high quality child care is often beyond the reach of low- and moderate-income families, making it difficult or impossible for some women to work.

- A young couple with two children, earning median salaries for their age group, would have to pay 32 percent of their income for child care.

- There are as many as seven million latchkey children aged 5 to 13 routinely left without adult care before or after school each day.

- Of six million U.S. businesses, only 3,300 help their employees find or pay for child care.

### Establish a National Child and Dependent Care Office

The Family Investment Initiative establishes a National Child and Dependent Care Office to promote long-range planning, research, coordination and implementation of a national child-care policy. The Office will work closely with states to implement federal policies. We pledge to develop a comprehensive system of federal supports to expand the supply of child care and lower its cost while at the same time improving compensation and opportunities for daycare providers. The Office will also work with states to enforce standards for safe and high quality child care.

### Increase Subsidized Child Care

Our commitment to child care is real. We must significantly increase child-care assistance to low- and moderate-income families where parents are working, going to school, or receiving job training. Poor families should receive free child care; moderate-income families earning up to 115 percent of a state's median income (about $30,000 nationwide) should receive aid on a sliding scale. The Jackson Initiative proposes to expand the federal government's funding of subsidized child care by tenfold, removing child-care funding from Title XX of the Social Services Block Grant and creating a new spending category for subsidized child care. States will be assisted in increasing the supply of child care, improving reimbursements to providers, and subsidizing low- and moderate-income families. Over two million more children will receive care as a result of proposed new funding.

To lighten the financial burden of child care for middle-income families, we should continue the current system of child-care subsidies to families through the Dependent Care Tax Credit. At present, most of the tax reduction through this credit benefits 10 million middle-class families earning between $20,000 and $40,000.

### Use the Public School System

A National Child and Dependent Care Office should promote research and development on ways to effectively use our public school system to provide before-school, after-school and vacation care for school-age children. Currently the federal government spends nothing for such school care. The Jackson Initiative allocates $590 million in 1993 for this purpose. Staffing could be provided by teams of child development associates, recruited from the community and trained to provide high-quality child care. In addition to serving as the sites of child care, schools could serve as community-based resource and referral centers for parents and for family daycare providers.

### Improve Compensation for Providers

A key to quality child care is an improvement in the status and compensation of child-care providers. The majority of the two to three million child-care providers in the United States earned the minimum wage or less in 1984. A raise in the minimum wage is long overdue and will assist these workers who care for the next generation.

Low salaries for providers interfere with the provision of high-quality care: for instance, in 1980, the turnover rate for child-care providers in centers (the highest paid) was 42 percent. The Jackson Initiative requires states to develop plans for improving wages and benefits and makes funds available for ongoing training and technical assistance.

### Meet Adult Daycare, Respite and Crisis Center Needs

The Initiative also recognizes the growing need for adult daycare and respite services. The National Child and Dependent Care Office will be charged with the development of a national policy to meet this need.

The Jackson Initiative allocates $50 million to develop crisis centers where sick children can be cared for. At present, illnesses for children cause absenteeism for parents, lowering productivity at the workplace. Combined with parental and medical leave policies, these crisis centers will help alleviate the stress placed on families by even minor childhood diseases such as colds and upset stomachs.

### Parental and Medical Leaves

Our present implicit family policy discounts the economic value of family care and imposes penalties on those who provide it. The United States is the only industrialized country which forces parents to choose between their jobs and their families. Even though women are essential to the U.S. workforce, it is usually mothers who are forced to make this draconian choice. In other countries, paid parental leaves help alleviate the child-care crisis.

- Eighty-five percent of U.S. working women will have at least one child during their working careers. Half of all new mothers have to be back at work long before the child's first birthday. In 1984, 60 percent of all working women were not covered by any maternity leave provisions.

- Parents lose approximately eight working days per year caring for sick children, but only one-third of all companies allow sick or personal leave to be used to care for a sick child. Less than half of all workers are entitled to any job protections in the case of emergency family needs or the birth of a child.

The Jackson Family Investment Initiative recognizes that sometimes the most important job a worker can hold is in the home, caring for a child or ill family member. Therefore, we support job protection and fair compensation for parental and medical care leaves.

These changes would bring U.S. policies more into line with the rest of the world—industrialized and developing countries alike. Almost every other country in the world, including developing countries, provides maternity leave; 125 countries pay cash benefits to new mothers. Japan, for instance, provides 12 to 14 weeks of paid maternity leave with the guarantee of job protection.

The absence of a national family leave policy is costly to families and to employers. Lack of such leave causes parents to return to the workforce still exhausted after the birth or adoption of a new child; workers are distracted by anxiety over sick family members at home; and well-trained workers reluctantly quit their jobs because they see no alternative way to meet their family responsibilities.

A 1987 study by the Institute for Women's Policy Research estimated the cost of women not having parental leave at $363 million each year. The cost comes from earnings lost by women who must give up their jobs and in taxpayer contributions for welfare payments to women forced out of their jobs.

The Jackson Initiative institutes a national system of parental and medical leaves to protect the jobs and incomes of workers who temporarily leave the workforce to care for an infant or a sick dependent. As a first step, the Initiative supports the Parental and Medical Leave Act of 1987, which mandates unpaid family leaves.

However, unpaid leaves only protect jobs, not income. They cannot solve the problems faced by low-income and single-parent families juggling paid employment and family life, a disproportionate number of them minority families. In the short term, unpaid leaves must be supplemented with adequate income support policies. In the long run, we need to develop legislation that will establish a paid parental and medical leave system for all employees, drawing on unemployment insurance models of financing. The federal government must take the lead, by introducing such legislation and by extending wage protection to federal employees on parental and medical leave.

## II. The Family Investment Initiative: Family Security

For many families today, jobs do not provide enough income to maintain an adequate standard of living. Others are unable to find jobs or are unable to find child care which would permit them to enter the workforce. For these families, income supports are necessary to enable them to live in dignity and security. The Jackson Family Investment Initiative guarantees an adequate standard of living to families needing assistance.

### Real Welfare Reform

Welfare reform should provide for the basic needs of families as well as help families to enter the workforce. In 1971, the combined value of Aid to Families with Dependent Children (AFDC) and Food Stamps brought families within 85 percent of the poverty line. Since then, the purchasing power of welfare benefits has fallen by over *one-third*.

The Family Investment Initiative restores the anti-poverty effectiveness of the AFDC system by raising benefits and extending eligibility to working poor families, drawing on the Omnibus Anti-Poverty Bill introduced by Representative Charles Rangel in 1984.

The Initiative recommends a national minimum benefit at 70 percent of poverty level, liberalizes asset restrictions, increases the federal share of costs, and extends benefits to two-parent families and the working poor. Roughly half of the federal dollars would accrue to the South, where benefits are the lowest in the nation.

The Initiative restores dignity and security to older and disabled poor people, who have suffered during the Reagan years under punitive regulations designed to deny them eligibility for benefits. It increases payments under Supplemental Security Income (SSI), the welfare program for older and disabled poor people, to the poverty level. It also makes the program available to the one million people who are currently eligible for but not receiving SSI.

These changes are costly and will be phased in over time as our economic expansion plan puts the country back on a sound economic footing. Nonetheless, family economic security must be a priority; between 1989 and 1993, the Jackson Initiative commits an average of $7.5 billion each year as a down payment on our promise to restore dignity to families receiving public assistance.

A few simple changes in the burdensome regulations governing the Aid to Families with Dependent Children program would go a long way toward helping low-income working families. The Jackson Initiative begins by restoring the program to the rules in place prior to 1981, when the Reagan administration made it nearly impossible for working poor families to supplement their earnings with public assistance and Medicaid. Specifically, the Initiative restores the earnings disregards which once permitted families to earn some income in the labor market without losing AFDC and Medicaid eligibility. In addition, to further remove the economic barriers to employment for welfare recipients, the Initiative proposes to disregard income saved through the Earned Income Tax Credit for purposes of AFDC and food stamp eligibility and benefit calculations.

### Comprehensive Child Support

Most single mothers receive no financial assistance from their children's fathers. The 1984 Child Support Enforcement Amendments could remedy much of this situation, but states have been slow to implement the new system. The Jackson Initiative continues federal government support to states to increase child support collections, both by better collection of current obligations and by working toward greater equity in child support awards.

However, child support enforcement cannot adequately provide for families when the father is unemployed or employed at low wages. Too often calls for child support enforcement have merely been excuses for the federal government to avoid its responsibility to help support poor families. The Family Investment Initiative places child support within a broad set of policies which includes good jobs at fair wages, adequate income supports, comprehensive child care and a national health program. Such a policy truly provides for comprehensive child support by giving parents access to the jobs they need to support their children, by easing the economic stresses which can tear families apart, and by giving young people the basic skills they need to choose meaningful work and family options for their lives.

### Investing in Families in Crisis: Social Services, Housing, AIDS and Drugs

Over the past decade, rising poverty, homelessness, unemployment and substance abuse have thrown more families into crisis, adding to juvenile delinquency, mental health problems and greater family violence. But at the same time, social programs which provide help to families in crisis have suffered under the Reaganomics budget axe. The Jackson Initiative restores federal cutbacks made since 1981 to social services for families in crisis.

In many states, poverty and homelessness, the spread of AIDS, and the drug abuse epidemic have caused an increase in the number of children and youth living in foster homes, residential centers and other institutions. A disproportionate number of minority children live away from their families. Thus, the Initiative proposes reauthorizing, with additional funding, the Child Abuse Prevention and Treatment Act, the Runaway and Homeless Youth Program, the Family Violence Prevention and Services Program, and the Juvenile Justice and Delinquency Prevention Program.

But it's not enough to deal with the symptoms of the problem. We have to deal with the root causes of homelessness, AIDS and substance abuse. The Jackson Initiative funds a four-pronged approach to the housing crisis. It provides funds for the emergency needs of the homeless by providing housing allowances to pay for housing where they live. It meets the immediate needs of low-income people by modernizing public and other subsidized housing and by providing housing allowances to help low-income families who are paying an excessively high percentage of their income for rent. It expands the supply of affordable housing by providing capital grants for new construction. The latter will emphasize construction by non-profit community-based organizations. Finally, the Jackson Initiative will aid first-time homebuyers by creating a low-cost revolving loan fund to help with downpayments.

The illness of AIDS presents a grave challenge to modern technology, to our health system as well as to our compassion. It can be effectively countered. It requires a massive public education and prevention campaign, an intensive (and costly) effort to discover an effective vaccine, as well as a program of national health care to help those who contract the disease to get the care they need. The Jackson budget will meet this challenge head-on— by providing the required resources.

We need a war on drugs just as we need a war on AIDS. Our children, families and cities are being invaded by drugs at home while governments are teetering all over the world because of drugs. It is not enough to say *no* to drugs. The Jackson Initiative says *yes* to action by substantially increasing the budget for a war on drugs. Priorities include cutting off drugs at the source, increased interdiction and law enforcement efforts, expanded education programs as well as providing treatment on demand for addicts.

### Investing in a Healthy Future

The most important asset for families is good health. Good health makes possible participation in the workforce, learning in schools and training programs, and participation in family and community life.

We need a National Health Program to make health care a right for all Americans regardless of their income. Such a program will provide comprehensive health care coverage, including preventive, curative, long-term, rehabilitative and occupational. The program will be universal, covering everyone under a single plan to assure equal access to care and to reduce administrative complexity and cost. Cost containment and savings will come from a streamlined system with less bureaucracy. Patients will have a free choice of providers.

In the short term, while a National Health Program is in the process of implementation, the Family Investment Initiative takes some specific steps to broaden coverage and ensure better prenatal care under the current system.

First, we must extend Medicaid coverage to all pregnant women and children whose families fall below 185 percent of the poverty line, one- and two-parent families alike. At present, less than half of all poor children and pregnant women have access to Medicaid. In the long run, this program will save money as well as lives. Every $1 invested in comprehensive prenatal care returns $3.38 in lower health-care costs later in life. Today, we must invest at least $2 billion more per year if we are to achieve these long-term savings in the future and create a healthy start for our youngsters.

Second, we should expand the Special Supplemental Food Program for Women, Infants and Children (WIC), which has proven its effectiveness in preventing premature births, infant mortality, low birthweight babies and child malnutrition. At present, this program only reaches one-half of those eligible. The Jackson budget proposes additional funding of $5.6 billion to WIC over the course of the next administration.

In addition, the Jackson Initiative proposes additional funding for child nutrition and the Food Stamp programs to ensure better health and development.

## III. The Family Investment Initiative: Looking to the Future

### Investing in the Future Workforce

We cannot afford to let the victims of economic violence fall by the wayside. They can become contributing members of society if we invest today in restoring their productivity. Displaced workers who have lost jobs, displaced homemakers who have lost the support of a husband and must now provide for themselves, young workers attempting to enter an ever more sophisticated workplace with ever

less adequate skills, people with disabling conditions, and welfare recipients—all need access to education and training and to meaningful work.

### Educating the Next Generation

We must undertake a bold new commitment to education, doubling the federal education and job training budget as an investment in the future of our families. A top priority is to establish an Office of Pre-school Education which would oversee an enlarged Head Start program and develop parallel programs in child-care centers and schools. The Jackson budget provides sufficient funding so that every three- to five-year-old child living in poverty receives a pre-school education. Currently fewer than one out of six kids is so fortunate. Yet the program makes good economic sense: every $1 that we spend on Head Start saves $5-$7 in later costs.

We need to restore Chapter I compensatory education funding to pre-Reagan levels, and provide money to rebuild deteriorating inner-city schools. We must invest in teachers by establishing a School Improvement Fund and by greatly expanding teacher training. The Jackson budget establishes a new $1 billion Teacher Corps to recruit new teachers, especially from minority communities and commits $150 million to launch a nationwide family literacy campaign. And the Jackson budget doubles current spending on student grants and loans, so that every high school graduate who qualifies for college assistance can get it.

### Job Training for the Future

Our economy is undergoing profound economic changes, yet the United States lags far behind other industrialized countries in developing a flexible job training/vocational education system. We face increased competition from a highly skilled world workforce, the restructuring and downgrading of jobs in America is still occurring, and a massive influx of new workers into the workforce is taking place. The result is workers in manufacturing plants being displaced or downgraded when their industries relocate, go out of business or undergo mass layoffs. Many new workers, especially welfare recipients, have never been able to enter the mainstream labor market because jobs are not available to them or because they lack the skills required for our more technological age. Our youth, especially minority youth in the inner city, get tracked early on into a cycle of unemployment for the rest of their lives because they lack the basic skills and fail to get the work experience of earlier generations.

We need to overhaul our job training system and establish a modern vocational education system which provides training to workers throughout their lives. We can look to Sweden and West Germany for successful models. The Jackson Initiative meets this challenge head-on by providing coordination and funding—an additional $4.5 billion per year—to develop programs which train workers for good jobs which are tied to community economic development needs and enable participants to reach their full potential.

Between 1979 and 1985 millions of American workers were displaced from their jobs due to plant closings and cutbacks. Business should pick up the bulk of their retraining and job search assistance. However, the federal government must aid those regions of the country most affected by economic restructuring. In 1980, the federal government spent $1.6 billion assisting workers and communities affected by dislocations. In 1986 funding had been reduced to $287 million and served fewer than 100,000 workers. The Jackson Initiative triples funding for dislocated workers to help them and their communities cope with economic change.

In addition to decent and affordable child care and health care, families trying to move from welfare to stable employment at adequate wages also need job and vocational training, improved academic skills, language proficiency job placement assistance and other services that provide long-term employment gains. Thus, the Jackson Initiative proposes spending an extra $1.5 billion per year by 1993 to help people on welfare learn such basic skills. These programs are highly effective. The latest government statistics (1984) show that welfare payments in one federal welfare-to-work program (the Work Incentive Program) were reduced by $587 million while only $271 million was spent to assist participants.

Finally, we need to give our youth hope and opportunity for the future. Remedial education, vocational training and programs of work are crucial for improving the chances of low-income and minority youth to get and maintain employment at decent wages. At present, students who don't finish high school and/or are not college-bound are tracked into outdated programs or risk wasting time and money in for-profit training schools with poor track records on placement. The Jackson Initiative nearly doubles spending for the Job Corps program to help disadvantaged youth. Every $1 invested in the program saves $1.45 due to increased employment and earnings and reduced welfare costs. We also need to significantly expand the summer youth training and employment program. Currently it's serving 300,000 fewer kids than it did in 1981. Yet there are more kids in need of remedial education and work experience now than back then. New funding in the Jackson Initiative would provide summer jobs with remedial education to one million more youth per year.

### Combatting Teen Pregnancy

Investing in families today through better education and training will help alleviate the crisis in teen pregnancy and contribute to stable families in the future. Nearly half of all poor youths between the ages of 15 and 18 have reading and math skills in the bottom fifth of the skill distribution. Compared to students with average skills, a young woman with poor basic skills is five times as likely to become a mother before age 16, and 18- and 19-year-old men with poor skills are three times as likely to be fathers.

### Beyond Welfare

Besides expanded federal funds to ensure access to real training and educational opportunities the Jackson Family Investment Initiative supports a voluntary employment readiness program. Many states are now experimenting with programs to help welfare recipients find paid employment, and several bills are pending in Congress. Unfortunately, these programs are inadequate: underfunded, often punitive, and unconnected to meaningful job creation. Few programs provide assistance for child care or transitional Medicaid. As a result, recipients are forced to sacrifice their children's health and safety in order to comply with what passes for "welfare reform."

## Medicaid Extensions and Welfare Reform

Meaningful welfare reform must ensure that families who leave the rolls for the workplace retain Medicaid eligibility for as long as they lack health coverage on the job. In the short run, extended Medicaid eligibility is needed for those who leave AFDC for jobs. In the long term, we need a National Health Program which will provide comprehensive care and universal coverage to all Americans, regardless of whether or not they receive public assistance.

Evidence from current welfare-to-work programs demonstrates the necessity of Medicaid extensions. Most placements in existing job programs are in service sector jobs, only one-third of which provide any access to health coverage. Even in the widely publicized Employment and Training Program (ET) in Massachusetts, health coverage is a problem. Only half of ET graduates have employer-provided health care. Nationally, studies have shown that 40 percent of people who leave AFDC for jobs are still poor after they get off the welfare rolls, which means that they cannot afford even the most minimal employee contribution to health coverage.

## An End to Workfare

Current programs and pending legislation permit states to require mothers to put in long hours of work at unpaid jobs, often displacing paid employees. The Jackson Initiative eliminates unpaid workfare requirements and stresses education—adult literacy, English as a Second Language, GED certification and post-secondary education—so that welfare recipients can achieve wages adequate to support their families when they are ready to enter the workforce.

We recognize that welfare reform aimed at finding paid employment for recipients cannot succeed without a federal commitment to economic opportunity and economic expansion. In areas where unemployment is already high, welfare-to-work programs raise expectations which cannot be fulfilled, create a game of mu-

sical chairs for those competing for jobs, and, at worst, penalize families for their failure to find work. By combining voluntary job readiness programs with economic expansion, access to child care, and full health coverage, we create real welfare reform which permanently moves families out of poverty.

## Taxing for Justice and Security

Over the past decade, the overall U.S. tax system has become more regressive, taking a greater share from poor and moderate-income families than from the rich. A recent study by the Congressional Budget Office found that families in the bottom 10 percent of the income distribution are paying nearly 20 percent more in federal taxes today than they did in 1977, while the top 1 percent of taxpayers are paying over 20 percent less.

This Robin Hood in reverse policy must end. Low- and moderate-income Americans must not continue to subsidize the rich and corporations. We can restore tax fairness, stabilize our economy and provide new revenues for the Jackson Family Initiative by returning taxes on the wealthy and corporations to their pre-Reagan levels, as well as by freezing military spending for the next five years.

We can use the federal tax system to help low- and moderate-income families with children achieve a better standard of living—one where family needs are adequately addressed and where families can even begin to save for their futures. We can use our tax system to promote economic justice and to provide economic security to hard-hit low- and moderate-income families.

Every industrialized country except the United States subsidizes children through a family allowance (a cash benefit from the government to *every* family with children). The United States should authorize a study of the effectiveness of family allowances. These allowances could easily be instituted in the form of a refundable dependent credit administered through the tax system, creating no new federal bureaucracies. This system would be no more cumbersome than the present system of deductions in the federal income tax.

## Can We Afford the Jackson Family Investment Initiative?

Some may argue that we can't afford to spend so much money on families. But it is wrong to see this as an expenditure—it is an *investment* in the future. As the U.S. population ages and as the world marketplace becomes more competitive, we cannot afford an untrained, undereducated workforce.

Our national security depends upon the children growing up today—children at risk through a decade of neglect. Most physical and mental development is determined by the time a child is five years old. The children in America's families cannot wait until there is a federal budget surplus.

We must support and protect all our families, whatever their form. Older people need support no less than young families; single parents need support no less than married couples. All are deserving of federal government leadership.

We reject the notion that the budget deficit forces us to choose among our families, to let some suffer economic violence while we help others. We can dramatically reduce the deficit even as we make the investments proposed in the Family Investment Initiative. It's a matter of political will. It's time for the President and the Congress to redirect our priorities so that we can build an America in which we invest in families today for the sake of our tomorrow.

## Sources

Thomas A. Bates, *The Changing Family to the Year 2000: Planning for Our Children's Future*, California State Assembly Human Services Committee, 1987.

Gordon Berlin and Andrew Sum, *Toward A More Perfect Union: Basic Skills, Poor Families, and Our Economic Future*, Occasional Paper 3, Ford Foundation Project on Social Welfare and the American Future, New York, 1988.

Children's Defense Fund, *A Children's Defense Budget, FY 1989: An Analysis of Our Nation's Investment in Children*, Washington, D.C., 1988.

Congressional Budget Office, *The Changing Distribution of Federal Taxes: 1975-1990*, Washington, D.C., 1987.

Family Policy Panel of the Economic Policy Council of the United Nations Association of the United States of America, *Work and Family in the United States: A Policy Initiative*, New York, UNA-USA, 1985.

Sheila B. Kamerman, "Women, Children, and Poverty: Female-Headed Families in Industrialized Countries," *Signs*, 1984.

Service Employees International Union, *1988 Presidential Candidate Issues Briefing Book*, 1988.

Ruth Sidel, *Women and Children Last: The Plight of Poor Women in Affluent America*, New York, Viking Press, 1986.

Working Seminar on Employment, Welfare, and Poverty, Institute for Policy Studies, *Women, Families, and Poverty: An Alternative Policy Agenda for the Nineties*, Washington, D.C., 1987.

**The Jackson Family Investment Initiative Budget**

|  | ($ in Millions) | | | |
|---|---|---|---|---|
|  | 1988 Reagan Actual | 1993 Baseline[1] | 1993 Jackson Proposed | 1993 Increase Over Baseline |
| **PROGRAMS** | | | | |
| Income Security | | | | |
|     AFDC | $10,874 | 13,282 | 18,882 | 5,600 |
|     Social Services[2] | 3,571 | 4,349 | 8,449 | 4,100 |
|     Supplemental Security Income | 12,636 | 15,550 | 20,250 | 4,700 |
| AIDS[3] | 1,525 | 1,857 | 4,857 | 3,000 |
| Child Care[4] | 3,985 | 4,691 | 11,191 | 6,500 |
| Drug Enforcement, Education & Treatment[5] | 3,463 | 4,217 | 7,417 | 3,200 |
| Education[6] | 20,002 | 25,075 | 40,520 | 15,450 |
| Job Training | 3,812 | 4,549 | 9,099 | 4,550 |
| Housing | 13,895 | 18,956 | 35,956 | 17,000 |
| Health/Nutrition | | | | |
|     Medicaid[7] | 30,494 | 52,194 | 54,894 | 2,700 |
|     WIC | 1,816 | 2,191 | 4,191 | 2,000 |
|     Child Nutrition | 4,405 | 5,943 | 8,443 | 2,500 |
|     Food Stamps | 12,551 | 15,520 | 20,520 | 5,000 |
| **TOTAL** | **$123,029** | **168,374** | **244,669** | **76,300** |

[1]Amounts are based on Congressional Budget Office (CBO) estimates and are not available at the program level.

[2]Social Services includes Social Services Block Grants (excluding child care portion); Community Services Block Grant; Alcohol, Drug Abuse and Mental Health Block Grants; Maternal and Child Health Block Grant; Community and Migrant Health Centers; child abuse and family violence programs; child welfare services; juvenile justice and delinquency prevention programs; and homeless youth programs.

[3]CBO does not have a calculation for AIDS funding. Amount is based on inflation adjustment of Reagan FY88 figures.

[4]Child care includes the Child and Dependent Care Tax Credit and the portion of the Title XX Block Grant estimated to be dedicated to child care.

[5]CBO does not have a calculation for this category. Amount is based on inflation adjustment of Reagan FY88 figures.

[6]Includes Head Start, currently part of the Health and Human Services budget, under a new National Pre-school Education Program.

# WAGING A WAR AGAINST DRUGS

*The drug crisis is the number one threat to our national security. Democracies are teetering all over the world because of drugs. Our children and cities are being invaded by drugs. And our foreign policy is undermined by drug dealing by friend and foe alike. It's not enough to just say* **no**. *It's time to say* **yes**—*to action.*

—*Jesse Jackson*

Today the drug crisis is a greater threat to our national security than our traditional enemies abroad. Drugs destroy healthy bodies leading to physical deterioration and death. Drugs interrupt educational and career goals. Drugs are dream-busters and hope-destroyers. Drugs destroy trust and rupture family ties. Drugs are directly related to crime. Drugs threaten democracy and development around the globe.

Yet the administration's response to this crisis has been haphazard, emphasizing slogans over action. To wage a "war on drugs," we need a comprehensive plan of action and we need leadership at the presidential level to help us change our minds, our morals, our economy and our conduct.

To wage this war, I propose to:

### Establish a National "Drug Czar"

Federal drug-related activities are now fragmented among at least 17 major agencies. A "Drug Czar" is needed to coordinate all of these efforts, someone with the authority and the funds to implement a comprehensive plan of attack.

### Cut Off Drugs at the Source

The stability of many of our allies is severely threatened because of drugs. We may already have lost the government of Colombia to bribes, threats and murders by the drug traffickers. Extraordinary measures are needed to break this international drug cartel which is making drug dealers more powerful than governments. We must:

- **Make Stopping Narcotics Production and Trafficking Our Number One Foreign Policy Priority with Drug-Producing Countries**

  Secretary of State George Shultz never publicly discussed the international drug problem—yet it is the most serious national security problem faced by our nation. We must persuade and assist drug-producing countries to implement a massive, comprehensive multifaceted program to stop drugs at the source. If they agree to do so, the United States should substantially increase its programs of drug-enforcement training, equipment and material assistance, as well as aid for economic development and crop diversification. If they do not commit to such an effort, we must enact substantial trade and diplomatic penalties.

- **Hold a Western Hemispheric Summit on Drugs**

  Action in the United Nations and the Organization of American States is needed to determine the best course of action required to protect our sister democracies from going under. In countries like Colombia, international troops may be needed to deal with the crisis.

- **Give Life to the Mexico-United States Commission on Narcotics**

Mexico is the source of more than one-third of our drug traffic. We need a strategic plan, developed in concert with the Mexican government, to restore the effectiveness of Mexico's marijuana and opium eradication programs and to control the flow of drugs over the border into the United States.

- **Stop Banks from Laundering Drug Money**

Drug dealers are able to take their profits from our pain and launder them through banks around the world. We need to negotiate international banking agreements in order to freeze and seize the assets of drug pushers and put an end to their enterprises.

## Secure Our Borders

We are being overwhelmed at our borders by the invasion of drugs. It does not make sense to have 325,000 troops stationed in a Europe at peace, while, at home, we have a Coast Guard and a Customs Service incapable of protecting our citizens in the war against drugs. We need to increase interdiction spending by 50 percent over proposed 1989 levels.

## Bust the Dealers

State and local law enforcement officials have become gridlocked with the number of narcotics prosecutions and by violent and petty crime related to drug trafficking and abuse. Drug dealers know their chances of getting caught, or if caught, of being prosecuted, are slim, because the courts are so clogged. A recent Justice Department study found that nearly three-quarters of all men who were caught committing crimes in 12 major urban areas tested positive for drugs. Yet President Reagan's 1989 budget proposes *no* federal funds to assist in local law enforcement efforts. We must fully fund the $230 million mandated by the Narcotics Control Assistance Act and double that amount to aid local law enforcement.

## Provide Treatment on Demand

Our lack of drug treatment programs means suffering, death, crime, the spread of AIDS, increased health care costs, loss of productivity and much more. About 50 percent of drug abusers would like to kick their habit; perhaps 50 percent of these people would successfully complete a program if it were available. But now they have almost nowhere to go. The few programs that exist have long waiting lists. When they are turned away, they go back on the streets and back on the drugs. We must support the Presidential AIDS Commission proposal to increase spending on drug treatment programs to $2 billion per year.

## Expand Drug Education and Prevention Efforts

We must move beyond mere slogans urging us to "say no to drugs." We must put our money and our effort where our mouth is and begin drug education as early as possible. The Secretary of Education must lead the effort to set national standards for drug education and promote curriculum development. Because our best chance to control drug abuse is through education, we must significantly expand funding for education and prevention above the proposed 1989 level of $611 million.

From the president on down, we need strong leadership in an anti-drug campaign. If the federal government can embark on a successful public relations campaign to reduce cigarette smoking, we can wage a similar effort against drugs. In conjunction with the private sector, we should develop public service announcements and other anti-drug messages as part of a comprehensive program.

It is time to put up the necessary resources to meet this national security threat head-on. Current federal funding for all drug-related efforts is less than $4 billion—about five days of the Pentagon's budget. We must change priorities. We need Drug Wars far more than Star Wars.

**The Jackson Proposed War Against Drugs Budget**

| PROGRAMS | $ in Millions | | |
| --- | --- | --- | --- |
| | 1989 Reagan Proposed | 1989 Jackson Proposed | Difference |
| Law Enforcement & Interdiction | | | |
| Justice | $ 1,504 | 1,964 | +31% |
| Treasury (Customs) | 523 | 784 | +50% |
| Dept. of Transportation (Coast Guard) | 625 | 938 | +50% |
| Dept. of Defense | 98 | 98 | — |
| State Department | 111 | 300 | +270% |
| Other | 17 | 17 | — |
| **Subtotal** | **$2,878** | **4,101** | **+42%** |
| **Prevention** | 611 | 917 | +50% |
| **Treatment** | 425 | 1,685* | +396% |
| **TOTAL** | **$3,914** | **6,703** | **+71%** |

*This represents the federal portion of increasing treatment spending to $2 billion. We propose that the remaining 20% come from state and local governments.

# MEETING AMERICA'S HOUSING NEEDS

*We can see the homeless on the grates, but we cannot see the millions of families paying 40 percent or more of their income for rent. It is a disgrace that in the world's wealthiest nation, housing is a privilege, not a right.*

*—Jesse Jackson*

We are the best housed nation on earth. Yet millions of Americans are on the streets, with no place to call home. Millions more are only one paycheck or emergency away from eviction and homelessness. Countless others are doubled- or tripled-up in small apartments. And first-time homebuyers are fewer and fewer, as our incomes fail to keep pace with the rising cost of a new home. The once great American dream of a decent home and living environment is no longer achievable for too many Americans.

The causes of this crisis are many. Stagnant or declining real income is one, high real interest rates another. Gentrification, which provides housing to the highest bidder and an eviction notice to everyone else, is another cause. Finally, there's the wholesale withdrawal of the federal government from housing. Federal assistance to low-income housing declined by more than 75 percent since 1981—a national disgrace. Meanwhile, federal subsidies for middle and upper-income housing, in the form of homeowner income tax deductions for mortgage interest and property taxes, continue to cost the Treasury four times as much as the government spends on housing for the poor.

We need a president who is committed to the goal of decent, affordable housing for all Americans, who provides a practical program for meeting our housing needs, and who offers a sensible way to fund it.

To meet America's housing needs, I propose to:

## Meet Immediate Needs for Shelter

The root cause of homelessness for two to three million Americans is the lack of housing they can afford. People need jobs and sufficient income to pay current housing costs, and they deserve to live in dignity. As an immediate, stopgap measure to combat homelessness, emergency shelters and social services for the homeless must be adequately funded. Homeless families and individuals seeking emergency shelter should be offered housing allowances enabling them to pay for decent housing. Counseling should be available to help them find suitable homes. Lastly, we need a foreclosure relief program to step in and temporarily stave off eviction or mortgage foreclosure for people unable to pay their mortgage because they have lost their jobs or become ill. We had such a mortgage relief program in the 1930s—it even made money. We can have such a program again.

## Protect Subsidized and Public Housing

Fully half of the present stock of public and subsidized housing is threatened by conversion, sale or demolition. Over the next 15 years, as many as one million units of federally subsidized housing built during the 1960s and 1970s could vanish. Its disappearance would eliminate a large portion of the highest quality low-income housing in the nation—housing that would cost $130 billion to replace. Loss of federal subsidies, decisions by owners to pre-pay their subsidized mortgages, thus opting out of low-income housing and converting their units for rent or sale to wealthier tenants, and lack of adequate money for maintenance, repair and renovation can and will cause subsidized housing to vanish. With over ten million low-income Americans paying over 50 percent of their income for rent, America can't afford to lose these homes.

We must modernize public and assisted housing and bring it up to decent, livable standards. We must impose a moratorium on pre-payment of subsidized units and expiration of Section 8 subsidies. Additional subsidies, incentives to keep the housing subsidized or sell it to non-profits and co-ops, and disincentives to convert (such as a windfall profits tax) are all needed to stem the loss of these units. These measures are justified by the huge investment that the government has already put into the buildings and by the profit that developers have already made from them.

### Ensure Housing Affordability

Everyone ought to be able to afford the costs of decent, moderately-priced housing in their own community. Yet millions of Americans pay more than half of their incomes for rent, leaving them little for the other basic necessities of life—food, clothing, health care. We must provide a housing allowance or an income supplement to make up the difference between the fair market rent and a reasonable percentage of the renter's income. In cities with vacancy rates below five percent this should be coupled with a vigorous rehab and construction program to control inflation in housing costs.

The best way to make housing permanently more affordable is to produce it at lower cost. This can best be done by expanding the pool of non-profit housing developers and operators, who see their task as providing decent housing at the lowest possible cost. Our cities have vacant buildings and land and plenty of community groups willing to rehab and build. To meet our housing needs, we must bring the federal and local governments together in partnership with neighborhood-based community development corporations, labor unions, churches and synagogues, and tenant cooperatives. Capital grants from the government covering a portion of the construction costs can reduce the need for long-term financing. Profits on development costs can be limited or non-existent. Under this plan, housing will remain in the hands of the non-profit groups, preventing speculation on its resale.

### Help First-time Homebuyers

High mortgage interest rates and large downpayments are the single greatest obstacles to homeownership for low- and moderate-income Americans. We need to help this generation own a home. We must revise the low limits on Federal Home Administration mortgages to keep pace with rising home prices, thus enabling many homebuyers to be eligible for assistance once again. We also need to lower FHA downpayment restrictions from 20 percent to 10 percent. We should create a revolving loan fund for downpayment assistance. Such a fund could loan money for downpayments at a low rate of interest, to be paid back over five to ten years. The government could also share in any cost appreciation realized as a result of the sale of the house.

Such an ambitious housing program can begin right now. Before Reaganomics, the federal government used to spend $33 billion per year on housing. In today's dollars, that's well over $40 billion. We currently spend $8 billion. We can make a huge downpayment on our housing needs by cutting military spending, without cutting our defense, and by restoring tax fairness. We can also use public pension funds—with federal guarantees to protect workers' retirement income—to invest in low-cost housing.

Builders need contracts. Construction workers need jobs. Millions of Americans need decent, affordable housing. It's time to reestablish the national housing goal set by Congress in the 1949 Housing Act, "a decent home and suitable living environment for every American family." We must and we will.

# THE JACKSON EDUCATION PLAN:

## A Commitment To Action

*If our schools are failing our children, it's because our government is failing our schools. The real underachievers are those in power—from the statehouses to Washington, D.C.—who are not willing to make education this nation's top priority, its first line of defense, its ultimate weapon for national security.*

*—Jesse Jackson*

Among the truths we hold self-evident in this country is that education is a human right and a public good. We believe that every child has the right to learn, regardless of creed, class or color. We believe that educated citizens are essential to a productive economy and a healthy society. We believe that educated citizens are the foundation and the safeguard of American democracy.

Knowing all this, we must ask in the late 1980s: what has happened to our commitment to public education? After so many decades of progress in expanding educational opportunity, of enriching the next generation, have we stopped moving forward?

The answer depends on where we look. At the top of the educational ladder, where there are indeed many excellent schools, some children are doing very well. But millions of others are floundering at the bottom, in the inner cities and in impoverished rural America, where schools have been abandoned.

In between, in the aging suburbs and small cities, the majority of children attend schools that struggle to stay ahead of shrinking tax revenues and rising numbers of families in need. These schools have little left over for excellence.

In education, as in the economy, opportunities are polarizing. Some crucial rungs are missing in the middle of the educational ladder as well as at the bottom. Too many children are being left out or left behind. As a nation, this is not progress—it is the beginning of a crisis.

According to a recent study by the Committee for Economic Development, 30 percent of young children are currently at risk of school failure. By the year 2000, if current trends are not reversed, half of our children will be at risk. These are not somebody else's children, living far away. These are *your* children, or your neighbor's or your cousin's. They live down the road or down the block. They are the next generation, and we are at risk of losing half of them to ignorance and waste.

Experts cite multiple reasons for the alarming number of children at risk: among children entering school this year, 30 percent will be latch-key kids, 14 percent will be born out of wedlock, 40 percent will come from broken homes, 15 percent will speak English as a second language, 10 percent will have poorly educated parents, 15 percent will be physically or mentally handicapped. Our family structures, social support systems and population patterns have changed radically in recent years, placing new kinds of stress on our schools.

But the fundamental reason that problems turn into failures is that we are not equipping schools to meet the needs of today's children and tomorrow's world. These problems are not insurmountable—but schools are going to need a qualitatively new level of commitment and innovation if they are to meet the educational and social challenges they now confront.

We have found solutions before when this country has faced educational crisis. When two million GIs came back from World War II without jobs, we passed the GI Bill and sent them to trade school and college, and trained a modern workforce in the process. When the Soviets sent up Sputnik and challenged our national pride, we didn't turn to the Pentagon; we passed the National Defense Education Act and enlarged the pool of college graduates.

When the Supreme Court put justice on the agenda and declared that separate is *not* equal, we integrated thousands of school systems across the country—and where the commitment to equality was sincere, integration has worked. When a growing economy gave working-class families the chance to send their kids to college for the first time, we expanded our universities and built hundreds of community colleges.

Educational problems can be solved—today we've got successful schools in every kind of neighborhood, working with every kind of child, in every social circumstance, proving that we can make schools work. Educators have learned a great deal in recent years about what needs to be done to improve mediocre schools and to turn failing schools around.

The question isn't really *how* to do it. The question is *why* it's not being done, in more places, for more children.

## Federal Responsibilities

One basic reason schools are falling behind is that the federal government hasn't answered the call for help. In fact, the main item on Ronald Reagan's educational agenda has been to undermine public education by turning funding over to private schools through vouchers and tax credits. His main message to educators

has been: you must do more with less.

Between 1981-87, the Reagan administration reduced social service funding for families and children by 53 percent. Between 1981-88, it reduced the federal educational budget by 15 percent, with the greatest cuts occurring in programs for the disadvantaged.

One result of these policies is that thousands of aspiring young people could not go to college. Although Congress defeated the worst proposals for cutting college aid, federal loans and grants have stagnated while college costs have soared. And since 1982, Reagan has eliminated $2 billion in Social Security benefits to college students. Their American dream got transferred to the Pentagon budget. Their tuition money is buying a B-1 bomber or weapons for the contras. This is educational violence against our youth and our country.

Another result of these policies is that children sit hungry in their classrooms because food assistance and school nutrition programs have been slashed. By 1985, three million children no longer received school lunches. This too is educational violence.

There is equal violence behind the cutbacks made in compensatory reading programs, services to handicapped children, after-school recreation programs and in-school job training. The Head Start program, by far the most successful of all government education programs since the GI Bill, today serves only 18 percent of all eligible children.

There is willful neglect in the fact that 70 percent of bilingual children receive no language assistance in school, and in the fact that 13 percent of all 17-year-olds are functionally illiterate. It's an unnatural disaster that 28 percent of teenagers drop-out of high school, and the drop-out rate reaches over 50 percent in some big city school systems. As many as half of all college entrants fail to graduate because they are not well prepared or do not have the money to finish.

There is shameful short-sightedness when half of the nation's teachers will leave or retire in the next decade, but teaching remains the most underpaid and devalued of all professions. The teaching crisis is even more stark when we realize that the number of minority teachers is severely declining just as the minority student population is sharply rising. We are blocking the pipelines to progress when talented students can't get educated as teachers, or find too little reward for choosing teaching careers.

Finally, there is a terrible price to pay when millions of children are deprived of skills, self-esteem, and sometimes life itself, because of drugs, teen pregnancy, street violence and a culture that tells them that greed is great. Across every socio-economic group, in every region of the country, children are faced with a crisis in values, a crisis of purpose, a crisis of caring. We will reap what we sow, and this society is sowing despair in too many places, including our schools.

But let's speak plainly: if our schools are failing our children, it is because our government is failing our schools. The real under-achievers are those in power—from the state house to the White House—who are not willing to make education this nation's top priority, its first line of defense, its ultimate weapon for national security. It's Ronald Reagan and William Bennett who have flunked the American education test.

Nor should we put our trust in the self-professed reformers who say they want excellence for all, but only put up the money for a few to excel. It's not enough to announce the good programs you endorse, if you're not willing to put resources and talent behind your proposals. It's time to put our money where our mouth is for public education.

## The Jackson Program For Education

The issue here is presidential leadership. Our children and our schools don't need any more broken promises. They need a program of action, and the priorities to make it work.

First and foremost, we need to *double* the federal education budget in the next administration.

Right now, nearly $300 billion of the federal budget goes to the military and only $19 billion goes to education. That isn't national security—it's a national disgrace. It's also a disgrace that the richest Americans are paying $55 billion less in taxes than they paid ten years ago.

If we only eliminated military waste—$30 billion a year by official government estimates, we could eliminate the educational waste of nearly one million high school drop-outs each year. If we re-allocated funds for military intervention in Central America, we could fund early intervention in our primary schools. If we correct tax regression from the top down, we can afford educational progression from the bottom up.

Now we all know that you can't just throw dollars at social problems. But we also know, if we're honest about solving those problems, that adequate funding is the foundation for effective programs. You get what you pay for.

We also know that the federal government can't do it all. In fact, the major role in education rightly belongs to the states and to local communities. Many states and local districts have been taking the lead in school reform in this decade. But their efforts have been held back, and others have not begun, because of two overwhelming obstacles: the lack of sufficient resources and the tremendous inequality of resources that do exist.

It is precisely the responsibility of the federal government to marshall national resources and to guarantee equal opportunity. In order to effectively enlarge resources and opportunities, however, the federal government must also contribute to the quality of our education system. We need to restructure the learning environment, to *modernize and humanize* schools, if we genuinely expect all children to thrive within them.

There are five areas for immediate action. Within each, program initiatives and spending targets are proposed to underscore our overall goals and to indicate what the federal government could achieve if current Department of Education spending levels were doubled over the course of the next administration.

### Priority #1: Invest in Children from the Start

We need to invest in our children from infancy up, not high-tech down. There is no other intervention that has proven to be as educationally effective or cost-effective as early childhood development programs. For every dollar spent in Head Start, we have saved $5-7 down the road in social service, criminal justice and remedial education costs.

Pre-school education programs must be expanded to reach every child in need. The Jackson education budget proposes $7.1 billion for a new Office of Pre-school Education, within the Department of Education, to enlarge Head Start as a community-based program and to develop parallel programs in child-care centers and schools. This commitment, nearly five times what we are now spending, would ensure a place for every one of the 2.25 million children, ages three to five, living in poverty in America today.

At the same time, federal health and human service policies must ensure that children entering school are healthy and ready to learn. The Jackson education budget restores cuts and expands programs for prenatal and infant care, school breakfast and lunch, and family health services. It also provides quality child care to working parents and those seeking jobs or job skills.

As children enter elementary school, we need to address educational disadvantage at the earliest possible moment. We need better and broader programs to help kids catch up in basic skills and language skills; to provide cultural enrichment and pride; to deal with special developmental or behavioral needs; to reduce the teacher load in overcrowded classrooms; to help parents encourage their children at home.

We must also start delivering these services in more enlightened ways that don't segregate or humiliate children. If we broaden the mainstream to deal effectively with a spectrum of needs, if we treat each child as a unique individual, we won't produce schools that are driven by tests and students that are stigmatized by tracking.

Our investment in children must create a level playing field, raising the ground for those who have too long been under-served. The Jackson education budget restores and expands Chapter 1 Compensatory Education funding to $6.5 billion to assist local schools in serving every disadvantaged child enrolled. It restores and expands funding to improve compensatory education techniques by revamping

the Follow Through program.

The Jackson program raises funding for bilingual education by four times the current level to aid states in meeting the sharply rising need for both language assistance and bilingual skills. The Jackson program restores full funding to education for handicapped children, doubling funds for pre-school programs for the handicapped. It doubles federal assistance for education of the homeless. The Jackson program restores Indian Education to full funding, after 40 percent cuts under Reagan, and restores the 66 percent cut from the Women's Educational Equity program.

In contrast with the Reagan Department of Education, we must provide the oversight and technical assistance needed to ensure that new resources produce effective learning approaches in all of these areas.

We also need to invest in the physical environment that greets disadvantaged children when they go to school. We need to change the unspoken messages that students receive in schools where paint peels from the ceiling, where the playgrounds are asphalt and broken glass, where 40 kids are packed into kindergarten classrooms, where schools are designed like industrial warehouses. Recognizing that much more will be needed over time, the Jackson education budget pledges an initial $200 million in incentive grants for an Urban School Rehabilitation program to help rebuild schools in the neediest inner cities.

### Priority #2: Invest in Teachers

The second priority for education is to invest in teachers. Every major report on the subject agrees: teachers need more pay and more say in how the schools are run. It's time for bottom-up reform, time to improve learning conditions by improving working conditions in the local school.

Federal dollars can help the states raise teaching benefits, reward innovative teaching approaches, and develop models for school improvement that give teachers greater creativity and responsibility. The Jackson education program creates a $100 million School Restructuring Research Program to assist local schools, districts and states in developing comprehensive, teacher-led school improvement models.

Federal dollars can also expand programs to upgrade teachers' academic and classroom skills, and to impart the cultural awareness and openness that is essential to effective teaching. The Jackson program increases teacher training funds to $400 million, several times more than current levels, to sponsor nationwide teacher centers, career development opportunities and teacher enrichment programs.

We need a massive recruitment drive for teachers, especially minority teachers, starting with high school college-bound programs. If colleges put the money and energy into teacher recruitment they put into recruiting and developing football and basketball players, we'd already be halfway there. The Jackson education program creates a $1 billion National Teacher Corps, providing college scholarships to talented young people in return for teaching service.

It's also time to recognize that educators are public service professionals, not public servants. Teachers deserve the full protection of labor law, as do other public employees. The federal government should play a leadership role in promoting collective bargaining rights for public school teachers nationwide. It should condition education aid to the states on upholding fair labor practices and should energetically endorse salary increases across the teaching profession.

### Priority #3: Connect Schools to Communities

To successfully address modern social and educational realities, schools need to renew connections with families, neighborhoods and workplaces.

The single-most important indicator of how well children will do in school is the education level of their parents and family members. Yet, 30 percent of American adults are functionally or marginally illiterate. The Jackson education program commits $150 million to launch a nationwide family literacy campaign, linking parent and child learning through community- and school-based programs.

In addition, the Jackson education budget proposes three federal demonstration programs to enhance: (1) parent participation in the schools; (2) the use of schools for community services; (3) the direct involvement of parents, teachers and citizens in local school governance. Such programs already exist in excellent schools, where community members work as aides or volunteer as tutors and mentors, where schools sponsor community cultural and recreational programs, where parent-teacher councils set local school goals. Our job is to see that these models for connecting schools to families and communities get out to the states and districts where this involvement does not yet exist.

Clearly, there is a pressing need to expand ways that schools address the pressures of adolescence. This society cannot bury its head in the sand, ignoring the risks confronting today's youngsters. The Jackson education budget proposes an initial $350 million to create: (1) a drop-out prevention demonstration program; (2) an adolescent support and drug-abuse prevention program; (3) a National Youth Community Service Corps, sponsoring local service projects.

Drop-out prevention programs need greatly expanded resources if they are to include the key ingredients for success: early intervention, parental cooperation, and personal as well as academic support for staying in school. We must also support re-entry programs for youth who have left school, building on the effective models provided by many small-scale, alternative high schools.

In addition, every middle and secondary school needs civics and counseling programs where teens can deal honestly and openly with problems of sexual responsibility, pregnancy, AIDS, drug abuse, alcohol abuse, child abuse, violence and suicide. These programs should draw on parents and community members as well as in-school health professionals.

Every high school should have a community service program where young people can gain skills—and feel productive and responsible—by helping others in their community. We need to start teaching democratic values by example and by experience, helping young people discover that they can make a difference in society.

Equally, we need to strengthen the links between school and work, links that are stretched thin in areas with high unemployment or too many dead-end jobs. The Jackson budget for vocational education restores funding cuts and also funds a major revamping of vocational programs.

Federal funds should support reforms to increase the academic components of vocational education—if we want to prepare youngsters for tomorrow's workplace, we need to develop problem-solving minds as well as skilled hands. We need to abolish sex stereotyping and discrimination, and to spur greater parent and worker involvement. We need to deepen the commitments of the business community to vocational education, so they can help schools provide up-to-date skills, appropriate training, and meaningful work experience.

### Priority #4: Open the Doors to Higher Education

Our investment in children, in teachers, in parents and communities won't meet the challenge unless we also open the doors to higher education and continuing education. The Jackson program calls for a student aid allocation of $16 billion by 1993, nearly double current spending.

This country should be able to say to every high school student: if you qualify for college, you can go—and you can finish. To accomplish this goal, we need to expand the numbers receiving aid, we need to raise the proportion of grants to loans, and we need to raise assistance levels.

In addition, student aid should be available to the long-term unemployed or the displaced worker who wants to re-train for a new job. Loan forgiveness programs should encourage both young people and working adults to enter human service careers in needy communities. Needy students whose Social Security survivor benefits were terminated by the Reagan administration should qualify for federally funded student aid.

### Priority #5: Ensure Equal Opportunity

Fifth and finally, the federal government has a special responsibility to safeguard civil rights and equal opportunity in education, both legally and fiscally.

We need to resume affirmative action in ed-ucation and end negative reaction. We need to promote equitable funding between states, between districts and between schools within each state. We need to protect students' rights to receive appropriate educational services and parents' rights to monitor school progress. We need to defend teachers' rights to academic freedom in a climate of free and open inquiry.

The Jackson education program allocates $650 million, redirected from the current Chapter 2 block grant, to form a State Equity Aid grant program to encourage more equitable local education funding and more vigorous school improvement programs.

The Jackson program redirects and restores funds to assist school systems in implementing desegregation plans that increase overall school quality. The Jackson program also expands funding to the Department of Education's Office of Civil Rights to insure that thorough monitoring of federal mandates and school compliance is carried out. It's time to put the Justice Department back to work for the Department of Education.

## Can We Afford This Commitment?

Our task is to combine quality and equality in every public school, where others have pitted excellence and equity against each other. Our task is to give every child the chance to be a productive participant in this society, where others have given up or given too little.

The ultimate issue is, of course, can the federal government afford it? Can we make a $40 billion commitment to education, over and above what states and localities are doing? Let's consider a hypothetical scenario.

What if the United States were struck by a mysterious and colossal national disaster, with the result that the children who are now in our schools were the only children we would have for a very long time, for more than a generation. What would we do?

We would suddenly feel that each of these children, these irreplaceable children, was very precious. We wouldn't care what color skin they had, or whether their parents spoke with an accent, or which side of the tracks they lived on. We would treasure all the potential they had to offer—we would celebrate the richness of their cultural diversity and individual uniqueness.

We would immediately stop running schools like industrial assembly lines, stamping out students in the molds of Cadillacs or Chevettes; there would be no margin for factory rejects.

We would rebuild schools as learning communities, where teachers and students had the time and space to interact as people. Students would be rewarded for initiative, cooperation, participation and self-discipline. Schools would be connected to local neighborhoods and to global concerns. We would honor teachers and parents as guardians of our future and we would ask them to tell us about each student and each school, to show us what works and doesn't work so that every child's education would be excellent.

We would help families nurture their children and make sure they were well-housed, well-fed and well-clothed. We would find every student a place in college or a productive job after high school, because we would have to count on them, and only them, to sustain economic growth. If today's school children were the only children we were ever going to know, we'd find a way to make a commitment to education; we would launch a national crusade.

That's exactly what the Jackson education program is—a national crusade for American education, from infancy to adulthood. Because even though there are more children to follow, the students in our schools today *are* irreplaceable. Each one of them is precious, each one is somebody's child and hope, each one is a human being and a national resource.

We can afford this crusade because nothing is more important than our children—because nothing is more important than their opportunity to live securely in a humane and democratic society. We can afford a decent education for every child because the alternative, mediocrity and neglect, carries far higher and far more tragic costs.

A good education is a much better investment in public security than prisons or welfare or unemployment benefits. A good education is a much better investment in national defense than Star Wars or Midgetman missiles. A good education is a much better investment in democratic values than covert wars in impoverished lands.

The American people believe in public education and are willing to support it. We know the schools aren't perfect, aren't as good as they should be. But we also know that the schools belong to us, they belong to our communities—and we know that with our government behind us, we can make them better.

We know that the future of our American dreams depends on the quality and equality we invest today in every child, teacher and classroom.

Having come all this way, we don't want to turn back, we don't want to stop. We want to move forward, so the next generation will see that we cared enough to set our priorities straight.

## The Jackson Education Budget

The Jackson Education Budget is provided as a guide to overall education priorities. Overall, the budget proposes a *doubling* of education funding over the course of the next administration, from approximately $18.8 billion in 1988 ($20.1 billion including Head Start from the Health and Human Services budget) to $40.5 billion in 1993.

The budget restores full funding to many programs which suffered significant cutbacks since 1981. In addition, the budget proposes new funding initiatives in a number of areas.

This budget reflects the need to re-organize several aspects of the U.S. Department of Education in order to improve program quality, and to target federal aid more strategically to schools in need. Chapter 2 block grants to states would be re-directed into a comprehensive teacher training package, and into state equity aid to equalize local funding and services to deficient schools.

A School Improvement and Restructuring grant package would consolidate existing programs and establish new programs to address, in complementary fashion: urban school rehabilitation, drop-out prevention, adolescent support and drug-abuse prevention, youth community service, parent and community participation, local school governance and desegregation. A School Restructuring Research Program, with a nationwide field capacity drawn from educators, would support these school improvement initiatives.

In addition, the Jackson Department of Education would create a new Office of Pre-school Education to oversee and coordinate the expansion of Head Start and equivalent pre-school education programs as a federal entitlement to low-income children, aged three to five.

## Sources

Ann Bastian, Norm Fruchter, Marilyn Gittell, Colin Greer and Kenneth Haskins, *Choosing Equality: The Case for Democratic Schooling,* Temple University Press, Philadelphia, 1986.

*Children in Need: Investment Strategies for the Educationally Disadvantaged,* The Research and Policy Committee of the Committee for Economic Development, New York, September 1987.

*Barriers to Excellence: Our Children at Risk,* Report of the National Board of Inquiry of the National Coalition of Advocates for Students, Boston, 1985.

Linda Darling-Hammond and Barnett Berry, *The Evolution of Teacher Policy,* The Rand Corporation, Washington, D.C., 1988.

*The Forgotten Half: Non-College Youth in America,* Report of the William T. Grant Foundation Commission on Work, Family and Citizenship, Washington, D.C., January 1988.

*Call to Action: A Briefing Book on the Status of American Children in 1988,* Report of the Children's Defense Fund, Washington, D.C., 1988.

Harold Hodgekinson, *All One System,* Institute for Educational Leadership, Washington, D.C., 1985.

**The Jackson Education Budget**

| | 1989 Reagan Proposed | 1993[1] Baseline | 1993 Jackson Proposed | 1993 Increase Over Baseline |
|---|---|---|---|---|
| | | ($ In Millions) | | |
| **PROGRAMS** | | | | |
| **Pre-School[2]** | | | | |
|     Head Start | $1,206 | | 4,140 | |
|     School-based | — | | 3,000 | |
| **Subtotal** | **$1,206** | **1,469** | **7,140** | **5,671** |
| **Elementary & Secondary Education** | | | | |
|     Compensatory/Chapter 1 | 3,833 | | 6,500 | |
|     Impact Aid | 756 | | 897 | |
|     Indian Education | 31 | | 121 | |
|     Chapter 2[3] | 487 | | 0 | |
|     Teacher Training | n/a | | 400 | |
|     State Equity Aid | — | | 1,000 | |
|     Family Literacy | — | | 150 | |
|     School Improvement & Restructuring | 202 | | 757 | |
|     Other | 29 | | 77 | |
| **Subtotal** | **$5,338** | **7,222** | **9,902** | **2,680** |
| **Bilingual & Immigrant Education** | **$163** | **227** | **647** | **420** |
| **Special Education & Rehabilitation** | **$3,387** | **4,145** | **4,286** | **141** |
| **Vocational & Adult Education** | **$979** | **1,174** | **1,500** | **326** |
| **Post-Secondary Education** | | | | |
|     Student Aid (Pell & SSI Survivors) | 5,319 | | 10,725 | |
|     Student Loans | 2,628 | | 3,997 | |
|     Teacher Corps | — | | 1,000 | |
|     Other | 529 | | 700 | |
| **Subtotal** | **$8,476** | **10,229** | **16,122** | **5,893** |
| **Research & Libraries** | **$245** | **270** | **574** | **304** |
| **Department Management** | **$308** | **339** | **354** | **15** |
| **TOTAL** | **$20,102** | **25,075** | **40,525** | **15,450** |

[1]Amounts are based on Congressional Budget Office estimates and are not available at the program level.

[2]Pre-school category (Head Start) currently exists under the Department of Health and Human Services, not the Department of Education.

[3]The Jackson budget redirects Chapter 2 funds into teacher training and state equity aid.

# THE JACKSON NATIONAL HEALTH CARE PROGRAM

*To be a good and a great nation—not just a strong nation—we must provide basic health coverage to all Americans. Only the United States and South Africa, of the industrialized nations in the world, do not have some form of national health care for all their citizens.*

—*Jesse Jackson*

Because they can't afford it, millions of Americans don't get the health care they need. Among industrialized nations, only our country and South Africa lack a health program that assures care for all. Health care must be established as a right, and this right, like our other constitutional rights, must be guaranteed at the federal level. The federal government must—and can—assure that high quality, comprehensive care is available to all Americans. But fulfilling this responsibility will require a bold initiative: a National Health Program (NHP).

Our health care system is failing. We have the most technologically advanced and expensive care in the world, yet we deny the most basic services to millions. We waste tens of billions of dollars on billing and insurance bureaucracy, while we skimp on prenatal care and immunizations. We squander $3 billion each year on health care advertising, while a million families are turned away from hospitals because they cannot pay. We are spending enough on health, but we are spending it on the wrong things. Patchwork reforms cannot solve these problems. Only an NHP can.

While millions of Americans are uninsured or underinsured, and our politicians declare that we cannot afford care for all, Canada has covered everyone under a program that costs 25 percent less than our system. Every Canadian has complete coverage for virtually all care; hospitals and doctors don't even send bills to patients. Canadians still enjoy high quality care and a free choice of doctors and hospitals, but they are free from the financial burden of illness.

Americans deserve no less. It is time to bring our best minds together to determine the best course of action for providing universal and comprehensive health coverage to all Americans at a price we *can* afford.

## The Problems with Our Current System

### Inadequate Coverage and Poor Health

Thirty-seven million Americans have no health insurance, and 25 million more have such inadequate insurance that illness could lead to bankruptcy. Most of the underinsured live in families headed by full-time workers; more than a third are children. As a result, 40 percent of all toddlers never get the immunizations they need to prevent illness.

For minorities and the poor, the situation is even worse—more than half of low-income African Americans and Hispanics are uninsured, and the proportion of the poor covered by Medicaid has fallen 20 percent in the last decade. As a consequence, more than a third of African American mothers and more than a fifth of white mothers receive prenatal care either too late or not at all.

Even people with insurance face rising costs and falling coverage; Medicare premiums for the elderly have increased rapidly and many employers are cutting back on coverage. The American people pay higher out-of-pocket expenses for medical care than the people of any other nation, yet they still lack adequate care.

The result of this poor health care is a disgracefully high infant mortality rate, and much suffering from preventable illness. Among industrialized countries the United States is tied for the worst infant mortality rate. For people of all ages, the death rate actually increased in 1985 (the latest year for which figures are available), an unprecedented deterioration of our nation's health. For minorities, the death rate, already 50 percent higher than for whites, is rising even faster, and the infant mortality rate is worse than in some Third World countries. Today in the U.S., a child dies needlessly every 50 minutes—from poverty, malnutrition and inadequate medical care.

## Wrong Priorities

Our health-care system is oriented toward fixing damage rather than preventing it. We spend $2,000 per person each year for health care and only $25 per person for medical research to prevent and cure illness. We pay $100,000 for intensive care for a premature baby, but we refuse to pay $800 for the prenatal care that could prevent prematurity. Thus, North Carolina has the same number of births as Sweden but much worse prenatal care, and needs twice as many neonatal intensive care beds. Most insurance policies won't cover routine preventive care like Pap tests; so, instead, we bear the human and financial costs of care diagnosed too late. We pay a billion dollars to care for the four million people injured at work, rather than expanding occupational health and safety programs to prevent workplace accidents. Because our efforts to prevent the spread of AIDS have been painfully, even criminally slow, we face a $16 billion bill for the care of AIDS patients in 1991. Three hundred thousand people die each year from smoking, while tobacco companies continue to entice young people to become addicted to nic-

otine. Reorienting our priorities to put prevention first can save lives and money.

## Excessive Costs

We spend more on health care than any other society, more than $500 billion each year. We are spending enough, but too little of that spending goes for appropriate care and too much is wasted on bureaucracy, billing, profits and on inappropriate and unnecessary care.

If the United States adopted a Canadian-style NHP we could save $60 billion per year on billing, bureaucracy and exorbitant profits, according to a recent Harvard study published in the prestigious *New England Journal of Medicine*. The report found that fully 22 percent of health care dollars go for billing and administration, twice as much as in the Canadian NHP. Eighteen percent of our hospital costs are consumed by billing and administration; Canada spends eight percent. Our health insurance companies collected $22 billion more than they paid out in 1985, five times the proportion spent for overhead in the Canadian program.

We also waste billions on unneeded hospitalizations, operations and tests. Studies have shown that as much as 20 percent of surgery may be unnecessary, adding more to doctor's incomes than patients' lives. Billions of dollars are spent on useless laboratory tests ordered only because doctors fear malpractice suits.

Costs are also driven up by the multi-billion dollar profits of health-care corporations. For-profit chain hospitals make profits by charging more—36 percent more than freestanding hospitals—giving less nursing care, and excluding the uninsured. Even the Peer Review Organizations (PROs), which contract with the federal government to monitor the Medicare program for abuse, are enjoying record profits—$27.5 million in the first two years—while average hospital profits on Medicare patients have more than doubled.

In the most extreme cases, the search for profits has led to criminal behavior. International Medical Centers (IMC), the largest HMO in the Medicare program, signed up thousands of elderly patients. It then refused to pay for their care: a sure-fire way to make money. The IMC president was finally indicted for fraud, and protracted investigations revealed that

IMC had hired nine ex-Reagan administration officials to smooth the way with the government.

IMC is not the only medical corporation with powerful friends in Washington. The powerful lobbies representing medical, insurance, hospital and corporate interests have enormous influence in Congress and the White House. The current Republican administration is crowded with individuals who worked for and were part of these business interest groups. For instance, Vice President Bush used to be a director of Lilly, one of the largest and most profitable drug and medical equipment companies. These interest groups are also very powerful in the Congress. In the last two elections PACs representing the health industry gave candidates for federal office 14 times as much money as did PACs favoring national health coverage.

Rather than instituting an NHP that would cut costs by slashing bureaucracy and unneeded care, the president and Congress have tried to control costs by stimulating "competition" in the medical-care sector. By having hospitals and other providers competing for patients, the price and overall costs of health services were supposed to decline. But they did not. The market does not work in medical care. The providers, such as hospitals, nursing homes, physicians and insurance companies, have enormous influence in shaping prices, costs and expenditures. Recent studies have shown that competition has exacerbated the problems of high costs; the rate of growth of national health expenditures (corrected for the overall inflation rate) has been larger in the 1980s (the "competitive" years) than in the 1970s. As costs have continued to increase, health benefits coverage has further declined.

### Public Money, Private Control

While government pays a great deal for health care in the private sector—more than a trillion dollars in all since 1965—it exercises little real control of the health industry that it funds. Private hospitals have rushed to accept government money, but they are unwilling to provide care when compensation isn't there— even though most hospital buildings and equipment were bought with government money. Even in so-called non-profit hospitals, the first person who greets a patient is a billing clerk put there to make sure that non-paying patients don't get in.

While government has paid for a massive expansion of private health care, the public sector has been starved for funds. Public hospitals have been left as pitiful remnants of their former selves, housed in aging buildings, equipped with outdated machines, serving largely those uninsured patients who are unprofitable for private hospitals. Since 1965, six of 19 public hospitals in New York City have been closed, as have 29 of California's 66 county hospitals and the only public hospitals serving Detroit and Philadelphia. Meanwhile, David Jones, head of the second largest for-profit chain, was paid $21 million in a single year (much of it coming from government funds), making him one of the highest-paid executives in the United States. The $21 million salary he pays himself would pay for health care for 10,000 people. We, through our government, already pay for most hospital care. It is time that our government assures that our money is more wisely spent.

## The Canadian Approach: Lessons for the United States

While in the United States tens of millions are uninsured and denied care, in Canada everyone is covered and there are virtually no out-of-pocket costs. While in the United States health care consumes 11.2 percent of the Gross National Product (GNP), Canada spends only 8.6 percent of GNP. We spend $500 more each year per person than Canada, but we get much less. The key to the Canadian success is a publicly administered NHP that covers everyone for all needed care.

Every Canadian is completely covered by the public insurance program administered by their provincial or territorial government. The federal government sets minimum standards for the provincial programs, and pays about half of the costs—more for poor provinces and less for the wealthy ones. Patients have free choice of hospitals and doctors, who collect their fees directly from the NHP. Since virtually all costs are covered by the public program, there is almost no private insurance.

Covering everyone in a province under a single comprehensive insurance plan assures equal financial access to care for all, and it greatly simplifies paying bills and other administration. In fact, hospitals don't even bill for each individual patient. Instead, they receive a single lump-sum budget to cover all of their operating expenses. This saves billions in hospital administrative costs annually.

Doctors' paperwork is also much simpler and cheaper—they bill a single insurance plan instead of 1,500 different ones as in the United States.

Public administration of the Canadian insurance system is much more efficient than the private U.S. insurance industry. Whereas U.S. insurers take as much as 16 percent of premiums for "overhead," overhead in the Canadian NHP is only 2.5 percent—about the same as our Medicare program. Finally, the Canadian NHP also has much more effective health planning measures than in the United States. In Canada, hospital facilities are expanded where there's a shortage and curtailed where there's a surplus. In contrast, 40 percent of U.S. hospital beds are empty, and hospitals compete to buy the latest high-tech gadgets—whether needed or not.

Overall, Canada spends 50 percent less of its health care dollars on billing and bureaucracy than the U.S. It also saves large amounts through improved health planning and lower rates of unnecessary surgery. In addition, doctors' incomes are about 10 percent lower than the $120,000 average in the United States.

As illustrated in Figure 1, the savings in Canada through a National Health Program have effectively contained costs (in comparison to the United States) despite vast increases in care. Prior to the passage of the NHP in 1966, Canadian health costs were almost identical to those in the United States. Since then, U.S. costs have risen more than twice as fast.

## Piecemeal Reform: A Prescription for Failure

Despite the obvious success of the NHP in Canada, most American politicians continue to advocate only piecemeal reforms—bandaids for our sick health care system when major surgery is needed. But the piecemeal approach simply exchanges one problem for another. Without more fundamental reform, we cannot improve access to care without raising costs.

For instance, the recently passed employer-mandated health insurance program in Massachusetts will cost about $1,500 per person per year (covering 100,000 people at a cost of $600 million over the next four years). Such a program nationally would cost $20-40 billion per year and still not meet the needs of the elderly, workers with inadequate insurance who face high co-payments, or the thousands bankrupted by the cost of nursing home care.

Though efforts in the individual states are laudable, a federal program is necessary to as-

Figure 1:

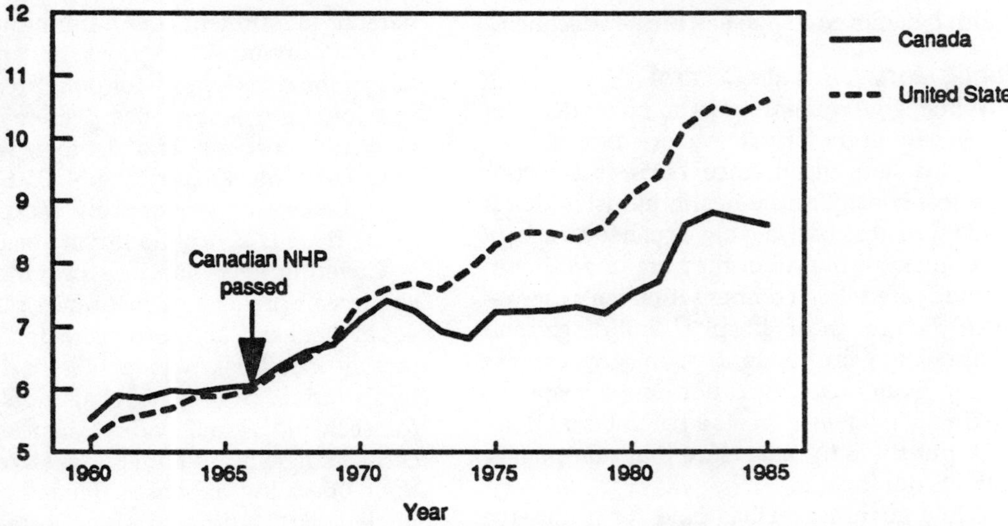

Health Expenditures as a Percent of GNP: United States and Canada, 1960–1985

sure that all Americans have the same chance to get good care. A federally-administered program is the only way to assure adequate funding in poorer areas and to prevent regressive state governments from blocking access to care.

In effect, since 1965, we have been conducting two experiments in national health programs. One, Medicare, provides health insurance for the elderly under the auspices of the federal government. The other, Medicaid, provides health insurance for the poor through a program funded jointly by the federal and state governments, and it is administered by the states. Although Medicare has a number of defects (especially failure to provide comprehensive coverage) the program has been efficiently managed and is popular with both patients and providers. The administrative costs are much lower than for similar programs in the private sector. Medicaid, on the other hand, suffers from limitations placed on it by different states, reflecting biases against minorities and the poor as well as differences in the health of the economy in the various states. Many states have demeaning eligibility tests, poor quality care for recipients, and inadequate access to many Medicaid-covered services even for qualified recipients (due, in part, to low reimbursement rates set by the states, so that providers are reluctant to care for Medicaid recipients).

Piecemeal reforms at the federal level, such as catastrophic health care proposals for the elderly, plans to mandate employer- provided insurance and proposals for expanded long-term care are well intentioned but insufficient. Catastrophic care proposals exclude coverage for some catastrophically expensive but much-needed health services like nursing home care and will leave the elderly with high out-of-pocket costs. Similarly, recent employer-mandated health-care coverage plans would still leave 14 million Americans uninsured, and 25 million underinsured. And long-term care proposals being debated cover some vital services but not other crucial needs.

More important, these patchwork proposals are expensive because they leave in place all of the waste and inefficiency of the current system. According to the *New England Journal of Medicine*, by 1993 we would pay $94 billion more per year in excessive billing, administration and advertising costs and in excessive profits than under a Canadian style NHP (see Table 1 on the next page). It is the fragmentation of our health care system that allows—indeed requires—this waste. As long as people are insured by 1,500 different programs, each with different eligibility rules, coverage and co-payments, the health care bureaucracy will remain enormously complex and expensive—and cost containment and access will remain in conflict. Only an NHP that covers everyone under a single program can end this fragmentation and waste. Only when all the funding flows through a single program can hospitals and nursing homes be paid on a lump-sum basis, virtually eliminating the cost of billing. Only an NHP can simultaneously solve the problems of access and cost.

## The Jackson National Health Program: Universal and Comprehensive Care

While the Canadians haven't solved all of their health problems their achievements offer a model for reform of the U.S. health system. Of course, the United States cannot simply import the Canadian model of health delivery directly. It needs to be studied more to determine its applicability to the U.S. Thus, the first act of a Jackson administration would be to empower a commission of experts to review the best possible way to implement a National Health Program. Whether or not the Canadian model, or that of another country, is used there are several characteristics that such an NHP should have.

The National Health Program (NHP) should be *universal*, providing coverage to all Americans regardless of income. The program should be *comprehensive*, and include acute, rehabilitative, chronic, long-term and home care; mental health and dental care; prescription drugs and medical supplies; and preventive and public health measures.

The program should be *federally administered* under a single plan to assure equal access to care, reduce administrative complexity and cost, and effectively contain costs through a

## Table 1:

**Savings on Administration, Marketing and Profits Under a National Health Program (NHP), 1993**

| CATEGORY OF EXPENDITURE | Projected Costs Under Current System | Projected Cost Under the NHP | Savings Under the NHP |
|---|---|---|---|
| | ($ in Billions) | | |
| Insurance overhead and central program administration | $40.2 | 21.1 | 19.1 |
| Hospital administration | 60.3 | 26.4 | 33.9 |
| Nursing home administration | 10.3 | 5.7 | 4.6 |
| Physicians' office overhead and billing | 78.8 | 63.1 | 15.7 |
| Hospital and health care advertising | 9.3 | – | 9.3 |
| Health industry profits | 32.0 | 20.3 | 11.7 |
| TOTAL | $230.9 | 136.6 | 94.3 |

The methods of estimating the above costs are detailed in "Cost Without Benefit: Administrative Waste in U.S. Medicine," *The New England Journal of Medicine*, D.U. Himmelstein and S. Woolhandler, February 13, 1986, 314:441-445. Estimates have been updated to 1993 using the latest figures and projections for health spending provided by the Health Care Financing Administration.

principal payer—the federal government. The complexity of our current insurance system, with its multiplicity of payers, forces U.S. hospitals to spend more than twice as much as their Canadian counterparts on billing and administration, and U.S. physicians to spend about 10 percent of their gross income on excess billing costs.

An NHP should give patients free choice of providers without any co-payments or deductibles. Co-payments and deductibles are unwieldy and expensive to administer, discourage the use of preventive care, and decrease the use of vital inpatient services as much as the use of unnecessary ones. Moreover, increases in co-payments and deductibles have failed to do what they are supposed to—moderate cost escalation.

An NHP should leave our current system of delivery in place—public, profit and non-profit hospitals as well as doctors who have their own practice. As in Canada, alternative insurance coverage for services included under the NHP should not be necessary and will be eliminated. An NHP should also ensure quality of care by establishing federal norms

and standards of good health to be followed by providers that receive funds from the NHP.

### Paying Providers

Under a federally-administered NHP, hospitals and nursing homes will no longer have to charge individually for each patient and service. Instead they would negotiate an annual operating budget with the NHP, based on the size and health-care needs of the population served by the facility. Capital funds for expanding or replacing health-care facilities would be allocated by the NHP and handled separately from operating budgets as in Canada. Hospitals and nursing homes receiving government funds would be governed by boards of trustees that are publicly accountable and representative of the communities they serve.

Physicians and other practitioners would be paid by a combination of salary, capitation and fees-for-service. They would be prohibited from sending bills for covered services directly to patients. HMOs and other prepaid health plans could continue to function, but would not be allowed to divert funds from patient care to expansion or profits.

## Funding the National Health Program

Funding for the NHP should come from the same sources that currently pay for health care. At present, of the more than $500 billion that we spend on health-related services about 40 percent is paid by government (derived from taxes on individuals and corporations), 25 percent is paid by corporate employers, and the remaining 35 percent is paid by individuals for insurance policies and out-of-pocket expenses. But instead of paying for Medicare or Medicaid or a multitude of public and private insurance plans, all funds should be administered through an NHP Trust Fund. It is critical that all funds flow through the NHP. Such a single-source (monopsony) payment has been the cornerstone of successful cost containment and health planning in the Canadian NHP.

Federal, state and local governments would contribute to the NHP Trust Fund in the same percentages that they currently contribute to the health sector. Corporations would contribute to medical care, on average, the same amount they pay today. Rather than paying through group insurance packages for their employees, they would pay the same amounts to the NHP Trust Fund. Individuals would pay the same or perhaps slightly less than under the current system of individual premiums, co-payments, deductibles and fees. Rather than paying the insurance companies or providers, they would pay a lesser amount to the NHP Trust Fund through earmarked health taxes based on personal income taxes. Collecting funds through taxes is both fairer and cheaper than collecting individual premiums, co-payments, deductibles and fees.

We estimate that the overall cost of an NHP will be little different than the cost of our current system—in fact we might even save money. Assuring everyone access to comprehensive care will increase the use of services, at least initially—improving our nation's health. It must be remembered that this is a benefit of an NHP, not a "cost"—more people will have access to the care they need. The resulting increased utilization of health services can most reliably be estimated from the findings of the Rand Corporation's massive five-year health insurance experiment. They estimate under a universal and comprehensive insurance system that overall utilization will increase by 14.6 percent and that death rates will drop so as to avert about 106,000 deaths per year in the United States. Since the United States currently has a surplus of hospital beds and an impending excess of physicians this increase in utilization could easily be accommodated by existing resources at modest cost. One estimate places the increased expenditures due to increased utilization at 9.4 percent if no other changes are made in the health care delivery system.

However, the cost of these additional services would be offset by the $94 billion it is estimated can be saved annually through greatly simplified billing and administration, as well as a decrease in health industry profits. And in the long-run, overall health costs will rise less rapidly because of improved planning and efficiency. Table 1 shows estimated savings in these areas for the year 1993 when an NHP could be fully phased in. Table 2 shows estimated total health spending for that year under the current system and an NHP. The estimates of savings are based on the *New England Journal of Medicine* report comparing current costs in the United States and Canada. As noted above, it is essential that the NHP pay virtually all health bills in order to realize these savings. Hospitals and nursing homes can only be paid on an annual lump-sum basis (which eliminates their enormous billing costs) if all of their funds come from a single source—the NHP. Single-source payment similarly simplifies billing by doctors and other providers and facilitates health planning.

A full NHP would need to be phased in over several years. Federal and state NHP boards would need to be established to oversee the program. Over the phase-in period, an increasing proportion of health-care funds could be funnelled through the NHP. Government funds currently going to the Medicare and Medicaid programs could immediately be allocated to the NHP fund. Employers could be assessed an NHP tax set so that the total collections equal the previous year's total employer expenditures for health care, adjusted for inflation. During the transition period, employers might deduct from their NHP tax con-

**Table 2:**

**Health Spending Under the Current Health System and Under a National Health Program (NHP) by Source of Funds, 1993**

| | ($ in Billions) | | |
| --- | --- | --- | --- |
| | Projected Spending Under the Current System | Projected Spending Under the NHP | Savings Under the NHP |
| **SOURCE OF FUNDS** | | | |
| **Government** | | | |
| Federal | $262.9 | 262.9 | — |
| State & Local | 91.7 | 91.7 | — |
| **Subtotal** | **$354.6** | **354.6** | **—** |
| **Corporations** | $210.6 | 210.6 | — |
| **Individuals** | $276.9 | 263.4 | 13.5 |
| **TOTAL** | **$842.1** | **828.6** | **13.5** |

The figures for total spending and government spending under the existing system were provided by the Office of the Actuary, Health Care Financing Administration. Estimates of corporate and individual spending were derived by assuming that the proportion of costs borne by each of these groups at present (corporate share 25 percent, individual share 35 percent) would remain unchanged in 1993. Estimates of cost savings under an NHP are derived from Rand Corporation data on increased utilization of health services with the abolition of financial barriers to care, and the savings on administration and billing that have been realized under the Canadian NHP. The estimates of costs to corporations and individuals under an NHP are based on the assumption that increased corporate taxes to fund an NHP would exactly offset savings on employee benefits, while increases in individual taxes would make up the remaining costs of the program.

tribution any money spent for health benefits. After the initial phase-in, individuals would stop paying insurance premiums, co-payments, deductibles and other medical bills. Instead, based on current cost and revenue estimates, they would pay earmarked health taxes levied to an amount estimated to be lower than the health spending currently derived from individuals' insurance premiums and out-of-pocket costs.

Overall, an NHP can decrease the health cost of individuals and of employers who currently provide health benefits. For instance, Ford Motors' health costs per employee could fall from $5,300 annually to about $2,000. Employers not currently providing health benefits would be required to contribute to the NHP fund, though special provision would have to be made for financially strapped small businesses. The insurance industry would receive the greatest adverse impact from an NHP. Indeed much of the savings used to expand care would come from the elimination of insurance

company overhead and profits. Although many employees would be re-employed through the state and local administrative apparatus, a program of job retraining and job placement for those who would be displaced must be an important component of the transition.

## Conclusions

We must assure affordable, high-quality health care for all Americans; we must make health care a right, not a privilege. Under the Jackson NHP, the security of a red, white and blue National Health Program card would replace the 1,500 different types of health insurance cards currently held by those people lucky enough to have coverage and would replace the financial threat of illness for those without. For health-care providers, the NHP would reduce costs and improve international competitiveness. For unions and workers, the NHP would mean guaranteed complete health coverage, even during layoffs and strikes, and a shift of focus in bargaining away from defending health benefits toward other issues.

The American people have long supported an NHP, but their elected representatives have denied it to them. According to polls, 72 percent of Americans favor a federal program that would assure comprehensive health care for all, a number which has remained stable for years. Until 1984, the Democratic Party platform always included a call for an NHP. Indeed the Kennedy-Griffiths Health Security Act, first proposed in 1969, was very similar to the proposed Jackson NHP. Today's proposal for mandated employer-provided health care—which would leave tens of millions uninsured or underinsured—is almost identical to Richard Nixon's proposal in the early 1970s.

The health needs of the American people are no less pressing today than in the past. Indeed, the crisis of affordability is much greater today than ever before. If our neighbors to the North can do it, as well as all the other industrialized countries except South Africa, so can we. We need to change direction and raise again our people's hopes and expectations for decent health care for all.

For the Democratic Party to regain its vigor it must regain its vision. The American people have a right to a real solution to the health care crisis: the Jackson National Health Program.

## Sources

Estimates of lives saved by universal access to care are based on the $78 million federally funded Rand Corporation Health Insurance Experiment. The method of extrapolation from the Rand data is detailed in "Free Care, Cholestyramine, and Health Policy," *The New England Journal of Medicine*, by D.U. Himmelstein and S. Woolhandler, December 6, 1984, 311:1511-1514. Estimates of current employer benefit costs are based on data from the Employee Benefits Research Institute.

Statistics about the U.S. medical care system were compiled primarily from *Health United States 1987*, National Center for Health Statistics; *Access to Health Care in the U.S.: Results of a 1986 Survey*, Robert Wood Johnson Foundation; *The Health of America's Children*, Children's Defense Fund, 1988; and *Medical Care Chart Book*, Health Administration Press, Ann Arbor, Michigan, 1986.

Data on international health expenditures were compiled primarily from *National Health Expenditures in Canada, 1975-1985*, Canadian Ministry of Health and Welfare.

# DEALING WITH
# THE AIDS CRISIS

*The illness of AIDS is a challenge to modern technology and to our health system. The fact of AIDS is a challenge to modern compassion and to modern behavior. The reality of AIDS is a challenge to our present, and to the future.*

*—Jesse Jackson*

Today, between one and 1.5 million Americans are believed to be infected with the virus presumed to cause AIDS. If we do nothing, this number is expected to grow to five million Americans over the next five years. We don't know exactly how many of those infected with the virus will become sick and die, but the Public Health Service predicts that by 1992, AIDS will be among the top ten killers in the country.

Solving a problem of such vast magnitude will require leadership that is both bold and compassionate. We need a massive coordinated effort to prevent the spread of AIDS and to meet the needs of those already infected—and we need this effort made now. All Americans must concern themselves with combatting this plague. The way we, as a people, respond to this crisis will test the strength of the fundamental fabric of our nation today, and in the years to come.

To combat AIDS, I propose to:

## Wage a Massive, Federally Funded Prevention and Education Campaign

We can prevent AIDS by public education. We can prevent AIDS by utilizing the mass media; by funding grassroots community educational initiatives (especially within the gay male and minority communities hardest hit by the epidemic); by providing for early public school education on drug abuse and sexuality; and by funding special outreach programs for those difficult to reach by traditional methods: drug users, prostitutes, prisoners and the homeless.

We can prevent the transmission of AIDS by making condoms available and making voluntary testing available for those who seek it. We must expand the quality of and availability of drug treatment programs so that intravenous drug users can kick the habit, thereby helping to prevent AIDS. Even more important, we must bring about an end to the underlying conditions that contribute to drug abuse by creating meaningful jobs and ending poverty and discrimination.

We can prevent panic over AIDS and the scapegoating of people with AIDS by stressing in all educational programs that AIDS is not transmitted through casual contact. We must confront the homophobia, the irrational and divisive fear, the victim-blaming that impede our efforts to combat this disease.

## Provide Sufficient Funding for All Aspects of Research

We must allocate sufficient dollars to wage an all-out effort to research AIDS prevention, treatment and cure. We must discover an AIDS vaccine and discover medicines to prevent those who already test positive from developing AIDS.

## Create a National Health Program to Provide Needed Health Care

The AIDS epidemic brings into sharp focus the flaws of the current U.S. health care system: its high cost, limited access and the massive numbers of people either uninsured or underinsured. We need a national health program to meet the needs of *all* people in this country. But, for people with AIDS, the need is particularly urgent and acute.

People with AIDS also have special needs. We propose a program that provides funding for hospice care for the terminally ill, social support for victims and their families, and child care for people too sick to care for their children. We need to provide the resources to support our public hospitals that bear the lion's share of the burden of caring for the poor and minority communities in our cities. We need to train health care providers on how to meet the needs of the terminally ill.

## Defend Civil Rights

We must end AIDS-related discrimination in employment, housing, education and health care. Mandatory testing and quarantine measures must be rejected both as a massive waste of resources, and as an ineffective solution borne out of panic.

## Follow Through on International Initiatives

As one of the wealthiest nations on earth we must fulfill our international obligations regarding AIDS prevention and research. With the World Health Organization (WHO) estimating that 10 to 12 million people are infected with AIDS worldwide, and with as many as 20 to 50 percent of all adults in hospitals in some regions of Central Africa identified as people with AIDS, the United States must no longer default on its payments to WHO. Rather, we must seek to coordinate all nations' activities and provide technical and financial assistance so that, together, the nations of the world can combat the AIDS crisis worldwide.

AIDS is not a disease imposed on those few who dare to disagree with conventional morality. It is a cruel and threatening disease which strikes across the lines of race, sex, class, age, religion and lifestyle. It is a national and international disease requiring the deepest compassion and the boldest leadership to achieve solutions.

# MEETING THE
# NEEDS OF THE ELDERLY

*Today, the federal budget deficit is pitting young against old and parents against children in the battle over social programs. We reject this politics of intergenerational conflict. Older Americans are not just our past—they are an essential part of our present and our future.*

*—Jesse Jackson*

A true test of the moral character of a nation is how it treats its citizens in the sunset years of their lives. The graying of our society should be anticipated with high expectations, not with fear. Unfortunately, in our youth-worshipping culture, the dread of aging is everywhere, feeding prejudice against the elderly and robbing them of their dignity.

Such prejudice has been fueled by an administration which has at best ignored and at worst abused the elderly. Twelve million elderly Americans today live in poverty or barely above the line. Older Americans now spend more out of their own pockets for medical care than they did before the passage of Medicare and Medicaid 23 years ago—forcing many to choose between eyeglasses, dentures or a room with heat.

Our elderly are a vast, undervalued, and under-utilized resource. They are not to be cast off—as was done in some cultures—because the community chooses not to care for them. The United States can meet the needs of our seniors and our seniors can help meet America's needs. We must change society's perception of the elderly and we must elect leaders who recognize the rightful place of older Americans in guiding and shaping our future.

To meet the needs of the elderly, I propose to:

## Protect Pensions and Insure an Adequate Income

Today, over 34 million Americans receive benefits through the Social Security system. For low-income seniors, Social Security is their lifeline, making up almost four-fifths of their total income. Without Social Security, nine million more elderly would struggle below the poverty line.

We must build confidence in the Social Security system, not undermine its public support every time the budget is debated in Congress. Social Security did not create the budget deficit—doubling military spending in peacetime and huge tax breaks to the wealthy and corporations did. Since Social Security is not part of the general budget and is solvent for the foreseeable future, we must leave it out of the budget debate and stop striking fear into the hearts of our seniors. We must also guarantee annual cost-of-living adjustments and prevent means testing the program in order to maintain its broad appeal.

We also need to make private pension plans as safe and secure as Social Security. Pension plans represent the savings of workers, who passed up wage and benefit increases while they were working to ensure economic security in retirement. There must be stricter enforcement of employer contributions to ensure adequate funding of pension plans. Corporations cannot be allowed to raid their pension plans to aid their balance sheets by terminating one plan and starting another, usually less generous, one. Current retirees must be assured of continued pension and health benefits, even as employers file for bankruptcy to escape their debts to their employees. It is the role of government to ensure that these private arrangements offer genuine security for America's workers, retirees and families.

We must also significantly improve the Supplemental Security Income (SSI) program which assists the low-income elderly, blind and disabled. Today, only one-third of the impoverished elderly who could benefit from the program participate. Due to poor program outreach and education, the other two-thirds do not know it exists. Even those who do participate are only brought up to 75 percent of the poverty line.

## Provide the Health Care All Americans Need

It is immoral that 37 million Americans of all ages go without any health care. Millions more are forced into poverty to get the help they need to stay alive. Even with Medicare and Medicaid, we don't have a health care program that truly cares for our poor and elderly—much less cares for all who need care.

We need a national health program that is universal and comprehensive—to meet the needs of the elderly as well as every American. This program should emphasize disease prevention, not just treatment; cover chronic illness as well as acute needs; be federally funded, not left to the vagaries of the fifty different states; and allow a person the freedom to choose his or her caregivers.

A national health program should have as its top priority the *long-term care* needs of the elderly. Few elderly people realize Medicare does not pay for long-term care. Only if they impoverish themselves (and their spouses) will Medicaid pay for a nursing home. But the elderly should not be forced into poverty or into nursing homes. We need services that are community-based, that let the elderly stay independent and in their own homes in their own communities as long as possible. How? By providing home health care, nutrition assistance, chore service, transportation, whatever help is necessary to ensure they receive care where they want to be—at home.

In the immediate future, we must ease the elderly's financial burden of skyrocketing health care costs. Between 1980 and 1985, Medicare costs jumped 34 percent, about $162 per person. For older people with incomes below or even just above the poverty line, health care is unaffordable. In addition to the protection Congress is proposing against catastrophic costs, we must roll back the dramatic increases in the hospital deductible (Part A) and the physician premium (Part B) of Medicare.

## Meet the Needs of Family Caregivers

Contrary to myth, families provide 80-90 percent of all care received by elderly Americans living in the community. For the most part, these family caregivers are themselves middle-aged or older women, for many of whom the physical, emotional and financial strains of caregiving present significant problems. We must have accessible, affordable adult day care programs and respite care services to ease the burden of 24-hour caregiving. Employers should offer flexible pension, retirement and work hour policies that don't penalize family caregivers and force our elderly into institutions.

## Enforce an End to Age Discrimination in Employment

Older Americans continue to face discrimination in hiring and pressure to retire from work involuntarily. We can undertake both public education campaigns and federal enforcement of age discrimination legislation to prevent these unlawful practices which rob our elders of the right to work and our country of the skills and experience of its elder workers. We must expand retraining and job placement efforts for older workers displaced by a changing economy.

It's time to explode the myths and stereotypes about aging which have kept our society from realizing its full potential. We *are* an aging society. How we deal with this reality will have major consequences for our future greatness as a nation. We can afford security for seniors. We can afford justice for older Americans. And we can afford dignity for our elders.

# RENEWING RURAL AMERICA

*There is something wrong when it is more profitable to produce Mercedes Benz automobiles than it is John Deere tractors. Farmers need a helping hand, not a handout. If we can save Chrysler, Penn Central Railroad and Continental Bank of Illinois, we can save the family farm.*

*—Jesse Jackson*

A depression is gripping many parts of rural America. Since 1981 we have lost 650,000 farms and one million rural jobs. It is a cruel irony that in the midst of so much plenty, there is so much need. People are standing in breadlines among our amber waves of grain. In our bountiful cotton country, farmers can't afford new clothes for their children.

This farm crisis is not the result of bad weather or bad management. Rural America has been sold out as a result of Reagan administration policies that merge the ownership of the food and textile industry in this country, purge the family farms and Main Street businesses at the heart of rural America, and submerge the rural economy under a mountain of debt. Eighty percent of the grain trade is controlled by four corporations. Five companies have 58 percent of the beef industry. While family farmers are struggling to get out of the red, food processors are rolling in the green—they had a 13 percent increase in profits in 1986.

Rural America is a worthwhile investment. By investing in the family farm, we invest in families that can feed the world; we invest in rural jobs and community prosperity; and we invest in a way of life that has been the backbone of this nation and its notions of economic and social justice.

This investment does not require the $26 billion in farm subsidies the Reagan adminis-tration paid last year to prop up huge agribusiness conglomerates. Instead, it requires an investment of good faith by the government in the hard work and know-how of family farmers, the most efficient agricultural producers in the world.

To save the family farm, I propose to:

### Institute a Policy of Fair Prices and Supply Management

We need an aggressive government policy that puts the family farm at the center of American agricultural policy. We need to implement the Family Farm Act, a program of parity, not charity. The Act allows farmers a price equal to the cost of production. It allows farmers to produce the food needed for market and world hunger needs without creating the runaway surpluses that undermine the farm economy. It calls for debt restructuring, soil conservation, affirmative action programs for minority farmers, and increased funding for domestic hunger programs.

### Negotiate International Trade Agreements

The Family Farm Act brings stability to world markets. Right now, we have a trade war over food and all sides are losing. Instead, we propose a trade peace, built on international agreements in which all sides come out winners. Instead of pulling the subsidy rug out from under the feet of our farmers (as international trade negotiators proposed last summer), we need a price floor under which no farmer shall fall. We need a system of fair trade that will benefit all countries.

## Keep Land in Farmers' Hands

Farmers are the source of rural prosperity. We need a moratorium on family farm foreclosures. We need innovative new programs that take advantage of the 3.5 million acres of foreclosed farmland now in Farmers Home Administration and Farm Credit System inventory to make it available to beginning, re-starting and minority farmers at long-term, low-interest rates.

We must make mediation programs available to farmers across the nation to help them work out their problems with lenders. We must ensure borrower's rights. If farm families should tragically lose their land through foreclosure, they must be given the right to stay in their homes and retain their homesteads.

## Develop New Markets

Government must do more than rescue the family farm from its current crisis. It should act to make the family farm a stronger competitor in local, national and international markets now dominated by the giant conglomerates. We need to assist family farmers seeking to diversify out of the mono-crop rut in order to respond to new market demand.

This year over 76 cents of every food dollar will go to middlemen. We need a government that is in the business of helping the producers of raw commodities band together to become their own processors so they can reap some of the profits derived from processing the food they've grown. We need a government that assists family farmers and ranchers to gain direct access to international markets that now operate as the private domain of international shippers.

The family farm produces more than just crops and livestock. It produces strong families and stable communities. It produces a devotion to the conservation of land passed on from generation to generation. If we institute policies that promote the economic development of the family farm, our government can produce prosperity in rural America and the entire nation.

# SAVING THE FAMILY FARM

Greenfield, Iowa, January 25, 1987

*(Note: This speech was delivered on Superbowl Sunday at kickoff time to an overflow crowd of over 900 people in a rural town of 2,000.)*

It's a pleasure to be here in Greenfield tonight, to enter this new year with some of America's most productive farmers, with some of my dear old friends, and with many new friends to be.

To Reverend Olmstead and the congregation here at Greenfield Methodist Church, my heartfelt thanks for opening up your church to us tonight. I thank Dixon Terry for that thoughtful introduction. I am delighted to spend the night with the Terry family here in Adair County. Dave Ostendorf has been most helpful in preparing for this Iowa visit, as have many of you here, including Jay Howe and Pat Eddy. I also must recognize Merle Hansen, board member of the National Rainbow Coalition, and a loyal and true supporter who has travelled many a mile with me, both across the United States and in Africa, in our joint struggle for international economic justice, peace and equality.

The crisis in agriculture, the misery and heartache felt throughout rural America is not new to you, nor is it new to me. In 1984, our campaign for the presidency was based on the need to go in a new direction. I stood with you for parity and not charity. Our campaign rang clear and true when we stated that America is blessed with fertile soil and hard-working, dedicated farmers. We said that government must reorder its priorities, must once again stand tall with and for its people.

In 1984, I stood with you for a new farm program, a program in direct contrast with that of the Reagan administration. It is a program calling for parity prices in the market, for well-structured supply management, for debt restructuring—including a moratorium on farm and home foreclosures—and for soil conservation programs to ensure that our children, and our children's children, could reap the benefits of our blessed land. I was the candidate who focused the nation's attention on the farm crisis and the need to go in another direction.

Today, we support the Save the Family Farm Act, which embodies those same principles, which offers an alternative to the suicide path of current farm policy. I need not remind you that 650,000 farmers have been forced out of business in the past six years, with a loss of 34,000 farms—almost 25 percent—here in Iowa. I need not remind you that 95,000 Main Street businesses, including 2,000 farm implement dealers, have closed their doors since 1981. I need not remind you that 55,000 farm implement manufacturing workers have been permanently laid off in the past five years.

Tomorrow morning I will visit with the locked-out John Deere workers of UAW Local 450. I know they appreciate the severity of the farm crisis, and how it affects their lives, and that you support them in their fight for their right to decent jobs and productive lives.

We must go in a new direction. Our solutions aim for stability and growth in the farm community, and a healthy, well-nourished world. The Save the Family Farm Act is a farm bill that proposes a permanent solution for today's farm crisis, for both family farmers and taxpayers alike.

The Save the Family Farm Act gives farmers a chance of success because it restores the essential ingredients that are missing from our current farm program. First, it gives producers a price that will cover an efficient farmer's cost of production; second, it gives producers a means to control the runaway surplus that has drained the federal treasury and kept interest rates high; and third, it provides an opportunity to restructure debts that have mounted during this depression. It includes significant provisions for increases in domestic hunger programs, as well as affirmative action for African American and other minority farmers.

According to an independent study by Texas A&M University, the Save the Family Farm Act is the only option that will give typical hard-working, productive family farmers in Texas at least an even chance of surviving in the next few years. The study compared all current alternatives and, by contrast, the Reagan approach gave the family farmer a poor chance of success.

Our solutions are based on a bedrock of justice and peace. It's no secret that the policies of the Reagan administration are based on disparity and war, at a tremendous burden to us all. Since 1981, our farm policy has cost American taxpayers more than the total cost of every farm program of Presidents Roosevelt, Truman, Eisenhower, Kennedy, Johnson, Nixon, Ford and Carter. In 1986, farm programs cost a record $25.8 billion, more than total net farm income. As my good friend Jim Hightower says, this administration has spent more money to cause more misery for more farmers than any administration in history.

Under Reagan's war policy, the deficit equals more than the total accumulated by all past presidents combined. He has chosen arms over farms and led the nation down the road to economic disaster. A single bomber program, the B-1, will cost more than one year's net farm income! This administration has squandered millions funding the terrorist contras who assassinate Nicaraguan farmers and health workers, while ignoring the economic and health needs of rural Americans at home. We must go in another direction, we must pursue a peace policy and choose life for all the people of the world. It is the moral thing to do. It makes economic sense and is the responsible thing to do. We must choose farms over arms and go in a new direction.

Over the last few decades the power of those very few who own and control the world's major financial institutions and corporations has grown tremendously. In the United States, 10 percent of our population now control 70 percent of the wealth, while 90 percent own only 30 percent. The top 40 percent get 68 percent of the nation's income: they get Broadway and limousines and million-dollar salaries. The bottom 40 percent get 15 percent of our income: the cellar with the stench, no lights, where despair abounds. This glittering of wealthy liberty without the substance of popular justice is the greatest challenge of our day.

Not only are the rich getting richer and the poor poorer, but the rich have become substantially more organized and the poor suffer more punishment and are less organized. The rich have turned their economic and organizational strength into political power that has no precedent in modern history.

Nowhere have these trends been more evident than in agriculture—than in the worldwide farm crisis that is daily undermining the very foundations of our society and people. Five corporate giants control 80 percent of the world's grain trade. None are subject to public scrutiny. All fall outside Securities and Exchange Commission reporting requirements. Similar concentrations of power exist in poultry, meat, sugar and beans.

A recent article in *Successful Farming* magazine listed the 400 largest farms in the United States. Believe me, these aren't farms like you have in Adair County. These are corporate farms that depend on a large force of low-wage labor and high-powered corporate managers. Some of these farms have familiar names: Cargill, Continental Grain, ConAgra, Castle and Cooke, and Tenneco. These 400 farms—often producing livestock fed with low-priced grain produced by family farmers—sold as much produce as all the farm products sold in the states of Iowa, Illinois and Florida combined. Today's *Des Moines Register* reported that ConAgra just merged with a huge cattle feedlot, another example of the sickness of merger mania fostered by the Reagan administration.

We are in an age when the world clearly needs trade peace and not trade war. The strong and independent cannot be allowed to protect their markets while inflicting the pain of unlimited competition on the weak and dependent. All countries, whether the United

States or Japan, must enter into fair and equitable trade agreements. Human harmony demands fair trade, not free trade. Nor is the arms race compatible with trade peace. Do we really believe the Soviet Union will continue to buy our wheat and corn if we jeopardize world survival with the insane Star Wars system? Do we really think the world is a better place if we refuse to trade with the people of Angola and Nicaragua?

Unfortunately, we are in an age where the value of grain and porkbelly futures—and corporate profits—are carefully calculated moment by moment, but where the future of our youth, our farmers, a sacred and essential way of life, and the land and other natural resources of our world are devalued and left out of the calculations, every day. We need a new equation, a new formula, where the dignity of a productive life for all people is the foundation of the equation.

The current farm crisis is not a crisis farmers brought on themselves. Our nation's farmers are not lazy, or stupid, or freeloaders. They work longer and harder than most people, pay their fair share of taxes, are extremely patriotic, defending this country in time of war. They are religious, respectful, humble Americans, trying to contribute what they can to make our nation strong, and to make an honest living doing it. America's farmers believe in hard work and sacrifice. They always have. The tragedy today is that, to escape the pain, farmers are turning to drugs and alcohol. The suicide rate among farmers has soared as they are forced to give up the way of life they have always known, a way of life that embodies our most traditional American values.

We must go in another direction. Farmers and displaced workers, urban and rural, African American and white, young and old, we must all join together to chart a new course. We must coalesce and fight back. The battle has just begun. The road is long, but together, our future is bright.

We can't let Howard Beach, New York, where an African American youth was killed while fleeing a white gang, or Forsyth County, Georgia, where the Klan is challenging the right of Americans to march and commemorate Dr. Martin Luther King, Jr., define who we are. Howard Beach and Forsyth County, Georgia, represent the poison and the pain, but not the solution.

If there must be a confrontation, let the confrontation not be at an open pizza parlor between African Americans and whites, but by all of us coming together at the gate of a plant closing on workers without notice because of corporate merger mania or moving to cheap labor markets abroad. Let's join together to prevent a sheriff's sale of our neighbor's foreclosed farm, and to pass the Save the Family Farm Act.

Let African Americans, whites, Hispanics, males and females understand that whatever we have in conflict socially, we have more in common socially and economically. We are all Americans.

Let the rejected stones coalesce to become the cornerstone of our nation—to restore the American dream.

Thus, let us join hands across lines of race and sex, whether we are urban or rural, and fight against the common economic threat to a better future for all of us. In the face of mounting tension, let us accept the challenge of turning to each other, and not on each other.

# ENDING HUNGER
# IN AMERICA

*Millions of people are starving throughout the world and going hungry in America. Meanwhile our grain silos are bulging and our family farmers are going bust. We need a new direction!*

—*Jesse Jackson*

Over 450 million men, women and children are hungry in this world. Surprisingly, 20 million of them live in the world's most agriculturally abundant country—our own. Significant progress was made in the fight against hunger in the United States from the mid-1960s through the 1970s. But Reaganomics has reversed that progress. Food programs are underfunded and soup kitchens and food pantries are overtaxed. The longest postwar economic expansion in U.S. history has passed by millions of our fellow citizens.

Hunger is primarily a result of poverty, and today, in America, over 33 million people are poor. Consequently, we have so many people who are hungry, most through no fault of their own. The majority are children. Many are among the elderly. An increasing number are farm families. A disproportionate percentage are minorities. Migrant workers, who pick food for our tables, and Native Americans, who first farmed this land, have the highest incidence of poverty.

Hunger can easily be ended in America, and in the rest of the world. It requires political will and making it a priority. The most important steps are those that attack poverty and its consequences. Ending hunger in America must be part of a comprehensive program to end poverty. But even with full employment, a decent minimum wage, a healthy agricultural economy, and a reformed welfare program, there will be those who need nutritional support.

And until we take these fundamental steps against poverty, other steps against hunger will be required.

To end hunger in America, I propose to:

## Establish a Right-to-Food Policy

Congress passed resolutions in 1976 declaring a right to a nutritionally adequate diet for every American—but programs to achieve that goal have never been implemented. We need a comprehensive national nutrition policy that implements the right to food and makes the elimination of hunger in America a national priority.

## Establish a Nutrition Monitoring System

We have no way of knowing for sure how many people go hungry in the United States because there is no ongoing system to gather nutritional information. President Reagan's Task Force on Food Assistance recommended a national nutrition monitoring system but the administration has failed to take its own advice. Better data will make for more effective programs and responses.

## Strengthen Food Programs

The most serious deficiency of domestic nutrition programs is underfunding. Most are highly effective. Some even save society money: The WIC (Special Supplemental Food Program for Women, Infants, and Children) program saves $3 in post-natal care for every

$1 invested. But WIC, like other food programs, serves only a fraction of those eligible—about one-third of those eligible; elderly nutrition and the largest nutrition program, Food Stamps, reaches less than one-half of those eligible. Specifically we need to:

- Fund nutrition programs so that all who are eligible are served and increase benefits for the Food Stamp program so that they cover the true cost of food.

- Strengthen outreach programs informing people of what assistance is available and for whom. In particular, the Food Stamp outreach program, cut by the Reagan administration, needs to be restored.

- Strengthen the nutrition education component of the Food Stamp program.

- Make it easier for people to obtain benefits by locating application offices in high-use neighborhoods and near public transportation, reducing red tape and providing adequate staffing of program offices.

### Make Special Efforts for Native Americans And Migrant Workers

A comprehensive approach to support social justice for both groups is needed. In the immediate term, migrants need to have easier access to food program benefits and Native Americans need to have access to a greater quantity and a better quality of food products.

### Protect Consumers

We need to promote a more competitive food industry to protect consumers and save family farmers. With 80 percent of the grain trade controlled by four companies and with 58 percent of the beef industry dominated by five firms, consumers are worse-off. We need farm policies that promote less use of pesticides and other chemicals and greater use of organic farming methods to make food safer to eat. Finally, changes are needed to ensure that nutritional information provided on food labels is more accurate.

No country should permit hunger within its borders, least of all a nation blessed with an abundant and productive agriculture and a nation founded on the right to life. The most basic right to life is the right to food. The American people understand this, and want hunger eliminated. It's time for our government to make the end of hunger a national priority.

# Ensuring the Dignity and Equality of Women

*Women are not a special interest group. They are the majority in our society and they have the right to a livable income, to freedom from discrimination in work and housing, to public policies which enable them to combine work and family life, and to respect.*

*—Jesse Jackson*

It is a disgrace that the United States, the richest and most technologically advanced nation in the world, continues to deny full and equal citizenship to women. When we fail to pass the Equal Rights Amendment, when we impoverish women (and children) by job segregation and budget cuts, when we exploit women's sexuality, this nation is deprived of the potential gifts a majority of its citizens have to offer.

Despite the media images of women in high-paying positions, most women have fallen deeper into poverty and despair in the Reagan years. As women have filled three out of five new jobs, they have joined the ranks of the working poor, which have nearly doubled in the 1980s. Women today still earn only 67 cents of a man's dollar in wages and they are still largely segregated into low-paying "women's jobs" in the clerical, sales and service sectors. Minority women, facing the "double jeopardy" of race and gender, are even worse off than white women—earning less, unemployed twice as often, and facing even greater job segregation.

No one should be forced to choose between work and family, between being able to afford to feed and clothe children and provide them proper supervision. Yet for all too many women this is their choice. We need a new set of rules—both at work and in law—that recognizes the importance of parenting and care-giving as well as work outside the home.

To ensure women's dignity and equality, I propose to:

## Pass and Vigorously Enforce Anti-discrimination Legislation

Women must be granted full protection under the law. We strongly support the passage and enforcement of the Equal (and Economic) Rights Amendment which would grant women the same constitutional rights as men. We must have an Attorney General who enforces the law of the land and a federal budget that gives greater funding to anti-discrimination agencies. We need the Civil Rights Restoration Act to guarantee that anti-discrimination laws will be broadly interpreted, ensuring full access and participation on the part of women and minority groups.

## Advance Economic Security

All workers must be guaranteed the right to a job at a living wage. We must significantly increase the minimum wage and link it to the average wage in the economy. We must reinvest in America, putting people to work to meet our needs in housing, health care, education, neighborhood revitalization and infrastructure repair. We need a new national commitment to strengthen workers' (especially service workers) rights to organize and represent their own interests. Women in unions earn a third more than women without unions.

We need a special effort to assure economic equality for women. We must break down the barriers in education, training and hiring which have created a sex-segregated workforce. "Women's work" must be eliminated. Vigorous affirmative action, with stated goals and timetables, must ensure equal access and participation for women in preparation for entrance into non-traditional fields and into higher paying and managerial positions. For the vast majority of women in traditional "women's jobs," we need a federal initiative establishing the principle of pay equity, so that jobs of comparable worth get similar pay. Part-time workers must be ensured minimum benefits, including pensions, on a pro-rated basis.

We must establish a uniform, national income benefit for needy families, most of whom are headed by women. We should explore a family allowance system which would supplement low earnings and ensure an adequate standard of living to families with children. Sixty-seven other countries around the world have such a system. Finally, we must seek changes in the Social Security system and in private pension plans. Women should not be forced into poverty in old age because of discriminatory wages or as a result of lost wages due to motherhood.

## Enable Women to Combine Work And Family

Women will never achieve equality in the marketplace until national and business policies on parental leave and child care change. Women—even women with small children—want work and not welfare. But to work they need decent pay, adequate health care and affordable child care. Thus, we oppose current welfare and "workfare" proposals that would force poor women with very young children to go to work at low wages in return for their welfare checks. Such proposals are punitive and dangerous to families.

We need a comprehensive national child-care policy, with an increased federal child-care tax credit, increased funding to states to develop and implement quality child-care programs, and the establishment of a national child-care office to promote long-range plan-

ning and implementation. We must also pass parental and medical leave legislation which would protect the jobs and incomes of workers who stay home to care for infants and for sick family members. The United States is the only industrialized country which does not guarantee women job-protected maternity leave. The lack of such a policy costs families and taxpayers nearly $400 million each year in lost earnings and public assistance.

## Support Reproductive Choice

Decisions on the timing and size of one's family are a private responsibility. We must respect that right of privacy, while supporting family planning and making information available to reduce infant mortality and unintended adolescent pregnancy. The federal government must expand funding for family planning clinics and for research into safe and reliable methods of family planning. We oppose any attempts to repeal a woman's right to choose and must make sure that poor women have the same reproductive rights available to them as the rich—including Medicaid funding of abortion and the enforcement of informed consent laws to prevent involuntary sterilization.

## Challenge Violence Against Women

The president does much to set the tone of a nation. The Reagan administration's cutbacks in social services for poor women and their families, his attacks on reproductive rights, and his reversal of affirmative action programs have all contributed to a climate allowing violence against women. We can create a different political climate, a climate in which women are treated with dignity and respect in every aspect of their lives. This includes adequately funding programs to stem violence against women and to protect those who have become the victims of such violence.

Women want equality, but equality cannot be achieved in a world in which the rules are stacked against them. Women want respect, but respect does not mean being put on a pedestal or into a gilded cage. Women want opportunity, not only in the home, but also in the workplace, the classroom and the athletic field. The time is now.

# DEFENDING AND PROMOTING LESBIAN AND GAY RIGHTS

*There are those who isolate differences, desecrate our humanity, and then justify their inhumanity, just as the Nazis did with yellow stars and pink triangles. It was not right in Nazi Germany, and it's not right in America.*

*—Jesse Jackson*

In the United States today, it is estimated there are nearly 25 million lesbians and gay men—nearly 10 percent of our population. Lesbians and gay men come from every part of society and from every stripe of the Rainbow, and are a vital part of the quilt that makes up America. They are African American, Hispanic, Catholic, Jewish, women, farmers, unemployed, homeless, disabled, students and parents. As citizens of this great country, lesbians and gay men must be afforded all the rights the Constitution provides.

Throughout the United States, however, lesbians and gay men live with the daily fear of discrimination because of their sexual orientation. Due to bigotry, and fear exacerbated by AIDS-associated hysteria, gay people have been kicked out of their homes, fired from their jobs, denied health and life insurance coverage, and assaulted on the streets. We must end this discrimination against lesbians and gay men. We must recognize diversity within the human family, and affirm the humanity and the legal and civil rights of all human beings.

In order to defend and promote the rights of lesbians and gay men, I propose to:

## Guarantee Full Civil Rights for Lesbians and Gay Men

We support the current Lesbian/Gay Rights Bill in the U.S. Congress, which calls for an end to discrimination based on sexual orientation. We support the implementation of a Presidential Order banning anti-gay discrimination in the federal government and the military.

The right to privacy must be guaranteed. No government—be it local, state or federal—has the right to regulate the private sexual behavior of consenting adults. The government has no place in the bedroom of its citizens—be they homosexual or heterosexual. The 1986 Hardwick decision, which violated the privacy of consenting adults, must be reversed through legislative action. Bigotry and prejudice have no place in the courts or legislative chambers of this nation.

The humanity of lesbians and gay people should be recognized and their rights fully respected. In Minnesota, a young woman lies in a hospital bed forbidden by the courts to see her long-term partner. That is not right. We support the rights of lesbians and gay men to child custody. Mothers and fathers must not be stripped of their custody rights because of their sexual orientation. The right to parent should be decided by the courts on a case by case basis. The love and quality of care provided to the child should be the basis of such a decision, not a person's sexual orientation. We support lesbian and gay partners being afforded other benefits granted to heterosexual couples, such as health care.

## Combat the AIDS Crisis

The AIDS crisis has had a profound impact on the lesbian and gay community. Too many have died, and too many more face an uncertain future. The bulk of the resources of the lesbian and gay community have been directed to meeting this crisis head-on due to the failure of the Reagan administration to adequately respond. We must take the burden off of community-based agencies and provide support for a federally funded war against AIDS.

Sufficient money must be allocated to wage an all-out effort to research AIDS prevention, treatment and cure. We must discover an AIDS vaccine and discover medicines to prevent those who already test positive from developing AIDS. It's time to provide funds for life, not for death.

We need a national health program to meet the needs of all people in this country—including people with AIDS. Our public hospitals and community health centers now bear much of the burden of care. They need immediately to get the resources from the federal government to care for people with AIDS and related conditions. We also propose a program that provides hospice care for the terminally ill, social support for patients and their families, and child care for parents too sick to care for their children.

As the gay community has so positively shown, the best weapon against AIDS is education. Education should include discussion of explicit sexual practices and risk reduction techniques. Mandatory testing, quarantines and other repressive measures are punitive and ineffective. We must develop appropriate public health policies that protect the population from this deadly virus while safeguarding civil rights. We must not allow the voices of panic and prejudice, homophobia, racism and fear to set public policy.

Historically, lesbians and gay men have made great contributions to humankind, yet they have often had to live under conditions of intense oppression. In the late 20th century, it's time we come together to insist on legal protection under the law for every American—for workers' rights, for civil rights, for women's rights, for the rights of religious freedom, for the rights of individual privacy, for the rights of sexual orientation. We must defend and promote the rights of all people.

# GUARANTEEING THE RIGHTS OF IMMIGRANTS

*It is ironic that as we recently celebrated the 100th anniversary of the Statue of Liberty and the 200th anniversary of the signing of the United States Constitution, the immigrant and refugee population in the U.S. suffered from untold acts of abuse, injustice, discrimination and violence. We must put a halt to anti-immigrant sentiments, laws, policies and practices.*

*— Jesse Jackson*

The strength of the United States has always been the diversity of our people and our constitutional commitment to equal protection under the law. Our commitment to diversity and democracy is more essential now than ever before. For in an interdependent world, the diverse cultures of our people provide a unique reservoir of understanding and talent, a reservoir our nation can draw upon to promote a positive world image, to foster international goodwill, to promote prosperity and world peace.

Yet the Reagan administration has shown little understanding of this commitment and these opportunities. Instead, thousands of refugees from the wars in Central America have been sent back to their countries to face violence and possibly death. An "English only" movement which delegitimizes immigrants' language and culture has been gaining momentum. The Reagan administration has fed anti-immigrant sentiment by challenging their constitutional rights and by nurturing the conditions conducive to acts of violence by the Ku Klux Klan and other such paramilitary groups.

Even the passage of the Immigration Reform and Control Act (IRCA) in 1986 was a product of this growing anti-immigrant sentiment. IRCA's combination of amnesty for immigrants who arrived in the country before 1982 and sanctions for employers who hire "illegal aliens" was touted as a way to make legal citizens out of millions of undocumented people and as a way to end employers' exploitation of undocumented workers. But IRCA has proven inadequate to the need. Instead, we need a new direction.

To guarantee the rights of all immigrants, I propose to:

## Extend and Expand the IRCA Legalization Program

The IRCA legalization program, as it is now being implemented, is doomed to fail. The Immigration and Naturalization Service estimates that close to four million people are eligible for amnesty. But less than one million have applied to date, and perhaps two to three million others are unable to even apply because of restrictive eligibility requirements, such as the 1982 cut-off date.

But, it is in our national interest to enable undocumented workers now here to come out of the shadows. They have established homes, have worked, paid taxes, they have contributed to the social and economic development of their communities. We must extend the amnesty program for at least one more year and move the cut-off date for eligibility to January 1, 1987. Immediate family of those who qualify must also be allowed to stay.

### Repeal Employer Sanctions

The new employer sanctions laws don't work. They discriminate against workers and burden employers. We must repeal sanctions and, instead, increase enforcement of labor laws, imposing treble damages on employers who violate laws forbidding exploitation of undocumented workers. Enforcing the labor laws will protect all American workers and remove the main reason some employers hire the undocumented: to exploit them.

### Eliminate All Temporary Foreign Worker Programs

We must eliminate all foreign "guest worker" programs. We must not again tolerate the "harvest of shame" of the Bracero program of the 1940s-1960s. In many parts of the United States unemployment among farmworkers is 20 percent or more. American agriculture needs to employ workers already here, not import guest workers who can't be organized or protected. What is true of agriculture is true of many other industries as well. If we need more immigrant workers, we must admit them on a permanent basis with full rights.

### Increase Permanent Legal Immigration Admissions

We should also increase permanent legal immigration admissions. Family reunification—including parents and brothers and sisters as well as spouses and children—should be our top priority. We must oppose any proposed law which would tightly restrict the concept of family and give preference to educated, English-speaking European immigrants. Immigration policy must not discriminate on any basis. Immigration for employment purposes should be based on job skills in demonstrably short supply.

### Protect Refugees and Asylum Seekers

There are over 20 million refugees and displaced persons throughout the world. They constitute a "fourth world"—the most impoverished and vulnerable of all; the innocent victims of war and persecution, pawns in the game of geopolitics. We have an obligation to protect all refugees, regardless of race, ideology or country of origin. We must strengthen our commitment to refugee rescue, immediately stop deportation of war refugees from Central America, and insure that protection and assistance is given on a non-discriminatory basis to refugees from Africa, the Middle East, Latin America and Asia as well as Europe.

### Address the Root Causes of Migration and Refugee Movements

Many refugees flee not just war but starvation. Migration is an important international and foreign policy issue. We need a foreign policy that addresses the conditions of poverty as well as wars which cause people to flee their homelands. The "Jackson Doctrine" will do this by redefining our relationship to the Third World and basing it on support for international law, self-determination, human rights and international economic development.

### Promote Naturalization and Citizenship

There are over six million permanent resident aliens living in the United States who are eligible for citizenship. We must encourage their citizenship and eliminate barriers to their naturalization. The federal government should provide funding and work closely with community organizations to strengthen naturalization and programs that encourage residents to take part in the rights and responsibilities of citizenship.

### Guarantee the Democratic, Political and Cultural Rights of Immigrants

The democratic rights of immigrants should not be denied because the United States government disagrees with their political viewpoints. We should repeal the McCarthy-era McCarran Act allowing the deportation of immigrants espousing political views the government finds objectionable. All charges against immigrants made under this Act should immediately be dropped.

We must vigorously oppose "English Only" initiatives. These actions aim to undermine bilingual and bicultural education and services. We must respect and protect the language and culture of all nationalities who live in the United States. The foreign born must not be discriminated against in education, in receiving services or benefits, or in their ability to participate in politics and union activities. We must support the concept of "English Plus," which would strengthen policies and programs for acquiring English language proficiency plus mastery of another language. In an interdependent world, multiple language skills are a definite asset to our nation, not a threat to our national security.

Finally, we must take action to prevent violence against immigrants, whether it is at the hands of private individuals, groups like the Ku Klux Klan, or under the aegis of the Immigration and Naturalization Service. We must not tolerate racism, harassment or physical abuse inside the government or in society at large.

Immigrants have built and enriched America from the time the first Europeans set foot on these shores. Whether fleeing political turmoil, religious persecution, or poverty and lack of opportunities in their homelands, these newcomers make tremendous sacrifices as they set up a new life in a new land.

Today's immigrants—mostly people of color from Latin America, the Caribbean, Asia and Africa—face similar, if not worse, political and economic conditions in their homelands. They come to America in the midst of a growing anti-immigrant, anti-foreign climate. They work in some of our poorest working conditions. They lack basic rights that we here already take for granted. They are paying a high price for the freedom and independence of America.

We must continue to welcome these immigrants—white, black, brown and yellow—into the American family. We must take advantage of what they have to offer without taking advantage of their economic vulnerability. We must appreciate their sacrifices and welcome their contributions to the mix that makes up America.

# INSURING JUSTICE FOR AMERICAN INDIANS

*America has an obligation to uphold and defend promises and commitments made to the American Indians. We must accord our treaty commitments the same respect that we, as a nation, have for our Constitution.*

—*Jesse Jackson*

No American racial group faces more economic and social injustice than the American Indian. On Indian reservations, where a majority of American Indians live, unemployment averages at least 40 percent, and double that in many areas. Three-quarters of Indian families on reservations live at or below the poverty level. Only one out of four of the wage earners there earns more than $7,000 annually.

There is a critical shortage of doctors; schools are seriously understaffed and underfunded; and housing is found to be substandard at three times the national rate. Such inhuman living conditions foster a suicide rate among young people that is nearly six times the national average.

Many of these problems are not confined to the reservation. Large numbers of Indians living off the reservation face discrimination on a daily basis and suffer from poor housing, poor health and low educational achievement.

The federal government has contributed significantly to these problems. It has stifled the will of the people through bureaucratic paternalism and inefficiency, perpetuating a cycle of dependency rather than promoting self-determination. The government has mismanaged its trusteeship of Indian resources, frequently tilting toward corporate interests. For example, the Interior Department has allowed corporations to illegally drain vast quantities of gas and oil from Indian land, depriving Indians—and the government—of as much as $5.7 billion worth of royalties.

We must reverse the federal policies that have created these conditions. In a spirit of true partnership and nationhood, the federal government must assist tribes in strengthening tribal governments, rebuilding tribal self-sufficiency, and establishing programs and projects developed in consultation with them.

To insure justice for the American Indians, I propose to:

## Recognize Our Treaty Obligations with American Indian Nations

The U.S. government signed 371 treaties with American Indian nations. All have been broken. This nation must honor the treaty commitments it makes to all nations, and we can do no less than honor those treaties made with American Indian nations. We should establish a presidential Treaty Commission to determine the obligations of the United States under treaties made with American Indian nations and report its findings to the U.S. Congress and the administration. As a first step in the right direction, we should pass the "Black Hills" bill which would return land to the Sioux. Another step is the redress of the wrongful termination of Indian nations—a shameful part of American history that must be reversed. Finally, individual states must not be allowed to assume postures of control over sovereign Indian nations and their enterprises.

## Promote Economic Self-Development

We need to insure that American Indian tribes are afforded the opportunity to determine their own course of economic development, a course which is respectful of their land and their culture. The government must act as a supportive partner to American Indian tribes. At a minimum, the Bureau of Indian Affairs must be restructured and streamlined to be more responsive to American Indian concerns.

We must restore development, management and utilization of Indian land resources to American Indians. We need credit reform policies to protect Indian land from foreclosure and liquidation. And we need increased technological assistance and training to identify opportunities for long-term, sustainable agriculture.

We must stimulate the development of Indian tribal economies by providing the necessary capital and technical assistance to Indian-owned business enterprises. We must do more than study the potential for reservation-based economic development. We must encourage private-sector participation in Indian country. To reverse the flow of wealth, we must stop businesses from misappropriating Indian-owned natural resources, such as oil, gas, minerals, timber and water, and assure adequate and timely payments for those rights and resources that are sold.

## Protect the Civil, Cultural and Religious Rights of Indians

In 1992, indigenous people throughout the Western hemisphere will observe the 500-year anniversary of recognized contact with the European culture. We must acknowledge and celebrate with them the integral part they have played in the social, cultural, historical and economic development of this country. Further, the unique relationship that American Indians have with the people of the United States must be recognized and reaffirmed. We must ensure that American Indians are protected from the ugly specter of racism that often disguises itself as seeking to mainstream Indian people. American Indians have the right to re-main who they are, and we must ensure this right is protected.

The right of American Indians to fully exercise their traditional religious beliefs and cultural practices must be protected and any barriers to the free exercise of traditional religion must be removed. Freedom of religion is a constitutional right afforded to the citizens of this nation, and it must fully apply to American Indians' spiritual beliefs.

## Meet the Educational, Housing and Health Needs of American Indians

Every American Indian child represents the hope for a better tomorrow, and that hope must never be locked out. We need to ensure that every person has equal educational opportunity. Therefore we must double federal spending for education, including Indian Education programs, to rekindle opportunity. We must also ensure that the right of American Indians to protect and foster their culture and language through education is honored.

We must provide every American Indian the opportunity to live in safe, decent, sanitary and affordable housing within their own communities. Special attention must be given to housing which is consistent with the culture and geographic area of every tribe. Consideration must be given to providing rent ceilings for Indian housing units in communities where no other market housing is available, affordable or in a safe and sanitary condition.

Access to health care should be a basic right in the United States. We need a national health care program that provides universal coverage to everyone regardless of income, that is comprehensive and covers the full range of health services, is culturally sensitive and allows people freedom to choose their health-care provider. Indians suffer particularly from the lack of health care. Quality health-care programs that address high infant mortality rates, low life span, substance abuse and unique health problems, such as diabetes mellitus and the high rate of suicide among teenage American Indians are an imperative.

There can be no justice in this nation until we right the wrongs committed against the American Indians. Legally, most of the 291 American Indian reservations are sovereign nations. Our relationship with these nations within our borders should be guided by the same principles that should guide our relations with nations outside our borders. These principles are self-determination, economic justice and abiding by our treaty commitments. We can do no less than follow these same principles in our relationship with the original nations of this continent, the American Indians.

# PROTECTING OUR ENVIRONMENT

*If a foreign power poisoned our air with acid rain, dumped toxic wastes in our water supply, and then took over the living space from our wildlife, we'd see this as a threat to our national security. But we are doing this to ourselves and it must stop.*

*—Jesse Jackson*

All nations face a huge challenge—many say a crisis—in managing the earth's natural resources and the quality of the environment. We face chemical warfare from hazardous wastes dumped into the environment which are finding their way into our bodies. Pollutants are destroying the ozone layer that protects us from harmful ultraviolet radiation. The ever-increasing level of carbon dioxide in the atmosphere threatens a devastating increase in world temperatures. We are destroying planet earth as we extinguish plant and animal species, raze tropical rainforests, and develop coastal wetlands around the globe.

Nearly 20 years ago, the United States made a firm commitment to protect the earth and clean up the environment. We passed laws and set up regulatory agencies. We spent billions of public and private dollars. But we have largely failed. Since the early 1970s, some pollutant levels have improved—but only by 10-15 percent; some stayed the same; others have become worse. In the 1980s, this environmental crisis was exacerbated by an administration committed to environmental deregulation. President Reagan attempted to sell off our national trust of parks, forests and other resources to big business; tried to gut the Clean Air Act; refused to prosecute polluters; and slashed the budget of the Environmental Protection Agency.

But restoring and preserving the environment for this generation and those to come will require more than a change in the administration. We need a shift in values—away from those that create technology designed for the mass destruction of people as well as the earth. We need a fundamentally new approach based on the following:

- **Prevention:** Environmental pollution is like a disease; it is best to prevent it. Our few successes at controlling pollution have not been achieved through high-tech control devices, but by common sense—simply stopping to put the pollutants into the environment.

- **Changing the System of Production:** Present environmental laws try to control pollutants that come out of the stack, the waste pipe, or the car exhaust. By then it's too late. To *prevent* pollution we must focus upstream, on the production process itself, changing it so to preserve the environment.

- **Restoration:** Besides protecting the air, land and water from future pollution we must restore, rehabilitate and wherever possible replace those natural resources which have already been harmed. Plenty of jobs can be created in the process.

- **International Cooperation:** We live in one world with international environmental problems that make no distinctions based on nation, ideology, race or class. The world's resources should be devoted to preserving and restoring the environment rather than to amassing ever greater armies.

To protect the environment, I propose to:

## Clean Up and Prevent Toxic Pollution

We demand the prompt elimination of unsafe toxic waste sites and the aggressive enforcement of the Toxic Waste Superfund program. Industry should be made responsible for future clean up costs as an incentive to stop polluting. We need regulations and federal research assistance to find new manufacturing techniques—to find substitutes for the most toxic chemicals. We must develop and promote new farming methods to reduce the use of pesticides and the destruction of our precious groundwater. Finally, we must strengthen and expand legislation informing workers and communities of the environmental hazards they face.

## Reduce Air Pollution

We need vigorous federal support for recycling as a substitute to the construction of new trash-burning incinerators. To prevent acid rain and reduce rising carbon dioxide levels, we need to transform how we produce power—starting with energy-conserving plants such as co-generators and shifting to alternative sources. To prevent smog we need to build and operate better mass transit and we must assist the auto industry to develop new engines.

## Achieve Energy Security

We need a Pan American Energy and Environmental Security Alliance to develop energy sources in this hemisphere. U.S. technology could be traded for oil from Latin America, thereby increasing trade, creating jobs and giving us a more secure source than we have now. To reduce dependence on fossil fuels we should make a major federal investment in renewable energy—from solar, hydro, wind and agriculture sources. To prevent nuclear acci-

dents such as Three Mile Island and Chernobyl and to reduce the hazards of radioactive waste we should phase out nuclear power. Finally, we need a major federal program to rebuild and insulate homes to reduce energy consumption and create new jobs.

## Protect Public Lands

We are in complete opposition to any attempt to weaken the protection of national parks, refuges and forests in Alaska and elsewhere. We oppose auctioning off our precious natural resources to the highest bidder. We must refuse to give in to oil companies seeking off-shore oil drilling rights in California, Florida and elsewhere for a few weeks worth of oil, because of the risk to fishing and tourist industries. Our coastal zones and national parks must receive increased funds to improve protection and management.

## Pursue International Environmental Cooperation

We need regular World Environmental Summits to freeze and reverse pollution, as much as we need Arms Control Summits to freeze and reverse the arms race—the worst environmental threat of all. A Marshall Plan for the Third World, combined with debt relief, would provide sorely needed income there and allow countries to afford environmental management. The United States should lead on the environmental front by setting the example, supporting the Law of the Seas treaty, eradicating acid rain, and finding an alternative to the fluorocarbons destroying the ozone.

The laying waste of the resources of our planet is only part of a larger social and economic system that sacrifices the welfare of the many for the short-term interests of the few. The next president of the United States, on his first day in office, must initiate a "Green Century." Our most precious gifts—the air we breathe, the water we drink, the oceans and soil that provide our food, the mountains and forests and the other living things that inspire awe in our hearts—must be preserved.

# THE CHALLENGE OF OUR DAY:

## Confronting Environmental and Economic Violence

Mendocino Headlands, California, March 20, 1988

I've been reading the papers and seeing on television what this coast means to you. I've heard about the 4,000 of you who showed up to speak in Fort Bragg and Eureka to protest the desecration of this ocean for a few weeks of oil. I have been impressed that people could care so much about the place where they live.

But not until today, not until viewing this incredible coast myself, have I fully understood the rapture in which you hold it, the depth of love you have for it, and the lengths you clearly will go to protect it.

Let me say from the outset, so that there is no confusion on this matter, that a Jackson administration will end Lease Sale 91. There will be no drilling for oil on the North Coast under a Jackson presidency. That is my promise to you today. My administration will strongly support Congresswoman Barbara Boxer's and Senator Alan Cranston's efforts to create an Ocean Sanctuary for the coast of California.

The laying waste of the resources of this coast, like those of the rest of the planet, are not part of my vision for our social and economic system. The welfare of the many must not be sacrificed for the short-term economic interests of the few. We must stop mortgaging the future to the present. We must stop destroying, or threatening to destroy, the most precious gifts of the Creator. Those gifts include the air we breathe, the water we drink, the food we eat, the mountains and forests that inspire awe in our hearts, and the companionship of billions of fellow travelers on this spaceship earth.

This plan to drill for oil, pollute the ocean

and dirty the air is environmental violence. It's also economic violence. We must say no to Big Oil and its friends at the Interior Department. We must not sell our resources to the highest bidder—nor, in the case of Lease Sale 91, the lowest bidder, at $25 per acre. The Reagan-Bush years challenged us merely to survive. The Jackson years will give us the opportunity to move beyond environmental and economic violence, beyond survival to restoration.

The Reagan-Bush years have been miserable for the environment, as well as for our economy and our communities. They've deregulated justice, and the civil rights banner of Ed Meese reads "We shall overturn." They've deregulated the stock market, and Wall Street crashed. They've deregulated the economy, and corporations have merged, workers have been purged, and the economy has been submerged under a mountain of debt.

Reagan and Bush deregulated the environment, and James Watt tried to sell off our national trust of land and resources at bargain basement prices to Big Business. Reagan and Bush deregulated the environment, and Ann Gorsuch tried to gut the Clean Air Act and refused to prosecute polluters under Superfund. Reagan and Bush deregulated the environment, and Donald Hodel told us the solution to ozone depletion was to wear sunglasses and extra clothing to protect our skin from the cancerous rays of the sun.

We need an environmental and an economic policy that makes sense. Restoring and preserving the environment for this generation and those that follow requires more than a change in any one administration. We need a shift in values. We need to prevent pollution at the source, not try to clean it up later. We need an Attorney General who will be in court enforcing the laws against polluters, not trying to dodge the law himself. We need to restore the damage that's already been done to the environment, not allow it to continue. We will either reduce, reuse, recycle and restore—or we will perish.

A Jackson administration will be about prevention, not reaction:

- To prevent the pollution of this coast, we need an energy policy that promotes conservation and renewable sources, not a "Drain America" policy at any environmental price.

- To prevent the assault of toxic chemicals, we need a long-term strategic plan. Industry must be redirected to manufacture products using less toxic materials.

- To prevent the growing pollution of our food and water supplies, we need to help farmers shift to organic farming and other safe production methods.

- To prevent waste incineration, we must mandate recycling.

- To prevent smog, we must manufacture cars which don't create it.

- To prevent another Three Mile Island or Chernobyl and to eliminate nuclear waste, we should begin now to phase out nuclear power.

Changing the way we produce goods and food can create economic benefits as well as environmental ones. Manufacturing less polluting, more fuel-efficient cars could revitalize the auto industry. New factories building cogenerators, solar collectors and photovoltaic cells would create new industries. Transforming farming would reduce the risk of contaminated food and water, while lessening the farmer's need for costly chemicals.

A Jackson administration will make the 1990s the decade to clean up the mess we made during the first 90 years of the 20th Century. America can enter the 21st Century with clean hands and a clean conscience. We will provide worldwide leadership and challenge the leaders of all nations to join with us in an historic effort to restore what we have plundered. And we must lead—so long as our five percent of the world's population continues to consume one-third of the resources of the entire globe.

We can restore the earth without the loss of work. My administration will put our unemployed people to work at the best jobs I can think of: restoring the planet. We need a new Civilian Conservation Corps, not as a make-work project, but to repair the environment. Let us mobilize our young to work for environmental restoration and the public good. Let's renew scarred timberlands with seedlings, reclaim lost wetlands with new grasses, and recover urban creeks for city parklands.

It's clear that the environmental crisis has no boundaries. All of us on this earth are victims of chemical warfare. If a foreign power poisoned our air with acid rain, dumped toxic wastes in our water supply, left dioxin in our earth, and threatened the ozone layer, we'd see this as a threat to national security. We would be right. But we are doing this to ourselves. And no matter who does it, it's chemical warfare and it must end. We oppose nuclear war and we must oppose environmental war. The environment is a national security issue.

We live in one world with international problems that make no national distinctions, no distinctions based on ideology, race or class. When Chernobyl first blew up, it was presented as a Soviet problem. It was. Then the wind blew, and European food was contaminated. The problem went even further, to Oregon, where cows were affected, and radiation got into the milk that we drink. Chernobyl became everyone's problem.

Chernobyl is a prime example of why a World Environment Summit is as important as a World Arms Control Summit. We need a summit meeting with nations like Brazil and Madagascar. We need to freeze pollution just as much as we need to freeze the arms race.

We will work together to protect the ozone layer, or the world's people will suffer disease. We will work together to stop the destruction of the rainforests in Brazil, or drought will come to Asia and Africa. We will work together to stop acid rain, or our streams and wildlife will die. We will regenerate our forests—implementing a policy of sustained yield in the United States and Canada and throughout the world—or we will be without wood and the jobs it provides.

We believe that by solving our environmental problems we can resolve many of the international problems and conflicts in the world. The Middle East is a flashpoint in the world because of the unnecessary dependence of our country, and the world, on non-renewable petroleum resources.

President Reagan's answer to energy security has been large-scale military intervention in the Persian Gulf—making the oil there the most expensive in the world. We have important relationships in the Gulf and we have interests there. But we need to develop alternative energy and security alliances. That's why I've proposed a Pan-American Energy and Environmental Security Alliance to work with our Latin American neighbors toward a peaceful and prosperous economic alliance.

Our neighbors, particularly Mexico, Venezuela, Colombia and Ecuador, are long-standing trading partners. They have oil reserves which dwarf those off your beautiful coast and can be accessed without damaging their environment. A Pan-American Alliance would provide an assured supply of oil among the nations of the Western hemisphere in times of crisis. It would also provide a means for our Latin American neighbors to reduce their terrible burden of debt. By exporting technology, instead of war, to our Latin neighbors, we make economic partners, allies and, indeed, customers of them. We must send environmental aid, not contra aid. We must offer Honduras engineers, not troops.

But one day the oil will dry up. Thus, the second part of my Pan-American Energy and Environmental Security Alliance is to vigorously develop non-polluting, renewable energy technologies. This is why I can promise to you today that we will not violate this ocean sanctuary. A sensible energy policy—including this new alliance—will make Lease Sale 91 obsolete, and it will make every other lease sale that despoils our oceans and coastlines—from Alaska to Florida to Massachusetts—obsolete as well. We need to turn our backs on the Reagan energy program—a program which has simply gutted every energy savings and development plan not controlled by the energy giants.

Before Reagan, we were the world's leader in the development of alternative energy, solar energy and conservation. Now, we may be last among the industrialized nations.

It is time for a new policy. It is time to remember that conservation is the cheapest and least polluting form of energy. And yet, under Reagan, we have seen Detroit encouraged to start building its dinosaurs again. We have seen weatherization funds for the poor gutted. We have seen incentives for conservation all but disappear.

The solution to our energy problem is not the amassing of ever greater armies to fight over dwindling resources. The number one environmental goal of any administration should be to end the threat of nuclear war—once and for all. It is time to dismantle the bombs, to turn our swords into ploughshares, to lift the nightmares out of the dreams of our children. There is no greater threat to our environment, to all the great goals we have talked about today, than the threat of annihilation by nuclear death. The next president of the United States has no greater responsibility, no greater mandate, than to end that threat for all time— and to turn over our scientists, our engineers and our research labs, which are unequaled in the world, to discovering the solutions to our many environmental threats.

Our campaign is a moral and political effort to transform the quality of American life. We want to restore a moral quality to the political decisions that affect our lives at home and the decisions that affect the lives of our brothers and sisters around the globe.

We want to set our nation on a course where the full spiritual, moral and physical resources of our people can be realized. We want to end the environmental and economic exploitation of the many by the few.

We need to come together. We need to recognize that the destruction of our environment is not distributed evenly throughout society. It is the poor, the elderly and minorities whose drinking water is the most polluted, whose air is the most dangerous to breathe, whose food is the least nutritious, whose jobs are the most hazardous. Here in Mendocino, it is the Indians whose fishing rights will be destroyed by oil exploitation.

We need to come together. We need to work in the southeast—a section of the country which has become the nation's industrial and toxic waste pay toilet. We must confront the poverty which allows them to accept toxic wastes. We must embrace their desire for empowerment that will help them develop local zoning laws to stop this pollution.

We need to come together. Our fight is not against the family farmer struggling to survive. It's against chemical companies and research bodies and government agencies that promote chemical farming that exhaust the land.

We need to come together. Our fight is not against the coal miner who suffers from levels of lung cancer seven times the national average. It is against the steel mill owner and the electric utility operator who fight legislation mandating the use of scrubbers to clean up a major cause of acid rain and who fail to research clean coal technology adequately.

We need to come together. Our fight is not against loggers who earn an honest wage for back-breaking work. It is against the lumber companies whose clear cutting and inadequate reforestation are despoiling some of the most beautiful land in the country.

We can choose a new direction. It requires bold leadership that proposes solutions as big as the problems: bold leadership that comprehends the urgency of the situation.

In this campaign, we have proved time and time again that while money is power, it is the people who are powerful. This campaign, in which we have garnered success after success while being outspent ten to one, is a campaign based on hope. Today, we share that hope. And at the end of my term in office, I know that I will be able to stand on these headlands again. The whales will still be alive and flourishing. The ocean will be so clear it will still be hard to tell where the ocean ends and the sky begins. We will have spent four or perhaps eight years improving our standard of living without destroying the standard of living for any other person or any other form of life.

We will have begun to transform our society into one in which people live in true harmony—harmony among nations, harmony among the races of humankind, and harmony with nature. Thank you.

# EXPLORING SPACE TO BENEFIT ALL HUMANITY

*For too long, our space program has been driven by military rivalries and corporate greed. The technology that can result from a space program oriented to public needs can be the economic backbone of our country and the world in the 21st century. It's time for new leadership, so that America's space program can go forward in partnership with all humanity.*

*—Jesse Jackson*

American technology has given us the ability to send people to the Moon and machines to the outer limits of the solar system. Through space exploration, we have gained an abundance of scientific knowledge about our earth and the solar system, greatly expanding our ability to forecast the weather and to communicate worldwide, and stimulating the development of new products and manufacturing techniques.

But space technology has its dark side. Military space technology is spurring the arms race and increasing the risks of a nuclear war which would destroy humanity. Our possession of this enormous technical capability carries with it the responsibility to ensure that it is used wisely for the benefit of all people.

The Reagan administration has failed to live up to that responsibility. Reagan has encouraged the development of space weapons to demonstrate superiority over the Soviet Union. He has misled the American people with absurd claims that the Strategic Defense Initiative, better known as Star Wars, can protect us all from the threat of nuclear war. At the same time, Reagan has failed to give leadership in shaping a long-term vision of what good things our country, in cooperation with other nations, could be doing in space.

To develop our space program to benefit, not destroy, all humanity, I propose to:

## Stop the Militarization of Space

A new direction in space policy requires abandonment both of the Star Wars program and of the development of anti-satellite weapons. Star Wars is a cruel hoax. It offers an impossible technological solution to a political problem. Pursuing Star Wars will cost $500 billion to $1 trillion and, in the end, produce not a defense but an arms race in the heavens. It will increase other nations' fears that we are building a shield to hide behind while we threaten a first-strike against them.

The anti-satellite weapons that have been under development also can only cause destabilization. They threaten the space-based surveillance systems which strengthen our security by providing the technical means to guarantee compliance with arms control treaties.

Space-based weapons fuel the fear of first-strike attacks. They generate counter weapons which generate counter-protective weapons. Our coffers will be robbed; our science distorted; our insecurity increased.

The Soviets have said that they are willing to curtail their own space weapons development. We ought to challenge them to sign a mutual and verifiable agreement to keep space free of all weapons and war fighting systems, an agreement that, like other arms control agreements, can be verified by satellite. At the same time, we must scrupulously adhere to the most significant arms control treaty of recent decades, the 1972 ABM Treaty, which restricts the development of anti-ballistic missile systems such as Star Wars. We cannot make peace while undermining existing treaties.

## Share Space Technology

Space technology is no longer the exclusive province of just the United States and the Soviet Union. Western European countries, Japan, China and India all have active space programs. Other countries use satellites for environmental monitoring and communications that promote their own economic development. In 1967, over 100 nations signed an Outer Space Treaty, saying that space ought to be used for peaceful purposes that benefit all humanity. Through the United Nations and other international bodies, the United States should take the lead to see that technological developments in space truly do benefit all people.

By sharing space technology, we can share information about the environment. Satellites can observe the fragile environment of the Earth in a systematic and efficient fashion. We can improve telecommunications. We can improve medical research. We must share our technology and the knowledge that comes from it, for we have only one planet we must share among all nations and all peoples.

## Explore the Planets

Planetary exploration by robot spacecraft has produced a golden age of astronomy. We have learned much about the mysteries of our origins. But now, due to mismanagement and shortsightedness, the pace of that exploration has slowed. We must start up again. We must turn to our planetary and space scientists for guidance and should support the goals of NASA's Solar System Exploration Committee Core program of planetary exploration. The attainment of these goals will require continued missions to Venus, Mars, Jupiter and Saturn and to selected asteroids and comets. Whenever practical, we should undertake these missions cooperatively with other na-

tions. Scientific exploration is not cheap, but it is an investment in our future. In the long-run, it may cost us dearly if we choose to just stay at home.

## Participate in a Joint U.S.-Soviet Space Project

A joint U.S.-Soviet mission to Mars is an idea with great potential to bring our peoples together in both practical and symbolic ways. Since Mars is the planet most like Earth, there is real scientific merit in learning more about it. Exploration of Mars is a logical outgrowth of growing capabilities in space. Both countries already plan unmanned missions to Mars. We ought to coordinate our efforts. We also should begin discussions with the Soviets on the feasibility of sending a human crew to Mars in a joint U.S.-Soviet mission, perhaps with involvement by other nations as well.

The United States is now planning a space station. The U.S.S.R. has enjoyed considerable success with their Salyut and Mir stations. We should direct the National Academy of Sciences to approach its Soviet counterpart with the intention of jointly leading an international effort to study the need for a large earth-orbiting space station. If such a station is deemed to be of value, we should jointly participate in its construction. With strong leadership, capable management and careful thought, a space station can produce great advances in communications, maritime and air traffic control, and astronomical, geological and geophysical exploration.

When the space shuttle Challenger exploded in January of 1986, two women, an African American man and an Asian American man were among the seven who died. The Challenger disaster symbolizes both the crisis of the U.S. space program and its future strength. In order to revitalize the U.S. space program, it must truly be a program that embraces all humanity and that all humanity can embrace. This can only be done by ensuring that the fruits of this research be used for the benefit of all of the Earth's inhabitants—not to strike fear in the hearts of those we proclaim our enemies nor to enrich those who claim to be our friends.

# IV

# RETHINKING
# NATIONAL
# SECURITY

# A NEW REALISM IN FOREIGN POLICY

Washington, D.C., April 14, 1988

Let me express my appreciation and delight at having the opportunity to meet with you today to share a few basic observations on security in the modern world.

The next president of the United States will face momentous choices about how to protect this nation, strengthen its people and preserve its democratic institutions. The decisions made will set the tone and the direction of American foreign policy for a new century.

A fundamental reassessment of our security priorities is long overdue. This must be grounded not in ideological presuppositions but on a new realism about the world in which we live, and a sober assessment of our real security concerns.

Our national security policy today is still based largely upon assumptions and institutions developed immediately after World War II.

Think of the world forty years ago. Stalin ruled in Moscow and communism appeared to be on the march. Western Europe and Japan were devastated by the war. What we now know as the Third World was just beginning its struggle against colonial rule. We were the world's preeminent power. We alone had the secret of the atomic bomb. We enjoyed an economic boom fueled by pent-up wartime demand and savings. We represented the voice of democracy and human rights across the globe.

From that reality came postwar strategy. Nuclear superiority would deter Soviet adventure. A grand alliance would contain Soviet expansion. A global commitment to intervene in civil wars and confront insurgencies from Greece to Indochina, from Iran to Central America, would forestall the spread of communism. We would police the world, even as we aided our allies and former enemies to re-build the global economy.

The world has changed dramatically since that time. The Soviet Union has built a nuclear arsenal equal to our own. Europe and Japan have recovered; their modern economies are competitive with our own. Communism holds no appeal to these democracies. Indeed, the Soviet system falls increasingly behind the modern economies of the West.

A Third World has been born, with over 100 countries coming to independence. They now struggle against grinding poverty and despair, torn by conflict born of tribalism, nationalism, religious fervor and financial austerity.

And we have changed. Our economy is still strong, but we are more and more dependent on a global economy over which we have less and less control. We are becoming overly dependent on foreign capital, foreign investment and foreign energy. Under Reagan and Bush, we have gone from the world's largest creditor to its largest debtor. Growing private wealth coexists with deepening public squalor as pressing investments in education, in children, in infrastructure, in health care go unmet. Our military is the strongest in the world, but we have learned at a great cost—in Vietnam, in Lebanon—the limits of military power.

Our challenges too have changed. Today, surely the number one threat in the streets of America is not alien ideologies, but illegal substances—drugs. Drugs are not simply a domestic problem, but a pressing dimension of our foreign policy, as well as either the most inept or the most corrupt aspect of our foreign policy. In terms of the security of our children, of our streets, indeed of ourselves, surely the threat of drugs is a clear and present danger to our national security.

Our policy must be changed to fit the new realities. We must change our course or lose our way. But change is always difficult. Institutional inertia stands against it. Conventional wisdom argues against it. Fearmongers rail against it. Too often politicians cater to prejudice and polls rather than mold opinion for the common good.

Over the last seven years, the Reagan-Bush administration has chosen virtually to ignore these realities. They have truly represented a reaction, a search for a nostalgic past, blind to the challenges of this day.

After seven years of Reagan-Bush, America's military budget has doubled, the largest peacetime military build-up in our history. Are we more secure now than we were at an earlier time? Have we expanded our influence in Latin America, Africa or the Middle East?

After seven years of Reagan-Bush, more Israelis are dead, more Palestinians and Arabs are dead, more Nicaraguans and South Africans are dead, and Americans are still held hostage.

After seven years of Reagan-Bush, our country has sacrificed much of its moral force and authority. The Reagan-Bush administration has sold missiles to the Ayatollah, illegally shipped guns to the contras, deceived our allies, spurned the law and lied to the Congress and the American people.

After seven years, we are losing the war on drugs, in part because it has not been our priority. Instead we have retained relations with dope-dealing generals, arms merchants and bandits in an obsession with three million Sandinistas who do not threaten us. Even if they did, 15,000 contras could not save us.

We have a strong military, but weak leadership; too many guided missiles and too few sensible minds. We need more than a new face in the White House; we need new realism and a new direction.

## The Nuclear Arms Race

We must address the fundamental threat to our survival— the nuclear arms race. Thus far, we have avoided Armageddon, but the threat of nuclear war poisons the dreams and blights the futures of our children every day.

Today, the United States and the Soviet Union have between us over 50,000 nuclear warheads. The Soviet Union poses a direct threat to our security and will continue to do so as long as it possesses weapons that can destroy all that has been built on the continent. Surely, the primary goal of U.S. security policy must be to reduce and ultimately to eliminate this threat.

History has demonstrated that no new nuclear weapons will make us safer or give us any meaningful advantage. The search for superiority is a dangerous illusion. No technical breakthrough can make us invulnerable. The Star Wars system is not a fantasy but a nightmare.

The INF accord is a small step in the right direction. Deep cuts in strategic arms represent a good second step. And even with deep cuts, we would possess an arsenal able to destroy the Soviet Union many times over. Both START and INF are too limited—neither would end the technological arms race. Under both, every new weapons system we can imagine could be developed. The same is true for the Soviet Union. The arsenals would grow faster, more accurate and more dangerous. If Star Wars takes the arms race to the heavens, it may soon become literally lunatic.

Agreements in which old weapons are dismantled and new ones developed will not make us safer. Agreements that spark a conventional arms build-up will not make us more secure.

We must seek another way. Arms control must become part of an arms reduction process, not a tactical ploy in a continuing arms race. Both sides must make a commitment to reduce nuclear and conventional armaments, to slow and eventually to stop the technological arms race. This requires that individual agreements be part of a broad conceptual framework for orderly reduction of both conventional and nuclear forces.

This is why, as president, I would initiate a nuclear testing and missile testing moratorium, challenging the Soviets to join. If we can then negotiate a verifiable comprehensive test ban treaty and a ban on new missile deployment, we can slow the modernization that drives the arms race. With negotiated conventional force reductions—necessarily asymmetrical to reflect our differing forces—we might begin to redirect the energy, imagination and zeal of the nation to rebuilding our cities, educating our children and re-kindling the hopes on which this society is based.

Any significant arms reduction will require a changed political relationship between the United States and the Soviet Union. Twenty-five years ago, President Kennedy called for a new beginning in U.S.-Soviet relations in a speech at American University. Today transformation of our relationship is both more necessary and more possible.

In the Soviet Union, Mikhail Gorbachev appears to lead a new generation of leaders intent upon making dramatic reforms. Gorbachev has explicitly stated that these reforms require a new course in foreign policy. His call for "new thinking" poses new challenges and new opportunities for bold leadership in the United States. For the first time since World War II, it may lie within our power to transform the global competition into a more cooperative and constructive relationship. Developing this relationship has its risks, but it is in the mutual interest of the United States and the Soviet Union, and it is the right thing to do.

We should take the leadership in forging a new era of cooperation and engagement with the Soviet Union. Arms negotiation should be accompanied by efforts to settle regional crises. The recent agreement on the withdrawal of Soviet troops from Afghanistan illustrates the possibilities. Joint ventures—in exploring space, in countering the threats to humanity, the depletion of the atmosphere, the destruction of the rain forests, the spread of malnutrition and disease, the plague of drugs—should be explored and launched where possible. Trade and cultural exchange must be expanded.

As we develop this new relationship, we must give high priority to engaging our European allies. The Reagan-Bush foreign policy is one of unilateralism—our allies are informed of actions already taken, rather than consulted on decisions yet to be made. We can and must do better, for greater cooperation is critical to our economy as well as our defense.

At the same time, our allies in Europe must assume greater responsibility for their own conventional defense. We spend some $150 billion a year on the defense of Europe and Japan.

In Europe, our allies have one and one-half times the population and more than twice the gross national product of the Soviet Union. They can share more of the burden. But our goal must be to reduce the burden for everyone. Major reductions in Western military forces can only occur as a consequence of major reductions in Soviet forces. Only sensible and verifiable arms reduction agreements can produce this. That must be the first priority of any president.

## The United States and the Third World

Let us not forget, however, that when the United States and the Soviet Union sit at the negotiating table only one-eighth of the world is represented. Most of the world is not white, not male, not prosperous and doesn't speak English. It is in the struggle for power and influence in the Third World that we have expended the greatest number of lives and resources in the Cold War, and nowhere is a new realism more necessary.

The Reagan administration has viewed the Third World as a chessboard in which a struggle for pawns and position is played with the Soviet Union. "The Soviet Union," President Reagan said, "lies behind all the trouble spots in the world."

From this perspective came the Reagan Doctrine, the commitment to intervene against any government or frustrate any movement which did not meet American approval. Inevitably, the Reagan Doctrine entailed open contempt for international law, illustrated in our withdrawal from the World Court after mining the harbors of Nicaragua. It entailed unilateral action, spurning the opinions and objections of our allies. It finally entailed secrecy and deception to avoid the protests of our people and the constraints of the Congress.

But the Reagan Doctrine is based on a fundamental misconception of the world. The countries of the Third World are not drawn to communism. They struggle against unimaginable poverty, against the legacy of colonialism, against underdevelopment, malnutrition and hunger. They contend with the mighty currents of nationalism and religion. They tend towards non-alignment, for they seek aid and investment wherever they can find it.

Any president must be prepared to use military force as a last resort to defend our nation and fulfill our treaty commitments. Yet surely by now we have learned that we do not gain influence or prestige by acting as midwife to governments in Iran, Guatemala or Chile or by propping up unpopular dictators in Haiti, Zaire or the Philippines. The Soviets have learned the limits of military intervention in Afghanistan, and they have clearly begun to realize that every government that calls itself communist and seeks aid from Moscow is not an asset.

That is why I call for a new doctrine—a Jackson Doctrine—to guide our policy, a set of guidelines far more pragmatic than the ideological fixations that have too often distorted our policy.

First, we must respect international law and support international institutions. Nowhere does the Reagan administration do our national interests greater disservice than in its contempt for international law and institutions. As a rich nation with global interests, we have the greatest stake in a legal order that legitimizes our presence. If our presence is seen as illegitimate across the globe, no military force will be powerful enough to protect us.

Similarly, as a great power, we must support the international organizations that can address transnational problems like malnutrition, AIDS, drought and acid rain.

Second, we must recognize the right of self-determination. Struggling people in the Third World will choose many forms of government and political economy. Some will not be to our liking, but we should respect their right to choose their own destiny.

Third, we must support human rights. Our foreign policy should reflect our values—our concern for freedom of speech and press, for freedom of religion, for due process and equal protection under the law. Gross and repeated violators of human rights should not be recipients of U.S. aid or trade preferences.

Finally, we must be a force for economic growth and justice. Development in the Third World is a security need of the United States. Without development, there will be no peace; without peace, there can be no growth. Without growth in the Third World, our own prosperity will be threatened. We will not succeed as an island of affluence in a sea of misery, and we will pay a heavy price for trying. Borders are too permeable. Drugs, terrorists, disease slip through. We cannot lock out the misery of the world.

We should not be enforcing austerity upon the impoverished, but taking the lead in lifting the debt burdens that have dashed any hope of economic growth in much of the Third World. We should be encouraging Japan and other industrial nations not to build more weapons, but to use their resources to create new development funds for the Third World.

At the same time, we should seek international cooperation to enforce basic labor rights abroad. Either the standard of living of workers abroad will rise or ours will decline. If workers abroad gain fairer wages, they can buy what we produce. We all grow together.

## The Crisis Areas

Against this backdrop of a new realism for American foreign policy, we can move constructively to address the most dangerous trouble spots in the world today.

In the Middle East, we have seen that a foreign policy that places more emphasis on military might than on respect for human rights, self-determination, international law and cooperation, is a foreign policy that neither serves our interests nor those of our allies.

After decades of conflict, neither the Israelis nor the Palestinians have security or peace. Each night we witness the human pain and suffering that generates only more anger and more violence. The Israelis and the Palestinians are locked in a death grip. Neither has the security to let the other go. We must do for them what they cannot do for themselves: move them from confrontation, occupation and despair to dialogue, mutual recognition and coexistence. We must challenge the Palestinian leadership to accept Israel's right to exist within secure borders, just as we must challenge Israel to recognize the Palestinian right to self-determination with security.

I welcome Secretary of State Shultz's initiation of a dialogue among the U.S. government and Jewish and Arab Americans. We urgently need their help and support to work towards a just solution in the Middle East. The Secretary's endorsement of an International Conference, his adherence to U.N. Resolutions 242 and 338 and the exchange of land for peace are all, in my judgment, positive steps towards ending the crisis.

To solve the crisis, we need active leadership. As President, I would appoint a personal emissary of the highest reputation to doggedly pursue the conversations to their conclusion. We must offer incentives for agreement—not threats against objection.

If we can move the Israelis and the Palestinians beyond war and beyond fear, think of the possibility. Beyond occupation and war, Israel could be a trading and manufacturing center for the Middle East and Africa. Beyond fear and war is the possibility of security, peace, economic growth and prosperity.

In southern Africa, we must take the lead in the struggle against apartheid. We must convene a summit of the Frontline states, to offer them the assistance they need to defend themselves from South African aggression and gain economic independence. We must work to get both South African and Cuban troops out of Angola and to free Namibia from occupation. Then we must engage our allies in full sanctions against South Africa. The bill introduced by Rep. Ron Dellums in the House provides the legal authority for full sanctions. We must act resolutely if we are to have any chance of avoiding an even greater tragedy in South Africa.

If we do these things—reverse the arms race, build international institutions, embrace the Jackson Doctrine in the Third World—we will dramatically increase our security. We can also cut our military spending without cutting our defense, and use that money to invest in America—in our children, in education, in health care and child care. If we just freeze our spending now, we can save $60 billion a year by 1993.

These views are consistent with our interests. They chart a new course through new realities, but are grounded in traditional values. Too often, convention and caution silence common sense. But leadership must seek the truth and stand for it even when it is not popular. A new direction can only come from a leadership bold enough to define it, and a citizenry confident enough to embrace it.

As I have travelled this land this election season, I can report to you that the American people are ready for a new direction. They are coming together across lines of race, color and religion to call for economic justice at home and peace abroad. A new majority will support a new realism in our foreign and military policy.

This is a moment of great change. It is time for the United States once again to take the initiative to use its power to promote a stable peace and real growth in the world economy. It is time to turn our energy to address the new threats facing this generation: the flow of drugs into this country; the environmental crisis; the deterioration of our air; the poisoning of the water supply; temperature changes that threaten floods or famine; and a world economic crisis that threatens to engulf our economy in a collapse triggered by the inability of poor countries to pay their debts. In these matters, the Soviet Union barely figures. Yet all are far less remote than a Soviet invasion of Europe or a thirty-day nuclear war at sea to which we devote so much of our treasure, our energy and our imagination.

The next president must know the world and have a realistic understanding of our possibilities. The next president must change direction and seek peace for our land.

# PROMOTING REAL SECURITY

*The time has come where we either freeze nuclear weapons or burn the people and freeze the planet. It's just that simple.*

—*Jesse Jackson*

In the twilight of the 20th century we need to reassess our national security needs. The United States has a weapons policy, not a security policy. It is based on a Cold War view of the world shaped by World War II, rather than recognizing that in the last 40 years economic and political realities have substantially changed.

Americans face a new world today. The nuclear arms race has produced over 50,000 warheads that can destroy the world at the touch of a button. Our World War II allies are now our economic competitors, yet we still spend over $150 billion a year to defend Europe against threats that even the military considers remote. A Third World with its own strengths and needs has been born of the old colonies of the First World. Multinational banks and corporations have forged a new global order which has replaced unionized labor at home with slave labor abroad. On top of it all, our economy is in hock to the rest of the world for at least $400 billion and the debt is rapidly increasing.

We need a foreign policy that promotes *real security* based on a new set of principles. We must take the lead in freeing the children of the world from the threat of nuclear war. We must reassess the threat in Europe and the Pacific and seek mutual reductions in Western and Eastern forces. We must export the best of our tradition and culture to the Third World—democracy, human rights, universal education and economic development—not arms, covert wars and a burden of debt that impoverishes those countries. With a *real security* policy we can dramatically reduce the military budget and use those funds to rebuild our economy, thereby increasing the security of all Americans.

To promote *real security*, I propose to:

## Reverse the Nuclear Arms Race

We need bold leadership to challenge the Soviets to move beyond a permanent Cold War relationship and to join us in building the common security arrangements we both need to survive. A first step would be a moratorium on the testing of nuclear weapons and flight testing of missiles. We must suspend deployment of new nuclear weapons—and challenge the Soviets to do the same. With a mutual halt to the arms race, we can sit down with the Soviets and negotiate mutual and verifiable agreements for deep cuts in both countries' arsenals and end the constant "modernization" that drives the arms race.

## Create Common Security in Europe

West European countries have twice the gross national product and one and one-half times the population of the Soviet Union. As Henry Kissinger has recommended, Western Europe should be responsible for its own conventional defense. Europe has been at peace since the Berlin crisis of the early 1960s, trade and travel have increased, and borders have been settled.

There is a real opportunity to bring the military situation in line with the political reality. With an intermediate-range nuclear weapons treaty as a starting point, we should respond to Warsaw Pact proposals for substantial conventional troop reductions. We should encourage European efforts to establish nuclear and chemical weapons-free zones. We can begin to limit the U.S. burden of defending Europe even as we seek to limit the long-run costs to our allies.

### Redefine Our Relationship to the Third World

Real security requires a new direction in policy towards the Third World based on the principles of the Jackson Doctrine.

- **Support and strengthen the rule of international law:** The Ayatollah is wrong when he mines the waters of the Persian Gulf and threatens world trade by preventing the free navigation of international waters. But President Reagan is wrong—and loses the moral authority to challenge him—when he illegally mines the harbors in Nicaragua. Because our interests are so broad the U.S. has the most to gain in a world that respects the rule of law in international relations.

- **Respect the right of self-determination:** The 130 countries of the Third World have different histories, cultures and economic conditions. They necessarily will have different social and political experiments. They have the right to choose their own destiny— to find their own ways to cope with poverty, illiteracy and political representation. We must respect that right, confident that democracy and freedom are spreading in the world.

- **Promote human rights:** Our foriegn policy should reflect and further our democratic values. Thus, we should condition our own aid and trade benefits on other countries respect for democratic rights, including the protection of the right of workers to organize. Our military should not be used to prop up undemocratic governments abroad. Slave labor anywhere is a threat to organized labor everywhere.

- **Support international economic justice and development:** Growth and prosperity in the U.S. requires raising the standard of living in the Third World, not lowering our own. We must work with Japan, West Germany and other trade surplus countries to fund a new "International Marshall Plan" for Third World development. By our providing capital and debt relief Third World economies will grow, their standard of living will increase, and trade with the United States will be revitalized, creating millions of jobs for Americans.

### The Military Price Tag

Our real security is grounded on a strong economy. But we cannot have a strong economy unless we redirect our public resources to invest in America—in education, in job training and child care, in roads, bridges and transportation so vital to a competitive economy. We will spend what is necessary for our security, but current spending wastes precious resources on unnecessary armaments.

We can cut the military budget without cutting our defense. We can save billions of dollars by reducing waste and mismanagement. If we reverse the nuclear arms race, tens of billions of dollars can be saved over the next five years. We do not need more MX missiles, the $40 billion Midgetman missile, the Stealth bomber or the Trident D-5 missile. The arms race should not be moved into the heavens. The United States should adhere to the limits of the Anti-Ballistic Missile treaty and not deploy Star Wars.

More than 40 percent of our military spending is for European security. We can make mutual reductions and achieve significant savings. We must limit the expenses we commit to intervention in far corners of the world. If we reduce our aircraft carrier task forces to the 12 that every president before Reagan found sufficient, we could save over $50 billion in the next five years. Our defense will not suffer.

We have a strong military, but weak leadership. We have guided missiles, but misguided minds. We have the power and the ability to enter into a new era of growth and opportunity at home and abroad. But our leadership has to come from the power of our ideas and the force of our example, not from the size of our arsenal.

# THE JACKSON DOCTRINE:

## Redefining Our Relationship to the Third World

*Regional conflicts should not be viewed through a lens clouded by superpower politics, but for what they really are—struggles against poverty, illiteracy and for self-determination. The Reagan Doctrine has failed. Our Third World relations must be based on a new doctrine, the Jackson Doctrine.*

—*Jesse Jackson*

For the past seven years, the Reagan Doctrine has misguided U.S. relations with the Third World. This Doctrine mistakenly assumes that most change and upheaval in the Third World comes from communist conspiracy, rather than from poverty, illiteracy and lack of political freedom. Because the Reagan Doctrine views the Third World as part of the U.S.-Soviet struggle, our foreign policy has mistakenly focused on rolling back "revolution" rather than moving forward with economic development.

Under President Reagan, the United States has played the role of the bully on the block. We've supported proxy armies, such as the contras in Nicaragua and UNITA in Angola, which waged war on governments that did not meet our approval. The result in practice, is the opposite of what was intended: countries that would naturally have close relations with the United States are forced in self-defense into a dependent relationship with the Soviet Union.

The Reagan Doctrine also promotes international law-breaking. Reagan officials have loudly displayed their contempt for international law and such international institutions as the United Nations. Found guilty of international law-breaking, we spurned the World Court which in the past we have relied on to protect our interests.

In region after region, the Reagan Doctrine has failed. When we aid UNITA in Angola, we do not confront communism; we affront all of Africa for we ally ourselves with apartheid and South Africa. When we aid the 15,000 contras in Nicaragua, we do not confront communism; we affront the 400 million people of Latin America, for we represent hegemony not self-determination. When we ignore the growing poverty in the Third World, we do not confront communism; instead, we undermine our own real national security needs.

It is time to redefine our relationship to the Third World. I propose a Jackson Doctrine based on the following principles:

### Support and Strengthen the Rule of International Law

As a global power, with diverse interests, the United States has the greatest stake in respecting and strengthening international law. Yet in Nicaragua we have pursued a policy which has trampled on international law, violated our own laws, alienated our neighbors and divided our citizenry. If our interests abroad are seen as legitimate, they will be protected by the society involved. If they are seen as an intrusion, there is no military force in the world strong enough to protect them. We would impoverish ourselves trying to do so.

In order to strengthen the rule of international law we must also recommit ourselves to strengthening such international institutions as the United Nations and the World Court. We must build new institutions to enforce and extend world legal order.

## Respect the Right of Self-Determination

Many pay lip service to self-determination, but refuse to apply it consistently. Some support self-determination for all but El Salvador—because it might choose the wrong form of government. Others support self-determination for all but the Palestinians, because they confront our closest ally in the Middle East. But to ignore self-determination is only to exacerbate the problem.

The countries of the Third World necessarily will have different social and political experiments. They have the right to choose their own destiny—to find their own ways to cope with poverty, illiteracy and political representation. We must respect that right, confident that democracy and freedom are spreading in the world. The use of military force abroad—which puts our military personnel at risk—should only be used as a measure of last resort. The United States will be more successful at preserving our values and interests if we use economic, political and diplomatic measures.

When we seek to determine the outcome of upheaval or revolution, we expend our resources and our reputation on an impossible task. Thus we should sharply reduce our military forces designed for intervention abroad. We should cancel all new aircraft carrier task forces—saving $36 billion. We should immediately halt U.S. aid to the contras in Central America and to UNITA in Angola. We should implement full economic sanctions against South Africa while promoting the economic development of the Frontline states. We must support a comprehensive political settlement in the Middle East which benefits both Arabs and Israelis and thus ensures the long-run prosperity of all countries in the region.

## Promote Human Rights

Our foreign policy should support those democratic values we hold most dear—free and equal political representation, freedom of religion, freedom of expression, and protection of the right of workers to organize. We must ensure that these basic rights are measured by one yardstick across the globe. It does us no credit when we criticize the Eastern bloc while we "constructively engage" South African apartheid. We should condition our foreign aid and trade benefits on other countries' respect for democratic rights.

## Support International Economic Justice And Development

The economic vitality of the developed and developing world are closely related. U.S. jobs depend on foreign markets. The enormous debt burdens and austerity development policies promoted by the International Monetary Fund leave Third World countries with little cash for purchasing U.S.-made goods. Economic stagnation in the developed world means less demand for Third World products and brings those countries close to debt default. Major defaults could easily trigger the collapse of many Western banks. Growth and prosperity in the United States requires raising the standard of living in the Third World, not lowering our own. We must support:

- **An International Marshall Plan for the Third World:** Rather than asking Japan to spend more money on weapons, let us ask Japan, West Germany and other trade surplus nations to create a new capital fund for Third World development projects.

- **Debt relief:** We must restructure debt to give the Third World a chance to grow. This includes: setting up an international mechanism to assume some of the debt at discount from private banks and convert it into longer-term notes; swapping some of the debt, for instance, in exchange for preserving land, such as the rain forests in Brazil, that is environmentally at risk; writing off the foreign debt least likely to be paid back.

- **A halt to International Monetary Fund austerity programs:** The IMF's austerity policies have placed a tremendous burden on Third World economies and have not improved the debt problem. A transformed program can enforce fiscal responsibility while promoting growth.

- **A code of conduct for American multinational corporations:** The playing field should be evened so that companies like General Motors find it difficult to close 11 factories in one week in the U.S., costing 30,000 American jobs, and open up two new plants in South Korea.

- **Democratic development strategies:** Economic development should promote Third World self-reliance and equitable distribution of resources. Third World elites should be prevented from depositing huge sums of money lent to their country to their personal bank accounts in the First World.

These are ambitious but achievable goals. The Jackson Doctrine is a foreign policy grounded in a more sensible view of the world. It reflects our values and serves our interests. And it will promote real national security.

# Achieving Democracy in South Africa

*The bloodshed, the violence, the suffering must stop. The challenge of this day is to end the Fourth Reich of South African apartheid, to end its terrorism against its own people as well as against its neighboring Frontline states.*

*—Jesse Jackson*

Southern Africa is in turmoil. For more than a hundred years, black South Africans have been repressed by a racist regime. Four million whites rule 25 million South African blacks, Asians and people of mixed race through a system of laws controlling peoples' travel, banishing them to poverty-stricken reservations, denying them the right to vote, and oppressing them through constant jailings, beatings, torturings and even death.

But today even this reign of legalized terror has not been enough to keep down the rising desires of South Africa's majority for freedom. They stood up to protest apartheid and they asked the rest of the world to bear witness. Many Americans have stood up to oppose apartheid—sitting in and going to jail, divesting pension and endowment funds, and passing state laws limiting economic relations with South Africa. Finally, in 1986 the U.S. Congress passed legislation requiring South Africa to make significant progress toward ending its system of apartheid.

The legislation required a repeal of the state of emergency in South Africa and respect for the principle of equal justice under the law. The legislation called for the release of black trade unionists and all political prisoners. The legislation set as a condition for continued trade the right of the black majority to form political parties, express political opinions, and participate in the political process. The legislation called for South Africa to end its

military and paramilitary actions aimed at its neighboring states. The legislation also called for the convening of a conference on international sanctions.

None of these conditions have been met and President Reagan continues to ignore the law. His administration has continued to pursue its business as usual policy of "constructive engagement," providing little incentive for South Africa to change. Weak economic sanctions are easily circumvented. America has closed its eyes to South Africa's illegal occupation of Namibia. Worst of all, we actually joined with South Africa and UNITA in attempting to overthrow the government of Angola by military force.

Such sabotage is South Africa's principal strategy for the region: destroy independent trade routes and militarily enforce the economic dependency of the region on South African rails, roads and ports. To break South Africa's military and economic stranglehold over its neighbors and over its own people, a comprehensive policy for the entire region is needed.

To achieve democracy in South Africa, I propose to:

## Declare South Africa a Terrorist State

Even as it terrorizes its people at home, South Africa conducts state-sponsored terrorism abroad as it seeks to destabilize countries throughout the region. We must act boldly against apartheid by declaring South Africa a terrorist state. Such a declaration will allow the President to quickly implement comprehensive sanctions and create a climate for our allies and international organizations to join us.

## Hold a Regional Summit

There must be a summit between South Africa's black neighbors—the Frontline states—the United States, and the European community. We all share in the responsibility to assist the millions of people in southern Africa to achieve a full measure of prosperity and independence. We need a coordinated policy to help bring about a merger of the economic and political forces in the region, to lessen their economic dependence on South Africa, and to defend themselves against South Africa's military aggression.

## Implement Comprehensive Economic Sanctions

We must encourage and support negotiations for a transition to democracy in South Africa. We support the organization that the majority of South Africans choose as their principal negotiator for freedom—the African National Congress. We recognize that the only way to bring South Africa to the bargaining table is to cut off its access to long-term trade, investment and capital. Current sanctions have been too easily circumvented. Responding to public pressure, and state and local legislation, many American corporations simply restructured their commercial relationships into leasing arrangements, instead of severing their ties to the apartheid regime. We must have a complete ban on trade with South Africa; cessation of intelligence links; and a date by which all U.S. corporations are forced to withdraw completely from South Africa. If the U.S. takes the lead we can join with our allies to create sanctions that work.

## Aid the Southern African Development Coordination Conference (SADCC)

The effects of international sanctions against South Africa will be limited as long as South Africa can maintain its military and economic stranglehold over its black neighbors, the Frontline states of Angola, Botswana, Mozambique, Namibia, Tanzania, Zambia and Zimbabwe. The United States, and our allies, should make a major development assistance commitment to the SADCC states. Such economic assistance must include a substantial increase in multilateral aid that emphasizes SADCC's priorities, including:

- Expanding trade and self-sufficiency in agriculture to reduce foreign debts, stabilize deteriorating environments, and reduce poverty and malnutrition in the region.

- Rehabilitation and reconstruction of the non-South African transportation routes in the region, particularly the Beria Corridor and the port of Maputo in southern Mozambique.

- Education and training of southern Africans for all levels of technical, scientific, managerial and administrative work.

- Coordination of regional industrialization policies to foster urgently needed job-creation and the production of industrial goods currently being imported from South Africa and overseas.

## Guarantee the Security of the Frontline States

It is foolhardy to talk about economic aid without realizing the external and military context in which that aid is to be utilized. The Frontline states must be provided the military security to defend themselves against South African invasion and terrorism. The United States must stop its financial and military support of the South African-backed UNITA forces in Angola and demand that South Africa withdraw its troops from Angola. Our failure to provide non-lethal support to Mozambique in their fight against the South African-backed RENAMO forces helps prolong a devastating war that is the primary cause of hunger there. The United States must also use our influence to pressure South Africa to withdraw its occupation forces from Namibia in accordance with U.N. Resolution 435. The message must be clear to Pretoria—respect the territorial integrity of your neighbors.

Our American agenda with southern Africa is not an African American agenda alone, although African Americans have strong ties to the continent. It is not simply a Democratic agenda, although many Democrats are deeply committed to a policy of international economic justice and human rights. It is an "American" agenda—one which is in our national interest and one which deserves the support of all our citizens. We can no longer afford to ignore the needs of 550 million Africans in favor of a few million Afrikaaners.

# Promoting Peace in Central America

*We face a challenge in Central America: can we move from a policy of war to a policy of peace, from force to diplomacy, from arrogance to respect? In Central America, the will for peace is clear. It's time we support the efforts of Central Americans to achieve negotiated solutions to the region's conflicts.*

*—Jesse Jackson*

Central America has been devastated by war. In the past decade, over 150,000 people have been killed, 2.5 million made refugees, and more than $5 billion in economic damage done. To put it in proportion, in the United States the cost of such warfare would be equivalent to wiping out the population of the city of Chicago, making refugees of all the people in California, and destroying one-quarter of our Gross National Product.

The Guatemala accords signed by the five Central American presidents on August 7, 1987 affirmed a Latin American identity and common history that binds these countries together despite their political differences. For his role in this effort, President Arias of Costa Rica received the Nobel Peace Prize. Upon accepting the prize Arias said that the future of Central America should be decided by Central Americans and that all countries should support efforts for peace instead of the forces of war in the region. Clearly, peace in Central America hinges on a change in U.S. policy.

We have already called for strong U.S. support of the Guatemala accords and the Contadora process, an initiative involving eight countries that make up four-fifths of Latin America's population. We have actively supported this initiative since its start and highlighted it in our special peace mission to Central America in 1984. Since then, we have outlined a framework for a new U.S. relationship with the Third World, a Jackson Doctrine based on four fundamental principles:

- Support and strengthen the rule of international law.

- Respect the right of self-determination.

- Promote human rights.

- Support international economic justice and development.

These principles are completely consistent with current Central American initiatives for peace. Within this framework, to promote peace in Central America, I propose to:

### End the Regional War

The United States must stop all military, economic and political efforts to destabilize or overthrow the Nicaraguan government, beginning with cutting off all assistance to contra forces and abiding by international law. U.S. troop maneuvers in Honduras should halt, and we should cease efforts to militarize Costa Rica. We should assist both governments to disarm the contra forces within their borders. Finally, American aid for governments waging war against their own people in El Salvador and Guatemala should be cut off and, instead, support provided to help negotiate national solutions to the conflicts in those countries.

## Forge A Durable Peace

We must support efforts to promote democracy in the region, including free elections in every country with guarantees of safety for all participants, as well as other forms of popular participation in community, labor and religious organizations. We should support the Contadora process which calls for signing a protocol to a treaty and non-aggression pact among all countries of the region. This treaty would ban foreign bases and military personnel, halt arms imports into Central America and arms smuggling within the region, and provide for reciprocal reductions in military forces. Bi-lateral talks need to be reopened between the U.S. and Nicaragua with our goal being the signing of a treaty committing both countries to a mutual, non-aggression pact and normalization of relations.

## Help Rebuild Central America

The U.S. should take the lead in assembling an international program of assistance to rebuild a postwar Central America and provide a basis for renewed, equitable and environmentally-sound growth. A rejuvenated Central American Common Market aimed at balanced regional development and the satisfaction of basic needs will also form the basis for trade and financial relations between Central America and the United States.

We must target our development assistance to programs that increase the participation of the poor in the region's economies. We must require genuine land reform, including credits and technical assistance for peasant cooperatives. U.S. aid should be conditioned on compliance with internationally recognized standards of human, political, and labor rights, as well as respect for indigenous people's culture and tradition. Direct humanitarian assistance should go to programs run by reputable, international organizations or domestic civilian groups—not military-dominated state agencies and programs tied to counterinsurgency activities.

## Work for International Reconciliation

To build the strongest relationship possible we need to increase understanding between the people of the United States and the people of Central America and provide assistance to those displaced by the war. To do this we must foster citizen-to-citizen contact between the United States and Central America through cultural and educational exchanges, "sister city" arrangements and similar programs designed to exchange skills and promote understanding. We should also grant Extended Voluntary Departure status to Central American refugees who want to stay in the U.S., instead of detaining and forcibly repatriating them. This is the least we can do for victims of a war our policies caused and prolonged.

Demilitarization is a first step toward achieving peace, and peace is a prerequisite for development. Peace and equitable development in turn can create the conditions for meaningful democracy, stability and genuine regional security. Let it be clear that a policy of peace is not a passive, isolationist policy, but an active policy that is the truest reflection of our national values. We have been ill-served by a military policy whose hallmarks are violence, deceit and scandal. We must turn the energies that we have directed to waging war into forging a durable peace.

# CREATING JUSTICE IN THE MIDDLE EAST

*After seven years of Reagan there are more Americans dead, more Israelis dead, more Arabs dead, more chaos, and now we are in a state of undeclared war in the region. The time has come where we must recognize that Israeli security and Palestinian justice are two sides of the same coin.*

—*Jesse Jackson*

U.S. policy in the Middle East is fatally flawed. The Reagan administration has failed to define U.S. interests in the region and landed us in an undeclared war. In Iran and Iraq we assisted both sides, thus prolonging their horribly self-destructive war. Reagan put between 25 and 40 U.S. ships and at least 25,000 American troops at risk in Persian Gulf waters to preserve undefined and conflicting interests. Hundreds of American lives have been lost.

The administration's failure to define a comprehensive Middle East policy has added to instability there and jeopardized both U.S. interests and the interests of our allies. How many more lives will be sacrificed before we define those interests more clearly, and work to build a consensus for the best *non-military* way to support them?

In all "hot spots" in the world, from the Middle East to Central America to southern Africa, the best foreign policy is based on the principles set forth in the Jackson Doctrine:

- Support and strengthen the rule of international law.

- Respect the right of self determination.

- Promote human rights.

- Support international economic justice and development.

To create justice in the Middle East, I propose to:

## Forge an Alternative Policy

We need an alternative policy in the Middle East which moves the process that began at Camp David to the next progressive step. A comprehensive political settlement which benefits both Arabs and Israelis is the only way to insure the security and prosperity of all countries in the long run. This policy should be built on several principles:

- The right of Israel to exist.

- The right of the Palestinian people to self-determination, including an independent state.

- The right of Lebanon to sovereignty and freedom from imposed partition.

- Normalized ties between the United States and all Middle East nations, based upon mutual respect for the sovereignty and independence of all countries.

- Demilitarization of the region and increased humanitarian aid that can enhance the stability and prosperity of all nations.

- An end to the U.S. military build-up in the Persian Gulf.

## Pursue Aggressive Diplomacy

The key to implementing these principles is

aggressive diplomacy based on bold leadership. We must use expanded diplomatic channels—rather than military aggression—to increase U.S. influence. We must seek the cooperation of the international community in solving the problems of the Middle East and get away from thinking that unilateral action by the United States is the key to peace. An international conference on the Middle East, held under the auspices of the U.N. and involving all parties concerned (including the chosen representative of the Palestinian people), will be a giant step towards peace.

Finally, the United States must improve relations with the Arab states. We should strive to expand economic, cultural, and trade ties amongst these states in order to weaken political barriers. This will lessen both the reasons and the willingness for war.

Establishing and maintaining friendly relations with Arab states need not require the United States to tilt away from Israel or abandon the special relationship it now has. Making new friends does not require abandoning the old.

America has a special relationship with Israel which must be preserved. America helped to found Israel, and American aid helps keep Israel strong. We believe, however, that in the long run America can best aid Israel by helping bring about a comprehensive political settlement seen as fair by both Arabs and Israelis. In order to do that, America needs to strengthen its relationship with *all* countries in the region.

# V

# THE
# REVIVAL
# OF HOPE

# THE PROMISE AND POLITICS OF EMPOWERMENT

Los Angeles, California, June 5, 1988

On this anniversary of Robert F. Kennedy's untimely death, how may we best remember him?

Let us honor him by committing ourselves to the cause that he and Dr. King worked for: the empowerment of all the people.

Empowerment. If before an election you ask candidates what they will provide for you, promises flow like momma's sweet syrup. After the election, too often the syrup turns sour. Suddenly, the politicians discover a deficit, or a "new consideration," or an "unexpected contingency," large phrases that mean broken promises.

I say real politics is not about providing for you. It is about empowering you so that you can provide for yourself.

Empowerment. This year experts predict that only half of all eligible Americans will go to the polls in November—a stark contrast to other major democracies where turnout ranges from 75 percent to 95 percent. And of course working and poor people are a disproportionate number of the no-shows.

Empowerment. From Iowa to California, this campaign has unleashed hope. It has expanded people's sense of the possible. It has built a coalition across ancient lines of race, religion and culture—common ground for empowerment.

Starting August 1, the Rainbow Coalition will launch a major registration drive. We will command the resources necessary to register African Americans, Hispanics, working men and women in large numbers to vote in November. Empowerment.

But we will go further than that. In Atlanta, the Democratic Party must make a commitment to empowerment—in the platform, in the party, on the ticket.

In the platform, we will ensure that the Democratic Party speaks forcefully against all impediments to registration and participation.

It is shameful—20 years after the death of Martin Luther King and Robert Kennedy— that we continue to deprive many citizens of the right to vote. Report after report documents discriminatory practices, barriers to registration, to voting, to hope.

Most recently the Citizens Commission on Civil Rights documented such practices.

In South Dakota, Indians from the Pine Ridge Reservation must travel 125-200 miles from the reservation simply to register.

In Dallas County, Alabama, African American deputy registrars were fired if they registered too many African Americans.

In Massachusetts, Florida and California, "Hispanic-looking" registrants were subjected to more stringent identification requirements than others.

Registration may be limited to a single location in a county, often the courthouse, distant from minority neighborhoods. Hours are limited, and often irregular. Offices are routinely closed for lunch. Registration deadlines expire a month or more before elections—long before many people even focus on the election.

These routine practices make it most difficult for working men and particularly working women to register and vote.

These registration requirements are not accidental. After the Civil War, the right to vote was extended to African American men. In 1920, it was finally extended to women. In the last half of the 19th century, some 75 percent of those eligible to vote did so. Falling turnout was the product of a movement to disenfranchise poor and minority people that swept the country at the turn of the century.

In the late 1880s the populist movement emerged among debt-ridden southern family farmers. African Americans were voting in large numbers in the early Reconstruction period. Poll taxes, literacy tests and registration restrictions were used to eliminate this challenge to the powers-that-be. By the early 1920s, southern turnout in presidential elections fell to a low of 19 percent.

In the North, businessmen pursued a similar strategy. Literacy tests and registration procedures succeeded in reducing turnout among urban workers and poor farmers. Northern turnout fell from over 80 percent in the late 1890s to 55 percent in the early 1920s.

In 1965, Dr. King led the struggle to reverse this trend in the South, to secure the right to vote. Despite the opposition of the Reagan-Bush administration, the Voting Rights Act has been extended.

Now we must go further. In Atlanta, the Democratic Party must make clear its commitment to universal voter registration, its support for the Universal Voter Registration Act, sponsored by Senator Alan Cranston and Representative John Conyers.

The Act provides for same-day registration, postcard registration and empowers service centers to act as registration centers. In Atlanta, the Democratic Party will make clear its commitment to the empowerment of all of the people.

Empowerment. We will register people to vote. We will fight to remove impediments to voting. We will also fight to remove impediments to making that vote count. Dual primaries, winner-take-all threshold, unelected super delegates and other party impediments to one person, one vote must be changed.

In Atlanta, we must ensure that the party's rules reflect the example of Dr. King, the inspiration of Robert Kennedy. We must also insure that the party's practice reflects the new voters coming into the process. The new coalition must be reflected in integrated slates. The new coalition must be reflected in reciprocal support. We have struggled too long and worked too hard to expect African Americans, Hispanics and women to support white male slates—with no reciprocal support for their candidacies. The party must make clear its commitment to the empowerment of all of the people.

Empowerment. We will remove impediments to registration. We will remove impediments to one person, one vote. We will change our ways to make room for new voters in the party. But we must go further than that.

We must remove the disproportionate influence of money on the political process. The U.S. Senate has become a club of white millionaires. Elected officials must spend the bulk of their time appealing to corporate PACs for the money they need to run for office. We have developed a system that protects incumbents and repels insurgents. A system designed to discourage new energy, new movement, new hope—at the very time our country must begin a new political era of experiment, innovation and expansion.

In Atlanta, I will put forward a comprehensive program to reduce the influence of wealth in politics, to open the process to all the people. The Democratic Party in Atlanta must make clear its opposition to plutocracy, its commitment to democracy.

It is not enough that people have the right to vote. It is not enough that the undue influence of money be reduced. People must have the reason to vote as well. Poor and working people do not vote in large numbers because they find no hope in either party. If the election offers a choice between two candidates of similar flavor and program—they have no reason to vote.

In Atlanta, the Democratic Party must keep hope alive. It must not only open the doors to voting, it must give working people a reason to vote.

That is why I have been so insistent that we offer a clear alternative to Reaganomics. That we make our priorities clear. That we make a commitment to invest in people—to provide hope. That we make a commitment that those who had the party under Reagan and Bush —the rich and the powerful—will pay for the party. That we make a commitment to change our priorities from building weapons that we can never use to investing in people whom we cannot afford to lose.

Let us not be the party of false dreams and broken promises. Let us not promise day care for working parents—and not commit the resources to provide it. Promise education for every qualified student, yes—but commit the resources to pay for it. Promise health care for all Americans, yes—but commit the resources to pay for it. Promise affordable housing, yes—but only if we commit the resources to back up the promise.

In Atlanta, I will fight to ensure that the party gives people reason to vote in the fall. That it offers the promise of America to every American. That it returns to its finest roots—the legacy of Franklin Roosevelt and the economic bill of rights, the legacy of Dr. King and the struggle for the right to vote, for economic justice, for peace; the legacy of Robert Kennedy and the promise of hope reborn among working and poor people.

I will fight not only for the promise, but for the commitment of new priorities that make the promise possible. The dream, and the program to pay for the dream. This is not about charisma, not about competence—but about the candor necessary to enlist the best aspirations of the people.

What does Jesse Jackson want? Empowerment—for all people in America. What will Jesse Jackson do in Atlanta? Know this—we will fight to ensure that the Democratic Party is the party of the people, the party of empowerment, the party of participation, the party of hope.

# THE STRUGGLE CONTINUES

Atlanta, Georgia, July 22, 1988

I greet you this morning with a sense of joy, a sense that because we've come this way we've maintained faith in the legacy of our forefathers and our foremothers. We're moving on up and have every reason to be hopeful, to be excited, knowing that we are close to where we are going, a long way from where we started, and in our lifetime—you and I—we'll be in the White House.

We must always put these struggles for change in historical context. I looked around last night and I thought about Atlantic City just 24 years ago—Fannie Lou Hamer and Aaron Henry on the outside, trying to get a seat in the Mississippi delegation. Last night the state chairman of the Regular Democratic Party in Mississippi was Ed Cole, an African American man. Black and white sat together, lion and lamb voted together, and none was afraid because we've progressed.

If you think there is some agony or hurt here today, you try Atlantic City in 1964 when the Democratic Party would not unseat the Regular Democratic delegation from Mississippi. But life moves on. From 1964 to 1968 Julian Bond and Channing Phillips and others took us a step higher and took the seats that were rightfully ours. Willie Brown rightfully got his delegates in Florida. Our Illinois delegation unseated Mayor Daley in 1972. The victory for Jimmy Carter in 1976 clearly represented the rise of the New South because of our votes and a new coalition.

Then we had the deluge of Reaganism and all of the diversion it has represented. But the fantasy is ending, the foolishness is ending and the air is coming out of the balloon. The struggle continues.

I told you on Sunday, let's measure where we are. Don't make Friday morning decisions on Sunday night. What were our objectives?

Expand the party. The Democratic National Committee was opened up this morning—there will be an additional vice-chair and 18 new positions, all of which we recommended. Expansion. Inclusion.

Look at our legislative agenda. This is so basic to the growth process of this country. The Conyers bill calling for universal on-site, same-day voter registration. It will save many millions of dollars in voter registration drives and put millions more people on the books.

I was down in Savannah, Georgia, a few months ago, where at 7 p.m. 9,000 people were gathered, many of whom wanted to register to vote. The registrar's office closed at 6:30, and we were not even allowed to pay the registrar overtime to keep the office open, or to have him come to the auditorium, which was exactly one and a half blocks down the street, to register people. The Conyers bill will end that. And that's progress.

The support of, without equivocation, the Dellums Bill on South Africa. The word went out that South Africa had been declared a terrorist state. All of Africa rejoiced. Because what does that mean? It means that either you declare there are no terrorist states, or South Africa is a terrorist state. And if it is a terrorist state, it then means anti-terrorist policy applies to it. It means that we do not trade with terrorist states, and we're not going to sell arms to countries that sell arms to terrorist states, and that we'll pull all American companies out of a terrorist state. That position alone shook the foundation of the whole apartheid system. And that's progress.

A commitment to economic set-asides, with the ability and will to enforce them. Economic set-asides by law are five to ten percent. Should it be ten percent across the board? What is five or ten percent of a $1 trillion budget? That's $50 to $100 billion a year set aside by law. It's a law, but it's like the Emancipation Proclamation—we got the proclamation without the emancipation. We have economic set-asides, but we have no apparatus to have them set aside, so the motion dies for lack of a second. We will implement that. It is urban reinvestment. It is business development. And that's progress.

The commitment to the ABC child-care legislation and to statehood for the District of Columbia, which means two U.S. Senators from Washington, D.C.—and a governor.

We've gotten Jim Wright, Speaker of the House, to commit himself to taking the Conyers bill and the Dellums bill to the floor. A Democratic majority means we can pass the Conyers voter registration bill. It means we can pass the Dellums South African sanctions bill. It means economic set-asides, ABC child-care legislation and statehood for the District of Columbia. Those are some of the commitments we've received. And that's progress.

A commitment to end the abandonment of the homeless. A commitment to end the abandonment of our children. A commitment to end the abandonment of women, infants and children. A commitment to reach out across lines of race, and sex, and religion, and affirm everybody's Americanness. It's time for a fundamental change in direction.

I said earlier in the week, the media came looking for a show, and found people serious. They said, "But where are the fireworks?" That was their business. We came looking for noble works, not fireworks. Not show business, but serious business.

The victory lies not in what Governor Dukakis and Lloyd Bentsen can do for us. That's not the victory. The victory lies in the fact that our minds have changed about ourselves, and our reasonable expectations have been expanded.

Mickey Leland can walk around, organizing a move to run for U.S. Senate in Texas, and not be looked down upon as being absurd. Lou Stokes can contemplate running for the U.S. Senate in Ohio, and not be dismissed as absurd. Andy Young can walk around here thinking about running for governor of Georgia, and not be dismissed as absurd. And David Dinkins can think about running for mayor of New York, and not be dismissed as absurd.

There's big business at stake here. Affordable housing. The stakes are high. Education for our children. The stakes are high. Stopping the dealing with dealers who are giving drugs to our children. The stakes are high.

I've had to learn the science of politics. I've watched it from its many angles. I'm often asked, what does the Lloyd Bentsen wing of the ticket mean to me? I tell you what it means. It represents a wing. We represent a wing. It takes two wings to fly. When all is said and done, hawks and doves are just birds. As long as they fly the same air, they cannot afford to have that air poisoned by pollution.

What does Bentsen being on the ticket mean to me in practical terms? It means that the contras have lost a vote. It means D.C. statehood has gained a vote. It means Mandela has gained an ally. And so, my friends, in this process we're transformed. We've become bigger people, and better people.

I am convinced we have reason to be hopeful, reason to build a coalition, reason to leave here and work, reason to have a record turnout, reason to keep this progressive campaign alive and building: in 1988 it's the White House; in 1990 it's the census; in 1991 it's reapportionment. We have reason to work.

We'll be blending Dukakis and Jackson supporters at the national, state and congressional district levels. We'll have access to where policies are made and priorities are set. Expansion, inclusion, relationships. Those have been the operative words for the week: expansion, inclusion, relationships, future, and the struggle continues.

I feel hopeful this morning. I feel delighted. I feel secure. I feel comfort that you will be protected in your role in the campaign, in the DNC, and I feel comfortable in the role I chose. That's why I don't want a job or a title. I want to be free to serve at my own pace. Free to support, and free to challenge. We have a role —to support, and to get respect according to our support. We have never had those two things before, a role and respect. And from that, everything else grows.

Throughout, this campaign has been about expansion, it's been about inclusion and about relationships. This morning, our enemies are sad and our friends rejoice because we've kept this campaign above the temptation of demagoguery, of racial divisions, and on a high and principled level. And friends, we're well on our way. The long-distance race doesn't go to the swift but to the strong—to those who can hold out. I don't feel tired. Even Reagan ran three times.

These last seven years have been especially painful. While our sons and daughters have died in Grenada and Lebanon and Europe, this President has not met with the Congressional Black Caucus one time. Denial of access. In these last seven years, this man suggested that those in South Africa who were shot in the back had provoked the shootings. In these last seven years, our complicity with South Africa, in Angola, in Namibia and inside South Africa, continues. In these last seven years, Reagan opened up his presidential campaign in Philadelphia, Mississippi, sending a signal that was missed by too many people. There's not even a railroad in Philadelphia, Mississippi, not even a small airport. The only thing it is known for is that it is where the civil rights activists Schwerner, Goodman and Chaney were found murdered. On that day of Reagan's announcement, even the Klan were there in their paraphernalia. I tell you from Philadelphia, Mississippi, to Bitburg, Germany, to Johannesburg, South Africa, it's been an unbroken line by Reagan, unchallenged by Bush.

My friends, I'm going to keep on arguing a preferable case to you about our live options. We might think now that in 1960 John Kennedy won unanimously. But he won by 112,000 votes—less than one vote per precinct. Kennedy won against Nixon with less than one vote per precinct difference in the American mind.

In 1960, we won by the margin of our hope, because Kennedy took the risks to relate to us publicly and to reach out to Dr. King.

In 1968, the psychology shifted. Dr. King was killed on April 4. Robert Kennedy was killed on June 5. There were riots at the Chicago Democratic Convention. With all of that death, all of that despair, all of those broken hearts, all of that lost blood, Nixon beat Humphrey by 550,000 votes.

The difference between Nixon and Humphrey was tremendous. But we could not make a distinction between the Great Society and the lost society. We lost by the margin of our despair what we had won eight years before by the margin of our hope.

Now we come forth in 1988, with much more strength and much greater capability. We've had to knock down doors in the DNC. It's not unusual. We give thanks that we have the ability to knock them down, and open them up. We can do that. We've always had the paradoxical burden of fighting to save the nation just to save ourselves.

If you're in the back seat of a truck, and you don't like the driver and the car's going over the cliff, don't take solace in the fact that he's going over the cliff, because he isn't going to push a button and eject you. You'll have to save the driver just to save yourself. And so here we are today, still knocking on doors. We're still winning every day and winning in every way.

Many things have changed this week in Atlanta—among other things, relationships. There have been serious meetings this week with Paul Kirk and the DNC leadership, and there will be serious changes in the DNC as of this morning because of you—not because those doors voluntarily opened up and certainly not because you stopped knocking. Some combination of your knocking and determination to get in has changed things.

I'm clear about it. John Kennedy supported the civil rights movement but the children in Birmingham wrote it. Lyndon Johnson didn't get the Voting Rights Act passed. Folks in Selma got it passed. And then Johnson wrote in ink what they had written in blood.

He had the will but not the capacity because there are checks and balances in this government. He told Dr. King, "I'm for it, but we can't get it because the Congress is too conservative. I just can't get it passed." But "street heat" in Selma gave him a new alternative. He then could say, "I'm for some change, now we shall overcome."

I'll tell you one reason I want to be close enough to serve and far enough away to challenge—because change requires a combination of new leadership and "street heat." John Kennedy and Robert Kennedy could not go to Birmingham and say, I feel ashamed, therefore I will enact a Public Accommodations bill. It took a combination of their leadership and our "street heat."

We've got to keep up the "street heat." My friends, if we put on two to three million new voters between now and October 8, there will be enough heat to cook our meat, and enough heat for George Bush to get out of the kitchen.

You do understand that the contra vote that comes up again next week—they can't get that vote now. You do understand that when Mayor Marion Barry and Rep. Walter Fauntroy try to get the D.C. statehood bill passed, that the wing of the party that's been holding it back—they have to deliver now. That's the art and science of politics. It takes different temperatures to cook different kinds of meat. That's "street heat."

I'm excited. There's going to be a change. Why are Republicans already talking about "They're running a three-man ticket—Dukakis, Bentsen and Jackson"? Well, they're trying to create some mess. That's a trick to drive us away, but we're not leaving.

There isn't a three-man ticket. Psychologically, I don't require it. A political ticket doesn't need it. We're more grown than that. We got this commitment on the Dellums Bill, and Mandela can rejoice, and on the Conyers Bill, and unregistered voters can rejoice, and on two senators and a governor in D.C., which could completely change the balance in the U.S. Senate, and we can all rejoice.

Let's look at a few more things here. I suppose the first victory for us is that we're together. People who didn't support us in 1984 supported us in 1988. There are those who didn't support us in 1988 who are going to support us from now on because it's clear what time of day it is.

We're also in major league politics now. This isn't softball. The next step is to go back to your states—to every state we won, every district we won—and see how your congressperson voted, see how your senator voted, and see how your DNC member voted. That's the basis for new politics right where you live.

That's the first thing you've got to do. In Mississippi they got themselves lawyers, or-

ganized over the long haul and now they are the leaders of the state Democratic Party. Our Mississippi delegation ran a ticket and won the leadership positions in the state party. We must do this in every state we won—from Maine to Delaware to Virginia to South Carolina to Georgia to Alabama to Louisiana—in every one of those states where we the people were humiliated on Wednesday night because we won the popular vote but the superdelegates imposed their will on us.

Some people say what did we get? Well, we got new rules and the party can't run over us again in 1992.

When you win Michigan two-to-one, and then come out 80-80 at the convention, it's time to go back home and do some work.

If you decide to go back home and not work, you're doing your enemy a favor. The threat is not that we might leave, the threat is we might stay. We're just an attitude away from winning. Just an attitude away.

When you go back to your states, remember that we are trying to put together a campaign state-by-state not just for Dukakis and Bentsen, but for ourselves. If you went to the grocery store and folks at your house were hungry, and you came back home with an empty grocery bag and a pocket full of money, they would say, "What's wrong with you?" You'd say, "Well, I went to the grocery store and they didn't have any steak." But they would rightfully ask about pork chops, sausage and the other stuff you can get there. When you go shopping in a presidential election, you're not just shopping for the top of the ticket. There's also city council races, school board elections and lots of other seats at stake. There's a whole grocery bag of elections.

Now we're going to do something else too. We must follow Michigan's lead and get your state legislature to pass same-day, on-site voter registration. It's a central civil rights issue.

Why did we win Michigan? I know why we won Michigan. Because my sons Jesse Jr. and Jonathan, and the actress Kim Fields, went into the high schools speaking to students and registering them to vote. They turned out to vote—about 150 high school senior classes with 300 to 400 seniors per school. These high school seniors weren't in anybody's computers.

The same youth that now are using their power against themselves have the power to completely change this nation. Change never does come about until our youth come alive. We've got to stop them from using their power in self-destructive ways.

The next thing is to run for office. Run for governor, run for U.S. senator, run for a local judgeship, run for everything that's open. Integrate slates—black, brown and white, male and female. If you don't win, you will at least create a new equation. And, if you get nothing out of it but learning how to run, you learn.

You know most African Americans who live in Chicago don't know Illinois. They know Chicago. They don't relate to folk in East St. Louis or Springfield or Peoria—they have Chicago on the brain.

The fact is we are putting too much focus on the city council people and not enough on state legislators, because city council folks by and large are there where the daily newspaper is and the television cameras are. They put city council issues on TV at night because the city council has got the day-to-day burden. But it's the state legislatures that have the budget.

I understand the psychology of it. Once you get to Chicago, you do not want to go to Springfield. You've paid your Springfield dues. You've left Springfield to get to Chicago. The fact is, my friends, the power is in Springfield, not in city hall.

New York—once you get to the bright lights! Big deal—the power's in Albany, not in New York City. Once you get to Philadelphia—right on! But the power is in Harrisburg, because that's where the budget is. Go to your state legislatures.

When should the Rainbow Convention meet in your state? Go find out from your state legislature when budget time is. Have your convention at budget time. Then you can lobby about the budget. They cut up a multibillion dollar budget in those little towns called Springfield, Harrisburg, Albany, but you can't get thirty people there. The city council will have a meeting on dog mess, and it's city council here I come. The TV cameras will be rolling, people will be jumping up and down for and against the dog. But in state

capitals, when it's time to discuss the budget reforms or education and everything else, you can't get thirty people there. The lights are too dim in state legislatures. We've got big mayors on the brain. But the best of mayors can't spend money they don't have—that's the business of state legislatures.

I want us to become more politically sophisticated. We should have thousands marching and meeting at budget time. The budget's the real issue with the Dukakis ticket. We must keep "street heat" on the budget because it is fundamental.

We must continue to build our own political organizations at the state level. We must meet and work together with their campaign people. Don't just be picked off one by one—let's relate in a disciplined fashion and keep our organization together. Learn from the campaign, don't disintegrate. Don't go away. We've got some big elections in 1989, the census in 1990 and reapportionment in 1991.

We will leave here with a bigger, better, stronger Rainbow Coalition. We've proven it can happen. It wasn't easy, but look around this room. There are white farmers in here, African Americans and Hispanics, Arabs and Jews, peace activists—this is our dream.

You look at the Democratic platform— most of the policies are our language—that's Jackson action. That stuff about South Africa being declared a terrorist state—that's Jackson action. That stuff about reinvest in America— that's Jackson action. You put 13 minority reports on the table and you win on nine of them—that's winning.

The fact that we were able to raise the issue of U.S. policy in the Middle East so the whole party could discuss it and think about it— that's profound change.

Now, if we have come this far—half asleep and half walking—you know what's next. We got 1,200 delegates and didn't even hardly believe it ourselves.

I have to keep looking on the bright side. On the day that we were in Oregon, they locked up two folks that threatened to assassinate me. We got 40 percent of the white vote in Oregon on that day. Do you know what that means? In Oregon? On that day?

And so our strategy was simple—expand

217

our options without tearing up the party, because it's the key vehicle we've got for the fight. We cannot fight by walking away from it. That will not win. I know better than that. We've got better judgment than that. We're long-distance runners.

The media keeps on wanting to project us as being an emotional, irrational, irascible, enigmatic kind of movement. But we stayed on Wednesday night and Willie Brown went up to the podium and, with grace, supported Michael Dukakis by acclamation. That's good judgment. And Mickey Leland, from Texas, went up there last night and by acclamation supported Lloyd Bentsen for vice president. That's good judgment.

And do you realize what we did this week in this town? Do you know the impact we've had? The whole world has been watching us all week, because we never stopped campaigning and we're not going to stop.

I want some of the party's resources to register more of us to vote. I want a record turnout. We cannot be bypassed. We can't be locked out. And, when you're too tough and mature to cry when you're hurting, I'll suffer for you. I'll die for you. I want you to suffer with me, and together our suffering will not be in vain. We're going to win. We're winning every day. Winning every day. Every day. Every day! Every day!

# ADDENDUM

# FROM IOWA TO CALIFORNIA: WE'RE WINNING EVERY DAY

From New York City to McFarland, California, from Cleveland, Ohio, to the Democratic National Convention in Atlanta, Georgia, Jesse Jackson told his supporters "We're winning every day." A campaign that won seven million votes and 1,200 delegates changed the American political landscape every day, in small towns and big cities, farms and factories, high schools and housing projects across the country.

Some of those changes were told by the *Flathead Courier* or the *Mountain Eagle*, but never made it into the *Washington Post* or the *New York Times*. Others went unnoticed altogether by the press. It would take a whole book, seven million stories, to fully describe what was won. The following state-by-state account highlights a few of the victories that Jesse Jackson—and we the people—won in the 1988 primary campaign.

### Iowa—February 8

On Superbowl Sunday, 1987, Jesse Jackson visited the small town of Greenfield, Iowa. Over nine hundred people ignored the biggest game of the year on TV and set out through the snow to hear him. Jackson promptly chose Greenfield as the headquarters for his Iowa Exploratory Committee. The people of Greenfield put up the national press corps in their homes when there weren't enough hotel rooms to accommodate them. Jackson won the entire county in the caucuses.

The Jackson campaign spent one-sixth of the money and had about one-eighth of the staff of the other candidates in Iowa, yet only Jackson won delegates in every single county.

*This section was written by Joanne Durham, Deputy Delegate Coordinator, 1988 Jesse Jackson for President Campaign.*

CBS exit polls showed that only 38 percent of Jackson's voters had been directly contacted to come vote, 10-20 percentage points lower than any other candidate's. But the people came out anyway. In a state with a one percent African American population, where he had won about 1.5 percent of the vote in 1984, 11 percent voted for Jackson in 1988. Dozens of African American churches held caucus trainings, and hundreds of people became precinct delegates who had never attended a caucus before. Farm networks, student organizations, peace and justice groups all organized for Jesse. In the end Jackson came out of Iowa second in national convention delegates—with 23 percent of the total—more than Gephardt, the Iowa winner, and Simon, who was in second place.

### New Hampshire—February 16

New Hampshire was a "neighbors approaching neighbors" campaign, with local residents comprising nine of the twelve staff people in the state. Jackson won eight percent of the vote in this all-white state and the first primary of the season. In New Hampshire, Jackson boldly articulated many of the themes that were to become central to his campaign, including an anti-drug program, national health care, and the need to unite to stop economic violence.

In Portsmouth, he condemned a wall built to separate a low-income housing project and adjoining luxury apartments. "These walls must come down," Jackson told the project's residents. "They have no place in Berlin and no place in America." Supporting striking railroad workers, Jackson capped his New Hampshire campaign by riding the "Rainbow Express" on a whistle-stop train circuit through many parts of the state, where even in the freezing cold people crowded the stations along the way to hear him.

## Minnesota—February 23

Minnesota was Jackson's first second-place finish. He won two of eight congressional districts, and beat everybody but the uncommitted vote in the largely rural first congressional district. Minnesota showed what a truly rainbow grassroots organization can accomplish. Volunteers worked in 80 percent of Minnesota's 90 mostly rural counties, with a major door-to-door operation in the urban centers beginning in December.

The campaign held caucus training at 4 a.m. after the night shift at Ford. For the first time in history, the plant actually closed down on caucus night because so many Jackson supporters requested leave to vote. Huge crowds turned out for Jackson's swing through rural Minnesota. Eighteen hundred people showed up at an event in Osakis, a town with a population of 1,300!

Jesse won the local caucuses in some white well-to-do suburbs of Minneapolis; he won the county caucus in conservative Brown County. The breadth of his support was reflected in the 29 members of Minnesota's Jackson delegation: African American, white, Native American, Hispanic, gay, the physically challenged, farmers, students, peace activists, women's advocates, environmentalists, unionists—three quarters of whom had never been to a Democratic convention before.

## South Dakota—February 23

Despite the 20-state Super Tuesday race looming ahead and no expectations for victory, Jesse Jackson visited Rapid City, arriving at 2 a.m. in a snowstorm. Three hundred people travelled from miles around, still in the snow, to hear him at 7 a.m. that Saturday morning. Jackson endorsed the Bradley Bill, calling for Indian land rights, again bucking conventional wisdom for success in a conservative, mostly white state.

He solidly won Shannon County, home of the Pine Ridge Indian Reservation, despite polling places which had been changed from the last election and people who had to wait half the day for a ride to the changed site. He came in second in Todd County on the strength of the votes from the Rosebud Indian Reservation.

## Maine—February 28

Halfway through Jesse Jackson's speech to over 3,000 striking International Paperworkers, friends and families in Jay, Maine, the slogan "Scabs out, union in" was transformed to "Reagan out, Jackson in." Jesse Jackson also transformed a six percent showing in Maine in 1984 into a strong second place finish with 39 percent of the final delegation to the national convention in 1988. He won the caucuses in the major cities of Portland and Bangor, as well as in smaller towns such as Cumberland, North Berwick, and Newcastle, winning six out of Maine's 16 counties. "Jackson Cuts into Dukakis' Backyard" read the headline in the *Portland Press Herald* the day after the caucuses. But it was not what Jesse took away from anyone that will be remembered in Maine, it is the message of hope he brought with him.

## Wyoming—March 5

In another state that received little money or national campaign support, Jesse Jackson scored 25 percent of the final delegation. Jackson delegates increased from 13 percent of the local delegates in March to 23 percent of the state convention delegates in May even after the press had anointed Mike Dukakis the sure nominee. Jackson won two counties, both rural, in the northern part of the state, based on the efforts of local volunteers who organized by phone and word-of-mouth. The campaign brought together a network of progressives from around the state, with at least half of the Jackson state delegation new to Democratic Party politics.

## Super Tuesday—March 8

On the day with more primary contests than any other, Jesse Jackson won more votes than any other candidate. The campaign spent $100,000 on the media, compared to millions of dollars lavished on it by other candidates. With hardly any paid staff, Jackson nonetheless captured the wholehearted support of the African American population of the South, winning a spectacular 95 percent of the African American vote (compared to 60 percent in 1984). His share of the white vote also increased in the region of the country where he and other civil rights activists had marched, protested and gone to jail 20 years earlier. Jackson's message of economic justice and hope rang true and his call for a New South healed many racial wounds by uniting people based on economic interests. According to CBS exit polls, he won the vote of the least educated (42 percent of those with a high school education or less voted for him); 60 percent of the unemployed or laid off; and 59 percent of the poorest ($5,000 or less income).

## Alabama

In Alabama, Jackson rallied with his supporters on the Edmund Pettus Bridge, where in 1965 civil rights marchers were turned back by state troopers. "And 23 years later," Jackson told his supporters the night of his Super Tuesday victory, "we have won that state—the same state that wouldn't even let us vote, that wouldn't even let us walk across the bridge."

Jackson more than doubled his vote from 1984, winning five of seven congressional districts and just over half of Alabama's 67 counties. Exit polls showed Jackson winning almost twice the African American vote and six times the white vote he won in 1984. African American voters turned out to vote in record numbers, comprising 44 percent of Democratic voters. In Birmingham, where Jesse spent $4,950 on TV advertising compared to $68,420 for Gore and $35,870 for Gephardt, Jackson totaled 63 percent of the sixth congressional district vote!

## Arkansas

With scarce resources, the Arkansas campaign brought in 17 percent of the state's vote for Jesse Jackson, spending approximately five cents per vote. Its broad-based coalition included statewide women's and peace networks, ACORN, African American churches, students and labor. In Pine Bluff, which Jackson won, the Students for Jackson network reached out to everyone working and studying on campus as well as the surrounding community, and registered more people than were enrolled in the school!

Jackson also won four counties in the Arkansas Delta. Voters' Leagues in these counties had worked for Jesse and consolidated their strength through the 1984 campaign. They

continued in 1988, electing African American officials to school boards, city council and other local positions along with their victories for Jackson on Super Tuesday.

## Florida

Jesse Jackson went from one delegate in Florida in 1984 to 33 in 1988. With an 11 percent African American population, Jackson took 20 percent of Florida's Democratic vote on Super Tuesday, beating both Gore and Gephardt and winning three congressional districts, including Miami. In the third congressional district, which Jackson won, 50 percent of the registered Democrats turned out to vote—the highest percentage turnout in the state. The campaign forged a statewide network, with new organizing skills and determination to increase minority empowerment in upcoming legislative and congressional races.

## Georgia

For the Jackson campaign, coming to Atlanta for the Democratic National Convention meant coming to the state of one of its finest victories. Jackson won Georgia with 40 percent of the vote; six of 10 congressional districts; double his percentage of votes from 1984; and more than twice as many counties as in 1984. He swept the fifth congressional district, taking every delegate. The Georgia campaign covered all the bases, from a field organizer travelling throughout the rural counties of the eight congressional districts to the first presidential candidate's rally ever in the small mill town of West Point. Students from the University of Georgia helped win Clarke County, and Jackson even won 121 votes in Klan-dominated Forsyth County.

Jackson won 94 percent of the African American vote in Georgia. His appearance at Ebenezer Baptist Church, flanked by Coretta Scott King, Andrew Young and John Lewis, foretold the united African American support Jackson would receive nationally throughout the rest of the campaign.

## Hawaii

The Jackson campaign gave Hawaii its first real contest for the Democratic presidential nomination and the strongest turnout in history. Of the 3,000 Democratic voters registered prior to Super Tuesday, about 2,000 were Jesse Jackson supporters, bringing new vitality into the party. The state party broke its tradition of going uncommitted and backed Dukakis, but Jackson still won 35 percent of the vote. In one of the closest contests in the country, he ran 17 votes behind Dukakis in the first congressional district.

### Idaho

Three delegates proudly represented Idaho for Jesse Jackson at the 1988 Democratic National Convention: one African American, one white, one Native American. Gore put the most effort in the state and Gephardt attempted to build a base in the high-tech industry. But Jackson's message and grassroots organization won him 21 percent of the caucus vote to Dukakis's 36 percent, with no other candidate breaking double digits. Jackson won caucus delegates in places like Idaho Falls and Twin Falls, with virtually no African American population.

### Kentucky

Jackson pulled 16 percent of the vote in Kentucky. African American voters, who only make up seven percent of the population, consistently came out to vote. While statewide turnout was only about 22 percent, African American precincts ran much higher, an average of 35-40 percent and as high as 50-60 percent in some areas of Louisville. The Jackson campaign also reached out for the first time into the mountain regions of eastern Kentucky, pulling 16-17 percent in some of the all white counties in this area. Five thousand people cheered Jackson in the mountain town of Hazard, where he was the first presidential candidate to appear in twenty years.

### Louisiana

Louisiana was another solid Jackson victory. He won over half the parishes in the state and almost doubled his vote from 1984. African American tenant organizers from New Orleans' huge housing projects played a major role in Jackson's 61 percent victory in the second congressional district. Volunteers went door-to-door in almost every public housing

development in the city, and residents not only came out to vote but also provided an avenue to the rural areas of Louisiana through their relatives and church connections.

The struggle for African American empowerment was deeply woven into the Louisiana campaign. Two African American women, strong Jackson supporters who played major roles in organizing the campaign, ran in the primary for U.S. Congress from Baton Rouge and Shreveport.

### Maryland

Expectations were high for Jackson to win Maryland until Gore, Simon and Gephardt support fizzled and Dukakis made the state one of his selected targets for Super Tuesday. Jackson still pulled 29 percent of the vote to Dukakis's 46 percent, winning two of Maryland's eight congressional districts.

Jackson's strong African American support in Baltimore and Prince George's County aided the ongoing process of African American empowerment in the state and the campaign won the co-chair of the state delegation. Youth involvement was significant statewide, from the mostly white campuses of Johns Hopkins and the University of Maryland (College Park) to majority African American schools in Baltimore and the eastern shore.

### Massachusetts

Jesse Jackson showed unexpected strength in winning 19 percent of the vote in Massachusetts, four times his 1984 showing. Jackson won delegates across the state, in nine of 11 congressional districts. Jackson supporters won ten townships in the first congressional district, including the college town of Amherst. The Massachusetts Jackson effort also mobilized over 300 volunteers to campaign for Jesse in neighboring New Hampshire.

### Mississippi

In his speech to the Democratic National Convention, Jackson pointed proudly to the changes over the years in the Mississippi delegation: "Twenty-four years ago, Fannie Lou Hamer and Aaron Henry—who sits here tonight—were locked out on the streets of Atlantic City, the heads of the Mississippi Freedom

Democratic Party. Tonight, an African American and white delegation from Mississippi is headed by Ed Cole, an African American."

Mississippi was one of Jackson's biggest wins on Super Tuesday, with 45 percent of the vote. Al Gore couldn't close the gap even with six trips to Mississippi and 150 endorsements from state officials. Mississippi's 31 percent African American population stood firm behind Jesse Jackson, and Jesse won four of five congressional districts and two-thirds of the counties in the state. In the Mississippi Delta, the poorest rural congressional district in the country, the majority African American population pulled in 65 percent of the vote for Jackson. And even in Lafayette County, home of Ole Miss and the site of bitter struggles in the civil rights movement, Jackson pulled 34 percent of the vote for a second-place finish.

## Missouri

Jesse Jackson beat the favorite son, Dick Gephardt, in his own hometown of St. Louis, and won the entire congressional district as well. A record turnout among African American voters made the difference. Winning 20 percent of the vote statewide, Jackson was the only other candidate besides Gephardt to make the 15 percent threshold for at-large delegates.

## North Carolina

Gore narrowly beat Jackson to win North Carolina, 35 percent to 33 percent. Jackson's impact on minority empowerment, coalition building, and expanded participation was evident throughout the state. Jackson won 38 out of 100 counties, more than double the number he won in 1984. He won every county in the seventh congressional district, including Robeson County, a 61 percent minority county with the largest American Indian population east of the Mississippi. The African American/Indian coalition built by the campaign defeated the overwhelmingly white Board of County Commissioners and replaced it with minority candidates in the May primary.

Jackson also won 12 percent of the vote in 24 counties with less than a five percent African American population, due to a well-organized campaign with efforts in every county in the state. He won a majority in Durham County, beating both Gore and Dukakis more than two-to-one thanks to a strong coalition of African American voters and progressive whites. The campaign also had a decisive impact on youth in the state. Jackson's visit to a high school in Asheville sparked the development of a Jackson network among Young Democrats, Teen Democrats and other youth, both for the presidential campaign as well as ongoing involvement in local and statewide races.

## Oklahoma

Jackson's 13 percent of the primary vote in Oklahoma was a marked contrast to his four percent in 1984. He won delegates from three congressional districts (1, 5 and 6). All three delegates were first time national convention participants. In addition to the congressional districts where he made the threshold, Jackson received over 15 percent of the vote in ten other counties. In two counties, Logan and Oklahoma, he finished in second place. Over 1,200 students waving "We Can Win" banners crammed a high school gymnasium to hear him on his visit to the state.

## Rhode Island

Jackson finished second in Rhode Island, beating everyone but Dukakis. In a New England state with a three percent African American population, Jackson again demonstrated his broad, national appeal. Jackson won almost one fourth of the vote in Providence, 28 percent in South Kingstown (with a varied population including Native Americans and retired military), and he was the top vote-getter in the small, all-white town of Foster. Running on the ballot for his delegate positions were African Americans, whites, union representatives, gays, a writer, a retired teacher, an Arab American, and state elected officials. Jackson's candidacy sparked an upsurge in progressive politics in Rhode Island, encouraging minorities to run for local and state office and bringing together a strong new coalition.

## Tennessee

In Al Gore's home state, Jesse Jackson won Memphis and the entire ninth congressional district with 72 percent of the vote, pulling 21 percent of the vote statewide. Jackson won 23 percent in Nashville's Davidson County, due largely to the grassroots effort of volunteers who registered over 2,000 youth in schools and housing projects and canvassed the surrounding rural areas wearing Jackson t-shirts and buttons to attract new supporters. Jackson also won Fayette and Haywood counties and took 35 percent of the vote in Hamilton County (Chattanooga).

## Texas

Jackson was second in the Texas primary, with 26 percent of the vote to Dukakis' 34 percent. He won delegates in all but four of Texas' 31 senatorial districts, won five senatorial districts, eleven counties and as many votes as George Bush! Relying on commitment and organization, Jackson beat Dukakis in local caucuses in the second part of the Texas delegate selection process.

The endorsement of Texas Agriculture Commissioner Jim Hightower, who campaigned with Jackson from the Farm Aid concert in Texas all the way to California, gave a clear signal of the progressive coalition the Jackson campaign had developed. In addition to his solid base among African American voters and significant Hispanic support, Jackson won 14 percent of the white vote according to CBS exit polls. He got as many white votes in Texas as Al Gore!

Jackson's message of economic justice broke through many barriers in Texas, such as among striking Mobil Oil workers in Beaumont, a traditionally conservative area. He even won some parts of east and west Texas that went for George Wallace in 1968.

## Virginia

Virginia brought in 45 percent of its votes for Jesse Jackson in another of Super Tuesday's big wins. African American voter turnout was generated in both rural areas and major cities by African American churches, radio stations and volunteers, with Jackson winning all five congressional districts with an African American population over 20 percent. Jesse won 70 percent of the vote in the fourth congressional district, and 19 out of its 20 counties!

His white support was estimated in exit polls at 14 percent, the highest in the South. He won the Shenandoah Valley's seventh congressional district, with a 12 percent African American population. In that congressional district, Charlottesville students and activists won their city, and rural supporters sponsored a Jackson "phone-in" rally that attracted farmers and workers from several surrounding counties, including Louisa, Madison and Orange, all of which Jackson won. Steelworkers joined the African American community in organizing for Jesse in the Tidewater area, Arab Americans and whites campaigned in addition to his African American base in northern Virginia, and he even took 12 percent of the vote in the predominantly white mining areas of western Virginia.

## Washington

In this state targeted by the Aryan Nation to be part of its "white nation," four days before Super Tuesday *The Seattle Times* predicted Jesse Jackson would receive four percent of the vote. Instead, first place was so close between Jackson and Dukakis that a winner couldn't be called for days, and Jackson eventually wound up with 40 percent of the delegates. That delegation included the presidents of three state labor unions—Hospital Workers, Inland Boatmen and United Farmworkers; the chair of the Quinnault Indian tribe; and the only African American city councilman in the state of Washington.

Competing against 15 paid organizers from the Dukakis campaign, the Jackson organization relied, as always, on the people, who came through at every turn. Students from Western Washington University volunteered to organize their campus, spread out to the surrounding community and won the entire county. Jackson made the 15 percent threshold for delegates from every county and every congressional district in the state.

## Alaska—March 10

Winning Alaska made a lot of people sit up and take notice of Jackson action. With the only help received from the national office being a bag of buttons, Alaskan supporters launched a grassroots campaign via telephone conference, with twelve coordinators spread over the vast expanse of the state. Alaskan natives contributed significantly to Jackson's success. He won the town of Bethel, which is 95 percent Alaskan native, as well as many other exclusively native precincts in western Alaska.

### South Carolina—March 12

Jesse Jackson's home state came in strong for him in its caucus, with 55 percent of the votes cast. Jesse won every county in the first and sixth congressional districts, and 80 percent of the counties statewide. Almost twice as many voters came out for him in 1988 as did in 1984.

Jackson's strength in South Carolina caused U.S. Senator Fritz Hollings to become in June the first white congressional superdelegate to endorse Jackson. In addition to his solid support among African American voters, the campaign rallied white progressives and won new allies among white farmers in South Carolina.

### North Dakota—March 13-27

With the help of organizers from the Minnesota campaign, North Dakota Jackson campaigners crisscrossed the state to build support for their candidate. Students, Native Americans, labor, farm advocates, women and peace groups all combined to make a Jackson campaign with literally hundreds of volunteers. As a result, Jackson won 19 percent of the straw poll of caucus goers, winning in diverse areas from the six combined legislative districts of Grand Forks, including the Unversity of North Dakota; the district of striking mineworkers in west-central North Dakota; Jamestown, a notably conservative small town; and the rural southeast district, including Sargent and Ransom Counties, hard-hit by small farm foreclosures.

### Illinois—March 15

Chicagoans welcomed Jackson home from Super Tuesday with an impromptu rally of 700 people at the General Electric plant where the late Mayor Harold Washington had endorsed him. Jackson took 32 percent of the Illinois vote, with Simon, also a favorite son, winning with 42 percent. Jesse won Cook County, including Chicago, which accounted for over 60

percent of the state's Democratic turnout. He increased his vote by more than 100,000 over 1984.

The African American community in Chicago, which was deeply torn apart following Mayor Washington's death, united behind Jesse. He won 92 percent of the mostly African American first congressional district, and 87 percent of the second. Based on his support in the Latino community, his vote in Chicago's eighth congressional district went from seven percent in 1984 to 22 percent in 1988. In a state with a long history of racial polarization, Jackson improved his white vote particularly among students and youth, winning the under-30 vote.

Jackson served as a focal point for labor struggles, with labor represented on his delegate slates in every congressional district. A Bloomington labor rally drew together workers from three unions on strike: International Association of Machinists, Teamsters, and Bakery and Confectionery workers, who in turn were addressed by the Farm Labor Organizing Committee.

### Kansas—March 19

Jesse Jackson placed second in the Kansas caucuses, 31 percent to Dukakis's 37 percent. He won the caucuses in three of five congressional districts. Kansas was another state where Jackson significantly broadened the Democratic Party—the majority of his supporters and delegates had never participated in the caucus procedure before.

In the rural first congressional district which covers more than half the state, Jackson organizing began only three days before the caucuses. In 11 counties grassroots farm organizers were contacted, including activists from Catholic Rural Life, Farmers' Union, Kansas Organic Producers and the American Agricultural Movement. As a result, Jackson tied with Dukakis for winning total delegates in those counties.

In the African American community in Wichita, over 400 people overflowed the caucus site and won all 20 delegates from the 29th legislative district, in an area which usually had low caucus turnout. Jackson won the Riley County caucus at the home of the traditionally conservative agricultural campus of Kansas State.

## Michigan—March 26

The Michigan caucus will be remembered with pride by every Jackson supporter throughout the country. Jackson's landslide in Michigan—54 percent to Dukakis's 29 percent—in a major northern industrialized state, could not be dismissed the way analysts and the press had dismissed so many earlier victories. Michigan forced the whole country to admit the simple fact that Jackson supporters had known from the start: Jesse Jackson was running because he wanted to be President of the United States, and millions of people across the country black, brown and white, urban and rural—wanted him to become president too.

Jesse won every major city in Michigan—Detroit, Flint, Kalamazoo, Grand Rapids, Lansing, Pontiac, Ann Arbor. He won Detroit with huge turnouts in predominantly African American precincts, despite Mayor Coleman Young endorsing Dukakis. He won three times Dukakis' vote in predominantly white Ypsilanti Township. He won Ann Arbor and other college towns. He won Dearborn where one of the country's largest Arab American communities came out in full force behind him.

## Connecticut—March 29

Connecticut, neighbor to Dukakis's home state of Massachusetts, has a seven percent African American population and the highest per capita income in the country. These factors helped Dukakis to recoup his losses from Michigan and win the state with 58 percent, but Jackson nonetheless won 28 percent of the vote. Al Gore, who was still in the race, only came up with eight percent. Jackson more than doubled his 1984 vote, going from one delegate in 1984 to delegates in every congressional district in 1988, a total of 16. Exit polls put his white vote at 22 percent. Jackson beat Dukakis more than two-to-one in Hartford, with heavy turnout in both the African American and Puerto Rican communities. He also won districts in the predominantly white West End and in racially mixed neighborhoods, as well as winning five other cities across the state.

## Puerto Rico—March 21
## Virgin Islands—April 3

These two wins for Jackson showed how far and wide his message had spread. Jackson won over 100,000 votes in Puerto Rico and won the non-binding primary with 29 percent of the vote. He won the Virgin Islands caucus with 86 percent of the votes cast, including that of the Governor, and won all the delegates. Jackson supported self-determination for both of these U.S. territories in his campaign.

## Colorado—April 4

Colorado was a close race between Jackson and Dukakis, with the final results giving Dukakis 43 percent and Jackson 34 percent of the caucus delegates. Held on the eve of the Wisconsin primary, the Colorado Democratic Party chose to release results from previously selected precincts to the news, which showed Jackson further behind. But Jackson won Denver and Colorado Springs, as well as seven counties in diverse parts of the state. Jackson inspired the Chicano community in Denver at an Easter Sunday service at Our Lady of Guadalupe Church, and he rallied with striking Chicano meatpackers in Greeley. Caucus participation in the Chicano communities was significantly higher than normal due largely to his appearances. In a state with only a four percent African American population, Jackson also won considerable white support.

## Wisconsin—April 5

Jackson won more votes in Wisconsin in 1988 than Gary Hart did in 1984, when he won the state. The excitement of Jackson's candidacy brought out huge crowds, and over a million people went to the polls, 400,000 more than in 1984. ABC exit polls showed Dukakis actually beat Jackson only by four percent among Democrats, but Dukakis picked up enough Republican and independent crossover voters to wind up with a 48 percent to 28 percent win over Jackson.

This was a remarkable showing for Jackson in a state with a three percent African American population. But the media, after building up expectations from Michigan, played it as a crushing defeat. Jackson more than tripled his 1984 showing and took approximately one-fourth of the white vote in the state. He won over 20 percent of the vote in every congressional district. He won the fifth congressional district with the largest African American voter turnout in the state's history, over 70 percent. His second best showing was in the second congressional district, where students in Madison contributed to his success. He won 29 percent of the vote in the third congressional district, the most rural part of the state. Jackson's support for auto workers in Kenosha who were faced with their plant closing won him the endorsement of the UAW local and caused Simon, Gore and Dukakis to all follow his lead to campaign there.

### Arizona—April 16

Arizona was typical Jackson Action '88. With the endorsements of the majority of the state's Democratic Party officials, large financial resources and over a dozen staffers, Dukakis was favored by the press to win two-to-one. Meanwhile, a rainbow of undaunted Jackson volunteers organized across a state with a three percent African American population and won 38 percent of the vote (to Dukakis's 54 percent). Navajo Indians trudged through knee-deep mud to cast their ballots. African American and Hispanic turnout in Phoenix was high despite major confusion over caucus sites. Jackson inspired a crowd of over 7,000 at Northern Arizona University in Flagstaff and won two of the rural counties in that part of the state. He also won Prescott and Tempe and nearly tied Dukakis in conservative, white Yavapai County. Jackson went from one delegate in 1984 to 14 in 1988, winning delegates in every region of the state.

### Delaware—April 18

Jackson added Delaware to his list of victories, walking away with 46 percent of the caucus delegates and winning the votes of about 55 percent of the participants. When the state party did little to publicize the 41 caucus locations, Jackson supporters went on cable TV and put the word out in a major door-to-door, church and telephone effort. In two of Wilmington's districts, Jackson won every single vote cast. In one district, Jackson supporters moved the caucus to a larger site in order to accommodate the overflowing crowd of senior citizens and others waiting out in the rain.

The day after their victory, a busload of Delaware Jackson supporters changed their "Vote April 18" signs to "Vote April 19," drove to New York, and chanted and sang their way through Harlem's housing projects in a last minute campaign effort in New York City.

### Vermont—April 18

Jesse Jackson won the caucus in the whitest state in the union, winning 46 percent of the delegates. Jackson won Burlington, the largest city in the state, as well as numerous caucuses in small towns and rural areas. The Jackson campaign once again stimulated turnout, with most towns reporting the highest attendance in history. Montpelier's caucus, which Jackson won almost two-to-one, couldn't fit in its assigned room, and many others were overcrowded. The campaign went on to influence ongoing state politics as well, with two Jackson supporters—a gay rights activist and a teachers union organizer—winning Democratic National Committee seats at the state convention over party regulars.

### New York—April 19

Nowhere was the high road that Jesse Jackson travelled in 1988 more apparent than in New York, where the most vicious attack of the campaign was unleashed against him by Mayor Ed Koch. Yet despite Koch's divisive tactics, Jackson won New York City, with more votes in 1988 than he won in the whole state in 1984. Jackson won the support of every African American and Hispanic elected official, an unparalleled accomplishment which has tremendous implications for empowerment of progressives in New York politics.

Together with labor, white liberals, gays, peace activists and others, African Americans and Hispanics put together a highly efficient election-day operation utilizing thousands of volunteers. Statewide, Jackson won 37 percent of the vote to Dukakis's 51 percent. Jackson won Rochester, Syracuse and Buffalo in addition to New York City. Exit polls indicated that he won 15 percent of the white vote, double his 1984 share, and nine percent of the Jewish vote, again twice his 1984 vote. He won more white votes than Al Gore, whom Koch endorsed. Jackson won half of the blue-collar vote statewide, and 64 percent in New York City, due in large part to support from many sectors of the labor movement.

## Utah—April 25

In a state with less than one percent African American population, where Jackson received about three percent of the vote in 1984, he qualified for delegates with 15 percent in the caucuses this year. Jackson's delegation included the first African American and Hispanic in Utah's history to be members of the Utah delegation.

## Pennsylvania—April 26

In a Democratic field which began with seven candidates, after New York only two had proven themselves able to remain in the running: Jesse Jackson and Mike Dukakis. Jesse Jackson had won 30 percent of the popular votes in primaries, and Mike Dukakis had won 34 percent. Yet the press crowned Dukakis the Democratic nominee with his New York win, and with only two candidates running, Dukakis pulled 66 percent of the Pennsylvania vote.

The popular belief that the contest was over resulted in a turnout in Pennsylvania 300,000 votes lower than 1984. Jackson, however, still managed to increase his vote by more than 100,000, winning 27 percent of the vote contrasted to 16 percent in 1984, and tripling his white vote. Jackson won 44 percent of the youth vote (under 30), and brought out 38 percent of those voting for the first time, according to CBS exit polls.

## Ohio—May 3

Jackson won 27 percent of the vote statewide, with Dukakis pulling 62 percent. Again Jackson increased his own vote by over 100,000 votes, even though overall turnout was slightly lower than 1984. Jackson continued to show strength among youth, winning 43 percent of the under 30 vote to Dukakis's 50 percent. His impact on youth in Ohio was seen in his appearances at several high schools, both white and African American, where he moved large crowds of students to leap to their feet

cheering. He beat Dukakis in Franklin County, (which includes Columbus and Ohio State), with a rally in Columbus drawing 10,000 people. He won over 40 percent of the vote in six congressional districts. Jackson's message of economic justice also hit home in Ohio, where 36 percent of those seeking work voted for him, according to CBS exit polls.

## Indiana—May 3

Indiana was a difficult state for the Jackson campaign. With only a seven percent African American population and known for its overall conservatism, Indiana held its primary immediately following Pennsylvania. Nonetheless, Jackson pulled 22 percent of the vote, adding 50,000 votes to his 1984 total. Jackson qualified for delegates in seven of ten congressional districts, including five with less than five percent African American population. He won the tenth congressional district in Indianapolis.

## Washington, D.C.—May 3

Jackson brought a special pride to the nation's capital, which knew it could deliver a victory. He won a landslide, with 80 percent of the vote, up from 67 percent in 1984. His solid support among African American voters was obvious as volunteers from all over the city rallied behind him for election day, with Jackson buttons worn by everyone from the mayor to the many homeless on Washington's streets. He won seven of eight wards in the city, winning four with over 90 percent of the vote. He also picked up more white votes than in 1984, winning 21 percent in predominantly white Ward 3, compared to 14 percent in 1984.

Jackson consistently championed the issue of statehood for D.C. in his campaign, not only in Washington but throughout the country. He made it one of his platform issues and addressed it in his speech at the Democratic National Convention.

## Nebraska—May 10

Jackson tripled his vote in Nebraska from 1984, winning 26 percent of the vote statewide. He won delegates in each congressional district of the state. Jackson won approximately one-fourth of the white vote statewide, and got

30 percent of the vote (more than four times his 1984 vote), in the mostly white first congressional district. And in the third congressional district, a rural district with only one city of more than 25,000 people and less than a 1 percent African American population, he won 24 percent of the vote. African American voters in Omaha came out strongly as well, with a 50 percent increase in turnout for Jackson over 1984 in the primarily African American second ward.

### West Virginia—May 10

Spaghetti dinners and leaflets to laid-off workers, Students for Jackson tables and Jesse Jackson days in churches characterized the West Virginia Jackson campaign. The delegates who came together to represent Jackson on the ballot in early February included African Americans, whites, Arab Americans, Jews, seniors, unemployed, clergy and workers from many unions, including the United Mine Workers, Hospital Workers, Postal Workers, UAW and AFSCME.

Jackson nearly doubled his vote in West Virginia from 1984, although he came up less than a percentage point short of the 15 percent needed to win delegates. Nonetheless, in a year in which overall turnout declined by 35,000 votes, Jackson's total picked up 20,000. A high school senior in Wyoming County, in the Appalachian coal area of the state, wrote to the West Virginia campaign: "I have already convinced one of my fellow students to vote for Mr. Jackson. I am attempting to convince my grandmother to register, so that she too can cast a Jackson ballot."

### Oregon—May 17

Jackson called the Oregon results "a mandate for change, and we will continue." He won 148,000 votes to Dukakis's 226,000. He won his strongest white vote of the season, 35 percent, in a state with less than a one percent African American population. Jackson also pulled his biggest crowds of the primary season in Oregon—13,000 at Oregon State at Corvallis and 15,000 at the University of Oregon at Eugene, where 10,000 people filled the hall and 5,000 more were left outside. Jackson won both of these counties where he spoke.

His grassroots organization covered the entire state, and reflected the enthusiasm only Jackson generated in 1988. His Coos Bay organization, for example, was started by tourists who came there on vacation and decided to stay and organize!

### New Mexico—June 7

On the last day of the primary season, Jackson doubled his 1984 showing in New Mexico, winning 28 percent of the vote. Jackson's strong stand on Indian rights helped him win McKinley County, the only Indian majority county in the state. He also won approximately 45 percent of the Hispanic vote in Santa Fe and San Miguel counties. Jackson's support in New Mexico ranged from former Governor Toney Anaya, who stumped the state for him, to field organizations in many small towns like Taos, to intensive phone banking and literature drops by high school students in Albuquerque.

### New Jersey—June 7

New Jersey's delegate system was one of several that prompted Jesse Jackson to fight and win rules changes in future primaries. The "winner take all" primary required winning more than 50 percent of the votes to qualify for any delegates. On top of this, paired legislative districts combined minority votes with white suburban ones and limited Jackson to winning only two of 20 districts, despite winning 33 percent of the popular vote.

However, despite the discouraging effect of the rules, Jackson action was evident in the state. He won almost every major city in New Jersey: Newark, Patterson, Trenton, Atlantic City, New Brunswick and many others. He won Essex County. He won 46 percent of the under 30 vote compared to 50 percent for Dukakis, and 45 percent of the 30-44 year old vote. He more than doubled his vote in rural and blue collar Salem County.

### Montana—June 7

Jackson increased his vote in Montana from five percent in 1984 to 22 percent in 1988. In April, he had been the first African American ever to address the Montana State Legislature. In May, he was greeted at the Flathead Indian

Reservation in Arlee by 4,000 people. Many were members of the Confederated Salish and Kootenai Tribes living there; others were whites and Indians from surrounding areas. In the June 7 primary, Jackson won the precincts of the Flathead reservation, as well as 45 percent of the vote on the Crow reservation. Jackson won delegates in both congressional districts in the state, sending a delegation to the Democratic convention that included his Native American state chair, a white university professor and a female farm activist.

## California—June 7

The California campaign analyzed its June 7th primary by saying, "The Jackson campaign achieved a big 'victory'...by getting 35 percent of the statewide popular vote total, despite the fact that the press, the party and the pundits had for seven weeks declared Dukakis the 'winner' and 'inevitable nominee.'" Just as he had in Iowa, Jackson won delegates in each of California's 45 congressional districts, from Del Norte to San Diego. He won at least 20 percent of the vote in every congressional district. Jackson won five congressional districts, including the city of San Francisco and parts of Los Angeles.

The rainbow of support was obvious in California: he won 95 percent of the African American vote, 46 percent of the Asian American vote, 36 percent of the Hispanic vote, and 22 percent of the white vote. Gays and lesbians, students, labor, environmentalists, Arab Americans, American Indians and many other constituencies participated in the campaign and were represented in California's delegation, the largest Jackson delegation to the Democratic convention.

In California, Jackson visited the small town of McFarland, where the children of Chicano farmworkers are dying of cancer at an extraordinary rate, due to the poison of pesticides. Five thousand people rallied there with Jackson, environmentalists joining with African American citizens of Watts and Los Angeles, movie stars joining Cesar Chavez and Chicano families of the town. Like most Jackson stops from Greenfield, Iowa to Atlanta, Georgia, this was much more than a campaign event. It was a reaffirmation of the Rainbow. It was a confirmation of why Jesse ran.

Jackson, as usual, expressed it best, speaking to supporters the night of the California primary: "Together we have ushered in a new political era. The years of Reagan's reaction are ending. A new era of citizen action, of concern and care, of hope and change is beginning."

## DEMOCRATIC TURNOUT & JACKSON VOTE:
## COMPARISON OF 1988 & 1984 PRIMARIES:

| STATE | 1988 TOTAL DemVote | 1988 JACKSON %Vote | 1988 JACKSON PopVote | 1984 TOTAL DemVote | 1984 JACKSON %Vote | 1984 JACKSON PopVote | DIFFERENCE Dem Vote | DIFFERENCE JACKSON %Vote | DIFFERENCE JACKSON PopVote |
|---|---|---|---|---|---|---|---|---|---|
| AL | 405,9443 | 43.5 | 176,764 | 428,283 | 19.6 | 83,787 | (22,340) | 23.9 | 92,977 |
| CA | 3,138,734 | 35.1 | 1,102,093 | 2,724,248 | 20.1 | 546,693 | 414,486 | 15.0 | 555,400 |
| CT | 241,395 | 28.3 | 68,372 | 220,842 | 12.0 | 26,395 | 20,553 | 16.3 | 41,977 |
| DC | 86,052 | 80.0 | 68,840 | 102,731 | 67.2 | 69,106 | (16,679) | 12.8 | (266) |
| FL | 1,273,298 | 20.0 | 254,912 | 1,160,713 | 12.4 | 144,263 | 112,585 | 7.6 | 110,649 |
| GA | 622,752 | 39.8 | 247,831 | 684,541 | 21.0 | 143,730 | (61,789) | 18.8 | 104,101 |
| IL | 1,500,928 | 32.3 | 484,233 | 1,659,425 | 21.0 | 348,843 | (158,497) | 11.3 | 135,390 |
| IN | 645,978 | 22.4 | 145,021 | 716,955 | 13.7 | 98,190 | (70,977) | 8.7 | 46,831 |
| LA | 624,450 | 35.5 | 221,532 | 318,810 | 42.8 | 136,707 | 305,640 | -7.3 | 84,825 |
| MA | 713,447 | 18.7 | 133,141 | 630,962 | 5.0 | 31,824 | 82,485 | 13.7 | 101,317 |
| MD | 531,335 | 28.7 | 152,642 | 506,886 | 25.5 | 129,387 | 24,449 | 3.2 | 23,255 |
| MT | 121,871 | 22.1 | 26,908 | 13,895 | 5.0 | 723 | 107,976 | 17.1 | 26,185 |
| NE | 168,684 | 25.7 | 43,380 | 148,855 | 9.1 | 13,495 | 19,825 | 16.6 | 29,885 |
| NC | 679,958 | 33.0 | 224,177 | 960,857 | 25.4 | 243,945 | (280,899) | 7.6 | (19,768) |
| NH | 120,754 | 8.0 | 9,615 | 101,131 | 5.3 | 5,311 | 19,623 | 2.7 | 4,304 |
| NJ | 654,302 | 32.7 | 213,705 | 678,893 | 23.5 | 159,788 | (24,591) | 9.2 | 53,917 |
| NM | 188,610 | 28.1 | 52,988 | 186,635 | 11.9 | 22,168 | 1,975 | 16.2 | 30,820 |
| NY | 1,575,186 | 37.1 | 585,076 | 1,387,950 | 25.6 | 355,541 | 187,236 | 11.5 | 229,535 |
| OH | 1,411,986 | 26.8 | 378,866 | 1,444,797 | 16.4 | 237,133 | (32,811) | 10.4 | 141,733 |
| OK | 392,727 | 13.3 | 52,417 | 42,800 | 3.7 | 1,584 | 349,927 | 9.6 | 50,833 |
| OR | 393,932 | 37.6 | 148,207 | 377,939 | 9.8 | 37,106 | 15,993 | 27.8 | 111,101 |
| PA | 1,507,690 | 27.3 | 411,260 | 1,656,294 | 16.0 | 264,463 | (148,604) | 11.3 | 146,797 |
| PR | 356,178 | 29.0 | 103,391 | 143,039 | n/a | n/a | 213,139 | n/a | 103,391 |
| RI | 48,959 | 15.2 | 7,445 | 44,511 | 8.7 | 3,875 | 4,448 | 6.5 | 3,570 |
| SD | 71,606 | 5.4 | 3,867 | 53,155 | 5.2 | 2,738 | 18,451 | 0.2 | 1,129 |
| TN | 576,314 | 20.7 | 119,248 | 322,063 | 25.3 | 81,418 | 254,251 | -4.6 | 37,830 |
| VT* | 50,791 | 25.7 | 13,044 | 2,000 | 14.0 | 280 | 48,791 | 11.7 | 12,764 |
| WI | 1,014,782 | 28.2 | 285,995 | 635,768 | 9.8 | 62,524 | 379,014 | 18.4 | 223,471 |
| WV | 340,097 | 13.5 | 45,788 | 359,744 | 6.9 | 24,697 | (19,647) | 6.6 | 21,091 |
| Subtotal | 19,458,739 | 29.7 | 5,780,758 | 17,714,722 | 18.5 | 3,275,714 | 1,744,017 | 11.2 | 2,505,044 |
| **1988 PRIMARY STATES WITH 1984 CAUCUSES** | | | | | | | | | |
| AR | 497,544 | 17.1 | 85,003 | 22,202 | 20.0 | 4,440 | | -2.9 | |
| ID* | 51,370 | 15.7 | 8,066 | n/a | 2.4 | n/a | | 13.3 | |
| KY | 318,721 | 15.6 | 49,667 | n/a | 19.0 | n/a | | -3.4 | |
| MO | 527,805 | 20.2 | 106,386 | 40,000 | 18.5 | 7,400 | | 1.7 | |
| MS | 359,417 | 44.7 | 160,651 | n/a | 27.0 | n/a | | 17.4 | |
| TX | 1,684,846 | 25.7 | 433,335 | n/a | 16.0 | n/a | | 8.5 | |
| VA | 364,899 | 45.1 | 164,709 | 25,505 | 26.7 | 6,810 | | 18.4 | |
| Subtotal | 3,804,602 | 26.5 | 1,007,817 | | | | | | |
| TOTAL | 23,263,341 | 29.2 | 6,788,575 | | | | | | |

*Idaho and Vermont held beauty contest primaries in 1988.

Source: ABC News Election Systems

# 1988 DEMOCRATIC PRIMARIES & CAUCUSES:
## CUMULATIVE POPULAR VOTES

| STATE | TOTAL | JACKSON | | DUKAKIS | | GORE | | GEPHARDT | | SIMON | | OTHER | |
|---|---|---|---|---|---|---|---|---|---|---|---|---|---|
| | | %Vote | PopVote | %Vote | PopVote | %Vote | PopVote | %Vote | PopVote | %Vote | PopVote | %Vote | PopVote |
| **PRIMARIES** | | | | | | | | | | | | | |
| AL | 405,943 | 44 | 176,764 | 8 | 31,306 | 37 | 151,739 | 7 | 30,214 | 1 | 3,063 | 3 | 12,857 |
| AR | 497,544 | 17 | 85,003 | 19 | 94,103 | 37 | 185,758 | 12 | 59,711 | 2 | 9,020 | 13 | 63,949 |
| CA | 3,138,734 | 35 | 1,102,093 | 61 | 1,910,808 | 2 | 56,645 | 0 | 0 | 1 | 43,771 | 1 | 25,417 |
| CT | 241,395 | 28 | 68,372 | 58 | 140,291 | 8 | 18,501 | 0 | 1,009 | 1 | 3,140 | 4 | 10,082 |
| DC | 86,052 | 80 | 68,840 | 18 | 15,415 | 1 | 648 | 0 | 300 | 1 | 769 | 0 | 80 |
| FL | 1,273,298 | 20 | 254,912 | 41 | 521,041 | 13 | 161,165 | 14 | 182,861 | 2 | 27,020 | 10 | 125,699 |
| GA | 622,752 | 40 | 247,831 | 16 | 97,179 | 32 | 201,490 | 7 | 41,489 | 1 | 8,388 | 4 | 26,375 |
| ID* | 51,370 | 16 | 8,066 | 73 | 37,696 | 4 | 1,891 | 0 | 0 | 3 | 1,409 | 4 | 2,308 |
| IL | 1,500,928 | 32 | 484,233 | 16 | 245,289 | 5 | 77,265 | 2 | 35,108 | 42 | 635,217 | 2 | 23,816 |
| IN | 645,978 | 22 | 145,021 | 70 | 449,765 | 3 | 21,865 | 3 | 16,777 | 2 | 12,550 | 0 | 0 |
| KY | 318,721 | 16 | 49,667 | 19 | 59,433 | 46 | 145,988 | 9 | 28,982 | 3 | 9,393 | 8 | 25,258 |
| LA | 624,450 | 35 | 221,532 | 15 | 95,667 | 28 | 174,974 | 11 | 66,434 | 1 | 5,155 | 10 | 60,688 |
| MA | 713,447 | 19 | 133,141 | 59 | 418,256 | 4 | 31,631 | 10 | 72,944 | 4 | 26,176 | 4 | 31,299 |
| MD | 531,335 | 29 | 152,642 | 46 | 242,479 | 9 | 46,063 | 8 | 42,059 | 3 | 16,513 | 6 | 31,579 |
| MO | 527,805 | 20 | 106,386 | 12 | 61,303 | 3 | 14,549 | 58 | 305,287 | 4 | 21,433 | 4 | 18,847 |
| MS | 359,417 | 45 | 160,651 | 8 | 29,941 | 33 | 120,364 | 6 | 19,693 | 1 | 2,118 | 7 | 26,650 |
| MT | 121,871 | 22 | 26,908 | 69 | 83,684 | 2 | 2,261 | 3 | 3,369 | 1 | 1,566 | 3 | 4,083 |
| NE | 168,684 | 26 | 43,380 | 63 | 106,334 | 1 | 2,519 | 3 | 4,948 | 1 | 2,104 | 6 | 9,399 |
| NC | 679,958 | 33 | 224,177 | 20 | 137,993 | 35 | 235,669 | 6 | 37,553 | 1 | 8,032 | 5 | 36,534 |
| NH | 120,754 | 8 | 9,615 | 37 | 44,112 | 7 | 8,400 | 20 | 24,513 | 18 | 21,094 | 11 | 13,020 |
| NJ | 642,302 | 33 | 213,705 | 63 | 414,829 | 3 | 18,062 | 0 | 0 | 0 | 0 | 1 | 7,706 |
| NM | 188,610 | 28 | 52,988 | 61 | 114,968 | 3 | 4,747 | 0 | 0 | 1 | 2,821 | 7 | 13,086 |
| NY | 1,575,186 | 37 | 585,076 | 51 | 801,457 | 10 | 157,559 | 0 | 2,672 | 1 | 17,011 | 1 | 11,411 |
| OH | 1,411,986 | 27 | 378,866 | 62 | 869,792 | 2 | 29,931 | 0 | 0 | 1 | 15,524 | 8 | 117,873 |
| OK | 392,727 | 13 | 52,417 | 17 | 66,278 | 41 | 162,584 | 21 | 82,596 | 2 | 6,901 | 6 | 21,951 |
| OR | 93,932 | 38 | 148,207 | 57 | 226,048 | 1 | 5,445 | 2 | 6,772 | 1 | 4,757 | 1 | 2,703 |
| PA | 1,507,690 | 27 | 411,260 | 66 | 1,002,480 | 3 | 44,542 | 0 | 7,254 | 1 | 9,692 | 2 | 32,462 |
| PR | 356,178 | 29 | 103,391 | 23 | 81,502 | 14 | 51,205 | 3 | 10,511 | 18 | 64,812 | 13 | 44,757 |
| RI | 48,959 | 15 | 7,445 | 70 | 34,211 | 4 | 1,939 | 4 | 2,028 | 3 | 1,395 | 4 | 1,941 |
| SD | 71,606 | 5 | 3,867 | 31 | 22,349 | 8 | 5,993 | 44 | 31,184 | 6 | 3,992 | 6 | 4,221 |
| TN | 576,314 | 21 | 119,248 | 3 | 19,348 | 72 | 416,861 | 2 | 8,470 | 0 | 2,647 | 2 | 9,740 |
| TX | 1,684,846 | 26 | 433,335 | 34 | 579,713 | 20 | 357,764 | 14 | 240,158 | 2 | 34,499 | 2 | 39,377 |
| VA | 364,899 | 45 | 164,709 | 22 | 80,183 | 22 | 81,419 | 4 | 15,935 | 2 | 7,045 | 4 | 15,608 |
| VT* | 50,791 | 26 | 13,044 | 56 | 28,353 | 0 | 0 | 8 | 3,910 | 5 | 2,620 | 6 | 2,864 |
| WI | 1,014,782 | 28 | 285,995 | 48 | 483,172 | 17 | 176,712 | 1 | 7,996 | 5 | 48,419 | 1 | 12,488 |
| WV | 340,097 | 14 | 45,788 | 75 | 254,289 | 4 | 11,573 | 2 | 6,130 | 1 | 2,280 | 6 | 20,037 |
| Subtotal | 23,263,341 | 29 | 6,788,575 | 43 | 9,901,067 | 14 | 3,185,721 | 6 | 1,398,867 | 5 | 1,082,946 | 4 | 906,165 |

* Idaho and Vermont held beauty contest primaries in 1988.

| STATE | TOTAL | JACKSON | | DUKAKIS | | GORE | | GEPHARDT | | SIMON | | OTHER | |
|---|---|---|---|---|---|---|---|---|---|---|---|---|---|
| | | %Vote | PopVote | %Vote | PopVote | %Vote | PopVote | %Vote | PopVote | %Vote | PopVote | %Vote | PopVote |
| **CAUCUSES** | | | | | | | | | | | | | |
| AK* | 2,600 | 35 | 900 | 30 | 770 | 2 | 49 | 1 | 30 | 1 | 18 | 32 | 833 |
| AZ | 38,263 | 38 | 14,502 | 54 | 20,700 | 5 | 1,951 | 0 | n/a | 1 | 459 | 2 | 651 |
| CO** | 35,022 | 34 | 11,837 | 43 | 14,919 | 3 | 946 | 0 | n/a | 0 | 73 | 21 | 7,247 |
| DE** | 4,660 | 46 | 2,120 | 28 | 1,295 | 2 | 98 | 0 | n/a | 0 | n/a | 25 | 1,147 |
| HI | 4,975 | 35 | 1,739 | 55 | 2,716 | 1 | 58 | 2 | 98 | 1 | 46 | 6 | 318 |
| IA*** | 123,496 | 11 | 13,564 | 21 | 25,894 | 0 | 192 | 28 | 34,525 | 24 | 29,593 | 16 | 19,728 |
| ID | 4,633 | 21 | 996 | 36 | 1,689 | 7 | 324 | 1 | 59 | 6 | 292 | 27 | 1,273 |
| KS | 8,837 | 31 | 2,713 | 37 | 3,243 | 16 | 1,423 | 2 | 41 | 0 | 6 | 14 | 1,311 |
| ME | 10,996 | 27 | 2,945 | 42 | 4,641 | 2 | 168 | 3 | 339 | 4 | 465 | 22 | 2,438 |
| MI | 212,668 | 54 | 113,832 | 29 | 61,750 | 2 | 4,321 | 13 | 27,190 | 2 | 4,468 | 1 | 1,107 |
| MN** | 130,000 | 20 | 25,740 | 34 | 44,070 | 1 | 1,300 | 7 | 9,620 | 18 | 23,400 | 20 | 25,870 |
| ND** | 2,530 | 19 | 479 | 27 | 692 | 5 | 136 | 17 | 442 | 6 | 150 | 25 | 631 |
| NV | 5,048 | 26 | 1,298 | 27 | 1,344 | 30 | 1,537 | 1 | 62 | 1 | 34 | 15 | 773 |
| SC** | 45,000 | 55 | 24,660 | 6 | 2,835 | 17 | 7,560 | 2 | 810 | 0 | 180 | 20 | 8,955 |
| UT | 11,097 | 15 | 1,712 | 74 | 8,216 | 0 | n/a | 0 | n/a | 0 | n/a | 10 | 1,173 |
| VT**** | 6,000 | 46 | 2,742 | 45 | 2,682 | 1 | 60 | 0 | n/a | 0 | n/a | 9 | 516 |
| WA** | 108,000 | 35 | 37,368 | 45 | 48,600 | 4 | 4,320 | 2 | 2,160 | 6 | 6,480 | 8 | 9,072 |
| WY** | 3,100 | 13 | 400 | 26 | 809 | 27 | 831 | 23 | 713 | 3 | 105 | 8 | 242 |
| Subtotal | 756,925 | 34 | 259,547 | 33 | 246,861 | 3 | 25,274 | 10 | 76,189 | 9 | 65,769 | 11 | 83,285 |
| TOTAL | 24,020,266 | 29 | 7,048,122 | 42 | 10,147,928 | 13 | 3,210,995 | 6 | 1,475,056 | 5 | 1,148,715 | 4 | 989,450 |

Note: In many cases the caucus turnout and vote totals are rough estimates. Amounts may not be exact due to rounding.

*Caucus delegates — only available numbers

**Estimate

***70% vote results calculated to 100% turnout

****State caucus delegates; see also beauty contest primary

Sources: ABC News Election Systems; State Democratic Parties; Secretaries of State; and *New York Times* and *Washington Post* reports where no official results are available.

# 1988 DEMOCRATIC PRIMARIES: VOTER CHARACTERISTICS

| | % TOTAL VOTE | | | | NUMBER OF VOTES (Millions) | | | | % OWN VOTE | | |
|---|---|---|---|---|---|---|---|---|---|---|---|
| | Total | Dukakis | Jackson | Other | Total | Dukakis | Jackson | Other | Dukakis | Jackson | Other |
| | 100% | 43% | 29% | 29% | 23.3 | 9.9 | 6.8 | 6.6 | 100% | 100% | 100% |
| Men | 47 | 41 | 29 | 30 | 11.0 | 4.5 | 3.2 | 3.3 | 46 | 47 | 50 |
| Women | 53 | 43 | 30 | 26 | 12.4 | 5.3 | 3.7 | 3.2 | 54 | 54 | 49 |
| White | 75 | 54 | 12 | 35 | 17.5 | 9.5 | 2.1 | 6.1 | 96 | 31 | 92 |
| African American | 21 | 4 | 92 | 4 | 4.9 | 0.2 | 4.5 | 0.2 | 2 | 66 | 3 |
| Hispanic | 3 | 48 | 30 | 20 | 0.7 | 0.3 | 0.2 | 0.1 | 3 | 3 | 2 |
| Age 18-29 | 14 | 35 | 38 | 27 | 3.3 | 1.2 | 1.3 | 0.9 | 12 | 19 | 14 |
| 30-44 | 31 | 37 | 36 | 26 | 7.2 | 2.7 | 2.6 | 1.9 | 27 | 38 | 29 |
| 45-59 | 25 | 42 | 30 | 28 | 5.8 | 2.4 | 1.7 | 1.6 | 24 | 25 | 24 |
| 60 + | 30 | 53 | 19 | 29 | 7.0 | 3.7 | 1.3 | 2.0 | 37 | 19 | 30 |
| Liberal | 27 | 41 | 41 | 19 | 6.3 | 2.6 | 2.6 | 1.2 | 26 | 38 | 18 |
| Moderate | 47 | 47 | 25 | 28 | 11.0 | 5.2 | 2.8 | 3.1 | 53 | 41 | 47 |
| Conservative | 22 | 38 | 23 | 38 | 5.1 | 1.9 | 1.2 | 1.9 | 19 | 18 | 29 |
| Democrat | 72 | 43 | 33 | 24 | 16.8 | 7.2 | 5.5 | 4.0 | 73 | 81 | 61 |
| Independent | 20 | 44 | 20 | 34 | 4.7 | 2.1 | 1.0 | 1.6 | 21 | 15 | 24 |
| Catholic | 30 | 60 | 18 | 22 | 7.0 | 4.2 | 1.3 | 1.5 | 42 | 19 | 23 |
| Protestant | 36 | 43 | 10 | 47 | 8.4 | 3.6 | 0.8 | 4.0 | 36 | 12 | 61 |
| Jewish | 7 | 75 | 8 | 17 | 1.6 | 1.2 | 0.1 | 0.3 | 12 | 2 | 5 |

Source: Based on *New York Times* total vote percentages. Amounts may not be exact due to rounding.